T0323407

The Psychology of Journalism

The Psychology of Journalism

Edited by

SHARON COEN AND PETER BULL

OXFORD
UNIVERSITY PRESS

OXFORD
UNIVERSITY PRESS

Oxford University Press is a department of the University of Oxford. It furthers
the University's objective of excellence in research, scholarship, and education
by publishing worldwide. Oxford is a registered trade mark of Oxford University
Press in the UK and certain other countries.

Published in the United States of America by Oxford University Press
198 Madison Avenue, New York, NY 10016, United States of America.

© Oxford University Press 2021

Library of Congress Cataloging-in-Publication Data
Names: Coen, Sharon, editor. | Bull, Peter, editor.
Title: The psychology of journalism / edited by Sharon Coen and Peter Bull.
Description: New York, NY : Oxford University Press, 2021. |
Includes bibliographical references and index.
Identifiers: LCCN 2021001745 (print) | LCCN 2021001746 (ebook) |
ISBN 9780190935856 (hardback) | ISBN 9780190935870 (epub) |
ISBN 9780197578612
Subjects: LCSH: Mass media-Psychological aspects. |
Journalism-Psychological aspects.
Classification: LCC P96.P75 P794 2021 (print) | LCC P96.P75 (ebook) |
DDC 070.4/49-dc23
LC record available at https://lccn.loc.gov/2021001745
LC ebook record available at https://lccn.loc.gov/2021001746

DOI: 10.1093/oso/9780190935856.001.0001

1 3 5 7 9 8 6 4 2

Printed by Integrated Books International, United States of America

Contents

Acknowledgements

We are very grateful to Oxford University Press (particularly Abby Gross and Katharine Pratt) for its interest in what we believe is an important contribution to knowledge. We also thank Jonathan Hardy, Catherine Thompson, Maria Elizabeth Grabe, Ozen Bas, Sarah Bachleda, Stuart Soroka, 'Wale Oni, Catherine Lido, Leyla De Amicis, Ariel Swyer, Nathalie Van Meurs, Zira Hichy, Grazia di Marco, and Joanne Meredith. The book wouldn't exist without you.

—The Editors

I thank my co-editor, Peter Bull, and all the contributors, whose competence and professionalism have been outstanding. I am grateful to Professor James Curran, Professor Rupert Brown, Professor Anne Maass and Professor Mara Cadinu for teaching me what it means to be an academic. Thanks to my friends and colleagues Joe Brooks, Leyla De Amicis, Claudia Manzi, Masi Noor, Carole O' Reilly, Anne Pearson, Ashley Weinberg and all my colleagues in Psychology at Salford. Thanks to the University of Salford for giving me a home and a second family and for awarding me a sabbatical to complete the book. Thanks to James Alex Gabriel for his help on proofreading and Nick Potts, Chris Gallagher and Trev Butt for their help.

And, as always, but not less meaningfully, I thank my three rocks: mamma Sonia, papà Claudio, and sister Jessica Coen—it's because of you that I think that everything is possible, and I don't give up that easily on my dreams ☺

—Sharon Coen

Contributors

Sarah Bachleda
University of Michigan
Ann Arbor, Michigan, USA

Ozen Bas
Kadir Has University
Istanbul, Turkey

Peter Bull
University of York
York, UK
University of Salford
Salford, UK

Sharon Coen
University of Salford
Salford, UK

Leyla De Amicis
University of Glasgow
Glasgow, UK

Graziella Di Marco
Universita' degli Studi di Catania
Catania, Italy

Maria Elizabeth Grabe
Indiana University
Bloomington, Indiana, USA

Jonathan Hardy
University of the Arts London
London, UK

Zira Hichy
Universita' degli Studi di Catania
Catania, Italy

Catherine Lido
University of Glasgow
Glasgow, UK

Joanne Meredith
University of Wolverhampton
Wolverhampton, UK

'Wale Oni
University of Salford
Salford, UK

Stuart Soroka
University of Michigan
Ann Arbor, Michigan, USA

Ariel Swyer
University of Glasgow
Glasgow, UK

Catherine Thompson
University of Salford
Salford, UK

Nathalie Van Meurs
Middlesex University
London, UK

1

Introduction

Sharon Coen and Peter Bull

In contemporary Western societies, journalism often comes under fire. This is due in part to the increased economic threat posed to the profession by a steady decline in the consumption of news but also to increasing scepticism in the value of news and the media in general. The latter is certainly not helped by claims of news media corruption, deception, and dishonesty by prominent social and political figures. Nor is this helped by scandals such as 'phone hacking' or 'Fake News'.

This book is an attempt to contribute to the debate concerning the role of news journalism in modern society by providing insights based on psychological theories and research on psychological processes that may play an important role in 'news-making'.

By the end of the book, we hope readers will have gained greater insight into the complex and multi-layered process that is the mediated communication of news. We view this as a nonlinear phenomenon, where there are no straightforward causal connections between the production, content, and reception of news. Instead, we propose a process of co-construction between the systems involved in the creation, delivery, and consumption of news, a process that is solidly embedded in the larger social and cultural context (Crigler, 1998).

In deciding to edit a book on the psychology of journalism, we grounded our understanding of the issue in media psychology. We understand *media psychology* as the study of the processes underlying individuals' interaction with media [intended, in line with the statement by the Media Psychology Research Centre (n.d.), as 'all forms of mediated communication, interaction and experience']. In particular, we are interested in processes related to the communication of news in a mediated environment. We recognize that this is an enormous task, as researchers in media, political communication, and psychology have produced many equally interesting and useful insights. Although not exhaustive, we hope this book will provide some useful

Sharon Coen and Peter Bull, *Introduction* In: *The Psychology of Journalism.* Edited by: Sharon Coen and Peter Bull, Oxford University Press. © Oxford University Press 2021. DOI: 10.1093/oso/9780190935856.003.0001 pointers for readers who would like to explore psychological approaches to news and journalism.

A Media Psychological Approach

In 1935, Cantril and Allport published a book titled *The Psychology of Radio*. In this seminal work, the authors suggested that in order to progress, psychology in general—and social psychology in particular—needs to start engaging with media and contribute to an understanding of this powerful tool and its impact on the society at large. The authors provided an incredibly 'modern' approach to media understanding in which they identified three different levels of analysis.

At the first—most inclusive—level, Cantril and Allport (1935) proposed an analysis of the structure of ownership and legislation concerning the medium. Similar approaches have been applied in the context of news and political communication, with attempts to arrive at a classification of media systems[1] across countries (see, e.g., Hallin & Mancini, 2004, 2011). In this book, we discuss how psychological research on, for example, social norms, ideology, and culture can complement that on media systems[2] to provide further insights at this broad level of analysis (see Chapters 6 and 8).

The second level of analysis is what we call product. At this level are analysed factors playing a role in the selection of programmes to be aired in a specific outlet and the type and content of the various programmes. In the context of news journalism, similar approaches have been taken in analyses of the amount and type of news provision across outlets. For example, Esser et al. (2012) analysed the opportunities for news provision on the main public and private television channels across 13 European countries. They were interested in understanding how television programming included opportunities for citizens to encounter political news and discussions. They found that there are significant differences in the amount of opportunities offered to citizens for politically relevant information, with Norway (and Israel) offering more opportunities than the other countries. Meanwhile, Curran et al. (2013) analysed the content of online news in 10 countries and found that online news outlets are remarkably similar to press and television

---

[1] Intended as the range of media, how they are organized, regulated, used, and understood within a particular cultural context.

[2] For a brilliant discussion on the definition of media systems, see Sonczyk (2009).

in their content. This is contrary to what had been expected by scholars, who argued that the internet would offer opportunities for a wider range of news, with a broader outlook on the world (for overviews of academic debates concerning the internet and its impact on news journalism, see Berger, 2009; Curran et al., 2012).

What can media psychology add to this already impressive body of work? Psychologists are interested in processes underlying news coverage, particularly the selection and sense-making of events and current affairs, as well as their relationship with people's behaviour. We hope this book will help in this respect.

At the third level, Cantril and Allport (1935) proposed an analysis of 'tastes and habits'. At this level, we are interested in what people are looking for when using media and whether media use is capable of gratifying those needs. This has been studied in what has been termed media 'uses and gratification' (Blumler & Katz, 1974). For example, Diddi and LaRose (2006) investigated news media usage among college students and found that the gratifications of surveillance (i.e., the extent to which media is used to aid decision-making and learning about the world as well as oneself) and escapism (i.e., the extent to which media is used to take one's mind off other things) were most commonly sought out by students in consuming news. In Chapter 3, we consider how such motivations may drive our attention and selection of news material.

Finally,, Cantril and Allport (1935) considered a series of experiments examining the features of the media and their impact on audiences. They then concluded with considerations of the implications of the reported studies for different areas of application, such as broadcasting, education, advertising, entertainment, or as a socialization tool. This approach has been echoed within the media and communication field by the so-called effects tradition, the approach to the analysis of persuasive messages pioneered by Carl Hovland and colleagues at Yale University (e.g., Hovland et al., 1953). The basic theme of this research can be summarized as 'who said what to whom with what effect'. There is an extensive research literature following the so-called Yale approach to persuasion, where scholars have systematically studied (in carefully designed experiments) the effects of different features of a persuasive message on people's understanding, memory, and attitude change in relation to a persuasive message (see, e.g., McGuire, 1968). Media psychologists are interested in understanding how media affordances[3]

---

[3] That is, what does a medium allow you to do, and in what format does it provide information?

influence the way in which we construct information. For example, this book discusses how different forms of delivery of information (e.g., in press vs. online media) affect people's attention (Chapter 3) and also the importance of both verbal (see Chapters 9 and 10) and nonverbal (see Chapter 11) elements in the way in which news is constructed and interpreted by users.

Overall, the work of Cantril and Allport (1935) is an excellent example of the role that psychology can play in complementing and expanding our understanding of mediated communication and its influence on an individual's mental and social life—for example; how the interaction with media can affect our cognitive functioning (attention, memory, and learning), the way we think about ourselves (identity, self-esteem, and body image) and others (stereotypes and intergroup relations), and the way we think about broader social issues (politics, the environment, and health). Indeed, this type of approach is also present within more 'sociological' approaches to the study of the role of the 'social' in human psychology.

For example, in a chapter on social representations and media communications, Sommer (1998) presents a powerful analysis of how social representation theory[4] plays out in the context of television-mediated communication. Sommers shows how the properties of the medium (e.g., its ability to deliver audio-visual information in motion) make it easier for the audience to perceive its content as more authentic, as it is delivered in a way that is closer to the way in which humans perceive 'primary' reality (p. 188). Thereby, it facilitates the key processes of objectification (i.e., associating abstract concepts to concrete objects) and anchoring (i.e., associating unknown concepts to known ones) typical of a social representation perspective (e.g., Moscovici, 1981).

A concern for the understanding of media has been a constant undercurrent in the history of psychology (e.g., Tuma, 2013). One example is Arcuri and Castelli's (1996) *La Trasmissione dei Pensieri* (*The Transmission of Thoughts*, SC translation), subtitled *Un Approccio Psicologico alle Comunicazioni di Massa* (*A Psychological Approach to Mass Communication*). Particularly relevant here is Chapter 5 of that book, in which Arcuri and Castelli propose a cognitive model of news reception and effects. However, this model, like many others,[5] can be placed in the so-called effects tradition of research,

---

[4] The term *social representation* refers to values, ideas, metaphors, beliefs, and practices that are shared among members of groups and communities.

[5] See, for example, Eveland and Seo's (2007) account of extant work on the news from a psychological perspective.

whereby scholars examine the impact of different news formats (often in the form of artificially created news items) on people's recall and interpretation of the events. A broader media psychological approach might help in integrating this work with research considering the particular mediated context in which news information is received, interpreted, and constructed, as in the previously mentioned example of Sommer (1998).

In addition, many psychologists interested in media have migrated outside the discipline and joined other fields that are concerned with the understanding of media and society (e.g., sociology, media studies, political communication, and media and communication), in which they have made remarkable contributions. A telling example is Sonia Livingstone's 1990 seminal work titled *Making Sense of Television*, in which the author draws— among others—from literature in social psychology to understand processes underlying the way in which people make sense of the programmes they see. The examples cited previously (and others that we mention throughout this book) show that psychologists in general—and social psychologists in particular—have the potential to contribute significantly to our understanding of the way in which individuals interact with—and make sense of— the mediated world.

The American Psychological Association has had a recognized division of Media Psychology and Technology since the 1980s, thus legitimizing and promoting the understanding of media as an integral part of the discipline. Simply stated, media psychological research is intended to understand how individuals interact with—and make sense of—technological advances in communication (see, e.g., Dill, 2013). Since the establishment of the division, we can count on many excellent examples of the application of psychology to the understanding of mediated communication. For example, the social psychologist Albert Bandura published a paper in 2001 applying his famous sociocognitive theory to understanding mass communication. According to this theory, people learn to perform both desirable and undesirable behaviours through observing such behaviours being performed by others. Bandura argues that these processes of social learning and modelling can be applied to mediated communication with (real or fictional) characters. In 2015, Jeffrey Zacks published a book applying research and scholarship in cognitive neuroscience to explain how we make sense of cinema. In this fascinating contribution, the author illustrates how psychological mechanisms that explain our perception of—and emotional reaction to—events in real life can be fruitfully applied to understand why and how we react to cinema and how particular production choices associated with film-making mean it is more likely for us to react in a way that is in line with what the director intended.

When taking a media psychological approach to understanding journalism, two constructs that are uniquely media psychological—in the sense that they concern exclusively the way in which humans deal with the mediated world and its impact in their everyday lives—need to be considered: parasocial relationships and the third-person effect.

The idea of parasocial relationships stems from Horton and Wohl's (1956) work on parasocial interactions—that is, the interaction audience members have with characters and individuals they see on television or cinema screens. In their work, Horton and Wohl show how—while watching a movie or a television programme—people react as if the events and characters portrayed were present. Moreover, they show how particular features of the programme (those aimed at 'breaking the fourth wall'),[6] such as camera angles and particular shots, are designed to foster these type of reactions. Research on parasocial relationships demonstrates how audience members not only react behaviourally to what is portrayed in the media but also are able to establish relationships with (real or fictional) media characters. Media psychologist David Giles (2002) has championed the argument that the interaction with mediated characters and the relationships we establish with them are comparable in their nature to the type of interactions and relationships we may develop with others in our day-to-day interactions. In other words, the relationships we establish with mediated characters are just as real in our minds as those we have with friends and family in our everyday lives. This is why, for example, people feel free to approach actors in cafés and chat with them as if they were old friends or ask actors why they (i.e., the characters they were playing) behaved in a particular way.

When thinking about journalism and news, we have argued elsewhere (Coen, 2015) that it is important to consider that both the increasing personalization of news and the focus on celebrities and scandals have real consequences for the ways in which we relate to, for example, politicians. The same argument can be applied when thinking about groups of people (see Chapter 7 on social identity and stereotyping). Moreover, changes in the contexts in which we consume news (e.g., via Facebook, which is the place

---

[6] The fourth wall metaphorically refers to an invisible, imagined wall separating actors from their audience. Although the audience can see through this 'wall', the actors act as if they cannot (see Brown, 2013).

where we tend to interact with people we know in the offline world and where extensive identity-related work takes place) may foster the development of these parasocial relationships. The emergence of cyberpsychology as a field of enquiry is a recognition of the importance of providing psychological input to an understanding of issues related both to technological design and to its wider social impact (especially the internet). As such, cyberpsychologists explore how all aspects of our psychological lives (e.g., cognitive functioning, identity, group and intergroup dynamics, and pro- and anti-social behaviour) can play out in the online world and how they relate to our offline cognitive, affective, and behavioural functioning (see, e.g., Attrill-Smith et al., 2019). A good example is the so-called *online disinhibition effect* (Suler, 2004), according to which the anonymity, asynchronicity,[7] and lack of physical interaction with others typical of computer-mediated communication can facilitate a sense of disinhibition in the users. This can result in them opening up to others in a way that they would not do in face-to-face interaction (benevolent disinhibition) but also becoming much more aggressive.

A second key construct of which we need to be aware when trying to understand mediated phenomena is the third-person effect (Davison, 1983). Fundamentally, this phenomenon shows how we tend to underestimate the impact media messages have on us as single individuals while overestimating the impact it has on other people. This might explain how most research examining the direct effects of media messages tends to show how an effect is usually found on the perception of social norms (i.e., what we think is acceptable in society) and not on individuals' own beliefs and behaviours (e.g., Paluck, 2009). When we as researchers, readers, journalists, and citizens reflect on the power of media, we may view others as (willing or unwilling) victims, believing that 'others' will be more susceptible to propaganda than us—that the effects will be stronger for them than for ourselves. But part of the message we hope to deliver with this book is that the processes we observe in action when individuals interact with media are part of our 'normal' psychological functioning, and we are all therefore subject to them. The Nobel laureate Daniel Kahneman (2011) confesses—after a lifelong career exploring the ways in which our brains work in processing persuasive messages—that

---

[7] Asynchronicity—not simultaneous or co-occurring in time.

except for some effects that I attribute mostly to age, my intuitive thinking is just as prone to overconfidence, extreme predictions, and the planning fallacy as it was before I made a study of these issues. . . . And I have made much more progress in recognising the errors of others than my own. (p. 417)

This awareness is crucial in our opinion, when we think of mediated communication as a social issue: We need to be aware that we as scholars, the audience, and journalists are all equally working with common psychological tools in exploring, receiving, or designing news.

However,, although there has been a great deal of work on the audience impact of mediated communication, relatively little attention has been given to news as a unique cultural product and to journalism as a practice. In this book, we try to fill this gap by exploring the psychological mechanisms concerned with both the production and the reception of news. We argue that although it is important to understand how the audience receives and makes sense of news in a changing media landscape, we cannot forget that the same psychological processes affect the way in which journalists select and communicate events in producing news.

The Importance of News in Democratic Societies

A question may arise at this point: Why should we as psychologists care about journalism and news, and why should journalists care about the psychological processes involved in news? For media and communication scholars, the answer is simple: Because news matters when it comes to understanding the functioning of modern democratic societies. In fact, Curran and Seaton (2002) ascribe to news and journalism a disproportionate power, which unfortunately is often not met with a proportional level of accountability.

The way in which political issues are communicated to the public can have a significant impact on how these are constructed and acted upon in society, an effect that is often underestimated due to the lack of methodological tools or cross-disciplinary integration of extant knowledge (e.g., Crigler, 1998; Beattie, 2019). In Beattie's (2019) words, psychological processes can be viewed as part of the 'invisible hand' in the 'marketplace of ideas'. We hope this book will contribute to render (at least in part) visible what has been so far invisible.

In his book on the democratic value of news, Stephen Cushion (2012) reviews an extensive amount of work demonstrating how the 'public service' function of journalism—so crucial in fostering informed citizenship—is often lost in media systems in which market-driven, commercial logic prevails. Cushion argues that systems in which there is a strong public service mandate, and with a strong public service media (public broadcasting systems), are ultimately more successful in contributing to democracy as it is understood in Western democratic societies. Thus, any psychologist interested in people's understanding of, attitude toward, or engagement with politics and/or social issues may be interested in the role played by news in these areas. At the same time, journalists may be interested in understanding how their work is perceived by their audience and how their own psychological functioning shapes (consciously or unconsciously) the way in which they identify and report events.

In a world in which journalism is in constant flux (see Chapter 2) and debates concerning 'fake news' (see Chapter 4) and 'media bias' (see Chapter 8) have arisen, we hope this book will provide answers and—more important—will give rise to questions about journalistic practice and its function in fostering democratic debates.

Understanding Journalism from a Psychological Viewpoint

In this book, we review theories and evidence in psychology to promote an understanding of key psychological processes involved in the production, consumption, and impact of journalism on individuals and society. The overarching assumption here is that we can view journalism as a complex system in which basic cognitive processes (e.g., perception, attention, and memory) interact with higher order factors (e.g., identity, culture, and ideology) in shaping the way in which individuals perceive, attend to, and make sense of the world around them. Crucially, this applies to both journalists and audiences alike.

Thus, for example, journalists' work is affected in a number of ways. These include their ability to identify (perceive), select (attend), and recall (remember) events they deem newsworthy (culture and emotion) and to communicate them in a way (discourse and nonverbal communication) that is understandable to their audiences (identity and stereotyping) and conducive to their professional standards (journalistic role conception). Likewise, the way in which news impacts their audiences depends on their exposure (perception) and attendance to it (attention), as well as their ability to remember (memory and knowledge) and make sense of it (discourse and nonverbal communication). Issues surrounding audiences' emotional state, ideology, culture, and identity will affect both the likelihood of individual choice to consume news and the way in which they make sense of it.

In this book, each chapter contains a comprehensive and in-depth overview of the state of the art of psychological research in each of the relevant subject areas. In addition, each chapter includes theories and research from related academic disciplines relevant to psychological enquiry in the areas of journalism, news production, and popular understanding of the media. Each chapter is summarized next.

Chapter 2: Journalism in the 21st Century

Chapter 2 presents a snapshot of the main characteristics of 21st-century journalism, examining changes in its organization, practice, and performance. It is also intended to contribute to the main themes of the book by outlining links between structural changes in the news industries and shifts in journalists' activities, attitudes, and self-perceptions. Of particular concern is the impact of the internet and more generally of digitalization. This chapter first considers the impact of the internet on traditional print media, television, and radio. The chapter then discusses the internet's impact on journalists' practices, which have undergone dramatic, rapid change and disruption. Next, the chapter focusses on journalistic content, where according to some critics, traditional journalistic standards have been weakened by the growing ascendancy of entertainment values and by the financial pressures of the need for advertising revenue. Finally, the chapter discusses identity and how journalists' traditional concepts of self-identity have responded to the pressures described previously.

Chapter 3: Perception and Attention

In Chapter 3, the application of psychological theories relating to visual perception and attention to our understanding of journalism is considered. Four specific topics are discussed. The first is the influence of so-called limited capacity processing—that humans are limited in the amount of information they can process at any one time. Arguably, journalists should take account of such limitations if they want to ensure their audience comprehends their stories. The second is the use of visual images by journalists. Although a picture may be worth a thousand words (or more!), journalists in their choice of images also need to take account of so-called wishful seeing—that people may see only what they want to see. Third is the phenomenon of 'priming'. The way in which a story is framed may trigger particular concepts or stereotypes, which may be either positive or negative. Finally, there is the role of emotional processing within journalism, both with regard to how the emotional state of an individual may impact their perceptions of a story and how journalists may utilize emotion to influence engagement and comprehension of their audience.

Chapter 4: Memory and Knowledge

The focus of Chapter 4 is on how changes in the media landscape have forced us to reconsider the way in which we understand, define, and research 'memory', 'knowledge', and 'informed citizenship'. Thus, for example, journalism needs to take account of the recent phenomena of so-called news grazing (the active consumption of news that involves flipping through channels and skipping unwanted material). Similarly, there is the phenomenon of 'incidental news exposure', based on studies that have shown global trends in unintended exposure to news when media users go online for non-news functions.

It is argued that traditional views of informed citizenship as simply acquiring appropriate information and facts are challenged by calls to recast it to include applied understanding and comprehension of social issues and also emotional responses to and emotional involvement in those issues. Chapter 4 is also highly critical of an excessive reliance on verbal tests of memory, and it stresses the need to develop visual measures, given that the human brain is better adapted for visual than verbal processing.

Chapter 5: Emotion

Two questions concerning the role of emotion in news coverage are discussed in Chapter 5. First, to what extent does emotion appear in news coverage? The authors have devised an automated content analytic strategy, which they applied to the analysis of editions of *The New York Times* from 1980 to the present day. Their results showed that expressed emotion is a regular feature of news events and that it has increased in frequency over time. Second, the authors consider why (and how) emotions matter in news content. Their analysis supports the widespread view that expressed emotion increases reader attentiveness. On the other hand, there is also a view that news might benefit if the expression of negative emotions (especially anxiety and anger) was less prevalent. However, the authors question this, given that news consumers appear to be more activated and attentive to emotion-laden content. Hence, the authors conclude that engagement with political news may depend on a certain amount of emotionality, while acknowledging that an excess of emotional intensity may be counterproductive.

Chapter 6: Norms and Roles

Chapter 6 provides an overview of the literature on the function of social norms and roles in shaping emotions and beliefs. Particular attention is paid to how social norms shape journalistic professional practice. Through the concepts of accountability, transparency, truth, and social responsibility, journalism is presented as a norm-driven socially constructed profession. For example, journalists' intrinsic personal norms are found to be stronger in predicting their behaviour compared with extrinsic influences, such as regulatory laws or organizational policies. The chapter also focusses on journalists' changing concepts of their own occupational role. A case study, based on journalism in Nigeria, is presented on the acceptance and use of digital technologies; which are presented as a double-edged sword. Thus, although broadcast journalists may be significantly empowered by their use, there is also a perceived dumbing down effect on journalistic practice, such that certain normative roles (e.g., sourcing information and expertise) may be jeopardized and professional ethics violated.

Chapter 7: Social Identity and Stereotyping

In Chapter 7, a social psychological perspective on how the media may influence societal attitudes and behaviours is presented, with a particular focus on media coverage of refugees and asylum seekers. Traditional social psychological approaches to core concepts of identity, categorization, and prejudice are discussed, followed by a review of relevant current models, such as intergroup emotion theory, integrated threat theory, and the so-called BIAS map (Behaviours from Intergroup Affect and Stereotypes). From these theories, it is proposed that refugees might be met with greater warmth and increased perceptions of competence if in the news they were reframed not as stealing jobs but, rather, as future citizens, supporting the countries in which they reside by doing necessary work and by creating new employment avenues. The chapter concludes with a proposal for five evidence-based strategies both for audiences to be more overtly aware of misleading media bias (e.g., through the creation of 'us versus them' identity narratives) and for developing a more responsible journalism.

Chapter 8: Ideology and Culture

In Chapter 8, theories and methods based on cross-cultural psychology are applied to a discussion of the impact of ideology and culture in journalism. The chapter begins by reporting a case study based on a cross-cultural analysis of media systems. One major finding is that in countries where the media has a strong public service mandate and public broadcasting systems, there is a better quality of news provision and a correspondingly higher level of informed and engaged citizenry. The chapter continues with a discussion of cross-cultural research both by Hofstede, who has identified six major dimensions whereby cultures can be compared and contrasted, and by Schwartz, who has identified value dimensions with universal meaning, such as security, happiness, and benevolence. In addition, the chapter discusses social identity theory, particularly the way in which the media may be responsible for creating and fostering an us versus them mentality. In conclusion, the chapter affirms that there is no one nation that holds the gold standard for journalism and can be used as a reference point for all others. In other words, there is no such thing as 'Greenwich Mean Time journalism'.

Chapter 9: Language and Social Identity

Chapter 9 is focussed on linguistic biases, particularly with regard to intergroup relations. It is based on the linguistic intergroup bias model, according to which individuals use different words to describe people and their behaviour on the basis of group membership. In particular, they tend to use more abstract terms (e.g., 'helpful' and 'aggressive') to describe positive behaviours of their own (in-group) and negative behaviours of those of 'out-groups'; conversely, they use more concrete terms (e.g., 'hit' and 'help') to describe negative behaviours of in-group members and positive behaviours of out-group members. Thereby, they attribute positive behaviours of in-group members and negative behaviours of out-group members to stable enduring characteristics while attributing negative behaviours of in-group members and positive behaviours of out-group members to transitory characteristics dependent on situation or context. This kind of linguistic bias may occur not only in informal communication but also in the mass media, where it can reinforce positive or negative social stereotypes without viewers or readers necessarily being aware how this process is taking place. The authors conclude that recognizing and limiting the use of such biased language is an important component in producing quality journalism.

Chapter 10: Language and Discourse

In recent decades, discourse analysis has had a major influence on social psychology. One of its major themes is that traditional concepts in psychology (e.g., memory, thought, emotion, or attitudes) can be comprehended through the analysis of talk. Discursive psychology (one particular form of discourse analysis) is focussed on the micro-analysis of the language—how specific words and practices can perform specific actions and how alternate ways of describing the situation are omitted. In Chapter 10, a review is presented of discursive psychology and its application to media research. This is followed by an illustrative case study based on newspaper headlines relating to 'Brexit' (the process of the United Kingdom leaving the European Union following the referendum on UK membership in June 2016). This analysis is focussed on the well-publicized claim that 'We send £350m a week to the EU. Let's fund our NHS [National

Health Service] instead'. The slogan was written on the side of the Leave campaign 'battle bus' and was highly contested both during and after the referendum campaign. In concluding this chapter, the author proposes that discursive analyses can not only help readers explore how particular events, people, and texts are constructed in the news but also help journalists in seeing how readers might interpret their words and what inferences may be drawn from this.

Chapter 11: Visuals and Nonverbal Behaviour

Nonverbal behaviour plays an important role in journalism because of its heavy reliance on visual forms of communication. Chapter 11 first discusses academic research on nonverbal behaviour in terms of the following topics: the communication of emotion and interpersonal relationships, the synchronization of nonverbal behaviour and speech, deception detection, and communications skills training. Next, this chapter focusses on the use of visuals and nonverbal behaviour in two specific journalistic contexts: print journalism and the television news. Photojournalism, the use of visual images to tell a story, is arguably the counterpart of print journalism. Illustrative examples are discussed, based on the impact of photos of the Vietnam War and the dead Syrian boy Aylan Kurdi; celebrity photos are also considered. This is followed by an analysis of the television news, focussed primarily on recent changes in audio-visual editing techniques. Next, a case study based on television news coverage of the British parliamentary expenses scandal of 2009 is presented. In conclusion, it is proposed that academic research on nonverbal behaviour has manifest applications and implications for our understanding of journalism, particularly to enhance our understanding of the impact of visual images and nonverbal behaviour on the wider society as a whole.

Chapter 12: Conclusion

In the final chapter, we summarize the lessons learned throughout the book and discuss the important role that psychological processes at the individual (e.g., identity), interindividual (e.g., attribution), and collective (e.g., intergroup dynamics) levels play in journalism in light of these lessons learned.

References

Arcuri, L., & Castelli, L. (1996). *La trasmissione dei pensieri: Un approccio psicologico alle comunicazioni di massa*. Decibel.

Attrill-Smith, A., Fullwood, C., Keep, M., & Kuss, D. J. (Eds.). (2019). *The Oxford handbook of cyberpsychology*. Oxford University Press.

Bandura, A. (2001). Social cognitive theory of mass communication. *Media psychology*, 3(3), 265–299.

Beattie, P. (2019). *Social evolution, political psychology, and the media in democracy*. Palgrave Macmillan.

Berger, G. (2009). How the internet impacts on international news: Exploring paradoxes of the most global medium in a time of 'hyperlocalism'. *International Communication Gazette*, 71(5), 355–371.

Blumler, J. G., & Katz, E. (1974). *The uses of mass communications: Current perspectives on gratifications research*. Sage.

Brown, T. (2013). *Breaking the fourth wall*. Edinburgh University Press.

Cantril, H., & Allport, G. W. (1935). *The psychology of radio*. Harper & Brothers.

Coen, S. (2015). The age of celebrity politics. *The Psychologist*, 28(5), 372–375.

Crigler, A. N. (1998). *The psychology of political communication*. University of Michigan Press.

Curran, J., Coen, S., Aalberg, T., Hayashi, K., Jones, P. K., Splendore, S., Papathanassopoulos, S., Rowe, D., & Tiffen, R. (2013). Internet revolution revisited: A comparative study of online news. *Media, Culture & Society*, 35(7), 880–897.

Curran, J., Fenton, N., & Freedman, D. (2012). *Misunderstanding the internet*. Routledge.

Curran, J., & Seaton, J. (2002). *Power without responsibility: Press, broadcasting and the internet in Britain*. Routledge.

Cushion, S. (2012). *The democratic value of news: Why public service media matter*. Macmillan.

Davison, W. P. (1983). The third-person effect in communication. *Public Opinion Quarterly*, 47(1), 1–15.

Diddi, A., & LaRose, R. (2006). Getting hooked on news: Uses and gratifications and the formation of news habits among college students in an Internet environment. *Journal of Broadcasting & Electronic Media*, 50(2), 193–210.

Dill, K. E. (Ed.). (2013). *The Oxford handbook of media psychology*. Oxford University Press.

Esser, F., de Vreese, C. H., Strömbäck, J., Van Aelst, P., Aalberg, T., Stanyer, J., Lengauer, G., Berganza, R., Legnante, G., Papathanassopoulos, S., Salgado, S., Sheafer, T., & Reinemann, C. (2012). Political information opportunities in Europe: A longitudinal and comparative study of thirteen television systems. *International Journal of Press/ Politics*, 17(3), 247–274.

Eveland, W. P., Jr., & Seo, M. (2007). News and politics. In D. R. Roskos-Ewoldsen & J. L. Monahan (Eds.), *Communication and social cognition: Theories and methods* (pp. 293–318). Erlbaum.

Giles, D. C. (2002). Parasocial interaction: A review of the literature and a model for future research. *Media Psychology*, 4(3), 279–305.

Hallin, D. C., & Mancini, P. (2004). *Comparing media systems: Three models of media and politics*. Cambridge University Press.

Hallin, D. C., & Mancini, P. (Eds.). (2011). *Comparing media systems beyond the Western world*. Cambridge University Press.

Horton, D., & Richard Wohl, R. (1956). Mass communication and para-social interaction: Observations on intimacy at a distance. *psychiatry*, *19*(3), 215–229.

Hovland, C.I., Janis, I.L., & Kelley, H.H. (1953). *Communication and persuasion*. Yale University Press.

Kahneman, D. (2011). *Thinking, fast and slow*. Penguin.

Livingstone, S. (1990). *Making sense of television: The Psychology of Audience Interpretation*. Pergamon.

McGuire, W. J. (1968). Personality and attitude change: An information processing theory. *Psychological Foundations of Attitudes*, *171*, 196.

Media Psychology Research Centre. (n.d.). *Homepage*. Retrieved 22 October 2019 from http://mprcenter.org

Moscovici, S. (1981). On social representations. *Social Cognition: Perspectives on Everyday Understanding*, *8*(12), 181–209.

Paluck, E. L. (2009). Reducing intergroup prejudice and conflict using the media: A field experiment in Rwanda. *Journal of Personality and Social Psychology*, *96*(3), 574.

Sommer, C. M. (1998). Social representations and media communications. In U. Flick (Ed) *The psychology of the social*. Cambridge University Press, 186–195.

Sonczyk, W. (2009). *Media system: Scope—structure—definition*. Retrieved 22 October 2019 from http://studiamedioznawcze.pl/Numery/2009_3_38/sonczyk-en.pdf

Suler, J. (2004). The online disinhibition effect. *Cyberpsychology & behavior*, *7*(3), 321–326.

Tuma, R. M. (2013). Media psychology and its history. In K. Dill (Ed.) *The Oxford handbook of media psychology*, 62–74.

Zacks, J. M. (2015). *Flicker: Your brain on movies*. Oxford University Press, USA.

2

Journalism in the 21st Century

Jonathan Hardy

'The news business . . . is going out of business', declared Wolff (2007). Well, not quite, not all, not yet, but that aphorism captures a period of unprecedented turbulence. Waves of disruption have pummelled islands of newsmaking, ripping through business models, working arrangements, settled practices, and identities of journalists alike. In the United States, newsroom employment fell by 23% between 2008 and 2017, a loss of approximately 27,000 jobs in one decade (Greico, 2018). In newspaper newsrooms, the decline was 45%, and in radio 27%, but employment levels in television and cable news remained stable. In the decade since Wolff's pronouncement, news businesses have indeed been going out of business, but not all, not yet.

Across most countries, journalistic media forms have struggled with diminishing advertising revenues, falling fee-paying audiences, reduced operating budgets, and intensifying competition from online media and platforms that are undermining the business models and structures of the older, 'legacy' news companies—ones that existed prior to the digital age (Weaver & Willnat, 2012). Yet, for news journalism the pattern is highly uneven. The collapse of legacy newspaper businesses has accelerated alongside growth in digital-only journalism, albeit with fewer paid jobs than those lost. Across the many debates about what kind of journalism is developing, or possible to develop, under current conditions, there is a full range of perspectives and also emotions, from anxiety to elation.

This chapter presents a snapshot of the main characteristics of 21st-century journalism, examining changes in the organization, practice and performance of journalism. It also seeks to contribute to the themes of this edited collection on the psychology of journalism by outlining links between structural changes in the news industries and shifts in journalists' activities, attitudes, and self-perceptions. The chapter first outlines changes in industries and then changes in journalists' practices. Next, it discusses issues affecting content and, finally, questions of identity.

Jonathan Hardy, *Journalism in the 21st Century* In: *The Psychology of Journalism.* Edited by: Sharon Coen and Peter Bull, Oxford University Press. © Oxford University Press 2021. DOI: 10.1093/oso/9780190935856.003.0002

Journalism, the American Press Institute (2019) states, 'is the activity of gathering, assessing, creating, and presenting news and information'. Yet, Anderson and Ward (2007, p. 8) caution that conventional definitions of 'the practice of news gathering and presentation' are unsatisfactory, 'telling us little about the sophistication of much modern-day journalism'. The focus of this chapter is on news journalism, to the neglect of myriad specialist do mains of communication that journalism as a whole encompasses. We will, however, trace how news journalism has expanded and how it blurs into and merges with other forms of communication. The demarcation lines separating journalism from other communication forms and practices, such as advertising, have sometimes been tenaciously upheld, albeit with mounting difficulty, constituting an important part of the 'boundary work' (Carlson, 2019) of professional identity formation.

A hundred years ago, the contours of a modern form of journalism were being espoused, and slowly institutionalized in the United States, around ideals of objectivity, neutrality, and serving the public interest, in a manner that influenced the self-conceptions of journalists worldwide (Hallin & Mancini, 2004; Waisbord, 2013). There was a struggle to secure the new journalism, but core values were advanced with confidence. A hundred years on, at the start of the 21st century, many advocates of those values are more troubled and cautious of their realization. Increasingly, more journalists work as freelancers or otherwise outside traditional desk-based jobs. Multiplatform journalism, and the rising influence of social media in particular, 'has led many to question the very basic concept of who journalists are and what qualifications they should have' (Weaver & Willnat, 2012, p. 1). Changes in journalism are always changes that involve psychological processes: identifications, anxieties, aspirations, adaptability, and instability. The story of 21st-century journalism interweaves the structural, institutional, cultural, social, and personal dimensions of uncertain paths and prospects under constant repair and refashioning.

Industries

In 1994, news publishers were experimenting, sometimes disastrously, with the creation of online supplements, some 400 worldwide. In the quarter century since, the industrial production of news has faced unprecedented disruption, with the ruins of both legacy media and new business models 'piling wreckage upon wreckage', as before Walter Benjamin's angel of history, in his evocative response to Paul Klee's painting *Angelus Novus* (Benjamin, 1970, p. 259). I outline key changes, but two preliminary statements are necessary. First, context matters. The 'crisis' of news media identified in advanced media systems is far from uniform worldwide, even if some factors have global relevance and reach. Long-standing structural decline in print readership in advanced economies sits alongside print growth in several regions, including Latin America and Africa. Second, all changes must be reviewed in the context of contested explanations of the problems, and opportunities, for journalism today. Key components of change are widely recognized and broadly agreed. The media, including journalism, has been profoundly affected by a series of transitions: from analogue to digital, and from stationary to mobile platforms (McNair, 2009). Consumers with internet access can pull content whenever they wish, from available sources, transforming patterns of scheduled supplies of professionally mediated journalism. An ever-increasing share of news is now accessed online. In a survey of 26 countries, 44% of news readers used digital and traditional sources equally, while 23% used digital channels only as their main source of news (Newman et al., 2016).

Digitalization has profoundly affected all aspects of the creation, circulation, and consumption of content. In the pre-digital era, most print publishers and broadcasters competed in spatially confined market sectors, sharing advantages of economies of scale and scope, and with legal–regulatory requirements, that created barriers to market entry. The growth of internet communications enabled all those conditions to be undermined, although crucially the resulting pattern is one mixing sustained advantages for large firms with ongoing disruption for all market actors. The most straightforward and significant impact has been the shift of advertising revenue from news publishers to other content suppliers and increasingly to platforms (Bell & Owen, 2017). Online advertising became the leading advertising medium worldwide in 2017 (ZenithOptimedia, 2018).

However, it is important to deconstruct simpler narratives and explanations of change, as Benjamin's angel of history reminds us. The narrative of relative stasis before disruption has credence—things have got considerably more challenging after digitalization—yet it downplays the significance of pre-digital changes, including those that help explain the roots of current predicaments. Paid consumption of printed news was declining from its peak in the late 1950s in the United Kingdom, with local daily papers gradually losing readers as mass industry employment and commuting patterns changed. Focussing on digitalization also occludes longer term shifts during the 20th century from the written word toward image and sound: from print to radio and television news. Boczkowski (2005, p. 4) traces the development of online newspapers to 'broader socioeconomic trends' originating in the 1960s, including 'rising newsprint and distribution costs, growing segmentation of consumption patterns, and the increased appeal of audiovisual media among younger generations'. In order to grasp the patterns of disruption and continuity, the next section summarizes key changes in news media markets: digitalization, globalization, and financing.

Digital Plenitude

Pre-internet news businesses generally required large capital outlay. New technologies, contract printing, and other developments enabled production costs and, to a lesser extent, distribution costs to fall, but labour costs and promotional costs remained prohibitive, making news publishing a risky business venture requiring deep pockets. Economies of scale and scope arising from large-scale, multi-paper publishing benefited newspaper chain owners and constricted market entry. Digitalization undermined some of these advantages and introduced a greater diversity of online news reporting, commentary, and storytelling—enabling more multidimensional perspectives and voices.

The digital era has seen a proliferation of news providers and platforms, but the most profound change, arguably, has been disintermediation; the removal of intermediary editorial functions between readers and content. Although Negroponte (1995, p. 57) was spectacularly inaccurate in his prediction in *Being Digital* that the media giants would dissolve into an array of cottage industries, he was right to highlight the significance of the removal of gatekeepers, of editors and managers, and of journalists as mediators, with possibilities of unmediated communication scaled up between millions of people. Historically, those with the 'means of publication' have been few in number. From Web 1.0 publishing from 1994 to Web 2.0 social media and beyond, there has been a massive, unprecedented expansion of the presence and share of mass self-communication (Castells, 2009) activity and consumption of disintermediated content: images, video, blog postings, and commentary. This ever-growing share of communications production and consumption exists alongside legacy journalism, digital 'native' publishing (those originating in digital environments), and 'owned media'—communications self-published by corporate, public, or civil society organizations.

In 2019, approximately 2 billion people accessed Facebook worldwide, and 1.8 billion people accessed YouTube. A survey of UK news audiences found that 43% used social media sites for news (Ofcom, 2015). Half (51%) of those using the internet/apps for news used the websites/apps of television and radio companies, so legacy media types have retained a significant share but now compete with a greater range of sources. A 2018 survey found that over half of adults prefer to access news through search engines, social media, or news aggregators, interfaces that use ranking algorithms to select stories, rather than interfaces driven by humans such as homepages, email, and mobile notifications (Newman et al., 2018). There is a greater opportunity for readers to check between alternative sources of information, including fact-checking services, to assess the validity of news sources, although the percentage doing so is generally very small. Only 1 in 10 US adults fact-check information read on social media, according to one survey (Brown, 2017). With greater access to original sources, and alternative accounts, the nature of newsgathering is more exposed than ever before, putting claims of objectivity and impartiality under greater scrutiny (Fenton, 2010, p. 560). Within this environment, it has become more difficult for journalists to perform and claim privileged status as providers of information and arbiters of truth. The impact of these changes on journalists' attitudes and identities is explored further later. Here, however, the complex patterns of media concentration need to be added to amend the story of digital plenitude. More voices, more providers exist alongside ongoing, and in some instances increasing, concentration of ownership. In the United Kingdom, three companies control 83% of national newspaper circulation (Mediatique, 2018); 81% of local newspaper titles are owned by five firms (Media Reform Coalition, 2019).

Internationally, wholesale news is dominated by three corporations—Associated Press, Thomson Reuters, and Agence France-Press—that supply most of the source material for international stories carried on television and the internet (MacGregor, 2013). A handful of multinational conglomerates own the majority of major news websites, commercial television, and newspapers worldwide (Bertelsmann; Comcast; Disney, including Twenty-First Century Fox; News Corp; Time Warner; Vivendi; and Viacom). Although processes of consolidation in news have been underway since the 19th century, they intensified with the growth and dominance of transnational media conglomerates in the 20th century, facilitated by advancing neoliberalism in policymaking (Hardy, 2014).

Until the 1980s, the newspaper industry was largely owned by national capital, but since the 1990s, it has been increasingly part of global merger and acquisition activity. Thus, while news brands continued to serve predominantly national and regional markets, their ownership and management became integrated into transnational capital (Picard, 2008; Compton, 2010). The largest news companies by market capitalization are concentrated in the United States, including News Corp ($7.48 billion), the New York Times Company ($4.21 billion), the Tribune Media Company ($3.39 billion), Daily Mail and General Trust (UK-based; $2.82 billion), E. W. Scripps ($1.38 billion), and Gannett ($1.12 billion) (Seth, 2018).

The expansion of voices, information, and opinions facilitated by the internet has impacted on all forms of journalism. A series of studies have, however, cautioned that more content and communication exchange does not necessarily equate to more journalism. A Pew Research Center report (Pew, 2006) found that only 5% of US blog postings sampled matched the criteria of 'what journalists would call reporting'. A later report (Pew, 2008) concluded,

> Even with so many new sources, more people now consume what old-media newsrooms produce, particularly from print, than before. Online, for instance, the top 10 news web sites, drawing mostly from old brands, are more of an oligarchy, commanding a larger share of audience than they did in the legacy media.

Globalization

More affluent and connected users have unprecedented access to news from throughout the world. The advances of satellite telephony and audiovisual communications, alongside cable, and transportation systems, have enabled the increasingly rapid circulation of news and overcome barriers of space and time on which traditional news markets were predicated (Sparks, 2004; Elliot, 2008). Twenty-four-hour news channels, such as CNN, became a feature of national and international cable television services from the 1980s and then reached growing audiences online as broadband and mobile data capacity became more widely available. International news journalism grew within internet-enabled publishing from the mid-1990s, online radio, and podcasting. Nevertheless, news has remained 'stubbornly local' (MacKay, 2000, p. 48), both in provision and in content and orientation. In content, research shows that foreign news tends to be filtered through news prisms shaped by dominant national geopolitical concerns (Lee et al., 2005). This pattern, associated with major national newspapers and broadcast news, is also replicated in internet news, countering the optimistic assumptions of more globalized and cosmopolitan reporting (Curran et al., 2013). Worldwide, television remains the most consumed form of journalism (Kennedy & Prat, 2018; Cushion, 2012). Nonetheless, news consumption of older formats and platforms is declining. Audiences for evening newscasts on network television in the United States have declined by 1 million per year while increasing across cable news channels (Fox, CNN, and MSNBC) (Pew, 2010). Terrestrial news audiences are shrinking and ageing, albeit with much cross-national variation.

Financing News: Sales, Subscription, and Advertising

As former *Guardian* editor Alan Rusbridger (2018) conveys in his autobiography, newspapers faced an agonizing set of challenges at the onset of digital publishing. Traditional paid newspapers relied on a mix of sales and advertising revenue with modest supplementary income. With financing firmly rooted in the mix of paid sales and advertising (display and classified), moving to digital publishing was expensive and risked cannibalizing revenues for highly uncertain rewards. As is now much debated, the floods of free news content, including from newspaper groups following business advice on 'building scale' and achieving 'first mover advantage', meant that most digital news offered publishers a quick way to spend money for little, if any, direct return on investment. In this context, the reallocation by marketers of their advertising spending had a crucial impact.

Initially, the challenge of digitalization was to classified ads as online markets blossomed. The internet's share of classified advertising in the United Kingdom increased from 2% in 2000 to 45% by 2008. In the same period, the local press share declined from 47% to 26%, while national newspapers' share of classified declined from 14% to 6%. The lucrative display ad revenue also gradually eroded. The deal whereby advertisers paid for journalism to attract readers who would see their ads has been unravelling since the early 1990s, as marketeers found more direct, information-rich, and cost-effective ways to track and target consumers online. UK local papers had reaped profits from their quasi-monopoly control over local advertising for vehicles, housing, and jobs into the mid-2000s, only to see that model collapse as classified ads moved online and advertisers followed users to Facebook and Google. Advertising revenue for the three largest UK regional publishers declined from £2.8 billion in 2006 to £832 million in 2016 (Waterson, 2019a). Online advertising revenue for publishing has become a significant revenue stream for some, but for the majority of news publishers, the 'dollars' lost from print advertising have been replaced by 'cents' earned from digital advertising (McChesney, 2013). Globally, 93% of all newspaper revenues in 2015 came from print [World Association of News Publishers (WAN-IFRA), 2016]. According to UK trade body News Media Association (Deloitte, 2016, p. 8), 81% of revenue comes from the print side of business and just 12% from digital.

Efforts to make good the loss of advertising by more effective retailing, through paywalls, micropayments, and subscriptions, have so far had only modest success. *The Guardian* had 500,000 regular subscribers worldwide in 2018, a significant achievement but one outweighed by continued heavy losses as the paper struggled to break even (Waterson, 2018). Successful monetization online has been mostly restricted to products serving elite or specialist audiences, where there are attributes of high-value content (relatively nonreproducible and/or fast), scarcity in supply, a valued user interface, and enhanced cross-platform availability. The Nikkei-owned *Financial Times*, which introduced a metered paywall in 2007, announced 1 million subscribers in 2019, with most growth in international markets in which it competes with *The Wall Street Journal*, which has 2.5 million subscribers (Greenslade, 2019). Yet, while subscriptions secured the *Financial Times'* profitability, print advertising declined by 5% and digital advertising declined by 3% in the previous year.

For newspapers overall, in the absence of significant growth in subscriptions, 'news organisations are focussing on maximizing revenue from those who are prepared to pay' (Newman & Levy, 2015, p. 12). A Reuters Institute (2018) study found that 66% of the 171 most important news organizations in 6 countries (Finland, France, Germany, Italy, Poland, and the United Kingdom) operated a pay model, with charges for premium content most common, followed by metered paywalls. For general, public-facing journalism, cultures of 'free' prevail and are expected to continue (Chyi & Lee, 2013). A survey by the Internet Advertising Bureau (Jackson, 2015) found

UK adults were prepared to pay only 92p a month to access news websites, less than they were prepared to spend on email, search engines, or online video. In a 10-country survey (Newman & Levy, 2015), only 11% of respondents reported they had paid for digital news in the past 12 months. A more recent cross-national study found that the average number of people paying for online news has edged up in many countries, especially in small markets where a majority of publishers pursue paywalls, yet in more complex and fragmented markets many publishers continue to offer free news online (Reuters, 2018). Pay models have tended to stall after reaching a small segment of their total consumer market willing to pay for content.

Thus, news revenues have been affected by the increased availability of free online content. Digital readership has increased, but digital revenue growth has largely failed to compensate for print decline, while adding to costs (Pew, 2015). Any increase in reader revenue is often offset by continuing declines in print and digital advertising (Newman et al., 2018). In most markets in Europe and America, printed newspapers sold to the public have seen an inexorable decline in sales and, with that, advertising revenue. The main exception has been free newspapers distributed in urban areas, which have provided a profitable advertising vehicle reaching commuters, including those whose consumption of other offline media tends to be light.

Assessing the 'Crisis' in News Businesses

Between 2008 and 2017, an estimated 39,000 US newspaper jobs were eliminated—a 45% decline (Greico, 2018). Across the five news industries, there were 114,000 newsroom employees—reporters, editors, photographers, and videographers—in 2008; by 2017, this workforce had declined to 88,000 (Greico, 2018). In the United Kingdom, the number of workers describing themselves as journalists declined by 11,000, from 84,000 in August 2016 to 73,000 in August 2017, according to Labour Force Survey estimates (Ponsford, 2017). The survey found a modest increase in the number of employed journalists, but a sharp decline among freelancers. One freelance journalist, Paul Donovan, described how the internet 'has generally meant more work for journalists but less pay', with publishers either not paying for online journalism or offering lower rates than 10 years ago: 'My own experience has been very much of seeing journalism go from my main job, earning a reasonable living, to hobby status' (as quoted in Ponsford, 2017). Across UK print as a whole, the number of journalists declined by more than a quarter, from 23,000 in 2007 to 17,000 in 2017 (Mediatique, 2018, p. 5).

Against these downward employment trends, digital news publishing has been a source of jobs growth. Start-ups such as Buzzfeed, Huffington Post, Vox, and Business Insider were the generators of most new jobs in the US news industry (Jurkowitz, 2014). Between 2008 and 2019, approximately 6,000 jobs were created in digital-native newsrooms, a 79%. However, 'too few newsroom positions were added to make up for recent losses in the broader industry' (Grieco, 2018). Digital native publishers have themselves faced considerable turbulence in recent years, after initially strong growth. A Pew Research Center report found that nearly one-fourth of digital publishers laid off workers during 2017 and 2018, despite the increase in employment in this sector overall. At the start of 2019, Buzzfeed laid off 220 staff, approximately 15% of its total workforce, and Vice cut 10% of staff in a restructuring of the business after missing revenue targets in 2018 (Willens, 2019).

Debates about the 'crisis' in news media intensified in the mid-2000s. Since then, some aspects at least are clearer. First, variability across countries and regions challenges ethnocentric generalization and requires more fine-grained analysis. For example, a survey of 10 countries (Newman & Levy, 2014, p. 55) found economic disruption was greatest in countries in which the majority of sales were from newsstands or shops (the United Kingdom, Spain, Italy, and Brazil) compared to home delivery via subscription (Japan, Denmark, Finland, and Germany). Secondly, Euro-American literature has tended to ignore the growth of paid newspaper markets across fast-growing economies in Asia, Africa, and Latin America (Franklin, 2009). Global printed newspaper circulation (including free titles) was 7.7% higher in 2009 than it had been 5 years previously; declining circulation in mature markets was countered by growth in Latin America, Africa, and in Asian markets, notably India (WAN-IFRA, 2009, 2016). An estimated 40% of the world's adult population read a newspaper on a regular basis (WAN-IFRA, 2016, p. 6). Global audience revenues grew by 7% between 2012 and 2016; although global advertising revenues declined by 21% overall in the same period, rates of decline varied greatly across different markets (WAN-IFRA, 2016). Third, even across advanced economies, the general trend has been decline and restructuring rather than collapse, which highlights the importance of differentiation between news sectors and competing enterprises (Franklin, 2009). The crisis debate tends to conflate print-based and broadcasting-based media, which makes some sense in examining trends across the convergent, commercial media of the United States but less so when addressing the mixed systems of Europe with relatively strong public service media alongside commercial publishers. Nevertheless, the common feature across media systems whose newspaper market was larger before digitalization has been an irreversible decline in print revenue, accompanied by cost cutting to manage that decline. In the United Kingdom, circulation declined by 25% between 2005 and 2010 in the 'quality' press and by 17% in the popular press (Enders Analysis, 2011).

Explanations for the crisis of the press indicate a range of perspectives on the various causes, and possible solutions, with debates reflecting

> not only different degrees of real impact by the crisis and national policy traditions but [the diffusion of...] an evolving transnational paradigm that dominates public discourse. [...] The state is supposed to play the role of a benevolent but mostly passive bystander, while commercial media outlets should tackle the problem by developing innovative content and business strategies. (Brüggemann et al., 2016, p. 547)

If internet disruption has been the chief explanatory narrative of commercial business managers, underinvestment has been the counternarrative of their critics. Owners were maximizing profits by cutting staffing and production costs while revenue declined, allowing newsbrands to plummet in a spiral of neglect. Critical scholarship highlights the processes by which corporations have come to dominate markets and pursue profit maximization at the expense of public interest news provision (McChesney, 2013). The literature describes the advancement of market values within commercial news media, what McManus (1994) calls 'market-driven journalism' and McChesney (1999) 'hypercommercialism'. The balancing of commercial and journalistic imperatives in for-profit news businesses, present since the 17th century, tilted toward profit extraction under corporate and investor pressures, within conditions of increasing market volatility, acquisitions activity, and financialization. In corporate decision-making structures, news editors and journalists formed a 'shrinking proportion of corporate personnel' (Anderson & Ward, 2007, p. 23). Commercial news owners 'privileged profit over reinvention' (Carlson, 2017, p. 181). Waves of corporate consolidation, aided by liberalization of ownership regulations, left commercial news production in the hands of debt-laden, financialized corporations with decreasing tolerance to subsidize loss-making reporting and whose corporate logics undermine journalistic independence and investigative capacity alike (Almiron, 2010).

The US newspaper market entered a 'death spiral', summarized by Rusbridger (2018):

> Circulation decline led to advertising decline. Management cut back editorial employees to stem declining margins while, at the same time, asking them to work harder and adding new digital requirements to their roles. Newspapers shrank and became less compelling. Readers found less of interest and stopped buying them. With few readers came fewer advertisers. The margins declined further. Managements made further cuts. (p. 74)

As profitability declined, capital began to abandon news journalism, shifting to more profitable activities, including classified advertising websites (McChesney, 2013). The crisis, critics argued, laid bare fundamental tensions between capitalism and democracy, between 'communication groups subject to financial logics and who can, and indeed do, exercise political action, and . . . the need that democracy and society have for an independent, rigorous and professional journalistic practice' (Almiron, 2010, p. 158). In debate were two principal causes of cuts: profit maximization on behalf of shareholders and the collapse of profitability as advertising migrated online. Although the cause for the decline is contested, the outcome was downsizing the journalistic workforce combined with intensifying productivity across always-on, converged newsrooms, leading to reductions in the breadth and depth of commercial news output (Anderson & Ward, 2007, p. 23). In the United Kingdom, local papers declined from 1,687 in 1985 to 1,286 by 2005, with 242 closing between 2004 and 2011, while leading newsgroups maintained substantial profit margins averaging 15–20% (Ramsay & Moore, 2016). By 2017, the majority of UK adults (58%) subscribed to no local daily paper.

For audio and audiovisual news, there are some similar patterns, but also differences in market conditions. Common features were increasing commercial pressures, increasing competition to secure audience share, and increasing engagement in an 'attention economy'. For public service media (PSM), insulation from market pressures eroded as financial and political settlements weakened. The rising tide of neoliberalism meant that the defence of nonmarket provision was pushed back. PSMs were increasingly 'disciplined' (Freedman, 2008) and subject to marketization and corporatization—the incorporation and privileging of private sector management goals into public institutions. However, these pressures were mitigated by generally healthier market conditions than commercial newspapers experienced. While the share of news viewing on the internet has increased annually, television remains the dominant news source in most advanced economies. In the United Kingdom in 2015, television was the principal platform for news consumption (67% of UK adults), followed by the internet (41%), radio (32%), and newspapers (31%, Ofcom, 2015, p. 5). Television news also saw a significant expansion of outlets across transnational services and, to a lesser extent, local news services. The internet has supplemented, but not simply replaced, legacy platforms of television and radio, both of which remain very strong in global reach and influence. With the ongoing convergence of 'post-broadcasting' on-demand and streaming video services, there are ever-evolving forms of news capturing audience attention, from 360-degree storytelling to short-form and vertical video. However, beyond subsidized (or cross-subsidized) content, monetization remains challenging.

Practices and Purposes

The industrial and market changes outlined previously have all had an influence on journalistic practice, considered in this section, and in turn on journalistic identities and psychological makeup. The overriding themes are intensification of work and increasing uncertainty, including less secure and stable boundaries. What journalists do has undergone dramatic, rapid change and disruption. Up to the 1990s, most journalists worked in-house and produced content for a single outlet, in a single format, and honed their storytelling craft skills within a single mode of expression: print, photojournalism, radio, or television reporting (Singer, 2011). Newsroom 'convergence' was much discussed, and more tentatively applied, from the 1990s until becoming pervasive in the 2000s. News media businesses began creating 'converged' newsrooms and developing 'multimedia journalism', while print-based publications expanded their audiovisual content. Businesses that were wholly or principally mono-media up to the late 20th century have, of necessity, become multimedia and increasingly multiplatform operations.

Larger media companies brought together journalists from very different cultures in print and broadcasting to produce from these platforms and from the Web. Digital production entailed speeded up publication; scanning and responding to competition; truncating processes of origination, writing, editing, and layout; and reducing or removing the former divisions of labour across journalism, subediting, and layout. Within so-called desktop journalism, journalists may combine writing, sub-editing, page composition, as well as other tasks such as meta-tagging for search engine optimization. In audiovisual production, journalists have had to add recording, editing, tagging, uploading, disseminating, and promoting work. Under convergence, formerly separate tasks and work cultures were brought together and new ones added, such as social media production, optimization, and analytics. As well as institutional reorganization, journalists developed innovative multimedia storytelling (Singer, 2011). Multimedia production has also contributed to wider shifts toward increased personalization in journalism. Star writers and columnists have to maintain self-branding, as well as corporate promotional work, through blogs, postings, and other content production in addition to traditional reporting formats. This has created new opportunities, pressures, and conflicts around the intellectual property ownership and obligations of such communications. Yet core craft practices remain and inform self-identities; journalists are storytellers. Overwhelmingly, news journalists self-identify as truth-seekers and truth-tellers.

Interactivity with readers and users has been one of the most discussed changes, although the anticipated and actual impacts need to be carefully sifted in any specific analysis. Digitalization certainly facilitated a revolution in responsiveness. Up to the 1990s, interaction between journalists and readers was rarely direct and mainly ritualized through designated activities such as readers' letters, radio and television talk shows, sparse audience feedback programmes, public events, and complaints mechanisms. With digitalization came accessible, real-time comment and interaction. This meant another demanding role for many journalists, now required to respond or undertake online moderation. More profoundly, it meant open, publicly accessible, critical engagement with journalists' work in a manner that rarely existed in pre-digital environments. In television and radio, there was always a stronger, regular connection with audiences, but interactivity was challenging and often managed by incorporation into established journalism practice (Cushion, 2012, p. 27). The gains of deepening democratic engagement were qualified by the mobilization of hate. Like other public figures, journalists were targeted by 'trolls', as well as by organized 'flak' or more spontaneous, shareable protesting. A *Guardian* analysis (Gardiner et al., 2016) found that women were subjected to much more vilification than men, with misogyny and sexism commonplace, and that writers from ethnic and religious minorities and LGBT+ people suffered the greatest abuse, in efforts to undermine their confidence and capacity to speak out. As well as managing the labour, including emotional labour, of interactivity, journalists are also under mounting pressure to engage as part of the overall effort to build traffic and page views that could be monetized. This, too, generates resistance to what some journalists describe as 'traffic whoring' (Singer & Ashman, 2009).

Journalists are obligated, or incentivized, to engage in a broader range of extra-media activity. For instance, *The Guardian* engages its journalists in training events for aspiring writers and talks and conferences on direct revenue raising and to build the affiliation of readers and convert more to become subscribers in a manner akin to practices in relationship fundraising. Overall, there have been a series of added tasks on top of the routine work expected of pre-digital news journalists (Singer, 2011).

Journalism became more networked. This in turn contributed to the displacement of traditional forms of authority. Online news tended to include hyperlinks to other sources, with the news publisher 'becoming in effect a network of a variety of news sources, rather than the undisputed bearer of "the news" or "the truth"' (Hargreaves, 2003, p. 53). Journalists are facing challenges from across an increasingly diverse range of communicators that erode their privileged gatekeeping role (Bruns, 2005; Deuze, 2005; Carlson, 2017). Those changes in production were then extended and accompanied by the further revolution in data about readers and users, and engagements with them. Datafication, the transformation of social activity into quantified data, allows for a displacement of decision-making from journalists and editors to action derived from signals of audience engagement and editorial 'effectiveness'. This presents another form of disintermediation, generating concerns such as those expressed by Carroll (2006):

> Disintermediated news is . . . not selected by editors. [It is news based on the assumption that] markets are capable of making better decisions about news than editors. We're getting this from two sides. First, there are the Web people, who have ingeniously figured out how to decide what's important by tabulating the collective wisdom of online readers. How galling for us—to be replaced by algorithm. Second, we're getting it from our own corporate leaders, who believe in market research. Why not just edit by

referendum? They wonder. Why not just ask people what they want and give it to them? (p. 5)

Google and Yahoo developed personalized news, with content customized by algorithms, based on user preferences and search history. A 26-country survey of news consumers found that 40% of consumers discovered news via search engines, approximately 33% via social media and approximately 12% through news aggregators (Newman et al., 2016, p. 93). Later studies found that the move to distributed content via social media and aggregators was stalling in some areas, with a decline in the discovery, posting, and sharing of news on Facebook (Newman, 2018). Nevertheless, increasing numbers rely on news that is curated by algorithm, personalized based on information about the individual user and not as a result of a human editor's selection decisions (Haim et al., 2018). As a consequence, human editorial agency, although still critical, is diminishing in parts of news production. Some filtering is regarded as essential in helping users manage relevance, while algorithms are being developed to help identify 'fake news'. The shifts to personalization and algorithmic section raise profound issues regarding news diets and diversity amid strengthening concerns surrounding 'filter bubbles' (Pariser, 2011); echo chambers; confirmation bias; and the reinforcement of prejudices over information exchange, dialogue, and mutual understanding. Joining established critiques of the ways commercialization undermines news values (Bennett, 2016) are those that concern the dynamics of monetizing digital journalism. One report (Silverman, 2015) finds

the business models and analytics programs of many large news websites create an incentive for them to jump on, and point to, unverified claims and suspect viral stories. This approach is receiving some pushback and is by no means universal, but the sites pursuing this strategy are large and drive a significant number of social shares for their content. (p. 144)

Artificial intelligence-assisted news consumption is increasing. The market growth of voice-activated digital assistants such as Amazon Echo and Google Home opens new opportunities for audio news. The vast majority of respondents (65%) in a Reuters survey (Newman et al., 2018, p. 7) prefer to get news through a side door rather than going directly to a news website or app. More than half (53%) prefer to access news through search engines, social media, or news aggregators—interfaces that use ranking algorithms to select stories—rather than through interfaces driven by humans (homepage, email, and mobile notifications). The demographic push from people younger than age 35 years remains toward greater use of mobile aggregators and social platforms and less direct access to news providers' outlets.

Working Conditions

Changing working practices have been summarized in the adage 'speed it up and spread it thin' (Fenton, 2010, p. 562). News journalists have been under increasing pressure to release and update stories online (including without adequate checks). Given the changes outlined previously, it is not surprising that these are accompanied by an increase in occupational precarity. Firms have responded to the disruption and 'crisis' in news sectors by seeking ways to reduced fixed labour costs. Flexible labour arrangements have been introduced in the wider context of deregulation and de-unionization in labour markets (Ursell, 2004). There has been a rise in subcontracting and tertiarization (Quintanilha, 2019). Of course, such general trends need to be assessed within specific contexts. In a survey of journalists in Portugal in 2016, nearly 90% 'agreed with the idea that journalistic work is going to be increasingly precarious and uncertain in the future; only 2.6 per cent of respondents disagreed' (Quintanilha, 2019, p. 11). The professional insecurity was reflected in low expectations concerning employment: 41% of journalists thought it likely they would become unemployed in the future, and 80% believed that, once unemployed, they would be unlikely to secure a new journalism-related job.

Some scholars argue that journalism is undergoing a process of 'de-professionalization', reversing the processes underway through the 20th century (Örnebring, 2010). This de-professionalization is evident in the weakening of media trade unions, with declining membership, a shrinking proportion of unionized media workers, and erosion of employer recognition and bargaining power. While the applicability of de-professionalization is debated, an even stronger version advances the proletarianization of journalistic labour. Recognizing that most journalists self-identify as information professionals, the charge is that they misrecognize their decline in status, agency, and autonomy. By contrast, other scholars identify a restructuring of the division of labour, but one that involves new challenges for journalists, including having to 'cover more fields of knowledge, perform more tasks and become more versatile', requiring ongoing self-education (Quintanilha, 2019, p. 2; see also Compton, 2010). There is broader agreement that these higher skills are adopted in conditions of disciplining labour (Franklin, 2008):

> Virtually all print journalists are now required to work across multiple media platforms which involves not only delivering copy for print and online editions of their newspapers, but also shooting brief video clips, reading pieces to camera, as well as recording podcasts. (p. 635)

Publishers are increasingly adding short-form audiovisual content, while '58% of publishers say they'll be focussing on podcasts, with the same proportion looking at content for voice-activated speakers' (Newman, 2018, p. 5). Journalists face growing demands for multiplatform, multifunctional work. For Compton (2010), 'These changes work to discipline labor and threaten communal professional standards' (p. 598).

Changing employment conditions have affected the already slow pace of advancement of greater diversity in the workplace. A 60-country study found that women held only 27% of top management jobs and 41% of senior professional positions in journalism (International Center for Journalists, 2011). Another global survey (Weaver & Willnat, 2012) found women better represented in some countries (China, Finland, Malaysia, Russia, Singapore, and Slovenia), yet the estimated proportion of women in journalism overall only increased from 33% in 1998 to 41% in 2012. The typical journalist, according to Weaver and Willnat (2012), 'is still primarily a fairly young college-educated man who studied something other than journalism in college, and who came from the established and dominant cultural groups in his country' (p. 544). In the United Kingdom, the proportion of Black and minority ethnic workers in the creative industries has barely risen and in some instances has fallen despite the pervasive assumptions of an open, egalitarian, and cosmopolitan sector. The class composition of journalism in the United Kingdom is also hugely unrepresentative of the population. Approximately half of journalists received a private education, enjoyed by approximately 7% of the total population (Martinson, 2018).

The changes outlined previously have also created new divisions of labour and new classes of workers who do journalistic-type labour without enjoying the status and conditions of their journalist colleagues. The Press Association, Britain's oldest domestic news agency, has sharply differentiated between their newsgathering operation and their news processing operation—news process employees, or 'production journalists', are tasked to convert gathered information into saleable news products, and are not required to have journalism training (but must have good writing skills and be proficient in digital production technologies) (Örnebring, 2010, p. 571; see also Ursell, 2004).

Cost-cutting regional papers in the United Kingdom introduced 'hubs' or 'print centres', where junior staff repackage stories for multiple editions and formats. Journalists have been defined as those who have at least some 'editorial responsibility' for the content they produce (Weaver & Wilhoit, 1986, p. 168). Such demarcation lines have become more blurred with the growth of 'content farms', such as Demand Media (now Leaf Group), involving various forms of content production, including content recommendation engines and brand-sponsored editorial content (discussed later). Altogether, there has been a proliferation of various sub-journalisms. 'Professional' journalism, taking place within institutional and payment-based arrangements, now blends with commercial sub-journalisms and with the expanding sectors of civil society journalisms, including citizen journalism, hyperlocal reporting, blogging, and occasional writing.

Content Issues and Problems

Traditional journalism, argues Elliot (2008), took time:

> It took time to fact check a story. It took time for editors to review stories and determine placement in newspapers and broadcast news programs. But, every technological advance, from the Guttenberg press to computer to satellite, has cut down the time that journalists thought that they needed to do their work. (p. 29)

As this reminds us, we are describing an intensification of processes that long predate the 21st century. Any positing of a slow-paced, well-resourced past would be an injustice to the historical record and experience of journalists. Yet a common theme in many of the discussions of problems in journalism today is the intensification of pressures on output as time, labour power, and other resources decline. A chief casualty, according to numerous studies, has been the resources and support for investigative journalism. As a UK Parliamentary report (House of Lords Select Committee on Communications, 2008) summarizes,

> The result of these pressures is that newspaper companies are having to make savings and this is having a particular impact on investment in news gathering and investigative journalism. The number of foreign news bureaux is decreasing, and there is an increasing reliance on news agency feed and information derived from the public relations industry. (p. 7)

In place of in-house investigative reporting, there has been growing reliance on news agencies and other supplied sources. Serving a 24-hour news operation, many journalists are deskbound, producing copy for multiple media platforms, with no time to source or research news stories themselves. In what Davies (2008) calls the 'news factory', reporters are forced by workplace conditions and control to depend on public relations (PR) suppliers for their leads. As a consequence, the PR industry exerts increased influence over the news agenda, yet the public lacks ready means to identify which news items have originated as press releases, reproduced in whole or part. The recycling of information produces 'churnalism', described as 'a news article that is published as journalism, but is essentially a press release without much added' (Media Standards Trust, n.d.). Researchers found increasing dependence by journalists on 'pre-packaged news', with one UK study finding 60% of press articles and 34% of broadcast stories came wholly or mainly from PR or news agency sources (Davies, 2008).

What such tactics mean for journalism is illustrated by the influence of fossil fuel companies on the discussion of climate change. Davies (2008) describes how the European Science and Environmental Forum, a 'pseudo-group, created with the help of two PR agencies (APCO Worldwide and Burson-Marsteller) with the specific intent of campaigning against restrictions on corporate activity' (p. 193), was reported favourably in a series of pieces denouncing the concept of man-made climate change by *Daily Mail* columnist Melanie Phillips, without readers being made aware that its work was funded by Exxon. Against the significant reduction in professional investigative and reporting capacity, however, are some countertrends, including the rise of enterprises, often low-profit or non-profit, dedicated to longer form investigative reporting, such as the Bureau of Investigative Journalism, openDemocracy, and Byline in the United Kingdom.

The boundaries of journalism are challenged by the fuzziness and encroachments at border points, but also by the fact that these incursions contribute to the questioning and undermining of core values and assumptions. Principles of balance, objectivity, and impartiality have been under increasingly critical scrutiny. In the United Kingdom, strict rules of impartiality in broadcasting have coexisted with a highly partisan tabloid and midmarket ('red top') press, with broadsheets occupying a space in between, balancing editorial lines with commitments to objectivity norms in reporting. Both the efficacy and the presumptions of this traditional governance have come under increasing scrutiny, in part as political dissensus widens. In a study of BBC television news coverage of immigration, the European Union, and religion, Berry (2013) found that party political sources dominated, accounting for 49.4% of all source appearances in 2007 and 54.8% in 2012. Conservative politicians featured more frequently than Labour ones (24 vs. 15) across the two time periods on BBC News at Six. Reporting on the financial crisis, business spokespersons outnumbered trade unionists by more than 5 to 1 in 2007 and 19 to 1 in 2012: 'The fact that the City financiers who had caused the crisis were given almost monopoly status to frame debate again demonstrates the prominence of pro-business perspectives' (Berry, 2013).

Tabloidization

A key term, *tabloidization*, carries accumulated baggage that needs unpacking. At a denotative level, it can refer to the reformatting of larger, broadsheet papers to smaller tabloid formats. At a connotative level, it refers to the expansion of editorial values associated with mass, popular orientation across journalism as a whole. Tabloidization is associated with 'the sensationalization of news, the abbreviation of news stories, the proliferation of celebrity gossip, and the more intensive use of visual material such as large photographs and illustrations' (Rowe, 2010, p. 351). In debates on tabloidization in newspapers, attention focussed on the diminishing space devoted to 'hard' news; the privileging of sensationalist storytelling over 'serious' analysis; and concerns about 'dumbing down', 'infotainment', 'newsak', 'PR-isation', and the like. This critique of the privileging of entertainment values, celebrity and scandal-rich content is answered by others, notably cultural studies academics, who offer more positive accounts of the shifts in news values and editorial tone (see Pilvre, 2012). Discourses of 'dumbing down' advance cultural elitist views that offer an imprecise, romanticized, constructed past as the basis for a narrative of decline that fails to recognize the positive gains of a more engaged, accessible communication. Critical-cultural scholars counter that much of the optimistic reading of tabloidization endorses an uncritical cultural populism and fails to address how capitalist dynamics shape and limit the capacity of journalism to serve audiences and privilege commercial over societal interests. Studying tabloidization in Estonia, Pilvre (2012) argues the media position was ambivalent, shifting public–private topic borders but reinforcing prevailing patriarchal gender patterns.

For some critics, the weakening of journalistic standards is attributed to the ascendancy of entertainment values. In the United Kingdom, several newspaper editors reached seniority having previously worked on entertainment and celebrity sections. The charge is that they brought with them values derived from sensationalism, looser adherence to rigorous standards of fact-checking information,+ and cultures of image trading with PR, paparazzi photographers, and others. Such explanations, however, can detract from the more impersonal pressures and constraints shifting news journalism toward provision 'rewarded' by readers and marketers in economically significant and measurable ways. Economic pressures arising from increasing competition for revenue have led to increasing dependency on 'agency and other swap agreement products and more "saleable" news focussing on lifestyles and celebrities' (Anderson & Ward, 2007, p. 23).

Television journalism has also been accused of forms of tabloidization, adopting more entertainment-oriented styles, shifting from 'hard' news (politics, economy, business, and international affairs) to 'soft' news (entertainment, celebrity, lifestyle, and sports) as competitive pressures increase in commercial market environments (Cushion, 2012). For public service media, there has been a deepening set of problems finding ways to maintain and engage their national and regional audiences and so retain the legitimacy conferred by doing so. For Rowe (2010),

The tabloid phenomenon can be read as both a sign of critical and professional anxiety about finding a media audience without substantial loss to a sophisticated political democracy, and a product of that anxiety when converted, in the media industry, to systematic attempts to connect with audiences by all available means. (p. 359)

Branded Content and Native Advertising

If digital advertising is required to subsidize digital journalism, the poor per-formance of some ad formats has been a problem for both publishers and marketers alike. Declining click-through rates and 'banner blindness' en-couraged advertisers to test other formats such as pop-ups and interstitials and then animated advertisements, pre-roll and other video formats. These formats, however, have also generated negative responses from consumers and ad avoidance strategies, most notably ad blocking. This has been among the factors leading to a rise in advertising integrated into content and 'dis-guised or camouflaged' to blend into editorial environments. This includes 'native advertising', described as 'content paid for and controlled by brands, but which looks like news, features, reviews, entertainment and other content that surrounds it online' (Parker, 2016). Sponsored editorial content is mate-rial with similar qualities and format to content that is typically published on a platform, but which is paid for by a third party. Advertising that resembles editorials long predates the digital age, but brands are increasingly involved in the production of publisher-hosted branded content, such as the Netflix-sponsored *New York Times* cover story on women inmates in 2014 to pro-mote *Orange Is the New Black* (Johnston, 2018), including material described as paid content, sponsored content, native advertising, programmatic native, content recommendation, and clickbait. Amid declining display advertising and subscription revenues, brand-sponsored content has offered publishers the potential for increased earnings, and it has offered marketers a means to tackle ad avoidance and boost engagement (Harms et al., 2017). Sponsored content is now the second most important revenue generator (44%), after advertising (70%) and ahead of subscription (31%), according to a world-wide newsroom survey (International Center for Journalists, 2017). A cross-national survey of publishers found that 10% were preparing for a future with little or no display ads (Newman, 2018, p. 22).

The growth of native advertising reflects new pressures and opportunities, shifts in governing values across established media, and the spreading influ-ence of formats and business models from the inaptly named 'pure players'—digital-only publishers such as Buzzfeed, Vice, Vox, and Huffington Post that attract a younger audience via social media and mobile (Nicholls et al., 2016). Buzzfeed built its audience through a combination of shareable entertain-ment content and listicles (articles using lists as their structure) sponsored by brands, with no display advertising until it introduced programmatic ads on BuzzFeed News in 2018.

These new editorial and business activities are impacting on the role and practices of journalists and creating hybrid spaces and identities for sponsored content producers. Publishers offer the expertise of their editorial teams to serve paid advertisers, deploying editorial staff directly or developing more quarantined units such as the *Guardian*'s Guardian Labs to create brand-sponsored content (Hardy, 2018).

The most pertinent charge against brand journalism is that there is a powerful imbalance in the resources to fund effective public communications. Professional journalism promised to ameliorate that imbalance by producing communications according to values that serve democratic and cultural life, including accuracy, balance, and editorial independence from vested interests. Yet, branded content favours resource-rich, commercial sources; sponsor-friendly coverage; and 'best-selling' stories and soft news. The central dilemma of native advertising is that revenue gain comes at the expense of eroding reader trust and undermining core jobs for news media (Piety, 2016).

Among researchers who have examined the adoption of sponsored content in newsrooms, Carlson (2014) examined 'norm entrepreneurship' among professionals adopting more affirmative perspectives of content curation against critical conceptualizations such as erosion of the 'firewall' between 'church' and 'state'; that is, editorial and advertising. Others have examined the emergence of 'hybrid editors' (Poutanen et al., 2016), working at the intersection of brand promotion and journalistic work. The expansion of ever-evolving forms of branded content creates a blurring of storytelling craft and journalistic purposes that was more rigorously demarcated under previous governance arrangements.

Identities

Governance encompasses all the rule-making processes that influence behaviour, from formal law and regulation to norms, cultures, and practices. Increasingly, argues Singer (2011), journalists are 'defining themselves in terms of professional norms, standards, and practices that, they say, are only sporadically shared by those outside the newsrooms' (p. 105). These practices and norms are sources of social identity and self-definition for journalists, across personal, institutional, and media sectoral levels. Governance is one of the bridges between responses across societies to what journalism is and does and the self-perceptions of journalists.

Journalism is subject to a complex patchwork of legal controls, public regulation, and self-regulation by publishers and providers, members of professional associations, and trade unions. The various international organizations monitoring media (see https://ifex.org) highlight the formal and informal means by which states, political parties, media owners, and other powerful interests exercise controls on reporting and communications worldwide. From 2013 to 2019, more than 600 journalists were killed worldwide, including anti-corruption activist Daphne Caruana Galizia, murdered in Malta, and *Washington Post* journalist Jamal Khashoggi, assassinated at the Saudi consulate in Istanbul. High-purpose and deadly seriousness constitute part of the image repertoire shaping complex and contradictory identities for journalists, most of whose work does not engender the same risks. Yet the pride in, and defence of, journalism remains important and a widespread source of identification and affiliation. In response to President Trump's attacks on 'fake news' and condemnation of the media as 'the enemy of the American people', some 350 US newspapers collectively published editorials in defence of press freedom (Reuters, 2018).

Against positive affirmation, journalists must also contend with plummeting public trust in many regions. The Edelman Trust Barometer of public attitudes found the media was the least trusted institution in 22 of 28 countries studied (Edelman, 2018). More granular-level analysis shows differentiation, with popular newspapers the least trusted source among legacy media, and television news ranked higher. Television journalism in advanced democracies is subject to public service requirements, impartiality rules, and other regulations that have tended to ensure more balanced than partisan coverage, with the United States being the major exception, after public interest obligations, including the Fairness Doctrine introduced in 1949, were rescinded in the 1980s. The level of audience trust and engagement with television tends to reflect audiences' assessment of channels' performance over longer periods and those channels' associations, whether with statist control of programming, staid programming, or a lack of appeal to ethnic or other minorities.

Journalistic Authority

The dominant normative model for journalism in the 20th century was 'a trained professional delivering objectively validated content' (McNair, 2009). This ideal-type model of 'Anglo-American' journalism began to break down under multiple challenges in the second half of the 20th century. One factor was the rise of 'new' literary journalism, within Anglo-American journalism, although this has been a feature of other journalism cultures, notably Southern European (Hallin & Mancini, 2004). Across North America and Western Europe, trends include the weakening of authority and legitimacy for public voices with the erosion of consensually accepted forms of status derived from politics, public institutions, and culture. Within these wider shifts, journalism's legitimacy has become, more than ever, open to dispute. As media historians show, journalism has been contested at various 'critical junctures', notably in the 1900s, 1930s, and 1960s, as well as in the current phase of digitalization (McChesney, 2007). Yet, the processes of disintermediation outlined previously in this chapter contributes to a profound shift from journalists' control over the flow of public information to breaking news 'as likely to come from the cell phone camera of a participant or an accidental observer as it is from a journalist employed by a news organization' (Elliot, 2008, p. 29; Singer, 2011). Journalistic authority is subject to questioning, challenge, threat, reconfiguration, and relocation; as Carlson (2017) writes in a book-length study, 'This environment strikes fear in the hearts of many journalists, but it is also a moment of opportunity to think about what we expect from the news' (p. 26).

Citizen journalism is associated with untrained amateurs performing below professional standards, yet the phenomena includes practitioners and groups motivated by criticism of the poor standards of 'professional' journalism and efforts to raise standards in investigative journalism, provide longer form reporting of thematic over episodic news, and strengthen fact-checking. Together, this poses fundamental challenges to the self-confirmatory discourses of 'professionalism'. Professional journalists can define themselves in terms of professional standards, from broad norms of accuracy and ethical responsibility to specialist legal requirements such as those surrounding judicial processes and court reporting. However, it is precisely these values that critics argue are being flouted and undermined (Singer, 2011). For instance, much criticism has been directed at the mobilization of hate speech within mainstream journalism in the United Kingdom.

In 2019, the new editor of *The Daily Express*, Gary Jones, condemned the paper's Islamophobia and announced an abrupt shift in editorial policy on anti-immigrant stories for a paper that ran 70 front pages featuring migrants in 2016 (Waterson, 2019b; Stop Funding Hate, 2019).

The unsettledness for some journalists arises from the challenge of assumed authority and 'balance' as partiality, whether of white male subjectivity, shared elite perspectives, or other delimiters of experience and insight. The long revolution in tackling racism, sexism, and other forms of discrimination and celebrating difference has been aided and influenced by the opportunities for more diverse, multivocality across communications exchange. The progression toward more enlightened, inclusive, and diverse journalistic voices is very far from assured, however. For instance, the values of 'neutral' fact-based journalism in America were challenged by new forms of advocacy journalism, from shock-jock radio hosts to right-wing punditry on Fox News and other cable channels (Hallin & Mancini, 2004, p. 286), marking a revival of partisanship that has intensified across the supply, if not consumption, of digital news.

How journalistic authority is being reconfigured and how this may be assessed in relation to qualities of voice, access, reporting, and communication exchange need careful, situated examination. What is clear, however, is that journalistic identities are subject to a series of conflicting pressures. There is a blurring of boundaries between journalism and other communications; between professional and amateur; and between producers, prosumers, and users of content. There is blurring between human-based and automated journalism. There is blurring across content and between a journalism of information and entertainment in particular. There is blurring between journalism and paid (advertising), earned (PR), and third-party-owned communications. A host of other boundaries are dissolving or being reconfigured, including convergence across platforms and forms as well as across specialisms and subgenres of journalism. The condition has been described as one of increasing 'liquidity', drawing on Zygmunt Bauman's (2000) influential concept, not only of rapid change but also of the inability to form more stable identifications in response to such change. Bauman (2005) describes

a society in which the conditions under which its members act change faster than it takes the ways of acting to consolidate into habits and routines. Liquid life . . . cannot keep its shape or stay on course for long. (p. 1)

For Singer (2011), increasing 'fluidity' is applicable across the whole enterprise of journalism, from structures to products and processes. Deuze (2005) examines journalism in the context of shifts from solid to 'liquid modernity' (Bauman, 2000), where arrangements and identities, such as those of professional and amateur, blur and merge. Deuze (2005) notes, 'The high modernism of journalistic professionalization has moved to a liquid modern state of affairs of feverish journalistic differentiation across media genres (including popular, tabloid, and infotainment journalisms), platforms, and industries' (p. 450).

It is important to avoid an overly generalized account of liquidity. Not all boundaries are blurred; some remain sharp, and many are defended in ways that sustain collective values and identity-work. Singer (2011) highlights efforts to shore up identities: Journalists 'have sought to define who they are and what makes them distinct' and asserted 'boundaries between themselves and other content providers in the open environment of the Internet' (p. 105). Another route taken has been to embrace changing self-perceptions and definitions about what journalists do and their normative role in the world (Singer, 2011). This embraces shifts from gatekeeping to sense-making roles, or from notions of strict objectivity toward more personal, engaged, interpretative roles, involving greater reflexivity toward source information supply.

Journalism cultures are formed through the negotiation of professional standards, common practices, and shared values. Such cultures are 'constituted on the basis of a particular set of culturally negotiated professional values and conventions that operate mostly behind the backs of the individual journalists' (Hanitzsch et al., 2012, p. 474). Surveys of journalists' attitudes worldwide show broad ideological consensus around core propositions: 'Journalism is (1) a professional service to the public that (2) is carried out in organizational contexts, (3) is mainly oriented toward facts, (4) provides timely and relevant information, and (5) requires at least some intellectual autonomy and independence' (Hanitzsch et al., 2012, p. 474; see also Deuze, 2005). Alongside these collectively shared values, dissensus is identified in three main areas: role perception (the normative and institutional role for journalists in society), epistemology (access to reality, acceptable evidence, positivism, and relativism), and different responses to ethical dilemmas (Hanitzsch et al., 2012). Key divisions form around intervention, from socially committed and engaged journalism to detachment. Journalists' personal identifications are also affected by widely divergent normative models, which Christians et al. (2009) summarize as monitorial (media as watchdog), facilitative (media as public sphere), radical (challenging authority on behalf of reform), and collaborative roles (media acting in partnership with centres of power).

The majority of journalists regard themselves as professionally autonomous, with internal factors having greater perceived influence over their practice than external pressures from 'organizational constraints (ownership, profit expectations, advertising considerations, and management) and external constraints (business people, advertisers, censorship, government officials, and politicians)' (Hanitzsch et al., 2012, p. 487). However, that affirmation needs to be qualified in light of previous studies showing that constraints may go unnoticed by journalists distanced from higher managerial decision-making and may also be internalized and normalized as 'the external limits of professional autonomy often operate in the form of persuasive processes rather than forced compliance' (Donsbach, 2004, p. 144).

More in line with the industry changes outlined previously in this chapter, job satisfaction levels appear to be declining. Weaver et al. (2007) trace declining job satisfaction among US journalists, regarding perceived erosion of autonomy, from the 1970s onwards. In their later 22-country survey, Weaver and Willnat (2012) found the majority of journalists to be dissatisfied. Those who were 'very satisfied' averaged 27.5% across all countries, and the percentage was slightly higher at 33% in the United States.

Studies and surveys indicate how professional and personal identities can be affirmed and strengthened in response to boundary challenges, not just undermined. The psychological work needed to sustain identities and to 'resolve' tensions and contradictions, however, lies outside of most conventional surveys and journalism research. In addition, there has been considerable research on journalists' attitudes about their work and profession but much less on how their beliefs influence their own work and outputs (Weaver & Willnat, 2012). So the focus and contribution of this book are particularly welcome.

Journalism in the 21st century is characterized by disturbance and uncertainty, from the cracking of monolithic corporate structures to the ambivalence of individuals oscillating between privileged status and subjection. For many who have lost jobs or quit, the experience will have been more agonizing than ambivalent, although many too have migrated to allied fields such as public relations, with relatively greater security and remuneration. Disruption has heightened the 'uncertainty and angst felt in the structures of professional performance' (Quintanilha, 2019, p. 1). Yet the overall picture is mixed. There is no common culture across global journalism. Both journalistic values and working conditions remain predominantly shaped by local political, economic, social, cultural, and occupational contexts. Within any given sectoral or institutional context, there tend to be beneficiaries alongside those negatively affected, advocates and critics of change, and usually a complex mixture experienced by individuals. In debates, the same phenomena, such as native advertising, can be regarded as the saviour or destroyer of journalism (Hardy, 2018). Mobilized in these debates, for practitioners but also for academics, are norms, values, cultural dispositions, and attachments articulated and sublimated to varying degrees.

Journalism is surviving in the 21st century, but Benjamin's angel of history surveys accumulated wreckage too, with long-standing news institutions felled, digital saplings snapped, amid a mixed panorama of despoilment and growth. The commercial model that sustained city newspapers, local monopolies, and national institutions is in structural decline. The business solutions that can work include monetization arrangements that pull at the threads of public interest journalism. Yet the practices involved in seeking to establish and maintain relations with audiences involve innovation and ceaseless reinvention. The business of news is damaged, but the practices of journalism continue to adapt and change.

References

Almiron, N. (2010). *Journalism in crisis: Corporate media and financialization*. Hampton Press.

American Press Institute. (2019). *What is journalism?* https://www.americanpressinstitute.org/journalism-essentials/what-is-journalism

Anderson, P. J., & Ward, G. (Eds.). (2007). *The future of journalism in the advanced democracies*. Ashgate.

Bauman, Z. (2000). *Liquid modernity*. Polity.

Bauman, Z. (2005). *Liquid life*. Polity.

Bell, E., & Owen, T. (2017). *The platform press: How Silicon Valley reengineered journalism*. Tow Centre for Digital Journalism.

Benjamin, W. (1970). *Illuminations* (H. Zohn, Trans.). Fontana.

Bennett, L. (2016). *News: The politics of illusion* (10th ed.). University of Chicago Press.

Berry, M. (2013). *Hard evidence: How biased is the BBC?* The Conversation. https://theconversation.com/profiles/mike-berry-101302/articles

Boczkowski, P. (2005). *Digitizing the news: Innovation in online newspapers*. MIT Press.

Brown, E. (2017, May 10). *9 out of 10 Americans don't fact-check information they read on social media*. ZDNet. https://www.zdnet.com/article/nine-out-of-ten-americans-dont-fact-check-information-they-read-on-social-media

Brüggemann, M., Humprecht, E., Nielsen, R., Karppinen, K., Cornia, A., & Esser, F. (2016). Framing the newspaper crisis: How debates on the state of the press are shaped in Finland, France, Germany, Italy, United Kingdom and United States. *Journalism Studies,* 17(5), 533–551.

Bruns, A. (2005). *Gatewatching: Collaborative online news production.* Lang.

Carlson M. (2014) When news sites go native: Redefining the advertising–editorial divide in response to native advertising. *Journalism,* 16(7): 849–865.

Carlson, M. (2017). *Journalistic authority: Legitimating news in the digital era.* Columbia University Press.

Carlson, M. (2019). Boundary work. In T. P. Vos & F. Hanusch (Eds.), *The international encyclopedia of journalism studies.* Wiley.

Carroll, J. S. (2006, April 26). What will become of newspapers? Joan Shorenstein Center on Press, Politics and Public Policy. (Speech delivered at the annual meeting of the American Society of Newspaper Editors under the title 'Last Call at the ASNE Saloon')

Castells, M. (2009). *Communication power.* Oxford University Press.

Christians, C., Glasser, T., McQuail, D., Nordenstreng, K., & White, R. (2009). *Normative theories of the media: Journalism in democratic societies.* University of Illinois Press.

Chyi, H. I., & Lee, A. M. (2013). Online news consumption: A structural model linking preference, use, and paying intent. *Digital Journalism,* 1(2), 194–211.

Compton, J. R. (2010). Newspapers, labor and the flux of economic uncertainty. In S. Allan (Ed.), *The Routledge companion to news and journalism* (pp. 591–601). Routledge.

Curran, J., Coen, S., Aalberg, T., Hayashi, K., Jones, P. K., Splendore, S., Papathanassopoulos, S., Rowe, D., & Tiffen, R. (2013). Internet revolution revisited: A comparative study of online news journal. *Media Culture Society,* 35(7), 880–897.

Cushion, S. (2012). *Television journalism.* Sage.

Davies, N. (2008). *Flat-earth news.* Chatto & Windus.

Deloitte. (2016). UK news media: An engine of original news content and democracy. http://www.newsmediauk.org/write/MediaUploads/Investigation%20Gallery/Final_Report_News_Media_Economic_Impact_Study.pdf

Deuze, M. (2005). What is journalism? Professional identity and ideology of journalists reconsidered. *Journalism,* 6(4), 442–464.

Donsbach, W. (2004). Psychology of news decisions: Factors behind journalists' professional behavior. *Journalism,* 5(2), 131–157.

Edelman. (2018). 2018 Edelman Trust *Barometer.* https://www.edelman.com/research/2018-edelman-trust-barometer

Elliot, D. (2008). Essential shared values and 21st century journalism. In L. Wilkins & C. Christians (Eds.), *The handbook of mass media ethics.* (pp. 28–39). Routledge.

Enders Analysis. (2011). Competitive *pressures* on the *press*: Presentation to the Leveson Enquiry. http://www.endersanalysis.com/content/publication/competitive-pressures-press-presentation-leveson-inquiry

Fenton, N. (2010). News in the digital age. In S. Allan (Ed.), *The Routledge companion to news and journalism* (pp. 557–567). Routledge.

Franklin, B. (2008). The future of newspapers. *Journalism Studies,* 9(5), 630–641.

Franklin, B. (2009). Introduction. In B. Franklin (Ed.), *The future of newspapers* (pp. 1–12). Routledge.

Freedman, D. (2008). *The politics of media policy.* Polity.

Gardiner, B., Mansfield, M., Anderson, I., Holder, J., Louter, D., & Ulmanu, M. (2016, April 12). The dark side of Guardian comments. *The Guardian.* https://www.theguardian.com/technology/2016/apr/12/the-dark-side-of-guardian-comments

Greenslade, R. (2019, April 14). *Financial Times* thrives by focusing on subscriptions. *The Guardian*. https://www.theguardian.com/media/commentisfree/2019/apr/14/financial-times-thrives-by-focusing-on-subscriptions

Greico, E. (2018, July 30). *Newsroom employment dropped nearly a quarter in less than 10 years, with greatest decline at newspapers.* Pew Research Centre. https://www.pewresearch.org/fact-tank/2018/07/30/newsroom-employment-dropped-nearly-a-quarter-in-less-than-10-years-with-greatest-decline-at-newspapers

Haim, M., Graefe, A., & Brosius, H. B. (2018). Burst of the filter bubble? *Digital Journalism*, 6(3), 330–343. doi:10.1080/21670811.2017.1338145

Hallin, D., & Mancini, P. (2004). *Comparing media systems.* Cambridge University Press.

Hanitzsch, T., Seethaler, J., Skewes, E. A., Anikina, M., Berganza, R., Cangöz, I., Coman, M., Hamada, B., Hanusch, F., Karadjov, C. D., Mellado, C., Moreira, S. V., Mwesige, P. G., Lee, P. L., Reich, Z., Noor, D. V., & Yuen, K. W. (2012). Worlds of journalism: Journalistic cultures, professional autonomy, and perceived influences across 18 nations. In D. Weaver & L. Willnat (Eds.), *The global journalist in the 21st century* (pp. 473–494). Routledge.

Hardy, J. (2014). *Critical political economy of the media: An introduction.* Routledge.

Hardy, J. (2018). Branded content: Media and marketing integration. In J. Hardy, H. Powell, & I. MacRury (Eds.), *The advertising handbook* (4th ed.). Routledge.

Hargreaves, I. (2003). *Journalism: Truth or dare.* Oxford University Press.

Harms, B., Bijmolt, T. H. A., & Hoekstra, J. C. (2017). Digital native advertising: Practitioner perspectives and a research agenda. *Journal of Interactive Advertising, 17*(2), 80–91.

House of Commons Digital, Culture, Media and Sport Committee. (2018). *Disinformation and 'fake news': Interim report.* House of Commons.

House of Lords Select Committee on Communications. (2008, June). *1st report of Session 2007–08: The ownership of the news* (Vol. 1). http://www.parliament.the-stationery-office.co.uk/pa/ld200708/ldselect/ldcomuni/122/122i.pdf

International Center for Journalists. (2017). ICFJ survey: The state of technology in global newsrooms. https://www.icfj.org/our-work/state-technology-global-newsrooms

Jackson, J. (2015, April 9). UK adults willing to pay only 92p a month to access news websites. *The Guardian*. http://www.theguardian.com/media/2015/apr/09/uk-news-websitesiab-digital-ad-spend-2014

Johnston, M. (2018, February 8). *How to rock mobile native advertising.* Content Marketing Institute. https://contentmarketinginstitute.com/2018/02/mobile-native-advertising

Jurkowitz, M. (2014, March 26). *The growth in digital reporting.* Pew Research Center.

Kennedy, P., & Prat, A. (2018). *Where do people get their news?* Columbia Business School Research Paper No. 17-65. SSRN. https://ssrn.com/abstract=2989719

Lee, C.-C., Chan, J., Pan, Z., & So, C. (2005). National prisms of a global 'media Event'. In J. Curran & M. Gurevitch (Eds.), *Mass media and society.* (pp. 320–335). Arnold.

MacGregor, P. (2013). International news agencies. In K. Fowler-Watt & S. Allan (Eds.), *Journalism: New challenges* (pp. 35–63). Bournemouth University.

MacKay, H. (2000). The globalization of culture? In D. Held (Ed.), *A globalizing world?* (pp. 47–83). Routledge.

Martinson, J. (2018, April 29). Pale, male and posh: The media is still in a class of its own. *The Guardian*. https://www.theguardian.com/media/media-blog/2018/apr/29/journalism-class-private-education

McChesney, R. (1999). *Rich media, poor democracy.* University of Illinois Press.

McChesney, R. (2007). *Communication revolution: Critical junctures and the future of media.* The New Press.

McChesney, R. (2013). *Digital disconnect.* The New Press.

McManus, J. H. (1994). *Market-driven journalism: Let the citizen beware?* Sage.

McNair, B. (2009). Journalism in the 21st century—Evolution, not extinction. *Journalism,* *10*(3), 347–349.

Media Reform Coalition. (2019). *Who owns the UK media?* https://www.mediareform.org.uk/wp-content/uploads/2019/03/FINALonline2.pdf

Media Standards Trust. (n.d.). *Churnalism.com.* http://mediastandardstrust.org/churnalism

Mediatique. (2018). *Overview of recent dynamics in the UK press market.* Department for Digital, Culture, Media & Sport.

Negroponte, N. (1995). *Being digital.* Hodder & Stoughton.

Newman, N. (2018). *Journalism, media, and technology trends and predictions 2018.* Reuters Institute for the Study of Journalism.

Newman, N., Fletcher, R., Kalogeropoulos, A., Levy, D., & Neilsen, R. (2018). Reuters Institute digital news report 2018. Reuters Institute for the Study of Journalism. http://media.digitalnewsreport.org/wp-content/uploads/2018/06/digital-news-report-2018.pdf?x89475

Newman, N., Fletcher, R, Levy, D., & Nielsen, R. (2016). Digital news report 2016. Reuters Institute for the Study of Journalism. https://reutersinstitute.politics.ox.ac.uk/sites/default/files/research/files/Digital%2520News%2520Report%25202016.pdf

Newman, N., & Levy, D. (2014). Reuters Institute digital news report. https://reutersinstitute.politics.ox.ac.uk/sites/default/files/research/files/Reuters%2520Institute%2520Digital%2520News%2520Report%25202014.pdf

Newman, N., & Levy, D. (2015). *Reuters Institute digital news report.* http://www.digitalnewsreport.org

Nicholls, T., Shabbir, N., & Nielsen, R. (2016). *Digital-born news media in Europe.* Reuters Institute for the Study of Journalism.

Ofcom. (2015). *News consumption in the UK: Research report.* Author.

Örnebring, H. (2010). Reassessing journalism as a profession. In S. Allan (Ed.), *The Routledge companion to news and journalism* (pp. 568–577). Routledge.

Pariser, E. (2011). *The filter bubble.* Penguin.

Parker, G. (2016). *Hidden ads risk killing native not the ASA.* https://www.asa.org.uk/news/hidden-ads-risk-killing-native-not-the-asa.html

Pew Research Center Project for Excellence in Journalism. (2006). *State of the news media: Tough times for print journalism—and in-depth reporting.* Pew Research Center.

Pew Research Center. (2008). *The state of the news media 2008.* https://www.pewtrusts.org/en/research-and-analysis/reports/2008/03/17/the-state-of-the-news-media-2008

Pew Research Center. (2010). *The state of the news media 2010.* https://www.pewinternet.org/2010/03/15/state-of-the-news-media-2010

Piety, T. (2016). Killing the golden goose: Will blending advertising and editorial content diminish the value of both? In M. Edström, A. T. Kenyon, & E.-M. Svensson (Eds.), *Blurring the lines: Market-driven and democracy-driven freedom of expression* (pp. 101–108). Nordicom.

Pilvre, B. (2012). Gender aspects of media tabloidization process in Estonia. *Media Transformations, 8,* 102–124.

Ponsford, D. (2017, September 20). Labour Force Survey: Sharp drop in freelancers accounts for 11,000 fall in the total number of journalists in the UK. *Press Gazette.*

Poutanen, P., Luoma-Aho, V., & Suhanko, E. (2016). Ethical challenges of hybrid editors. *International Journal on Media Management, 18*(2), 99–116.

Quintanilha, T. L. (2019, February). Journalists' professional self-representations: A Portuguese perspective based on the contribution made by the sociology of professions. *Journalism*. doi:10.1177/1464884919828246

Ramsay, G., & Moore, M. (2016). *Monopolising local news*. King's College London.

Reuters. (2018, August 16). Newspapers across U.S. rebuke Trump for attacks on press. *The New York Times*.

Rusbridger, A. (2018). *Breaking news: The remaking of journalism and why it matters now*. Canongate.

Seth, S. (2018, November 22). *The world's top 10 news companies*. Investopedia. https://www.investopedia.com/stock-analysis/021815/worlds-top-ten-news-companies-nws-gci-trco-nyt.aspx

Silverman, C. (2015). Lies, damn lies and viral content. Tow Centre for Digital Journalism. http://towcenter.org/research/lies-damn-lies-and-viral-content

Singer, J. B. (2011). Journalism in a network. In M. Deuze (Ed.), *Managing media work* (pp. 103–110). Sage.

Singer, J. B., & Ashman, I. (2009). 'Comment is free, but facts are sacred': User-generated comment and ethical constructs at *The Guardian*. *Journal of Mass Media Ethics*, *24*(1), 3–21.

Sparks, C. (2004). The impact of the internet on the existing media. In A. Calabrese & C. Sparks (Eds.), *Toward a political economy of culture* (pp. 307–325). Rowman & Littlefield.

Stop Funding Hate. (2019). *Stop Funding Hate is reclassifying the Daily Express as 'under review'*. https://stopfundinghate.info/2018/07/27/stop-funding-hate-changes-its-stance-on-the-daily-express

Ursell, G. (2004). Changing times, changing identities: A case study of British journalists. In T. E. Jensen & A. Westenholz (Eds.), *Identity in the age of the new economy*, (pp. 34–54). Elgar.

Waisbord, S. (2013). *Reinventing professionalism: Journalism and news in global perspective*. Polity.

World Association of News Publishers. (2009). *World press trends 2009*. http://www.wan-ifra.org/microsites/world-press-trends

World Association of News Publishers. (2016). *World press trends 2016*. http://www.wan-ifra.org/microsites/world-press-trends

World Association of News Publishers. (2017). https://wan-ifra.org/2017/06/world-press-trends-2017-the-audience-focused-era-arrives/

Waterson, J. (2018, November 5). More than a million readers contribute financially to *The Guardian*. *The Guardian*. https://www.theguardian.com/media/2018/nov/05/guardian-passes-1m-mark-in-reader-donations-katharine-viner

Waterson, J. (2019a, May 8). Local media. Closure of Walsall's papers is a loss of pride as well as news. *The Guardian*, p. 19.

Waterson, J. (2019b, April 28). Gary Jones on taking over *Daily Express*: 'It was anti-immigrant. I couldn't sleep'. *The Guardian*. https://www.theguardian.com/media/2019/apr/28/gary-jones-on-taking-over-daily-express-it-was-anti-immigrant-i-couldnt-sleep

Weaver, D. H., & Wilhoit, C. G. (1986). *The American journalist*. Indiana University Press.

Weaver, D. H., Beam, R. A., Brownlee, B. J., Voakes, P. S., & Wilhoit, G. C. (2007). *The American journalist in the 21st century: US news people at the dawn of a new millennium*. Lawrence Erlbaum Inc.

Weaver, D. H., & Willnat, L. (Eds.). (2012). *The global journalist in the 21st century*. Routledge.

Willens, M. (2019, February 4). Following layoffs, Vice Media signals an end to its free-wheeling days. *Digiday UK*. https://digiday.com/media/following-layoffs-vice-media-pitches-a-more-mature-story-and-business

Williams, A., Barnett, S., Harte, D., & Townend, J. (2014). The *state* of *hyperlocal community news* in the UK: *Findings* from a survey of practitioners. https://hyperlocalsurvey.files.wordpress.com/2014/07/hyperlocal-community-news-in-the-uk-2014.pdf

Wolff, M. (2007, October). Is this the end of news? *Vanity Fair*.

ZenithOptimedia. (2018). Advertising expenditure forecasts March 2018. https://www.zenithmedia.com/wp-content/uploads/2018/03/Adspend-forecasts-March-2018-executive-summary.pdf

3

The Importance of Visual Attention and Perception in Journalism

Catherine Thompson and Sharon Coen

Journalists report on specific events, and they present these events in a variety of formats to the general public. The main aim is to inform but also, in many cases, to entertain the consumer. Consequently, a story needs to be engaging and needs to be understood. To support this, journalists need to know how to capture and hold an audience's attention and how information is processed and interpreted. Moriarty (1995) found that those working in the field of visual communication considered perception and cognition as the most important disciplines with regard to informing their topic area. This chapter covers a selection of psychological theories related to visual perception and attention, it also identifies how aspects of cognitive processing influence communication.

Although attention and perception can be applied to journalism in a variety of ways, we focus on four specific topics. The first is the influence of limited capacity processing on the consumption of media messages. The second is the use of visual images by journalists to attract attention and aid processing as well as the effect that images may have on an audience's perception of a story. We go on to show that the way in which an audience comprehends information can be due to its members' own motivations but can also be due to the way in which the information is framed and the methods used to prime specific concepts. Finally, we consider the role of emotional processing within journalism, with regard to both how the emotional state of an individual may impact on their perceptions of a story and how journalists may utilize emotion to influence engagement and comprehension of their audience. This is by no means an exhaustive coverage of the links between cognition and journalism, but it will demonstrate the importance of cognitive processing in the field of media communication.

Catherine Thompson and Sharon Coen, *The Importance of Visual Attention and Perception in Journalism*
In: *The Psychology of Journalism*. Edited by: Sharon Coen and Peter Bull, Oxford University Press.
© Oxford University Press 2021. DOI: 10.1093/oso/9780190935856.003.0003

Limited Capacity

One of the key concepts within cognitive processing is the argument that humans are limited in the amount of information they can process at any one time. One of the first proponents of this viewpoint was Kahneman (1973), who suggested that capacity limitations are closely associated with the amount of effort required to process the information. Processing can occur either in a top-down, goal-driven manner, which is voluntary, effortful, and resource-intensive, or in a bottom-up, stimulus-driven manner, which is automatic, effortless, and utilizes few resources (Schneider & Shiffrin, 1977; Shiffrin & Schneider, 1977). Automatic processing will allow more than one piece of information to be processed in parallel because it does not put pressure on capacity limitations. However, it is predicted that when trying to process more than one piece of information in a goal-driven manner, this overloads the information processing system and a 'bottleneck' occurs, meaning that the information has to be processed serially (e.g., Broadbent, 1958; Treisman, 1969).

An effect that illustrates capacity limitations is the attentional blink (AB). The AB shows temporal restrictions in our ability to process information and is measured using a rapid serial visual presentation (RSVP) paradigm. In an RSVP, participants are presented with a stream of items (usually letters or numbers) one after the other. The items are shown very quickly (approximately 10 items per second), and participants are asked to search for one or two targets from the stream. For example, participants may be shown a series of grey letters along with one or two coloured letters and they must identify the coloured target letters among the grey distractors. When identifying a single target from an RSVP, accuracy is usually very high (e.g., Broadbent & Broadbent, 1987). However, when identifying two targets, performance on the second target (T2) suffers if the target is presented within 500 ms of the first target (T1). This is the AB effect.

Early theories to account for the AB effect focussed on limited capacity. For example, Raymond et al. (1992) proposed an inhibition model suggesting that when T1 is detected, subsequent items have to be inhibited to ensure they do not compete for resources. Therefore, if T2 is presented before T1 has been processed, it will be missed. This explains why accuracy to T2 is high when presented more than 500 ms after T1: There is no longer competition for resources. However, it would therefore be expected that the AB effect would last longer as the complexity of T1 increases (using up more resources and taking more time to process), but results do not support this (e.g., Shapiro et al., 1994). Chun and Potter (1995) instead suggest a two-stage model, proposing that information processing consists of a low-level, unlimited capacity stage and a high-level, limited capacity stage. All information enters the low-level stage, and items that meet the 'target-defining features' will be transferred to the second stage for further processing. Because this second stage has a limited capacity, an 'attentional gate' prevents additional information from entering until processing is complete. The theory proposes that when T1 enters the high-level stage, the attentional gate closes, meaning that T2 remains in the low-level stage, where it is not processed fully. This is supported by findings showing that T2 can often be detected (it has been processed at a low level), but it cannot be identified (because identification requires additional, high-level processing).

There are many other theories that try to explain the AB effect, but it is generally accepted that the effect reveals how human performance suffers due to limited capacity. The effect has implications for journalists because it raises the issue of whether an audience is fully processing the story presented. Findings from the AB effect show that this will very much depend on how quickly the information is being presented, how long it takes the audience to process and comprehend the information, and whether their attentional resources are still being utilized by something they have previously seen. Traditionally, news stories were generally communicated via newspapers and a limited number of television channels. This meant that news broadcasters had some control over how, when, and in what order their stories were presented. They could limit the speed with which information was presented and so, to a certain extent, they had the opportunity to consider capacity limitations. Things have changed dramatically since that time, and now consumers have substantially more control over how they get their news, what order they read/watch/listen to stories, and how quickly they move between different stories. This in turn means that the journalist has less control and so needs to take additional steps to ensure their story is communicated to the widest audience in the most effective manner.

To illustrate this within current society; news is often accessed via links from social media and consumed (at times almost accidentally) while users are on the go or engaged in other activities (Bergström & Jervelycke Belfrage, 2018). The role of social media influencers in determining which news items will be more likely to reach the audience, and in what order, is potentially becoming more important than the role of newspaper editors. It is nonetheless imperative to consider that influencers mainly share and frame (i.e., propose particular interpretative angles) the news, whereas news outlets and editors are still the main gatekeepers of information. This has two main implications. On the one hand, editors and journalists are now confronted with the task of attracting the attention of influencers, both by selecting 'appealing' events that the influencers would be inclined to share and by presenting such events in a way that is likely to attract and maintain attention (see Chapter 2). On the other hand, and in keeping with what has been stated previously, people are consuming news at times inadvertently, in a context in which their attention is divided (they are on the go), and they often rely on influencers to guide not only their consumption but also their interpretation of the news (but see the case study on eye tracking presented later in this chapter).

Further support for capacity limitations comes from studies measuring divided attention. Whereas the RSVP is usually employed to measure temporal attention and investigates the ability to process details presented within the same stream of information, divided attention studies measure the ability to attend to and process information from multiple sources. One method to study divided attention is use of the dual-task paradigm, in which participants are asked to perform a single task and then perform two tasks simultaneously. Performance on the dual task is then compared to that on the single task. Divided attention studies have been used extensively in the field of driving because attention is crucial in the driving task. A study by Strayer and Johnston (2001) outlines the dangers of divided attention (and supports limited capacity theories). Participants completed a simulated driving task in which they had to apply the brakes each time they saw a red light. They either completed the task on its own or while speaking on a mobile phone. The results showed that participants missed twice as many of the red lights and braking times were significantly slower to the lights when speaking on the mobile phone. This shows that when performing two tasks, we have to divide our limited resources between the two, leading to deficits in performance.[1]

On the basis of the previously discussed research findings, it would seem logical for those involved in media communication to limit the amount of information they try to present to their audience. Yet this is not always the case. A notable change in media broadcasting took place on 1 August, 1981, with the launch of MTV (originally known as Music Television), an American

---

[1] In most countries, it is now illegal to drive while using a handheld phone. However, Strayer and Johnston (2001) found the same effects regardless of whether participants were using a handheld or a hands-free phone.

television channel aimed toward young adults. The creator of MTV, Robert Pittman, argued that younger viewers were looking for television that was more engaging than the traditional format. In 1990, Pittman suggested that younger viewers have the ability to process different sources of information at the same time and, crucially, they prefer media that incorporates a range of messages. In contrast, he argued that older viewers do not have the capacity to process multiple sources of information in parallel (Pittman, 1990). Despite a lack of concrete evidence to support these views, his suggestions coincided with broadcasters adopting multiple message formats that consisted of elements such as a news anchor, weather forecast, sports results, and news crawls all presented simultaneously. A news crawl consists of scrolling information usually in the lower portion of the television screen [see Pavolik et al. (2015) for a test of their effect on information recall and retention].

Use of the multiple message format is supported by viewership data. For instance, when CNN (Cable News Network, a 24-hour American news channel founded in 1980) changed its Headline News to include multiple messages, viewership among their target demographic (ages 18–34 years) increased by 104% (NewsHour Online, 2002, cited in Bergen et al., 2005). In support of Pittman (1990), McClelland and Kerschbaumer (2001) also found that although the format was appealing for younger viewers, this was not the case for older audiences. Yet the adoption of multiple message formats is in direct contrast to the findings from cognitive psychology that consistently show we are unable to process multiple sources of information in parallel. Bergen et al. (2005) suggested that comprehension of simultaneously presented multiple messages within the media may be associated with perceptual grouping, potentially allowing for comprehension of more than one message at a time. Perceptual grouping is the process of chunking visual information together in order to process this information more effectively. For instance, items that are close together in space tend to be processed as a single entity rather than individually. Perceptual grouping is based on the viewpoint from Gestalt psychology (a school of thought founded in the early 20th century which proposed that perception occurs via a series of basic laws) that we organize stimuli according to laws of grouping (Wertheimer, 1923; Koffka, 1935). Gestalt psychologists proposed the law of similarity, which states that similar information will be grouped together and processed as a whole rather than being processed as independent units. This will require fewer resources than having to process each item individually.

According to Bergen et al. (2005), if multiple messages are similar (e.g., semantically related), they may be processed as one unit, putting less strain on limited capacity resources. They conducted a series of studies to explore this theory, asking participants to pay close attention to a news presenter while also trying to remember 'pre-loads' that were presented in a visual or auditory format. The news stories were 12 seconds long and consisted of a news anchor (simple condition) and a news anchor accompanied by news crawls across the bottom of the screen (complex condition). The pre-loads were presented prior to each news story and consisted of a visual pattern (visual condition) or an alphanumeric string (auditory condition). After each story, participants were tested on their recall of the pre-loads and were asked five questions about the news story. In the complex condition, participants recalled the visual pre-loads more accurately than in the simple condition. This is surprising because it may be expected that increased information (in the form of the news scrolls) would overload attentional capacity, causing the pre-loads to be filtered out (particularly as participants were told to prioritize the news stories). This may support the idea that participants were able to group the news anchor and the scrolls together, therefore putting no additional pressure on resources compared to the simple condition in which the news anchor appeared alone. However, the results also showed that significantly fewer facts were recalled from the news stories in the complex condition. Perceptual grouping therefore does not appear to be taking place, although this is perhaps to be expected, given that Gestalt laws are related to low-level perceptual features such as shape, contrast, and proximity in space and not to higher level properties such as semantic relationships.

Bergen et al. (2005) concluded that although viewers may consider multimessage formats to be more engaging, they have a negative impact on processing. News broadcasters should consider this because although this format may capture attention, it is likely to place too many demands on an individual's limited cognitive resources. This will mean that certain features of news stories will not be processed. As a result, not only will the audience be unlikely to remember the information because it is not encoded fully but also the audience may misunderstand the information because it is processed in a fragmented manner.

In addition to the increased use of the multiple message format, advances in technology have prompted an increase in media multitasking (MMT), whereby a consumer will have access to a number of different media messages on a number of platforms at any given time. Evidence suggests that television viewers are increasingly making use of secondary media devices while watching a television programme (e.g., Rideout et al., 2010; Voorveld & van der Goot, 2013). For example, imagine a viewer watching a breaking news story on television while monitoring online updates on the story using their laptop and reading views of the story on Twitter. This is challenging for the journalist because they need to ensure their story is the one that is selected by the viewer despite competition from other sources; however, it is also a challenge for the viewer due to the competition for cognitive resources between the different tasks.

Wang et al. (2015) make the argument that depending on the nature of the MMT it can be achieved successfully with effective performance on more than one task. They propose 11 factors that influence MMT, and they group these into four categories. One category, 'task relations', links to the threaded cognition model (Salvucci & Taatgen, 2008). Despite limited capacity theories proposing that completing two tasks can impair processing on one or both tasks, the threaded cognition model (Salvucci & Taatgen, 2008) makes the argument that tasks can be 'represented as threads of processing' (p. 101), and if tasks can be incorporated into related threads, it may reduce the competition for resources (somewhat similar to the notion of perceptual grouping). The theory builds upon the multiple resource theory of Wickens (1984, 2002), which outlined that processing resources are separated into a series of domains and multitasking can occur, providing tasks draw on different resources. For example, it is possible to walk home from work while listening to a news podcast because each task draws on a different pool of resources, but it is much more difficult to listen to a news podcast while also reading a newspaper because the two tasks rely on the same sensory modalities.

One of the few studies to investigate MMT in related tasks (i.e., in which different sources of information could theoretically be combined into related threads) was performed by Kätsyri et al. (2016). Their primary aim was to explore how the emotional content of one task can influence performance in a second, concurrent task. Emotional information is perceived to be more salient (e.g., Ohman et al., 2001; Smith et al., 2003) and so is likely to attract attention and resources. Some studies show that this is particularly the case with negative information compared to positive information (e.g., Baumeister et al., 2001). Kätsyri et al. (2016) presented 38 participants with 24 news videos, half positive and half negative. Eight tweets were created for each video, again half positive and half negative, and participants watched the videos in a random order on a television while simultaneously monitoring the related tweets on a tablet. Self-reported attention to the tablet was higher for the negative tweets than for the positive tweets, and this was supported by objective measures showing increased eye fixations on the negative tweets and better recall for the negative tweets. When viewing positive news stories, the negative tweets were attended more often than the positive tweets; however, when viewing negative news stories, there was no difference in the amount of attention given to positive and negative tweets. This suggests that negative information attracts more attention compared with positive information, consistent with findings from the psychological literature (see Baumeister et al., 2001). Crucially, however, the semantic similarity between the two tasks did not moderate the detrimental impact of MMT on attention, suggesting that even when tasks are related it is not possible to process multiple messages at once.

The previous findings appear to contrast with the suggestions of Wang et al. (2015) regarding 'task relations'. However, this category also incorporates a factor they refer to as 'task hierarchy', which states that if one task is perceived as more important (or is more salient), then resources will be prioritized to that task, leading to detrimental performance on the other task. Based on the evidence showing that we pay more attention to negative stimuli than positive stimuli, it appears that the negative tweets were prioritized over the positive news stories. This would account for increased attention to the negative tweets when participants viewed positive news stories. However, because priority was always given to the negative news story, there was no difference between the attention given to positive and negative tweets when presented with a negative news story. Initially, this would still suggest that MMT is possible depending on the saliency of the new messages; however, overall Kätsyri et al. (2016) found reduced processing of the news stories at times when tweets were presented compared to times when there were no tweets. This means that regardless of the saliency of the messages, performance always suffered with the addition of a secondary task. This supports the concept of a limited capacity processing system. It clearly indicates that with increasing availability of technology, journalists need to work harder to capture and hold the attention of their audience in order to prevent distraction by other media sources.

It seems evident that humans have a limit to the amount of information they can process at any one time, but the variety and amount of media messages we are exposed to at any given time do not appear to reflect this.

Consequently, a question may be raised about how much information a journalist may be communicating to their audience. Yet this important aspect of human performance is being considered in the field of visual communication, most notably in the limited capacity model of motivated mediated message processing (LC4MP; Lang, 2000, 2017). One critical aspect of the model is the assumption that the human brain can only process a certain amount of information; capacity limitations can influence encoding (the processing of information), storage (holding information in memory to use later), and retrieval (recall of information). The findings described previously support the LC4MP, and they provide empirical evidence to show that cognitive capacity influences the way in which media messages are consumed. It is encouraging to know that media communication is being studied in relation to cognitive processing, and it is clear that journalists should take account of capacity limitations if they want to ensure their audience comprehends their message.

The Impact of Visual Images

In addition to limiting the amount of information they attempt to communicate, journalists may also want to consider how best to present their information. Given that humans have a limited capacity, we have to be selective with regard to what we choose to pay attention and to what we choose to ignore. This is achieved via selective visual attention, whereby resources are biased toward those things perceived to be relevant and away from those considered irrelevant (Johnston & Dark, 1986; Theeuwes, 1993). As previously stated, attention can be allocated in a top-down (endogenous) manner or a bottom-up (exogenous) manner. Top-down attention is based on task demands and the intentions of the observer, and it is associated with a voluntary allocation of resources to specific information. Bottom-up attention is based on the characteristics of the information and is related to the automatic capture of attentional resources by the most salient stimuli (Schneider & Shiffrin, 1977; Shiffrin & Schneider, 1977). Given the distinction between top-down and bottom-up attention, it may be proposed that to capture and hold attention, a journalist should ensure that their message is salient and that it aligns with the goals and intentions of their audience. One method to achieve this is through the use of visual images.

Bottom-up attention is also referred to as 'stimulus-driven' attention because it involves the allocation of attentional resources based on the properties of stimuli in the environment. Koch and Ullman (1985; see also Itti & Koch, 2000) proposed that low-level visual features of an environment (i.e., colour, orientation, and motion) are processed pre-attentively and a 'saliency map' is created. Focussed attention is then directed to information within the environment in order of saliency. This means that visual images are more likely to capture attention because they are usually bigger and more colourful than text. Pictures in news stories have been found to attract readers (e.g., Garcia & Stark, 1991), suggesting that the use of images is an effective way to initially gain the attention of an audience.

The automatic capture of attention by visual images is particularly evident with emotional pictures. Nummenmaa et al. (2006) have studied this using eye tracking, an objective method of studying overt visual attention. Eye tracking can consist of a range of individual measures, and eye movements are separated into fixations (where the eyes remain fixated on a stimulus) and saccades (where the eyes move between information). Fixations can provide a great deal of detail about the allocation of visual attention: The more we fixate toward something, the more we are interested in that particular item; the longer we spend fixating on an item, the more resources we are investing to process the information. Nummenmaa et al. (2006) made use of the fact that the initial fixation made to an image indicates the automatic capture of attention and therefore shows which information is most salient. They presented participants with pairs of natural scenes for 3000 ms and asked them to make a judgement about whether the two images were equally pleasant. Images involved either people (target images) or inanimate objects (control images). Those involving people were pleasant (e.g., individuals smiling), unpleasant (e.g., individuals suffering from harm), or neutral (individuals engaged in a neutral activity and showing no expression of emotion). The eye movement measures collected included the time taken to fixate the target image and the gaze duration on the target image. Participants were quicker to fixate on an emotional target image compared to a neutral target image, and they were significantly quicker to fixate the pleasant images (e.g., a beach scene) compared to the unpleasant images (e.g., a rubbish dump). This shows the automatic capture of attention by emotional images, indicating that humans are more likely to orient their attention toward emotional information. In addition, emotional images were fixated for longer, particularly the pleasant images. This also shows greater attentional engagement on the emotional images, suggesting that not only do certain images capture attention but also that they are more likely to hold attention. Journalists can make use of these findings by incorporating emotional images into their stories.

In addition to capturing (and holding) attention, visual images can also influence effectiveness of processing. According to the dual-coding theory of Paivio (1971, 1986), cognitive processing is separated into two systems—a verbal and a nonverbal (visual) system. The verbal system is responsible for processing language, and the visual system is associated with the processing of visual images. These two systems can interact, meaning that the combination of text and images can affect comprehension of a message. The dual-coding theory outlines that different sources of information activate these two systems in different ways. Language will usually be processed (and stored in memory) as a verbal code, but images can be processed both verbally and visually (i.e., we can create a verbal code for an image in addition to a visual code). It therefore follows that the use of images would support memory recall (because there are more ways to retrieve the information).

Compelling evidence for the dual-coding theory comes from the picture superiority effect, which is the improved memory performance for images compared to words (e.g., Paivio & Csapo, 1973). The dual-coding theory would explain this with the argument that pictures are processed in two different ways, thus increasing the chance of retrieval. However, an alternative viewpoint is the sensory semantic theory (Nelson, 1979), which suggests that (1) images are more distinctive and the ability to encode them on the basis of their uniqueness increases retrieval, and (2) pictures cue semantic memory better than do words. Semantic memory is memory for facts and information about the world, and activation of semantic memory increases the meaning we can associate with incoming information. This increases processing, which then leads to an increased chance of recall (Craik & Lockhart, 1972). Evidence for the sensory somatic theory comes from Nelson et al. (1976), who found that pictures were recalled more accurately than words but only when the pictures were sufficiently different from each other; when they were very similar, the picture superiority effect disappeared. Paivio (1975) also found that the effect disappeared when participants were asked to make a semantic judgement about words and pictures during encoding. This shows that encoding (and therefore memory) is better when we can process information in a more meaningful manner (regardless of the properties of this information).

Studies measuring the impact of images in media communication have shown that visual images are processed more efficiently (e.g., Graber,

2001) and recalled more effectively (e.g., Graber, 1996) than text. The importance of visual images in journalism is also evidenced by the fact that politicians are increasingly favouring 'image bites' or 'video bites' over the more traditional 'sound bites'. In the 2004 US presidential campaign, sound bites accounted for 14.3% of news coverage, and image bites accounted for 25.1% of coverage (Bucy & Grabe, 2007). Schill (2012) states that political communication has changed in recent years and is increasingly 'built on a visual foundation; images are primary and words and text are often secondary' (p. 119). Yet although visual images are considered to aid information processing, they can also have a substantial impact on audience perception of a story.

Schill (2012) makes the case that images are 'enthymemes'; they can provide information implicitly, and they encourage a viewer to make a specific judgement. When crafting their message, a journalist may therefore use an image to implicitly elicit a certain viewpoint from their audience. For example, the way in which a photograph is taken can have a significant impact on a viewer's perception; when photographed from a low angle, a subject is more likely to be judged as taller and more powerful by the viewer (Graber, 1996). Although journalists conform to strict ethical guidelines in terms of presenting the truth, because an image is enthymematic and only 'suggests', compared to messages that are presented linguistically, it is much easier to dispute the fact that pictures encourage an audience to draw a particular conclusion (Schill, 2012).

Prior to Schill (2012) labelling images as enthymemes, Abraham (1998, 2003) made the case that mass media used images to add new meanings and suggestions beyond those contained in the written or verbal information in a story. This is supported by a study showing that readers presented with a single, balanced news story were biased toward one viewpoint or another depending on the image that accompanied the story (Gibson et al., 1999). Abraham and Appiah (2006) argued that this 'implicit visual propositioning' is particularly concerning in relation to stereotyping in news stories because news stories are generally considered to be accurate. In a study conducted in the United States, White participants were presented with three race-neutral news stories—one about oil tankers, one about school vouchers, and one about three-strike laws.[2] The latter two topics are stereotypically

---

[2] Individuals convicted of a third serious crime are automatically sentenced to a minimum of 25 years in prison.

associated with Black populations, and the researchers aimed to investigate whether the use of images could influence audience viewpoints of the issues raised. The news stories were paired with no pictures, two pictures of Black individuals, two pictures of White individuals, or one picture of White individuals and one picture of Black individuals. After reading each article, participants were asked about the extent to which they thought Black and White populations would be affected by each issue. When no images were presented, participants thought Black populations would be more affected by the issues of school vouchers and three-strike laws, therefore conforming to racial stereotypes. This was also the case when the stories were presented with images of Black individuals. Crucially, however, when images of Black and White individuals were shown, there was no difference in the extent to which participants judged Black and White populations to be affected by the issues. Abraham and Appiah (2006) concluded that 'news media can perpetuate stereotypes in subtle and highly effective ways using implicit visual imagery' (p. 196). Mass media can therefore have a negative influence on our judgements.

It appears that journalists have the potential to influence public opinion without the audience being aware that they are doing so, yet there is also evidence that an individual's own motivations can influence the way in which they perceive visual images. Balcetis and Dunning (2006) conducted a series of studies to measure the impact of motivational state on visual perception. In one experiment, they invited undergraduate students to participate in a 'taste-testing experiment'. Participants were presented with two drinks: One (desirable) was an appealing-looking glass of freshly squeezed orange juice, and the other (less desirable) was a thick green drink with an unpleasant smell. Participants were told they would only taste one drink and were asked to smell each one and then spend 3 minutes making a prediction about what their experience would be if they had to drink a set amount of each one. Following this, they were seated at a desk and told that the computer in front of them would randomly determine which drink they would taste. Some of the participants were informed that if a number appeared they would taste the orange drink, and if a letter appeared they would taste the green drink. The others were informed that a number would mean they tasted the green drink and a letter would mean they tasted the orange drink. An ambiguous figure was presented that could be perceived as either the letter B or the number 13. When participants were hoping to see a letter, 72% reported they saw a B, whereas when hoping to see a number, 60.5% reported they saw a 13.[3] This demonstrates that the participants' desire (to avoid the less appealing drink) influenced their visual perception.

Dunning and Balcetis (2013) propose that these findings are an example of 'wishful seeing' (we see what we want to see). One explanation for the influence of motivational state on visual perception is the use of 'perceptual sets'. A perceptual set is a mental association that is activated before information is presented. This perceptual set then guides processing to specific elements of the information, and so it is more likely to be perceived one way than another.

The influence of our own goals and intentions on the way in which we think and behave is known as 'motivated cognition'. This is linked to top-down (or 'goal-driven') processing; however, whereas traditionally researchers investigating goal-driven processing have focussed on the way in which demands and expectations regarding a specific task will influence cognition, the field of motivated cognition explores how the demands and expectations of the individual impact cognitive processing. These may well be the same. For instance, if an individual is interested in climate change and wants to search for recent news stories about this topic, then the goal of the task (to find interesting pieces on climate change) matches their own personal goal (to find interesting pieces on climate change). If that is the case, then the journalist can easily align their content with the intentions of the audience. However, in some circumstances, our internal goals and desires may be different from the goals of the task we are completing. For example, a geography student may need to find interesting news stories on climate change for an essay they are writing (task goal), but their attention is drawn to news stories about travel because they are looking forward to the holiday they will take when they graduate (personal goal). In this situation, cognitive resources may be directed to stories about climate change and stories about travel due to conflicting goals.

Considering the variety of people who have access to the media and the variety of goals that they each may have, it is arguably very difficult for a journalist to take account of this and ensure that their story reaches the target audience. Although images may capture attention and may be easier to process than text, the way in which they are processed will be affected by the goals of the viewer, and this may then influence whether or not the viewer continues with the piece or moves to another news story. When using images, one very

---

[3] Note that no participants were asked to taste either drink.

simple thing journalists can take from the findings related to wishful seeing is that they should try to avoid ambiguity so that the information they are attempting to convey within a picture can only be interpreted in one way. However, they do need to be aware that visual images could be viewed in a number of ways depending on the motivations of their audience.

Priming

The implicit activation of a mental concept or category that then influences subsequent processing (Balcetis & Dunning, 2006) is referred to as priming. It is related to the way in which information is stored within semantic memory, with stronger links between closely associated concepts. When an item is presented to an observer, a concept is activated within semantic memory and spreading activation occurs, meaning that related concepts are also activated (Collins & Loftus, 1975). This activation serves to 'prime' the related concepts, making them easier to access than unrelated concepts that have not been primed. A classic example of this comes from Meyer and Schvaneveldt (1971), who presented participants with pairs of words and nonwords (e.g., 'ffyhrt') and asked them to respond to whether both items in a pair were words or nonwords (a lexical decision task). When words were presented, they could either be related (e.g., 'nurse–doctor') or unrelated (e.g., 'nurse–butter'). Participants were significantly quicker to respond when the words were related compared to when they were unrelated, providing evidence that activation of the first word in semantic memory primed associated concepts, therefore meaning that related second words were easier to access and identify than unrelated second words.

Scheufele (2000) suggests that priming can be used in media communication by helping set the agenda of a piece. Priming highlights particular aspects, making them appear more important to the audience. The use of priming can have negative consequences, however, as can be seen from the study by Abraham and Appiah (2006) discussed previously, with visual images priming racial stereotypes. Moreover, although Abraham and Appiah (2006) show the immediate effects of media primes on an individual's perception and judgement of a story, the negative impact can be greater than this due to the processes of memory. When related concepts are activated frequently, this strengthens the association between the concepts, increasing the chances that if one concept is activated, the related concept will also be activated. In addition; the more recently we have activated a concept, the easier it is to reactivate (Tversky & Kahneman, 1973). The use of frequent, similar primes within the media therefore has the potential to alter an audience's attitudes regarding certain issues (e.g., strengthening negative stereotypes) because it alters accessibility of semantic memory.

Early research on priming identified ways in which stimuli affect subsequent perception at a relatively simple level of processing—for example, one word activating a semantically related word. This illustrates relationships between mental concepts within memory; however, evidence for the priming of stereotypes indicates the activation of mental categories and schemas. This is arguably more relevant to media communication because media messages usually incorporate a large amount of information. A schema is a collection of concepts that are related to a specific event or person. For example, we may have a schema about going shopping to the supermarket or a schema about a particular celebrity. Schemas are stored in semantic memory. When activated, all the information associated with a schema is activated. The schema then influences processing because cognitive resources are directed toward schema-related information. A study by Brewer and Treyens (1981) demonstrates this process. In this study, participants were asked to wait in an 'office' for approximately 35 seconds before entering a laboratory for an experiment. The room contained items that one would expect to find in an office, such as a desk and a calendar, but it also contained some unusual items, such as a toy and a skull. When participants were given an unexpected recall test for the items, they recalled more of the consistent items than the inconsistent items. This shows that attention is directed toward information that is congruent to a schema. Participants also falsely recalled more schema-consistent items that were not present in the room but would usually be found in an office. This shows that activation of a schema will influence our ability to accurately recall information from memory.

Although they can lead to attentional bias and retrieval problems, schemas are useful because they help reduce the amount of cognitive resources needed to process a situation. Instead of approaching every experience as new, we can use existing knowledge and expectations to guide attention, therefore saving on resources. The formation of schemas represents an interaction between conscious (controlled) processing and unconscious (automatic) processing (Schneider & Shiffrin, 1977; Shiffrin & Schneider, 1977). Controlled processing is associated with the effortful allocation of resources to achieve a particular task goal; however, over time and with increased experience of a task, processing can become habitual. This means that it becomes automatic, no longer requiring top-down resources. The formation of habits can be beneficial because they allow for goal-driven behaviours to be completed automatically when cued by a specific context (e.g., Reason, 1984; Wood & Neal, 2007). Schemas are also cued automatically (e.g., by specific primes), and again, they allow for resources to be allocated to task-relevant information without the requirement for controlled processing.

Schemas can also help us make sense of information, allowing for the assimilation of new details into existing knowledge structures. By using primes to activate schemas, a journalist can therefore avoid overloading their audience, relying on the schema to support the information they are trying to communicate. The obvious drawback, however, is whether the audience has the required schema; this will very much depend on their past experience. Indeed, Domke et al. (2002) state that the ability of images to prime certain judgements is due to the interaction between the visual image and the viewer's 'pre-existing beliefs and experiences' (p. 134). This represents a challenge for journalists, and so knowledge of their target audience is crucial.

The use of existing knowledge to interpret information and form a judgement is known as 'pragmatic inference' (e.g., Brewer, 1977). The relationship between media primes and pragmatic inference has been investigated by Chan and Yanos (2018). They note that the media tends to portray a negative view of individuals suffering from mental illness (e.g., Corrigan et al., 2005; Stuart, 2006; Wahl, 1992), and there is evidence that this media bias influences public opinion about mental illness (e.g., Angermeyer & Matschinger, 1996). In the study conducted by Chan and Yanos (2018), participants were asked to read a relatively vague news report of a violent incident. For half the participants, there was no mention of mental illness in the report, whereas for the other half, a prime was included stating that the perpetrator 'has a history of schizophrenia'. The prime did activate mental illness stereotypes, and participants who were primed were more likely to state that mental illness played a role in the incident. When memory for the report was tested, participants who were primed falsely recalled details that were only implied in the report (not explicitly stated), therefore supporting the use of pragmatic inference. This shows that when a schema (in this case, a stereotype) is activated by a prime it will influence the way an individual allocates their attention, the way they interpret information, and their memory for the information. In particular, the inclusion of a prime will lead individuals to bring their own knowledge and experience (stored in the schema) to their interpretation of information. The influence of media priming is therefore a complex interplay between the characteristics of the prime, the information contained within a news report, and the preexisting knowledge of the audience. Journalists need to have an awareness of how these factors can interact to impact on public opinion.

In addition to affecting perceptions and judgements, priming has also been found to influence behaviour. This was explored by Bargh et al. (1996), who conducted a study asking participants to complete sentences using words that were neutral (e.g., 'thirsty' and 'private') or stereotypically related to the concept of elderly people (e.g., 'wrinkled' and 'retired'). Following the task, participants primed with the elderly words walked away from the laboratory room significantly slower than those primed with the neutral words. Research has also shown that priming can influence performance. In a study conducted by Dijksterhuis and van Knippenberg (1998), participants were asked to imagine what life would be like as either a professor or a football hooligan and were then asked to complete a trivia test. Those primed with the category of professor performed better on the test than a control group that was given no prime, and those primed with the category of football hooligan performed worse.[4]

Behavioural priming has been attributed to the link between perception and behaviour. For instance, according to the ideomotor account (e.g., Dijksterhuis & Bargh, 2001; Dijksterhuis & van Knippenberg, 1998), priming of a particular trait automatically activates behaviour associated with the trait. Appel (2011) proposes that the perception–behaviour link may have less relevance in explaining the effect of media primes because they often involve narratives that require individuals to create a mental model of a situation or person. This is potentially reflected by the fact that media primes can result in the consumer behaving similarly to the prime (behavioural assimilation) but can also result in behaviour that is different from the prime (contrast). Using the selective accessibility model, Mussweiler (2003, 2007) attempts to account for assimilation and contrast. The model proposes that when given a prime, an individual will use this as a point of reference and will then engage in either similarity testing or dissimilarity testing. Similarity testing occurs when the prime seems similar to the self, in which

---

[4] Although the 'Professor Prime' effect has been found in a number of studies, a large-scale replication of the experiment completed by Dijksterhuis and van Knippenberg found no effect of a prime on cognitive performance (O'Donnell et al., 2018).

case the comparison focusses on information consistent with the prime (i.e., the characteristics that the consumer shares with the prime). If the prime is judged more different from the self, this will encourage dissimilarity testing, which focusses on information that is inconsistent (i.e., the ways in which the consumer and the prime differ).

One way to influence the type of comparison made is to choose the prime carefully. Dijksterhuis and Van Knippenberg (1998) found that priming using a category led to assimilation, whereas priming using a specific example led to contrast. A second method is to encourage a specific comparison, manipulating whether the consumer identifies similarities or differences. This was investigated by Appel (2011), who found that after reading a story about a football hooligan (intended to prime the stereotype of 'stupid'), participants performed worse on a general knowledge test than a control group that did not read the story (behavioural assimilation). However, participants who read the same story but were asked to identify differences between themselves and the subject of the story performed better (contrast). Again, this shows that priming can have an impact on behaviour (and performance) but also that a journalist has the potential to encourage specific judgements and behaviours depending on the prime they use.

Often, the use of primes in media communication is considered to be manipulative, and studies conducted on priming generally focus on negative consequences, such as the priming of stereotypes (e.g., Chan & Yanos, 2018). Journalists have a responsibility to their audience to portray the truth, but in using primes in a considered manner, they may also be able to support and benefit their audience. An example of this is the finding of Abraham and Appiah (2006) that racial stereotypes were reduced when a racially neutral story was paired with pictures of Black and White individuals compared to when it was paired with pictures of Black individuals only. In addition, with knowledge of the way in which primes can cue certain behaviours, a journalist may be able to encourage and promote positive behaviours rather than negative behaviours. This has been considered within the field of health psychology—for instance, presenting images of healthy foods rather than unhealthy foods (Papies, 2016)—and could be incorporated into the mass media. The careful use of primes may therefore alter public opinion and behaviour in a beneficial way.

Using Emotion

A further way in which media primes can be used to influence an audience is to make use of emotion. Emotions affect cognitive processing; therefore, inducing an emotional state in an audience (affective priming) can impact the way in which a story is comprehended. Explanations for affective priming are again based on the structure of semantic memory. According to the network theory (Bower, 1981), emotions are stored as nodes within a semantic network, and spreading activation has specific influences on cognitive processing. For example, activation of a negative mood state would result in spreading activation to related negative concepts rather than positive concepts. One effect that supports the network theory is mood congruency, whereby individuals recall more mood-congruent information than mood-incongruent information. For example, Rinck et al. (1992) induced participants into happy or sad moods and asked them to rate the valence of a selection of words (how positive or negative each word was). When recalling the words in a neutral mood state (feeling neither happy nor sad), those who had originally been induced into a sad mood recalled more unpleasant words and those originally induced into a happy mood recalled more pleasant words. The effect is attributed to the fact that the emotional state of the observer activates the semantic network, biasing attention toward emotionally congruent information. This increases processing (and encoding) of that information compared to emotionally incongruent information, resulting in improved recall.

Mood congruency is an example of how emotional state affects what we pay attention to and therefore what we process, yet evidence also shows that emotional state can influence the way in which we process information (e.g., Basso et al., 1996; Fredrickson & Branigan, 2005). In particular, it appears that positive mood states enhance creativity (Baas et al., 2008), improve problem-solving (Isen et al., 1987), and expand the breadth of attention (Rowe et al., 2007). The broaden-and-build theory (Fredrickson, 1998, 2001) explains this, arguing that positive emotions will broaden the scope of attention and therefore allow more information to be processed at any given time. In contrast, negative emotions will narrow attentional scope, reducing the amount of cognitive resources available and therefore limiting information processing.

In a study designed to measure the influence of affective priming (and therefore emotional state) on the processing of news articles, Baumgartner and Wirth (2012) asked participants to read a positive article about football or a negative article about child soldiers. Mood was assessed to confirm that the stories had primed the required emotional state, and then participants read six more news articles, three positive and three negative. Finally, participants were given a cued recall test consisting of two questions about each of the six articles. Overall, participants recalled more mood congruent information (e.g., those who read the football article remembered more information from the three positive articles compared to the three negative articles). This supports the mood congruency effect. In addition, participants who read the football article showed better memory for all six articles compared to those who read the child soldier article. This supports the broaden-and-build theory because it shows that a positive mood enhanced processing resources, allowing more information to be encoded and therefore more information to be recalled.

Baumgartner and Wirth (2012) argue that news producers should consider the impact of affective priming when organizing their stories. Specifically, the allocation of attention to reports presented after a negative story could be very different from the allocation of attention to reports presented after a positive story. This will ultimately affect encoding of the message and will therefore influence comprehension and recall of the information.

Despite a wide variety of findings to support the broaden-and-build theory, more recent work indicates that the relationship between cognition and emotion is not as simple as the theory suggests. Gable and Harmon-Jones (2010a) made the argument that the effect of positive and negative mood will vary according to motivational intensity ('the impetus to act'; p. 211). In addition, they distinguished two levels of motivational direction, approach and withdrawal. Approach is the motivation to move toward something, whereas withdrawal is the motivation to move away from something. Whereas negative emotions are generally associated with withdrawal, positive emotions are associated with approach.

Gable and Harmon-Jones (2010b) used a global–local processing task (Navon, 1977) to assess the effect of motivational intensity on the scope of attention. In this task, participants are usually presented with large letters that are made up of smaller letters (e.g., a large letter F made up of small letter T's). Participants are asked to identify whether a particular letter is present in the image, and response times are measured on the basis of whether the letter (when present in the image) is presented as the global feature (large letter) or the local feature (small letter). It has been argued that faster responses to the global feature represent a wide scope of attention with greater processing resources, and faster responses to the local feature indicate a narrow scope of attention and limited resources (e.g., Fredrickson, 2001). Gable and Harmon-Jones (2010b) found that participants induced into a negative mood with sad pictures were quicker to attend to global features (Experiment 1), and participants induced into a negative mood using disgust pictures were quicker to attend to local features (Experiment 2). Although both emotional states are related to withdrawal, disgust is associated with greater motivational intensity than sadness, and so the researchers proposed that negative affect with high motivational intensity will lead to attentional narrowing, but negative affect with low motivational intensity will lead to broadening of attention.

Gable and Harmon-Jones (2008) also measured the impact of motivational intensity in positive mood states. They induced participants into 'low approach' positive affect using humorous films of cats, and they induced participants into 'high approach' positive affect using films of delicious desserts. They found that high approach positive affect led to narrowed attention and low approach positive affect led to a broadening of attentional focus. Gable and Harmon-Jones (2008) also found that the narrowing of attention in high approach conditions was particularly common for individuals who were high in trait approach motivation. In their motivational dimension model of affect, Gable and Harmon-Jones (2010a) were able to account for these findings because they take into consideration both the valence associated with an emotional state (how good or bad something is) and the motivation associated with an emotional state (the motivation we have to either approach or avoid something). This contrasts with the broaden-and-build theory, which focusses only on valence.

The importance of motivation brings us back to LC4MP (Lang, 2000, 2017). One of the key facets of this model is the way in which the human motivational system can impact on processing. LC4MP outlines two motivational systems—an appetitive (approach) system responsible for seeking out information and an aversive (avoidance) system responsible for avoiding threat. The model suggests that when encountering information, cognitive resources will be allocated toward the processes of encoding, storage, and retrieval, but the emphasis on each one will interact with arousal. The appetitive system is more active in rest states (in order to promote information seeking), and emphasis is given to encoding. As information in the environment becomes more motivationally arousing, more resources are invested into encoding to ensure that the information is processed fully. However, as arousal increases, activation of the aversive system will increase and resources will be invested in storage (to ensure sources of threat are remembered) and retrieval (to access previously stored information in order to help develop strategies for avoiding threat). On the basis of this, it has been suggested that the level of arousal within a news report can have an impact on processing of the message. For example, when processing an arousing story that is relatively simple, there may be sufficient resources to allow for encoding even though the aversive system will bias resources toward storage and retrieval. However, with a more complex story, the added processing demands of the story will lead to cognitive overload at the encoding stage, resulting in limited processing and therefore poor memory for the story.

Grabe et al. (2003) provide support for this aspect of LC4MP. They compared attention, arousal, and recall to six highly arousing stories (e.g., a report on a drive-by shooting) and six less arousing stories (e.g., repairs on a city drainage system) that were each presented as a short video. The stories were presented in either a tabloid (complex) format (e.g., adding sound effects, music, and slow motion) or a standard (simple) format. As intended, physiological measures showed increased arousal of participants when viewing the more arousing stories. More attention was also given to arousing stories than non-arousing stories. Findings additionally showed that cued recall was poor for the arousing stories when presented in a tabloid format, whereas recall of non-arousing stories was better when presented in a tabloid format. In accordance with LC4MP, Grabe et al. (2003) suggest that arousal redirects resources toward storage and retrieval processes, leaving fewer resources for encoding, and the added complexity of the message when presented in a tabloid format (i.e., when presented with many additional elements, such as sound effects and music) leads to cognitive overload and information is not processed effectively. In contrast, it is argued that the lack of arousal in the neutral stories puts less pressure on processing resources but the added complexity is required in order to encourage the focus of attention toward the information. This has implications for the presentation of news and implies that emotional stories are best presented in a simple manner, but more neutral stories may benefit from more complex presentation.

LC4MP indicates that effective production of media messages is a delicate balance between engaging the audience and not overloading them with information. One technique that can help with this is the use of news narratives. A news narrative consists of 'events that are chronologically ordered, situated in a detailed setting, and described from the perspective of an eye-witness' (van Kreiken, Sanders, & Hoeken, 2015, p. 221). According to past research, news narratives can increase engagement with a story (Knobloch et al., 2004; Sanders & Redeker, 1993) and can also increase comprehension and memory of a story (Machill et al., 2007). With regard to printed news, van Krieken, Hoeken, et al. (2015) propose that narratives help draw the attention of a reader and allow them to identify with those involved in the event. A narrative also means that the reader can gain a better understanding of a situation without actually experiencing it. In relation to this, Peelo (2006) suggests that narratives for shocking events encourage readers to take the role of a 'mediated witness'.

A study by van Krieken et al. (2015) investigated engagement with crime narratives by comparing narrative and non-narrative reports of a real-life shooting that took place in the Netherlands in 2011. The articles contained the same basic facts about the event (e.g., date, location, and the number of people injured), but the narrative article told the story from the perspective of eyewitnesses. Participants reported feeling more 'present' when reading the narrative compared to the non-narrative story, and they reported greater attentional focus on the narrative. This shows increased engagement with the narrative, and the researchers argued that narratives are effective because they engage the reader both cognitively and emotionally. Interestingly, the study compared a long narrative (1238 words), a long non-narrative (1215 words), and a short non-narrative (402 words), and whereas participants reported more attention to the long narrative than the long non-narrative, there was no difference in attention to the long narrative and the short non-narrative. This indicates that when writing a long article, a journalist should use a narrative style to increase engagement.

Encouraging the role of mediated witness appears to increase attention and engagement in news stories, and the popularity of this method is reflected in the number of journalists who use linguistic techniques to create the eyewitness viewpoint (van Kreiken et al., 2015). It therefore seems apparent that journalists have an understanding of how to capture the attention of their audience and how to increase emotional engagement to improve comprehension and retention of a story. Yet LC4MP (Lang, 2000, 2017) indicates that the use of emotional information has to be considered in reference to capacity limitations. Findings show that emotional information can be used to capture (and hold) attention (e.g., Nummenmaa et al., 2006), and affective priming can be used to influence the way in which a story is processed (e.g., Baumgartner & Wirth, 2012). However, the relationship between emotional processing and cognitive resources is complex, and journalists need to acquire an understanding of this to ensure that they can engage their audience without overloading them with information.

Case Study: The Importance of Attention in Understanding News—Lessons from Studies Using Eye-Tracking Techniques

In an exquisite and intrinsically media psychological fashion, in 1977 O'Bryan identified in the attention processes an essential ingredient to understanding the effectiveness of educational programs on television. O'Bryan reviewed a series of studies in which researchers explored the role of different production features of mediated messages in attracting children's attention, using eye movements as an indicator of attention. The review reports on a programme of research in which production features are employed to 'cue' the children into paying attention to crucial pieces of information. The argument of the paper in general seems to be that it is possible to align production features with theories of attention and learning in order to maximize the educational potential of media products. This key idea is echoed by Bucher and Schumacher (2006), who argue that in order to best understand the way in which people select news it is important to understand what attracts attention. Interestingly, in both cases the authors report studies in which attention is measured by observing their participants' eye movements. Eye tracking (a method employed to track oculomotor behaviour) can play an important role in understanding how we direct our attention when exposed to information in the media, on the assumption that we look toward the information we are attending. Of course, this is an approximation that uses a behavioural measure to infer a psychological process, and as such it is not perfect. For example, one can argue that even if we are looking at something, it does not necessarily mean we are attending to it. However, it is true that it is not possible to attend to a (visual) stimulus if we do not see it. Furthermore, research suggests a link between attention, working memory, and eye movements (Theeuwes et al., 2009). For this reason, researchers have successfully adopted eye tracking as a way to measure attention.

When it comes to media, Bucher and Schumacher (2006) report how eye-tracking research allows for

- describing distribution of attention to a media stimulus (Küpper, 1990; Garcia and Stark, 1991);
- following and comparing patterns of attention to a media stimulus as dependent upon its design features (Stenfors et al., 2003; Outing and Ruel, 2004; Holmqvist and Wartenberg, 2005; Holsanova et al., 2006);
- distinguishing at a micro level different phases of a media reception process such as orientating, scanning, or reading (Holmqvist, Holsanova, Barthelson, and Lundqvist, 2003);
- following patterns of interaction with Web sites (overview in Jacob and Karn, 2003). (p. 354)

The authors themselves report a series of studies in which eye tracking was employed to show how both bottom-up (stimulus-driven) and top-down (motivation-driven) processes seem to influence attention to news across media (print, online, and digital newspapers). They also make the case that when reading the news, the participant engages in a process of meaning-construction by directing attention to different elements of the stimulus (the newspaper).

However, the perceptual environment, context, and motivation vary when it comes to social media. It is arguable that the motivations behind news consumption would be very similar, whether these are offered online or in a press version. We have already mentioned how social media is also a platform of 'accidental' exposure to news. Research shows that there are differences across social media in the extent to which they are used to satisfy different needs (or seek different gratifications; e.g., see Phua et al., 2017), but the need for information, while often present, is generally not the main reason (to the best of our knowledge). So what happens when a news item appears in the feed? Will it attract attention? How will it be processed?

Once again, eye tracking research can help shed light on these issues. Vraga et al. (2019) use eye-tracking methods to show how news and political information presented in a Facebook news feed receive a portion of attention and are therefore processed at least on a superficial level. When it comes to political news, Sülflow et al. (2019) used eye tracking to explore whether participants would engage with posts that were more consistent with their political ideology. The experiment comprised 103 participants (93 for the eye tracking), all of whom were exposed to news items that originated from authoritative or less authoritative websites and were either consistent or inconsistent with the participants' attitudes on political issues. Finally, each article was accompanied by users' comments, which were either consistent or inconsistent with the argument presented in the article. The authors measured the amount of time participants spent looking at attitude-consistent versus attitude-inconsistent news and comments and authoritative versus not authoritative sources. Using self-report measures, they also assessed whether participants would express interest in clicking on the article. Once again, eye-tracking data provided a useful complement to the self-report measures. Results showed how participants (1) allocated attention to both attitude-consistent and attitude-inconsistent posts (thus supporting Vraga et al.'s findings) and (2) showed that they were more likely to click on consistent than inconsistent posts. Moreover, participants paid more attention to, and were more likely to select, news from authoritative sources. With regard to comments, the authors found a very interesting interaction, whereby participants tended to pay more attention to posts that were consistent with their own attitude when comments seemed to oppose that position, whereas cross-cutting news posts received more attention when they were accompanied by attitude-consistent comments.

In another contribution, Josephson and Miller (2015) showed, again using eye tracking, that question formats for news items on Twitter tend to be ignored when presented in primary positions, at the beginning of the feed. This result might need replication, given that there is no other evidence in this area, and it would be useful if it was combined with the uses and gratification perspective to explore the role of motivation in this type of selection. Interesting, however, is the fact that eye-tracking data in this case seems to indicate order effects in the likelihood of people paying attention to (let alone processing) information on social media. Future research could focus on perceptual aspects of social media news feeds and how they interact with attention patterns.

Overall, the research reported here seems to support the idea that the inclusion of theories and techniques derived from the literature on attention has the potential to complement and expand our understanding of news consumption patterns. Or to use Bucher and Schumacher's (2006) words, 'A theory of media selectivity needs a theory of attention, because attention to a media stimulus is the starting point of each process of reception' (p. 347).

Conclusion

The aim of this chapter was to outline a selection of theories relating to visual attention and perception and illustrate how they can be applied to engagement and processing of news stories. It is evident that knowledge of cognitive psychology can support effective journalism because it provides information about what captures attention and how to capture attention, the constraints on information processing, and the impact of emotion on processing. We have seen that the limited capacity processing system is a critical factor affecting engagement and comprehension of news stories. This is particularly concerning in an era in which the audience has a great deal of choice over how and when they access news. Journalists can make use of automatic processing by using salient images to capture attention, but they also need to ensure that their message holds attention and is interpreted in the appropriate manner. One method to influence interpretation is the use of media primes to implicitly activate certain perceptions and judgements. However, research shows that journalists need to manage these carefully to ensure that they are not ambiguous and that they have the desired effect. Journalists also need to consider the use of primes in relation to ethical considerations. Even when attempting to influence the way in which a message is interpreted, journalists still face challenges due to the internal motivations of the audience. Motivation interacts with processing capacity and emotional state, and without an understanding of this, it is difficult to ensure that information is communicated in the intended manner.

Although the focus of the chapter was on information processing from the perspective of the audience, it must be acknowledged that journalists are subject to the same influences. With greater pressure to engage with different media formats, are journalists able to divide their attention effectively or will this lead to poor performance? When going into a situation to report on a story, would the situation prime a specific schema, therefore affecting the way in which the journalist can process the information and the neutrality with which they communicate this information? Does being in a negative mood limit attention and creativity of the journalist? These are all important questions to consider, and in addition to developing an understanding of thinking and processing of their audience, the theories and research outlined previously suggest that journalists would benefit from an awareness of their own thinking and processing.

References

Abraham, L. (1998). *Subtle manifestations of prejudice: Implicit visual constructions of Black pathology.* PhD dissertation, Annenberg School for Communication, University of Pennsylvania.

Abraham, L. (2003). Media stereotypes of African Americans. In P. M. Lester & S. D. Ross (Eds.), *Images that injure: Pictorial stereotypes in the media* (2nd ed., pp. 87–92). Praeger.

Abraham, L., & Appiah, O. (2006). Framing news stories: The role of visual imagery in priming racial stereotypes. *Howard Journal of Communications, 17,* 183–203. doi:10.1080/10646170600829584

Angermeyer, M. C., & Matschinger, H. (1996). The effect of violent attacks by schizophrenic persons on the attitude of the public towards the mentally ill. *Social Science & Medicine, 43,* 1721–1728. doi:10.1016/S0277-9536(96)00065-2

Appel, M. (2011). A story about a stupid person can make you act stupid (or smart): Behavioral assimilation (and contrast) as narrative impact. *Media Psychology, 14*(2), 144–167. doi:10.1080/15213269.2011.573461

Baas, M., De Dreu, C. K., & Nijstad, B. A. (2008). A meta-analysis of 25 years of mood-creativity research: Hedonic tone, activation, or regulatory focus? *Psychological Bulletin, 134,* 779–806. doi:10.1037/a0012815

Balcetis, E., & Dunning, D. (2006). See what you want to see: Motivational influences on visual perception. *Journal of Personality and Social Psychology, 91*(4), 612–625. doi:10.1037/0022-351.91.4.612

Bargh, J. A., Chen, M., & Burrows, L. (1996). Automaticity of social behaviour: Direct effects of trait construct and stereotype activation on action. *Journal of Personality and Social Psychology, 71*(2), 230–244. doi:10.1037/0022-3514.71.2.230

Basso, M. R., Schefft, B. K., Ris, M. D., & Dember, W. N. (1996). Mood and global–local visual processing. *Journal of the International Neuropsychological Society, 2*(3), 249–55. doi:10.1017/S1355617700001193

Baumeister, R. F., Bratslavsky, E., Finkenauer, C., & Vohs, K. D. (2001). Bad is stronger than good. *Review of General Psychology, 5*(4), 323–370. doi:10.1037//1089-2680.5.4.323

Baumgartner, S. E., & Wirth, W. (2012). Affective priming during the processing of news articles. *Media Psychology, 15*(1), 1–18. doi:10.1080/15213269.2011.648535

Bergen, L., Grimes, T., & Potter, D. (2005). How attention partitions itself during simultaneous message presentations. *Human Communication Research, 31*(3), 311–336.

Bergström, A., & Jervelycke Belfrage, M. (2018). News in social media: Incidental consumption and the role of opinion leaders. *Digital Journalism, 6*(5), 583–598.

Brewer, W. F. (1977). Memory for the pragmatic implications of sentences. *Memory & Cognition, 5,* 673–678.

Brewer, W. F., & Treyens, J. A. (1981). Role of schemata in memory for places. *Cognitive Psychology, 13,* 207–230.

Broadbent, D. E. (1958). *Perception and communication.* Pergamon.

Broadbent, D. E., & Broadbent, M. H. P. (1987). From detection to identification: Response to multiple targets in rapid serial visual presentation. *Perception & Psychophysics, 42,* 105–113.

Bucher, H. J., & Schumacher, P. (2006). The relevance of attention for selecting news content. An eye-tracking study on attention patterns in the reception of print and online media. *Communications, 31*(3), 347–368.

Bucy, E. P., & Grabe, M. E. (2007). Taking television seriously: A sound and image bite analysis of presidential campaign coverage, 1992–2004. *Journal of Communication, 57,* 652–675.

Chan, G., & Yanos, P. T. (2018). Media depictions and the priming of mental illness stigma. *Stigma and Health, 3*(3), 253–264. doi:10.1037/sah0000095

Chun, M. M., & Potter, M. C. (1995). A two-stage model for multiple target detection in rapid serial visual presentation. *Journal of Experimental Psychology: Human Perception and Performance, 21*(1), 109–127.

Collins, A. M., & Loftus, E. F. (1975). A spreading-activation theory of semantic processing. *Psychological Review, 82,* 407–428. doi:10.1037/0033-295X.82.6.407

Corrigan, P. W., Watson, A. C., Gracia, G., Slopen, N., Rasinski, K., & Hall, L. L. (2005). Newspaper stories as measures of structural stigma. *Psychiatric Services, 56,* 551–556. doi:10.1176/appi.ps.56.5.551

Craik, F. I. M., & Lockhart, R. S. (1972). Levels of processing: A framework for memory research. *Journal of Verbal Learning and Verbal Behavior, 11,* 671–684.

Dijksterhuis, A., & Bargh, J. A. (2001). The perception–behavior expressway: Automatic effects of social perception on social behaviour. *Advances in Experimental Social Psychology, 33,* 1–40.

Dijksterhuis, A., & van Knippenberg, A. (1998). The relation between perception and behaviour or how to win a game of Trivial Pursuit. *Journal of Personality and Social Psychology, 74,* 865–877.

Domke, D., Perlmutter, D., & Spratt, M. (2002). The primes of our times? An examination of the 'power' of visual images. *Journalism, 3*(2), 131–159.

Dunning, D., & Balcetis, E. (2013). Wishful seeing: How preferences shape visual perception. *Current Directions in Psychological Science, 22*(1), 33–37.

Fredrickson, B. L. (1998). What good are positive emotions? *Review of General Psychology, 2*(3), 300–319. doi:10.1037/1089-2680.2.3.300

Fredrickson, B. L. (2001). The role of positive emotions in positive psychology: The broaden-and-build theory of positive emotions. *American Psychologist, 56*(3), 218–226. doi:10.1037/0003-066X.56.3.218

Fredrickson, B. L., & Branigan, C. (2005). Positive emotions broaden the scope of attention and thought-action repertoires. *Cognition and Emotion, 19*(3), 313–332. doi:10.1080/02699930441000238

Gable, P., & Harmon-Jones, E. (2010a). The motivational dimensional model of affect: Implications for breadth of attention, memory, and cognitive categorisation. *Cognition and Emotion, 24*(2), 322–337. doi:10.1080/02699930903378305

Gable, P., & Harmon-Jones, E. (2010b). The blues broaden, but the nasty narrows: Attentional consequences of negative affects low and high in motivational intensity. *Psychological Science, 21*(2), 211–215. doi:10.1177/0956797609359622

Gable, P. A., & Harmon-Jones, E. (2008). Approach-motivated positive affect reduces breadth of attention. *Psychological Science*, *19*(5), 476–482. doi:10.1111/
j.1467-9280.2008.02112.x

Garcia, M. R., & Stark, P. (1991). *Eyes on the news*. Poynter Institute.

Gibson, R., Zillman, D., & Sargent, S. (1999). Effects of photographs in news-magazine
reports on issue perception. *Media Psychology*, *1*, 207–228.

Grabe, M. E., Lang, A., & Zhao, X. (2003). News content and form: Implications for
memory and audience evaluations. *Communication Research*, *30*(4), 387–413.

Graber, D. A. (1996). Say it with pictures. *Annals of the American Academy of Political and
Social Science*, *546*, 85–96.

Graber, D. A. (2001). *Processing politics: Learning from television in the internet age*.
University of Chicago Press.

Isen, A. M., Daubman, K. A., & Nowicki, G. P. (1987). Positive affect facilitates creative problem solving. *Journal of Personality and Social Psychology*, *52*, 1122–1131.
doi:10.1037/0022-3514.52.6.1122

Itti, L., & Koch, C. (2000). A saliency-based search mechanism for overt and covert shifts
of visual attention. *Vision Research*, *40*, 1489–1506.

Johnston, W. A., & Dark, V. J. (1986). Selective attention. *Annual Review of Psychology*,
37, 43–75.

Josephson, S., & Miller, J. S. (2015). Just state the facts on Twitter: Eye tracking shows
that readers may ignore questions posted by news organizations on Twitter but
not on Facebook. *Visual Communication Quarterly*, *22*(2), 94–105. doi:10.1080/
15551393.2015.1042161

Kätsyri, J., Kinnunen, T., Kusumoto, K., Oittinen, P., & Ravaja, N. (2016). Negativity bias in
media multitasking: The effects of negative social media messages on attention to television news broadcasts. *PLoS One*, *11*(5), e0153712. doi:10.1371/journal.pone.0153712

Koch, C., & Ullman, S. (1985). Shifts in selective visual attention: Towards the underlying
neural circuitry. *Human Neurobiology*, *4*(4), 219–227.

Koffka, K. (1935). *Principles of Gestalt psychology*. Harcourt Brace Jovanovich.

Knobloch, S., Patzig, G., Mende, A. M., & Hastall, M. (2004). Affective news effects of
discourse structure in narratives on suspense, curiosity, and enjoyment while reading
news and novels. *Communication Research*, *31*, 259–287.

Lang, A. (2000). The limited capacity model of mediated message processing. *Journal of
Communication*, *50*(1), 46–70.

Lang, A. (2017). Limited capacity model of motivated mediated message processing
(LC4MP). In *The international encyclopedia of media effects Vol. 17* (pp. 1–9). Wiley.

Machill, M., Köhler, S., & Waldhauser, M. (2007). The use of narrative structures in television news: An experiment in innovative forms of journalistic presentation. *European
Journal of Communication*, *22*, 185–205.

McClelland, S., & Kerschbaumer, K. (2001). Tickers and bugs: Has TV gotten way too
graphic. *Broadcasting & Cable*, *20*, 1.

Meyer, D. E., & Schvaneveldt, R. W. (1971). Facilitation in recognizing pairs of
words: Evidence of a dependence between retrieval operations. *Journal of Experimental
Psychology*, *90*(2), 227–234.

Moriarty, S. (1995). Visual communication theory: A search for roots. Paper presented at
the Visual Communication Conference, Flagstaff, AZ.

Mussweiler, T. (2003). Comparison processes in social judgment: Mechanisms and consequences. *Psychological Review*, *110*, 472–489.

Mussweiler, T. (2007). Assimilation and contrast as comparison effects: A selective accessibility model. In D. A. Stapel & J. Suls (Eds.), *Assimilation and contrast in social psychology* (pp. 165–185). Psychology Press.

Navon, D. (1977). Forest before trees: The precedence of global features in visual perception. *Cognitive Psychology, 9*(3), 353–383. doi:10.1016/0010-0285(77)90012-3

Nelson, D. L. (1979). Remembering pictures and words: Appearance, significance, and name. In L. S. Cermak & F. I. M. Craik (Eds.), *Levels of processing in human memory* (pp. 45–76). Erlbaum.

Nelson, D. L., Reed, V. S., & Walling, J. R. (1976). Pictorial superiority effect. *Journal of Experimental Psychology: Human Learning and Memory, 2*, 523–528.

Nummenmaa, L., Hyönä, J., & Calvo, M. G. (2006). Eye movement assessment of selective attentional capture by emotional pictures. *Emotion, 6*(2), 257–268.

O'Bryan, K. (1977). Cues and attention to the visual display in children's television. *Journal of Educational Television, 3*(2), 42–45.

O'Donnell, M., Nelson, L. D., Ackermann, E., Aczel, B., Akhtar, A., Aldrovandi, S., Alshaif, N., Andringa, R., Aveyard, M., Babincak, P., Balatekin, N., Baldwin, S. A., Banik, G., Baskin, E., Bell, R., Bialobrzeska, O., Birl, A. R., Boot, W. R., Braithwaite, S. R., Briggs, J. C., et al. (2018). Registered replication report: Dijksterhuis and van Knippenberg (1998). *Perspectives on Psychological Science, 13*(2), 268–294. doi:10.1177/1745691617855704

Ohman, A., Flykt, A., & Esteves, F. (2001). Emotion drives attention: Detecting the snake in the grass. *Emotion, 130*(3), 466–478.

Paivio, A. (1975). Coding distinctions and repetition effects in memory. In G. H. Bower (Ed.), *The psychology of learning and motivation* (pp. 179–214). Academic Press.

Paivio, A. (1986). *Mental representations: A dual coding approach*. Oxford University Press.

Paivio, A. (1971). *Imagery and verbal processes*. New York: Holt, Rinehart & Winston. (Reprinted 1979, Hillsdale, NJ: Erlbaum).

Paivio, A., & Csapo, K. (1973). Picture superiority in free recall: Imagery or dual coding? *Cognitive Psychology, 5*, 176–206.

Papies, E. K. (2016). Health goal priming as a situated intervention tool: How to benefit from nonconscious motivational routes to health behaviour. *Health Psychology Review, 10*(4), 408–424. doi:10.1080/17437199.2016.1183506

Pavolik, B. L., Piwinsky, M. J., & Fulton, L. A. (2015). News crawls in local TV news: Do they help or hinder information recall and retention. *Advances in Journalism and Communication, 3*(04), 139.

Phua, J., Jin, S. V., & Kim, J. J. (2017). Uses and gratifications of social networking sites for bridging and bonding social capital: A comparison of Facebook, Twitter, Instagram, and Snapchat. *Computers in Human Behavior, 72*, 115–122.

Pittman, R. (1990). We're talking the wrong language to 'TV Babies'. *The New York Times*, A15.

Raymond, J. E., Shapiro, K. L., & Arnell, K. M. (1992). Temporary suppression of visual processing in an RSVP task: An attentional blink? *Journal of Experimental Psychology: Human Perception and Performance, 18*(3), 849–860.

Reason, J. T. (1984). Lapses of attention. In R. Parasuraman & R. Davies (Eds.), *Varieties of attention* (pp. 515–549). Academic Press.

Rideout, V., Foehr, U., & Roberts, D. (2010). *Generation M: Media in the lives of 8- to 18-year-olds*. Henry J. Kaiser Family Foundation.

Rinck, M., Glowalla, U., & Schneider, K. (1992). Mood-congruent and mood-incongruent learning. *Memory & Cognition, 20*(1), 29–39.

Rowe, G., Hirsh, J. B., & Anderson, A. J. (2007). Positive affect increases the breadth of attentional selection. *Proceedings of the National Academy of Sciences of the USA, 104*(1), 383–388. doi:10.1073/pnas.0605198104

Salvucci, D. D., & Taatgen, N. A. (2008). Threaded cognition: An integrated theory of concurrent multitasking. *Psychological Review, 115*(1), 101–130. doi:10.1037/ 0033-295X.115.1.101

Sanders, J., & Redeker, G. (1993). Linguistic perspective in short news stories. *Poetics, 22*, 69–87.

Schill, D. (2012). The visual image and the political image: A review of visual communication research in the field of political communication. *Review of Communication, 12*(2), 118–142. doi:10.1080/15358593.2011.653504

Schneider, W., & Shiffrin, R. M. (1977). Controlled and automatic human information processing: I. Detection, search, and attention. *Psychological Review, 84*(1), 1–66.

Shapiro, K. L., Raymond, J. E., & Arnell, K. M. (1994). Attention to visual pattern information produces the attentional blink in rapid serial visual presentation. *Journal of Experimental Psychology: Human Perception and Performance, 20*(2), 357–371.

Shiffrin, R. M., & Schneider, W. (1977). Controlled and automatic human information processing: II. Perceptual learning, automatic attending, and a general theory. *Psychological Review, 84*(2), 127–190.

Smith, N. K., Cacioppo, J. T., & Chartrand, T. L. (2003). May I have your attention, please: Electrocortical responses to positive and negative stimuli. *Neuropsychologica, 41*(2), 171–183.

Strayer, D. L., & Johnston, W. A. (2001). Driven to distraction: Dual-task studies of simulated driving and conversing on a cellular telephone. *Psychological Science, 12*, 462–466.

Stuart, H. (2006). Media portrayal of mental illness and its treatments: What effect does it have on people with mental illness? *CNS Drugs, 20*, 99–106. doi:10.2165/ 00023210-200620020-00002

Sülflow, M., Schäfer, S., & Winter, S. (2019). Selective attention in the news feed: An eye-tracking study on the perception and selection of political news posts on Facebook. *New Media & Society, 21*(1), 168–190.

Theeuwes, J. (1993). Visual selective attention: A theoretical analysis. *Acta Psychologica, 83*, 93–154.

Theeuwes, J., Belopolsky, A., & Olivers, C. N. (2009). Interactions between working memory, attention and eye movements. *Acta Psychologica, 132*(2), 106–114.

Treisman, A. M. (1969). Strategies and models of selective attention. *Psychological Review, 76*, 282–299.

Tversky, A., & Kahneman, D. (1973). Availability: A heuristic for judging frequency and probability. *Cognitive Psychology, 5*, 207–222.

van Krieken, K., Hoeken, H., & Sanders, J. (2015). From reader to mediated witness: The engaging effects of journalistic crime narratives. *Journalism & Mass Communication Quarterly, 92*(3), 580–596. doi:10.1177/1077699015586546

van Krieken, K., Sanders, J., & Hoeken, H. (2015). Viewpoint representation in journalistic crime narratives: An analysis of grammatical roles and referential expressions. *Journal of Pragmatics, 88*, 220–230. doi:10.1016/j.pragma.2014.07.012

Voorveld, H. A. M., & van der Goot, M. (2013). Age differences in media multitasking: A diary study. *Journal of Broadcasting & Electronic Media, 57*(3), 392–408. doi:10.1080/08838151.2013.816709

Vraga, E. K., Bode, L., Smithson, A. B., & Troller-Renfree, S. (2019). Accidentally attentive: Comparing visual, close-ended, and open-ended measures of attention on social media. *Computers in Human Behavior, 99*, 235–244.

Wahl, O. F. (1992). Mass media images of mental illness: A review of the literature. *Journal of Community Psychology, 20*, 343–352.

Wang, Z., Irwin, M., Cooper, C., & Srivastava, J. (2015). Multidimensions of media multitasking and adaptive media selection. *Human Communication Research, 41*, 102–127.

Wertheimer, W. (1923). Untersuchungen zur Lehre vonder Gestalt. *Psychologische Forschung, 4*, 301–350. Abridged translation: Principles of perceptual organization. In D. C. Beardsler & M. Wertheimer (Eds.), *Reading in perception*. Van Nostrand.

Wickens, C. D. (1984). Processing resources in attention. In R. Parasuraman, J. Beatty, & R. Davies (Eds.), *Varieties of attention* (pp. 63–101). Wiley.

Wickens, C. D. (2002). Multiple resources and performance prediction. *Theoretical Issues in Ergonomics Science, 3*, 159–177.

Wood, W., & Neal, D. T. (2007). A new look at habits and the habit–goal interface. *Psychological Review, 114*, 843–863.

4

Reconsidering Informed and Participatory Citizenship in the Current Media Ecosystem

Maria Elizabeth Grabe and Ozen Bas

More media content has been produced during the past 20 years than in the entire prior 2,000-year history of *Homo sapiens*. Citizens who are skilled at navigating the information tide are at an advantage to become socially and economically empowered. Disproportionately represented among those who struggle to navigate the information environment are citizens with lower levels of education, and women. To no surprise, these social inequities count among the most studied topics in the social sciences. Specifically, knowledge acquisition, informed citizenship, and civic engagement enjoy interdisciplinary attention from scholars in media, psychology, political science, informatics, and sociology. Despite the concentration of research interest, efforts, and funding, contemporary research in this area faces conceptual and methodological challenges to address the fast-evolving information ecosystem and its consequences for how contemporary citizens live their lives (Grabe & Myrick, 2016). This chapter offers some insights on how the evolving media ecosystem is shaping informed citizenship and the challenges for scholars of cognition—specifically those who work in the areas of memory, comprehension, and knowledge in this pursuit.

New Journalism: New Ways of News Consumption

Memory will likely remain central to understanding what citizens know about the world they inhabit, but the contemporary media environment demands more than efficient memory-making. Future research will have to identify, explicate, and operationalize information navigation skills (e.g., fast

Maria Elizabeth Grabe and Ozen Bas, *Reconsidering Informed and Participatory Citizenship in the Current Media Ecosystem* In: *The Psychology of Journalism*. Edited by: Sharon Coen and Peter Bull, Oxford University Press.
© Oxford University Press 2021. DOI: 10.1093/oso/9780190935856.003.0004

and accurate judgements of credibility and usefulness of information) that are wielded in service of information management. Thus, the *learning from news* research tradition (Eveland & Scheufele, 2000; Gunter, 1987; Neuman et al., 1992; Robinson & Davis, 1990) would benefit from incorporating a *navigation of news media* focus (e.g., see Albæk et al., 2014; Castells et al., 2009; Lindlof, 1991). Movement on fronts both qualitative (e.g., in-depth interviews and ethnography) and quantitative (e.g., physiological measures and media use tracking) is needed to explore how the human perceptual system is judging mediated content in real time. Beyond factors related to the current media environment, a few factors related to media users and content deserve attention.

News Grazers

Pew Research Center data identified an emerging group of media users who are relatively young (aged 18–34 years), locally minded, and mobile screen-using audiovisuals. Perhaps most striking, they find what they need rather than wait for it to be served. Such active consumption of news has been growing steadily with the proliferation of cable television that invites flipping through channels and skipping unwanted material. These fast sampling rates of the viewing environment, enabled initially by the television remote control (Walker & Bellamy, 1991), were dubbed news grazing for the first time in a 2004 Pew Research Center report (Morris & Forgette, 2007; Pew Research Center, 2004). Since then, the percentage of grazers has increased dramatically (Pew Research Center, 2010). Grazers are mostly ages 18–34 years, slightly more likely to be men, and stay attentive only to that which captivates their attention (Morris & Forgette, 2007).

It is approximately 60 years since Zenith introduced a television remote control called Lazy Bones. Yet, media researchers have made few inroads beyond audience self-reports to study the behavioural (clicking, zapping, channel surfing, and grazing) ramifications of this technology. The key findings from these audience self-report studies, some grounded in the *uses and gratifications* perspective, connect grazing behaviour to two main gratifications: to get more out of media use and to avoid unappealing material (e.g., advertisements and 'people you don't agree with') (Walker & Bellamy, 1991; Walker et al., 1993; Wenner et al., 1993). These findings line up with the contemporary demographic profile of a media grazer, but as invaluable as this early work was in uncovering changes in news consumption patterns, the changing media ecosystem demands innovation in self-report measures, comprehension, and perhaps observational studies to understand how much grazing happens and how that behaviour affects memory (Camaj, 2019; Bailey et al., 2013).

Cross-sectional studies have shown cognitive and behavioural effects of news grazing habits (Bennett et al., 2008; Morris & Forgette, 2007). Examining 2004 Pew Research Center data, Morris and Forgette (2007) found that when controlled for other demographic factors, American news consumers were found to be significantly less knowledgeable about political issues and less engaged in being involved in political decision-making than non-news grazers.

More recently, the news grazing behaviour associated with cable television watching has evolved into incidental news exposure on digital platforms and mobile devices. Molyneux (2018) examined this new digital news consumption habits on mobile devices and found that news consumption on these devices is shorter in duration compared to other platforms, but occurs more frequently and is spread throughout the day. Molyneux also found that contemporary citizens get news on multiple platforms.

Incidental News Exposure on Social Media

News consumption that accompanies another primary activity has been identified and operationalized as incidental news consumption (Boczkowski et al., 2018). An important distinction in this area of study concerns the *intent* to acquire information, with browsing, information seeking, and information encountering serving as some of the terms used to articulate the nuances in a citizen's volitional attempts at gaining information. The matter of intent (or information-seeking efficacy) has also surfaced with regard to vulnerability to information overload. One study of online information encountering (among Germans) reported that age and information-seeking efficacy are linked to information overload (Schmitt et al., 2018). Specifically, younger participants and those with lower information-seeking self-efficacy are more susceptible to information overload.

During the course of traditional news media use (i.e., newspaper and television), the linearity of browsing through a newspaper or watching a newscast promoted exposure to news stories that varied in interest to a news user.

Today's delivery systems (which allow news users to customize the type of content they are presented with) sidestep these unintentional information absorption opportunities. Yet, incidental exposure has become a central feature of social media use (Boczkowski et al., 2018). Studies have shown global trends in unintended exposure to news when media users go online for non-news functions (Newman et al., 2017). Importantly, an experimental study found that incidental exposure to news has significant effects on recognition and recall of news information (Lee & Kim, 2017). In addition, incidental exposure to online news has been found to be positively associated with knowledge (Tewksbury et al., 2001). Some scholars call attention to self-selection in information exposure during social media use (Newman et al., 2017). Still, 59% of Facebook users have reported incidental exposure to news on this platform every day or almost every day (Purcell et al., 2010). Interestingly, cognitive responses to information not purposefully sought out by social media users vary depending on the social traces of that information. Information encountered through a closely tied member of one's network significantly decreases incidental exposure to news compared to information encountered through a weakly tied member of the social network (Ahmadi & Wohn, 2018). The amount of time spent, the frequency of getting updates, and the frequency of clicking on links about news on social media were also found to be associated with increased incidental exposure (Ahmadi & Wohn, 2018).

Future work in this area could be instrumental in understanding the more subtle, unintended, and diffused information absorption that citizens are subjected to in the current media environments. This line of approach has old and deep roots in media research that favoured long-term and less tangible approaches to understanding the influences of media on citizens. Scholars approaching media as an agent of socialization (e.g., the cultivation tradition) could make substantial contributions to understanding how citizens acquire knowledge in unintended ways as they navigate a dense information landscape.

Social Media and Misinformation

Our understanding of how new pathways of information flow have impacted democratic life lags behind the pace at which the transformations are occurring. Today's news information flow via the social web is an algorithm-driven network with millions, or perhaps billions, of gatekeepers. Their influence often does not match their expertise (Lazer et al., 2018). Instead, their impact on the public agenda comes from clicking, liking, and sharing. It is tempting to view this connectivity as a leap toward democratizing news flow. After all, the agency of contemporary media users reduced the role of journalist as the authority on what counts as news—it also empowered citizens to distribute information through their social networks. Yet, there are a number of outcomes related to this diffusion of information that appear unconducive—or outright ruinous—to informed citizenship. An anecdote from a vehicle-ramming attack that occurred on April 23, 2018, in Toronto, Canada, showcased the vulnerabilities of contemporary news information flow. Natasha Fatah, a journalist, tweeted two eyewitness accounts, one wrongly identifying the attacker as angry and Middle Eastern and another correctly identifying him as White (Meserole, 2018). Unfortunately, the wrong tweet spurred more engagement and sharing than the correct one, exemplifying the concern about the lack of safeguards in distributing credible information.

The information that social web influentials produce is not held to the same newsworthiness, fairness, and truth standards of traditional journalism. The new threshold for news information flow does not discriminate opinion from verifiable fact, opening the contemporary news media ecosystem to misinformation, fake accounts, social bots, trolls, and other manoeuvres. Dissemination platforms that enabled these flow patterns are now lethargic in countering or filtering information for accuracy. Some technology companies have developed systems to identify and remove misinformation from their platforms (Ireton & Posetti, 2018). Nevertheless, Facebook's CEO Mark Zuckerberg said that Facebook cannot, as a company, be expected to safeguard against or clean up misinformation campaigns (Paul, 2019). The trends in fake news and misinformation sharing on social media show that user engagement with false content has increased on both Facebook and Twitter through the end of 2016 (Allcott et al., 2019). Since then, engagement with misinformation has decreased on Facebook, while continuing to rise on Twitter. Efforts of Facebook to combat fake news and the dissemination of misinformation on its platform after the 2016 election are seen as more earnest in attempting to address the problem (Allcott et al., 2019). Pinpointing the effects of misinformation through social media is not an easy task for researchers (Meserole, 2018). The widespread incidence of fake news in the age of social media has become an integral part of intentional misinformation. The Pew Research Center (2016) found that 23% of Americans shared fake news knowingly or unknowingly. Interestingly, overestimating the level of knowledge about fabricated historical events and topics in physical sciences was positively associated with the level of perceiving fake news as accurate (Pennycook & Rand, 2020, pp. 185–200). Exposure to false information tends to last—one experimental study found that memory for misinformation lasted for approximately 1½ years (Zhu et al., 2012).

The outcomes of the changing news information ecosystem include disagreement on what constitutes important political issues, polarization in opinion, disintegration of a shared reality among the populace, incivility, suspicion, and violence ignited by conspiracy theories. New tools and literacies must be developed to separate misinformation from credible information and trusted sources—be that applications for detecting misinformation, media literacy taught in school curricula, or empowering professionals or news-literate citizens who consume and share vetted stories on social media. The intricate interaction of cognitive, social, and algorithmic biases that mediate exposure to information via social media is not yet fully understood.

Informed citizenship is a vital part of the conceptualization of democratic life, and it is built on the flow of trustworthy information. Many contemporary scholars and public intellectuals have pointed to the failures of this idealistic view of how social life unfolds in democratic systems (Druckman, 2005; Somin, 1998). It is important to remind ourselves that misinformation—intended campaigns or unintended mishaps—is not new. It is a historical reality that has been part of human interaction since we invented the means to draw and write. The history of media points to the variety of ways in which both written and spoken word, as well as images, have been used as an apparatus of religious propaganda, tools to serve abusive commerce practices, and a means for elites to exercise social control over the lower classes (Briggs, 2005; Burke, 1994; Goody & Watt, 1963; Graff, 1987; Havelock, 1963). Yet, the current volume and the efficiency of dissemination platforms that serve misinformation pose arguably a higher threat to the integrity of free-flowing information than at any other point in human history. It is precisely the unchecked flow in information that will put new burdens on citizens to acquire media literacy skills to evaluate information for credibility. Research that tests the impact of identified media literacy skills is desperately needed.

Emotional Personalization as a New Form of Journalism

Tabloid, sensationalism, human interest, personalized news, infotainment, and soft news are all terms used to refer to less than desirable content and stylistic dimensions of journalism (Gripsrud, 2000). These journalistic forms are often seen as violating traditional ideals of generating informa tion through objective means in service of a rational populace. This way of thinking has pervasive roots. It can be traced back to the preoccupation of Hellenic philosophy with protecting reason from becoming infected by emotion (Nussbaum, 2001) and the Cartesian separation of reason from emotion that served Enlightenment ideals well into the 21st century. Part of this paradigm's legacy is the problematization of emotion in democratic politics and the insistence on objectivity as the ground rule of conduct for journalistic practice (Schudson, 2001; T. Van Dijk, 1988). So ingrained is this paradigm that the adoption of every new media technology prompts eruptions of concern about how objectivity in journalism will be affected (Wartella & Jennings, 2000; Conway, 2009; Gripsrud, 2000). For example, shifts in stylistic conventions and formats such as the penny press of the 1830s, yellow journalism at the end of the 19th century, and 1990s tabloid television and newspaper formats stoked cycles of apprehension about objectivity in journalism (Altschull, 1990; Bird, 1992; Grabe et al., 2001).

Emotional provocation is what critics of television view as undermining the information value of news by being subjective (Graber, 2001) or 'underdistanced' (Tannenbaum & Lynch, 1960, p. 382). The very idea of eliciting an emotional reaction such as empathy is problematized as interfering with the process of becoming a rationally informed citizen. At the same time, a number of scholars, following in the footsteps of neuroscientific findings, are gathering evidence in support of the idea that inserting emotion into news has gainful consequences for informed citizenship (Bas & Grabe, 2015, 2016; Marcus & Mackuen, 1993; Mujica & Bachmann, 2016).

Bas and Grabe (2015) experimentally tested the effects of exposure to emotional personalization, which is conceptualized as inclusion of testimonies of ordinary citizens who are victims of social problems such as sexual harassment, child labour, and corruption in public housing administration. Bas and Grabe recruited participants from both high ($n = 40$) and low ($n = 40$) educated groups, with the high education group comprising participants with at least a master's degree, and the low educated group holding no more than a 2-year associate's degree. Their results showed that regardless of education, when citizens view emotionally personalized versions of news stories, they are able to better recall and comprehend news stories compared to non-personalized versions of the same stories. Similarly, Mujica and Bachmann (2016) found that melodrama increases recall of news reports, and news that triggers enthusiasm, anxiety, or empathy also provokes political participation of citizens (Bas & Grabe, 2016; Marcus & Mackuen, 1993).

Against the backdrop of structural changes in news dissemination, consumption pattern mutations, and content shifts; the functions of journalism in democratic social systems have to be reconsidered. These changes have cognitive sequels that impact knowledge acquisition and informed citizenship.

Memory, Comprehension, and Knowledge

Some historians argue that American democracy was established as a real-world experiment in which the founding fathers put rules in place to create the institutional context for citizens to participate in governance. At the centre of this ideal is the notion of informed citizenship, protected by rights such as the freedom of expression and public access to information and a postal service (Starr, 2004). Even in subsequent revisions of democratic theory—across Western democracies—free flow of information is pivotal to democratic practice. Knowledge of social issues is viewed as a precondition for meaningful participation (Schumpeter, 1942), and the news media's role in facilitating informing citizenship is embraced by both the architects of democratic theory and journalists. Yet, over time and across research methodologies, findings of superficial knowledge and low levels of democratic participation surfaced.

A number of scholars have argued that in order to tame the information tide, users employ a processing strategy that decreases the information that is necessary to be stored, known as *schematic thinking* (Graber, 1988). News users discard chunks of information while also incorporating other pieces of information to existing knowledge. In this way, users develop an integrated knowledge of news events that aligns with their interests, as well as information processing, and emotional responses to news content. Graber's experimental studies on how participants learn from news showed they were not able to recall much detail from the stories they viewed. But surprisingly, participants remembered the meaning of stories beyond the factual details.

Although factual details of stories might be forgotten, judgements, impressions, and opinions based on stories remain as traces, integrated into existing schema and knowledge structures. Thus, news users acquire information selectively based on existing knowledge schemas that also facilitate the integration of new information (Graber, 1988).

Related to the work on schema processing, more than 200 studies have consistently (since the 1970s) documented different levels of knowledge gain across education or socioeconomic status groups (see Gaziano, 1997, 2010; Hwang & Jeong, 2009). Evidence is impressively robust across cultural contexts (Bonfadelli, 2002; Hwang & Jeong, 2009; Nguyen & Western, 2007; J. van Dijk & Hacker, 2003;), media platforms (Kim, 2008; Wei & Hindman, 2011), and content variables (Ettema et al., 1983; Jerit et al., 2006). Moreover, individual differences among audience members have been tested to explain the gap (Eveland & Scheufele, 2000; Kwak, 1999; Neuman et al., 1992; Price & Zaller, 1993), but education level has emerged as the leading predictor of variance in knowledge acquisition gaps.

Throughout the years, knowledge gap and related 'learning from news media' research also moved from surveys to experimental methodologies. Based on the mechanics of the limited capacity model of information processing (Craik & Lockhart, 1972; Tulving & Thompson, 1973; Schneider & Shiffrin, 1977), the knowledge gap and news learning studies tested memory formation at encoding, storage, and retrieval levels. Most studies focussed on encoding, using recognition tests (Grabe et al., 2009; Shoemaker et al., 1989; Tremayne & Dunwoody, 2001), confirming that lower education groups processed (encoded) news information less efficiently compared with higher education groups (Grabe et al., 2000, 2008; Yang & Grabe, 2011).

However, a number of scholars have grown uneasy about conceptualizing, quantifying, and measuring knowledge (Bonfadelli, 2002; Gaziano, 1997; Prior, 2014; Selwyn, 2004; Woodall et al., 1983) as encoding (recognition memory) rather than comprehension of news (Gaziano, 2010; Wahl-Jorgensen, 2019). Traditional views of informed citizenship as encoded memory for facts are challenged by calls to re-explicate informed citizenship to include applied understanding, comprehension, and even emotional response to and involvement with social issues.

This fault line is driven by ontological and methodological tensions. First, ontological shifts in cognitive neuroscience focusing on the entanglement of rationality and emotion are well deployed. Perhaps one of the key flares in this paradigm conversion was Damasio's (1994) argument, on the basis of neurological evidence, that humans are not primarily thinking beings who also feel but, rather, feeling beings who also think. This line of thinking did not escape political science and news research on informed citizenship.

Second, work in cognitive science that treated comprehension and memory as two distinct cognitive processes (Ortony, 1978) entered the new research realm. Comprehension measures were developed to move beyond memory and adopted among researchers who were interested in the process of learning from news media (e.g., Robinson & Levy, 1986; Woodall et al., 1983). Comprehension measures assess if participants have integrated information into a meaningful system of existing knowledge (Robinson & Levy, 1986; Tremayne & Dunwoody, 2001). Although measures vary across studies, comprehension tests are centrally concerned with how well participants grasp the gist of a story or can apply acquired information in other contexts. These outcomes are arguably more conducive to the ideals of informed citizenship than remembering peripheral details such as the names of people and places. In this line of inquiry, memory of details from a story is not viewed as evidence that the audience understood what the story is about. At the same time, comprehension of the story does not necessarily ensure memory of factual details contained in it (Graber, 1988). Yet, correlations between memory and comprehension are often reported (Basil, 1994; Edwardson et al., 1992; Findahl & Höijer, 1985), and high education groups have been shown to verbally recount and comprehend material from text-based media at higher rates compared with low education groups (Grabe et al., 2009; Yang & Grabe, 2011).

In a media environment in which information is available at the fingertips of users, it is open to discussion whether factual news details are more important than comprehending the gist of the social issues to which users are exposed. The idea that remembering factual details might become less important than having general gist awareness of social issues in living an informed life is somewhat controversial—but it might provoke much needed research interest and debate. Indeed, it seems plausible that the contemporary human brain, during early stages of cognitive developmental plasticity, might optimize navigational over storage capacity. Interestingly, an experimental study showed that citizens with lower levels of education (high school or less) tend to acquire general awareness of emotionally personalized stories, whereas higher educated participants (completed graduate degrees) fare better with forming memory for factual details from the stories that they watch (Bas & Grabe, 2015).

This shift in what might be considered in the future as 'knowledge that empowers' offers hope for narrowing knowledge gaps. Yet, the media environment that does not put instrumental access to information at the fingertips of all citizens equally is unlikely to become more inclusive than it is now. In February 2019, approximately 46% of American adults with a high school education or less had access to home broadband; the comparable percentage for college graduates was 94% (Pew Research Center, 2019). The inequities in physical and cognitive access to information across demographic groups— and the promise that audiovisual media hold for overcoming some of these barriers—have been the motivation for the focus on work that we have conducted over the past decade.

Case Study: Visual Knowledge

In evolutionary circles, explanations for why the human brain is better adapted for visual than verbal information processing are often based on the relatively short history of verbal language in the natural history of *Homo Sapiens*. In this regard, Paivio (1971) argues that words are processed in a linear fashion—one at a time—whereas visuals are processed faster and holistically as an entanglement of verbal and visual memory records. When one of these routes fails at the retrieval stage, the other can often successfully manage the task (Paivio, 1971). This acknowledgement of visual primacy in *Homo sapiens* has opened up the path for ontological shifts in cognitive and neuroscience thinking about visual processing as the dominant mode of learning (Barry, 2005; Damasio, 1994). Yet, knowledge gain has been consistently measured through verbal means. Visual memory and comprehension instruments are strikingly underdeveloped because knowledge is not operationalized in visual terms. Graber (2001) observes that 'the belief that audiovisuals are poor carriers of important information has become so ingrained in conventional wisdom that it has throttled research' (p. 93). Her calls (Graber, 1988, 1990, 1996, 2001) for revising the way media and political communication scholars think about the importance of images as information sources have not been answered earnestly.

Some notable exceptions are experimental studies examining the effects of candidate facial emotion on voter evaluations (Keating et al., 1999; Rosenberg et al., 1991), Graber's (1988, 1990, 2001) pioneering work on creating visual measures, and Prior's (2014) effort to establish visual political knowledge measures. In a series of studies, Graber (2001) found that viewers recalled more visual than verbal themes from television. Prior (2014) employed visual (faces) and verbal (names) recognition questions to uncover the encoding process of political knowledge. For example, a question such as 'Who is the current Senate Majority Leader?' represented a verbal prompt and featured four verbal (name) options. The visual version of the question featured the same verbal prompt but offered four visual representations of faces. Prior (2014) found that differences among college graduates and non-graduates declined significantly when knowledge was measured visually. This suggests that the potential of images as a knowledge equalizer might be unrealized due to the methods used to gauge knowledge (Prior, 2014).

Indeed, the low levels of knowledge routinely reported in survey and experimental research might partially be due to the kind of knowledge measures that are employed and the circular logic that underlies them. For example, education level has been linked to political knowledge that is measured through the written word, which requires literacy. It is therefore highly predictable that political knowledge and comprehension of political complexities—measured through the written word—are linked to formal education (Jennings, 1996; Nie et al., 1996). Graber (1996) interprets these findings as a matter of literacy in aid of verbal processing. We argue that literacy also serves verbal knowledge measures. On the other hand, visual information processing requires no literacy, develops practically at birth, and enables most citizens to learn about their social world from a very young age. For unclear reasons, visual processing and visual measures of knowledge remain customarily idle in scholarly pursuits to understand informed citizenship.

It is noteworthy that Tichenor et al. (1970), when they first formulated the knowledge gap hypothesis, shared the view that audiovisual learning might enhance knowledge levels among less literate groups:

> Since television use tends to be less correlated with education, there is a possibility that television may be a 'knowledge leveller' in some areas. Whether TV does in fact have such a levelling function seems to be an urgent matter for further research. (p. 170)

More than 50 years later, there is no consensus about the potential of audiovisual learning as an equalizer across education groups. Some studies have shown that memory is aided by visuals (Grabe et al., 2009; Gunter, 1987; Katz et al., 1977; McCarthy & Warrington, 1988), whereas others have found that they inhibit memory, especially when news stories contain discrepant information across visuals and verbals (Brosius et al., 1996, van der Molen & Klijn, 2004; Zhou, 2005) or when they are highly compelling (Grabe et al., 2003; Miller & Leshner, 2007; Newhagen & Reeves, 1992). Yet, these studies did not measure memory visually. They mostly tested the effects of audiovisual content using verbal information measures or, as Graber (2001) points out, 'In tests of what viewers learn from television news, scholars have usually asked only for recall of the verbal message, assuming that the visuals mirrored the verbal texts or conveyed no significant substantive information at all' (p. 93). Thus, because visuals are not considered to have much information value, they are not used as an index of consequential processes such as memory formation or comprehension of social issues (Graber, 1990).

Indeed, most existing knowledge tests do not measure image-based recognition and comprehension. If cognitive scientists are correct in arguing that *Homo sapiens* is generously endowed with visual information processing abilities—compared to verbal processing, which is a recent environmentally driven adaptation—the knowledge gap between higher and lower education groups might disappear if visual knowledge measures are employed. To test this idea, we embarked on a research project during the mid-2010s (see Grabe & Bass, 2015), recruiting 80 participants and exposing them to eight public affairs news stories. Consistent with survey and experimental research on knowledge gaps, we used education as an indicator of socioeconomic status. The high education group participants had all earned at least a master's degree. Participants in the low education group had no more than 2 years of vocational training.

Both visual and verbal memory were assessed using five-option multiple-choice questions, at two time points separated by 1 week. Simple verbal recognition questions featured a verbal prompt and verbal answer options, whereas visual recognition questions had a verbal prompt with visual options from which to choose. Each participant answered a total of 64 simple recognition questions—16 in each modality (32 total) at each time point (64 in total). Recognition measures, such as these, target familiarity with message content but fail to assess depth in how citizens understand social issues. We therefore developed questions with the goal to measure comprehension. To this end, we developed 2 visual and 2 verbal questions per story at each time point, adding up to another 32 questions in total—8 visual and 8 verbal at each time point of measurement. These questions required reasoning and also required participants to apply information that was presented in the experimental stimuli. For example, simple recognition (both visual and verbal) of who regulates debt collection was sufficient for a correct answer. Comprehension, on the other hand, required not only remembering information given in the story (i.e., advice to consumers on how to protect themselves against collector abuse) but also application of that information in selecting an answer. Verbal and visual questions for recognition and comprehension were designed so that content and difficulty levels were comparable across modalities.

We expected confirmation of an overall knowledge gap on verbal recognition tests of news information (H1) and verbal comprehension test scores (H2), such that people with higher levels of education outscore those with lower levels of education. The next step was to test if recognition and comprehension scores were higher when measured visually compared to verbally (H3), regardless of education levels of participants. A research question directed tests to compare education-based knowledge gaps when recognition and comprehension were measured through visual versus verbal modalities (RQ1). Some existing evidence points to education as inhibiting forgetting: The higher the education level, the slower the memory decay (Grabe et al., 2009; Karrasch & Laine, 2003; Morrow & Ryan, 2002). These findings offered impetus for a fourth hypothesis (H4) predicting that the low education group would be associated with more recognition memory and comprehension decay over the course of a week compared with the higher education group. Finally, given the sparseness of evidence related to audience education level, the modality of memory tests, and time delay, the last research question (R2) prompted a comparison of memory measures (recognition and comprehension) across modalities and participant education levels.

Table 4.1 provides a summary of our findings. In short, the first and second hypotheses were confirmed: The high education group outperformed the low education group on both verbal recognition and comprehension measures. Hypothesis 3 made a forecast for modality main effects on both recognition and comprehension tests, such that visual tests would

Table 4.1   *F* Test Results for Analysis of Variance on Simple Recognition and Comprehension Measures[a]

Variables	F	p	η^2
Verbal Measures Only			
Simple recognition			
Main effect, education (H1)	64.47	.001	.452
Verbal comprehension			
Main effect, education (H2)	92.230	.001	.542
Simple Recognition—Full Model			
Main effect, education	61.11	.001	.443
Main effect, modality (H3)	91.23	.001	.195
Education × modality (RQ1)	12.96	.001	.028
Main effect, time	32.69	.001	.075
Time × education (H4)	1.59	.211	.004
Time × modality	0.27	.605	.001
Time × education × modality (RQ2)	0.002	.962	.000
Comprehension—Full Model			
Main effect, education	72.88	.001	.487
Main effect, modality (H3)	13.77	.001	.025
Education × modality (RQ1)	27.81	.001	.050
Main effect, time	3.25	.075	.014
Time × education (H4)	3.25	.075	.014
Time × modality	8.55	.005	.008
Time × education × modality (RQ2)	0.64	.428	.001

[a]$df = 1$.

produce higher scores compared with verbal tests. This hypothesis was also supported. Research question 1 prompted a sequence of tests to assess the influence of visual versus verbal modalities on knowledge acquisition across education groups. As depicted in Figure 4.1, the low education group is more sensitive to modality differences. Testing memory visually narrowed the knowledge gap in both recognition and comprehension tests. Yet, the knowledge gap remained statistically present in both modalities and across recognition and comprehension measures. Interestingly, both education groups scored significantly higher in visual than in verbal recognition. Yet, in comprehension assessments, higher educated people did not differ significantly in their comprehension of news across the two

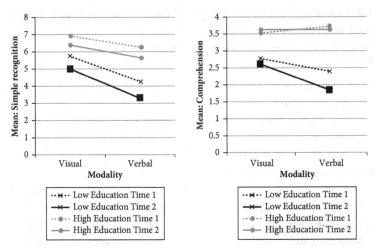

Figure 4.1 Three-way interaction effects for education level of participants, question modality, and time on simple recognition and comprehension.

modalities while the low education group did perform significantly better on visual than on verbal comprehension.

The inquiry into how time delay affects memory showed that recognition memory, regardless of modality, decayed across education groups at a similar rate. Moreover, regardless of participant education level, visual comprehension remained robust over time compared to verbal comprehension. However; comprehension decayed faster for the low education group. Indeed, high education participants appeared practically immune to variation in test modality over time. Low education participants, in stark contrast, had a significant decay over time in verbal compared to visual comprehension assessment scores. Thus, citizens with lower levels of education had diminished capacity in showcasing their comprehension of issues in verbal tests across two time points. Visual tests of comprehension did not produce a significant depreciation over time.

The robust main effects for recognition and comprehension test modality suggest that visual measures need to be taken seriously in future assessments of memory. Measures of memory and comprehension over time complicate research designs but afford a more thorough understanding of informed citizenship. The findings reported here also highlight the appropriateness of calls from political scientists such as Doris Graber and Markus Prior to use questions formulated in both modalities to measure news retention and levels of public knowledge (Graber, 1994, 1996; Prior, 2014). Yet, as Prior (2014) notes, it is not always possible to ask questions visually. In working to accomplish this goal, we discovered the extraordinary challenge of posing the same questions in two modalities, which might explain why researchers have avoided visual measures. Yet, as this study demonstrated, comparable measures, testing recognition and applied conceptual knowledge, can be accomplished.

The findings provide reason to be somewhat cautious about the size of knowledge gaps that have been reported over more than 40 years of research. To be sure, inequities in memory gain appear with more vigour when verbal compared with when visual measures are used. Differences in visual recognition memory between higher and lower education groups are clearly less pronounced than in verbal recognition memory tests. It is important to keep in mind, however, that although there is shrinkage in information acquisition gaps across test modalities, the gaps do not disappear. In fact, the knowledge gap remains robust regardless of test modality and time delay. In that sense, Tichenor et al.'s (1970) knowledge gap hypothesis has gained another evidentiary foothold in this data set.

As many scholars have noted, recognition memory tests might not offer an adequate assessment of knowledge that would promote informed citizenship. The findings of this study support this line of argument. Different patterns emerged for education groups in recognition memory and comprehension over time. Whereas recognition memory decayed at similar levels for both groups over the course of 1 week, comprehension declined only in the low education group. This finding deserves further investigation to determine if (1) comprehended material is more robust over time than encoded details once it is committed to memory and (2) if this information processing affordance is a byproduct of formal education. If the trend (education helps retain comprehension) holds up under further scrutiny, it might be indicative of a cognitive strategy not to exhaust finite cognitive means in the service of absorbing and retaining simple details. Perhaps this shows a preference for deriving insights (e.g., what to do when a debt collector is abusive) on how to navigate a complicated social environment. Further research is needed to test this differential in managing cognitive reserves. It might very well be that citizens retain what is conducive to productive manoeuvring through life (comprehension) more than scattered details (simple recognition).

Compared to other measures of information gain (e.g., simple recognition, cued recall, or free recall), comprehension of social issues is arguably the grandest of achievements in knowledge acquisition. It is probably not unreasonable to argue that this cognitive process is at the heart of the journalistic mission: to inform citizens, across all demographic lines, for participatory democratic practice. This study adds further evidence that images should be included in assessments of knowledge. The structural exclusion of citizens with lower levels of formal education from experimental studies through the overuse of convenient undergraduate subject pools is a matter of weak (but sometimes tolerable) external validity in social science practice. What is untenable, however, is the continued use of verbal-only measures of how citizens acquire information from media. This tradition engenders a type of measurement bias against citizens with lower levels of education who have a greater ability to exhibit what they encode and comprehend through visual assessments. At the risk of overstatement, it is time for an amicable ontological defection from the Gutenberg legacy.

Conclusion

In the current audiovisual screen-based media environment, it seems prudent to suspend normative traditions, take stock of available measures for knowledge acquisition, and expand on them to accommodate a more nuanced understanding of knowledge gain across demographic groups. Doing so will stray from the dominant research paradigm, grounded in convictions about the supremacy of rational thought, verbal information, and news as cold, hard facts. But this departure from tradition is necessary in a changing media environment in which the very notions of informed citizenship and democratic process are mutating. There is an urgent need for work that not only tests memory but also tests comprehension, applied knowledge, and information navigational skills. At the risk of committing an overdrawn statement—We might be at the cusp of a new democratic way of life in which memory for cold, hard facts will not prepare citizens for informed participation. Instead, skills to gauge information and source credibility and the capacity for expansive but course-grained mapping of the social landscape might become more conducive to savvy citizenship.

References

Ahmadi, M., & Wohn, D. Y. (2018). The antecedents of incidental news exposure on social media. *Social Media+ Society*, 4(2). doi:10.1177/2056305118772827

Albæk, E., Van Dalen, A., Jebril, N., & De Vreese, C. H. (2014). *Political journalism in comparative perspective*. Cambridge University Press.

Allcott, H., Gentzkow, M., & Yu, C. (2019). Trends in the diffusion of misinformation on social media. *Research & Politics*, 6(2). doi:10.1177/2053168019848554

Altschull, J. H. (1990). *From Milton to McLuhan: The ideas behind American journalism*. Longman.

Arpan, L. M. (2009). The effects of exemplification on perceptions of news credibility. *Mass Communication and Society*, 12, 249–270.

Atton, C., & Hamilton, J. (2008). *Alternative journalism*. Sage.

Bailey, R., Fox, J., & Grabe, M. E. (2013). The influence of message and audience characteristics on TV news grazing behavior. *Journal of Broadcasting & Electronic Media*, 57(3), 318–337.

Barry, A. M. (2005). Perception theory. In K. Smith, S. Moriarty, G. Barbatsis, & K. Kenney (Eds.), *Handbook of visual communication* (pp. 45–62). Erlbaum.

Bas, O., & Grabe, M. E. (2015). Emotion-provoking personalization of news: Informing citizens and closing the knowledge gap? *Communication Research*, 42(2), 159–185.

Bas, O., & Grabe, M. E. (2016). Personalized news and participatory intent: How emotional displays of everyday citizens promote political involvement. *American Behavioral Scientist*, 60(14), 1719–1736.

Basil, M. (1994). Empirical examination of modality-specific attention to television scenes. *Communication Research*, 21(2), 208–231. doi:10.1177/009365094021002004

Bennett, S. E., Rhine, S. L., & Flickinger, R. S. (2008). Television 'news grazers': Who they are and what they (don't) know. *Critical Review*, 20(1–2), 25–36.

Bird, S. E. (1992). *For inquiring minds: A cultural study of supermarket tabloids*. University of Tennessee Press.

Boczkowski, P. J., Mitchelstein, E., & Matassi, M. (2018). 'News comes across when I'm in a moment of leisure': Understanding the practices of incidental news consumption on social media. *New Media & Society*, 20(10), 3523–3539.

Bonfadelli, H. (2002). The internet and knowledge gaps. *European Journal of Communication*, 17(1), 65–84. doi:10.1177/0267323102017001607

Briggs, X. D. S. (Ed.). (2005). *The geography of opportunity: Race and housing choice in metropolitan America*. Brookings Institution Press.

Brosius, H., Donsbach, W., & Birk, M. (1996). How do text–picture relations affect the informational effectiveness of television newscasts? *Journal of Broadcasting & Electronic Media*, 40(2), 180–195. doi:10.1080/08838159609364343

Burke, P. (1994). *Popular culture in early modern Europe*. Routledge.

Camaj, L. (2019). From selective exposure to selective information processing: A motivated reasoning approach. *Media and Communication*, 7(3). http://dx.doi.org/10.17645/mac.v7i3.2289

Castells, M., Fernandez-Ardevol, M., Qui, J. L., & Sey, A. (2009). *Mobile communication and society: A global perspective*. MIT Press.

Conway, M. T. (2009). *The origins of television news in America: The visualizers of CBS in the 1940s*. Lang.

Craik, F., & Lockhart, R. (1972). Levels of processing: A framework for memory research. *Journal of Verbal Learning and Behavior, 11*(6), 671–684. doi:10.1016/S0022-5371(72)80001-X

Damasio, A. R. (1994). *Descartes error: Emotion, reason and the human brain.* Putnam's Sons.

Druckman, J. N. (2005). Does political information matter? *Political Communication, 22*(4), 515–519.

Edwardson, M., Kent, K., Engstrom, E., & Hofmann, R. (1992). Audio recall immediately following video change in television news. *Journal of Broadcasting & Electronic Media, 36*(4), 395–410. doi:10.1080/08838159209364189

Ettema, J. S., Brown, J. W., & Luepker, R. V. (1983). Knowledge gap effects in a health information campaign. *Public Opinion Quarterly, 47*, 516–527.

Eveland, W. P., Jr., & Scheufele, D. A. (2000). Connecting news media use with gaps in knowledge and participation. *Political Communication, 17*(3), 215–237.

Findahl, O., & Höijer, B. (1985). Some characteristics of news memory and comprehension. *Journal of Broadcasting & Electronic Media, 29*(4), 379–396. doi:10.1080/08838158509386594

Gaziano, C. (1997). Forecast 2000: Widening knowledge gaps. *Journalism and Mass Communication Quarterly, 74*(2), 237–264.

Gaziano, C. (2010). Notes on 'Revisiting the knowledge gap hypothesis: A meta-analysis of thirty-five years of research'. *Journalism & Mass Communication Quarterly, 87*(3–4), 615–632. doi:10.1177/107769901008700311

Goody, J., & Watt, I. (1963). The consequences of literacy. *Comparative Studies in Society and History, 5*(3), 304–345.

Grabe, M. E., Kamhawi, R., & Yegiyan, N. (2009). Informing citizens: How people with different levels of education process television, newspapers, and Web news. *Journal of Broadcasting & Electronic Media, 53*(1), 90–111.

Grabe, M. E., Lang, A., & Zhao, X. (2003). News content and form: Implications for memory and audience evaluation. *Communication Research, 30*(4), 387–413.

Grabe, M. E., & Myrick, J. (2016). Informed citizenship in a media-centric way of life. *Journal of Communication, 66*(2), 215–235.

Grabe, M. E., Yegiyan, N., & Kamhawi, R. (2008). Experimental evidence of the knowledge gap: Message arousal, motivation, and time delay. *Human Communication Research, 34*(4), 550–571.

Grabe, M. E., Zhou, S., & Barnett, B. (2001). Explicating sensationalism in television news: Content and the bells and whistles of form. *Journal of Broadcasting & Electronic Media, 45*(4), 635–655.

Grabe, M. E., Zhou, S., Lang, A., & Bolls, P. (2000). Packaging television news: The effects of tabloid on information processing and evaluative responses. *Journal of Broadcasting & Electronic Media, 44*(4), 581–598.

Graber, D. A. (1988). *Processing the news: How people tame the information tide* (2nd ed.). Longman.

Graber, D. A. (1990). Seeing is remembering: How visuals contribute to learning from television news. *Journal of Communication, 40*(3), 134–155. doi:10.1111/j.1460-2466.1990.tb02275.x

Graber, D. A. (1996). Say it with pictures. *Annals of the American Academy of Political and Social Science, 546*, 85–96. doi:10.1177/0002716296546001008

Graber, D. A. (2001). *Processing politics: Learning from television in the internet age.* University of Chicago Press.

Graff, H. J. (1987). *The legacies of literacy: Continuities and contradictions in Western culture and society.* Indiana University Press.

Gripsrud (2000). Tabloidization, popular journalism and democracy. In: C. Sparks and Tulloch, J. (Eds.) *Tabloid tales: Global debates over media standards.* Rowman and Littlefield Publishers Inc., pp. 285–300.

Gunter, B. (1987). *Poor reception: Misunderstanding and forgetting broadcast news* Routledge.

Havelock, E. A. (1963). *Preface to Plato* (Vol. 1). Harvard University Press.

Hwang, Y., & Jeong S. (2009). Revising the knowledge gap hypothesis: A meta-analysis of thirty-five years of research. *Journalism & Mass Communication Quarterly, 86*(3), 513–532. doi:10.1177/107769900908600304

Ireton, C., & Posetti, J. (2018). *Journalism, fake news & disinformation: Handbook for journalism education and training.* UNESCO Publishing.

Jennings, M. (1996). Political knowledge over time and across generations. *Public Opinion Quarterly, 60*(2), 228–252. doi:10.1086/297749

Jerit, J., Barabas, J., & Bolsen, T. (2006). Citizens, knowledge, and the information environment. *American Journal of Political Science, 50*(2), 266–282.

Katz, E., Adoni, H., & Parness, P. (1977). Remembering the news: What the picture adds to recall. *Journalism Quarterly, 54,* 231–239. doi:10.1177/107769907705400201

Keating, C., Randall, D., & Kendrick, T. (1999). Presidential physiognomies: Altered images, altered perceptions. *Political Psychology, 20*(3), 593–610. doi:10.1111/0162-895X.00158

Kim, S. H. (2008). Testing the knowledge gap hypothesis in South Korea: Traditional news media, the internet, and political learning. *International Journal of Public Opinion Research, 20*(2), 193–210.

Kwak, N. (1999). Revisiting the knowledge gap hypothesis: Education, motivation, and media use. *Communication Research, 26*(4), 385–413.

Lazer, D. M., Baum, M. A., Benkler, Y., Berinsky, A. J., Greenhill, K. M., Menczer, F., & Schudson, M. (2018). The science of fake news. *Science, 359*(6380), 1094–1096.

Lee, J. K., & Kim, E. (2017). Incidental exposure to news: Predictors in the social media setting and effects on information gain online. *Computers in Human Behavior, 75,* 1008–1015.

Lindlof, T. R. (1991). The qualitative study of media audiences. *Journal of Broadcasting & Electronic Media, 35*(1), 23–42.

Marcus, G. E., & Mackuen, M. B. (1993). Anxiety, enthusiasm, and the vote: The emotional underpinnings of learning and involvement during presidential campaigns. *American Political Science Review, 87*(3), 672–685.

McCarthy, R. A., & Warrington, E. K. (1988). Evidence for modality-specific meaning systems in the brain. *Nature, 334,* 428–431. doi:10.1038/334428a0

Meserole (2018). How misinformation spreads on social media—And what to do about it. *u/blog/order-from-chaos/2018/05/09/ho w-misinformation-spreads-on-social-media-and-what-to-do-about-it.*

Miller, A., & Leshner, G. (2007). How viewers process live, breaking, and emotional television news. *Media Psychology, 10*(1), 23–40. doi:10.1080/15213260701300915

Molyneux, L. (2018). Mobile news consumption: A habit of snacking. *Digital Journalism, 6*(5), 634–650.

Morris, J. S., & Forgette, R. (2007). News grazers, television news, political knowledge, and engagement. *Harvard International Journal of Press/Politics, 12*(1), 91–107.

Neuman, W. R., Just, W. R., & Crigler, A. N. (1992). *Common knowledge: News and the construction of political meaning.* University of Chicago Press.

Newhagen, J., & Reeves, S. (1992). The evening's bad news: Effects of compelling negative television news images on memory. *Journal of Communication, 42*(2), 25–41. doi:10.1111/j.1460-2466.1992.tb00776.x

Newman, N., Fletcher, R., Kalogeropoulos, A., Levy, D., & Nielsen, R. K. (2017). *Reuters Institute digital news report 2017.*

Nguyen, A., & Western, M. (2007). Socio-structural correlates of online news and information adoption/use: Implications for the digital divide. *Journal of Sociology, 43*(2), 167–185.

Nie, N. H., Junn, J., & Stehlik-Barry, K. (1996). *Education and democratic citizenship in America.* University of Chicago Press.

Nussbaum, M. (2001). *Upheavals of thought: The intelligence of emotions.* Cambridge University Press.

Örnebring, H., & Jönsson, A. M. (2004). Tabloid journalism and the public sphere: A historical perspective on tabloid journalism. *Journalism Studies, 5*(3), 283–295.

Ortony, A. (1978). Remembering, understanding, and representation. *Cognitive Science, 2*(1), 53–69.

Paivio, A. (1971). *Imagery and verbal processes.* Holt, Rinehart & Winston.

Paul, K. (2019). *Facebook says it can't handle election misinformation crisis alone.* https://www.theguardian.com/technology/2019/jun/26/facebook-constitution-supreme-court-zuckerberg

Pennycook, G., & Rand, D. G. (2020). Who falls for fake news? The roles of bullshit receptivity, overclaiming, familiarity, and analytic thinking. *Journal of Personality, 88*(2), 185–200.

Peters, C. (2011). Emotion aside or emotional side? Crafting an 'experience of involvement' in the news. *Journalism, 12*(3), 297–316.

Pew Research Center. (2004, June 8). *News audiences increasingly politicized. 4: Attitudes toward the news.* http://www.people-press.org/2004/06/08/iv-attitudes-toward-the-news

Pew Research Center. (2010, September 12). Americans spending more time following the news. http://people-press.org/2010/09/12/americans-spending-more-time-following-the-news

Pew Research Center (2016) *Many Americans believe fake news is sowing confusion.* Retrieved from:http://www.journalism.org/2016/12/15/many-americans-believe-fake-news-is-sowing-confusion/

Pew Research Center. (2019, June 12). Internet/broadband fact sheet. Retrieved 20 July 2019 from https://www.pewinternet.org/fact-sheet/internet-broadband

Pinker, S. (1997). Words and rules in the brain. *Nature, 387,* 547–548.

Power, S., Taylor, C., & Horton, K. (2017). Sleepless in school? The social dimensions of young people's bedtime rest and routines. *Journal of Youth Studies, 20*(8), 945–958.

Price, V., & Zaller, J. (1993). Who gets the news? Alternative measures of news reception and their implications for research. *Public Opinion Quarterly, 57*(2), 133–164.

Prior, M. (2014). Visual political knowledge: A different road to competence. *Journal of Politics, 76*(1), 41–57. doi:10.1017/S0022381613001096

Purcell, K., Raine, L., Mitchell, A., Rosenstiel, T., & Olmstead, K. (2010, March 1). *Understanding the participatory news consumer: How Internet and cell phone users have turned news into a social experience* http://www.pewinternet.org/2010/03/01/understanding-the-participatory-news-consumer

Regier, C. C. (1957). *The era of the muckrakers*. Peter Smith.

Robinson, J., & Davis, D. (1990). Television news and the informed public: An information processing approach. *Journal of Communication, 40*(3), 106–119. doi:10.1111/j.1460-2466.1990.tb02273.x

Robinson, J., & Levy, M. (1986). *The main source: Learning from television news*. Sage.

Rosenberg, S., Kahn, S., & Tran, T. (1991). Creating a political image: Shaping appearance and manipulating the vote. *Political Behavior, 13*(4), 345–367. doi:10.1007/BF00992868

Schmitt, J. B., Debbelt, C. A., & Schneider, F. M. (2018). Too much information? Predictors of information overload in the context of online news exposure. *Information, Communication & Society, 21*(8), 1151–1167.

Schneider, W., & Shiffrin, R. M. (1977). Controlled and automatic human information processing: I. Detection, search, and attention. *Psychological Review, 84*(1), 1.

Schudson, M. (2001). The objectivity norm in American journalism. *Journalism, 2*(2), 149–170.

Schumpeter, J. A. (1942). *Capitalism, socialism, and democracy*. Harper Perennial.

Selwyn, N. (2004). Reconsidering political and popular understandings of the digital divide. *New Media & Society, 6*(3), 341–362.

Shoemaker, P. J., Schooler, C., & Danielson, W. A. (1989). Involvement with the media: Recall versus recognition of election information. *Communication Research, 16*(1), 78–103.

Snoeijer, R., de Vreese, C., & Semetko, H. (2002). The effects of live television reporting on recall and appreciation of political news. *European Journal of Communication, 17*(1), 85–101. doi:10.1177/0267323102017001608

Somin, I. (1998). Voter ignorance and the democratic ideal. *Critical Review, 12*(4), 413–458.

Starr, P. (2004). *The creation of the media: Political origins of modern communications*. Basic Books.

Swados, H. (1962). *Years of conscience: The muckrakers*. World Publishing.

Tannenbaum, P. H., & Lynch, M. D. (1960). Sensationalism: The concept and its measurement. *Journalism Quarterly, 37*(2), 381–392.

Tewksbury, D., Weaver, A. J., & Maddex, B. D. (2001). Accidentally informed: Incidental news exposure on the World Wide Web. *Journalism & Mass Communication Quarterly, 78*(3), 533–554.

Tichenor, P. J., Donohue, G. A., & Olien, C. N. (1970). Mass media flow and differential growth in knowledge. *Public Opinion Quarterly, 34*(2), 159.

Tremayne, M., & Dunwoody, S. (2001). Interactivity, information processing, and learning on the World Wide Web. *Science Communication, 23*(2), 111–134. doi:10.1177/1075547001023002003

Tulloch, J. (2000). The eternal recurrence of new journalism. In C. Sparks & J. Tulloch (Eds.), *Tabloid tales: Global debates over media standards* (pp. 131–145). Rowman & Littlefield.

Tulving, E., & Thompson, D. (1973). Encoding specificity and retrieval processes in episodic memory. *Psychological Review, 80*, 352–373. doi:10.1037/h0020071 van der Molen, J. H. W., & Klijn, M. E. (2004). Recall of television versus print news: Retesting the semantic overlap hypothesis. *Journal of Broadcasting & Electronic Media, 48*(1), 89–107. doi:10.1207/s15506878jobem4801_5

Van Dijk, J., & Hacker, K. (2003). The digital divide as a complex and dynamic phenomenon. *The Information Society, 19*(4), 315–326.

Van Dijk, T. A. (1988). *News as discourse.* Erlbaum.

Wahl-Jorgensen, K. (2019). *Emotions, media and politics.* Wiley.

Walker, J. R., & Bellamy, R. V., Jr. (1991). Gratifications of grazing: An exploratory study of remote control use. *Journalism Quarterly, 68*(3), 422–431.

Walker, J. R., Bellamy, R. V., Jr., & Traudt, P. J. (1993). Gratifications derived from remote control devices: A survey of adult RCD use. In J. R. Walker & R. V. Bellamy (Eds.), *The remote control in the new age of television* (pp. 103–112). Praeger.

Ward, S. (2005). *The invention of journalism ethics: The path to objectivity and beyond.* McGill-Queen's University Press.

Wei, L., & Hindman, D. B. (2011). Does the digital divide matter more? Comparing the effects of new media and old media use on the education-based knowledge gap. *Mass Communication and Society, 14*(2), 216–235.

Wenner, L. A., Dennehy, M. O., & Walker, J. R. (1993). Is the remote control device a toy or tool? Exploring the need for activation, desire for control, and technological affinity in the dynamic of RCD use. In J. R. Walker & R. V. Bellamy (Eds.), *The remote control in the new age of television* (pp. 113–134). Praeger.

Woodall, W. G., Davis, D. K., & Sahin, H. (1983). From the boob tube to the black box: Television news comprehension from an information processing perspective. *Journal of Broadcasting & Electronic Media, 27*(1), 1–23.

Yang, J., & Grabe, M. E. (2011). Knowledge acquisition gaps: A comparison of print versus online news sources. *New Media & Society, 13*(8), 1211–1227.

Zhou, S. (2005). Effects of arousing visuals and redundancy on cognitive assessment of television news. *Journal of Broadcasting & Electronic Media, 49*(1), 23–42.

Zhu, B., Chen, C., Loftus, E. F., He, Q., Chen, C., Lei, X., Lin, C., & Dong, Q. (2012). Brief exposure to misinformation can lead to long-term false memories. *Applied Cognitive Psychology, 26*(2), 301–307.

5

Emotion

Sarah Bachleda and Stuart Soroka

This chapter is focussed on the role of emotion in news coverage. We are interested in two different questions about emotion. The first is a simple empirical issue: To what extent does emotion appear in news coverage? There is no lack of work detailing the use of emotion in political campaign advertising, of course, but there is relatively little work that captures the nature and frequency of expressed emotions in regular news content. Our work begins accordingly by introducing an automated content-analytic strategy for capturing discrete emotions in news coverage, and we implement that strategy on a sizeable body of news content in *The New York Times*, from 1980 to the present. Results confirm that even as journalistic norms encourage objectivity, that objectivity does not preclude emotionality, if not from the journalist than from the subjects of the news. Indeed, journalistic norms likely serve to increase rather than decrease the prevalence of emotion in news content, particularly negative emotion. Emotions are a regular feature of news events, and there is evidence that the frequency of discrete emotions found in news content is increasing over time.

We start this chapter by examining the frequency of emotions in news. After having demonstrated that emotions are a regular feature of news content, we turn to our second question: Why (and how) does emotion in news content matter? We consider first the *expression of emotion* in news content and the possibility that expressed emotion increases attentiveness from readers. This creates the incentive for audience-seeking journalists to include emotional content. The results of our data analysis are in line with what one would expect were journalists acting on established journalistic norms—not just in service of increasing audiences but also in line with views of media as a critical Fourth Estate. We then turn to the *feeling of emotion* from readers. Expressions and feelings of emotion need not match—indeed, it seems very likely that they are only tangentially connected. But felt emotions matter for the ways in which audiences consume and react to news coverage. In

Sarah Bachleda and Stuart Soroka, *Emotion* In: *The Psychology of Journalism.* Edited by: Sharon Coen and Peter Bull, Oxford University Press. © Oxford University Press 2021. DOI: 10.1093/oso/9780190935856.003.0005 short, emotions condition information processing. Here, we turn to well-established literature in communication and psychology on the relevance of emotion to information processing and behaviour. This work is useful in helping us understand how and why emotions are relevant to both the practice and study of journalism.

The Frequency of Expressed Discrete Emotions in News Content

There is a small but important literature that attempts to capture discrete emotions in news content (e.g., Back et al., 2011; Strapparava & Mihalcea, 2008; Soroka et al., 2015). Note that by 'discrete emotions', we refer to the range of different emotion categories, such as anger, fear, happiness, and so on. These are somewhat different quantities than the focus of work on 'negativity', for instance. Negativity is about the simple valence of news content. In later sections, we consider in more detail the valence and discrete approaches to emotion, and others as well. Here, however, we focus on identifying some discrete emotions expressed in news. Our current goal is simple: to establish the prevalence of expressed discrete emotions in news content.

Capturing discrete emotions, however, is relatively difficult. Past work regularly relied on expert coders to identify discrete emotions in news content (e.g., Uribe & Gunter, 2007). This method can be reliable, but obviously it has constraints for very large bodies of data. Fortunately, technological change has enabled two key advancements in content analysis research. First, media content is readily available in digital format, in massive quantities. Second, that content can be dealt with computationally. This has led to the development of content-analytic dictionaries that can be applied to analyse bodies of text nearly unlimited in size.

In the case of research on emotion, multiple dictionaries have emerged and been applied to examine the emotionality of open-ended survey questions, personal diaries, political speeches, and media content. Unfortunately, many of these dictionaries are just starting to distinguish discrete emotional sentiment (as opposed to positive–negative valence), and they lack tests of validity (see Soroka et al., 2015). For this reason, we focus here on the new Discrete Emotions Dictionary (DED) (Bachleda et al., 2021). We review the construction of this dictionary briefly, although a more thorough account is available in Bachleda et al. (2021).

The first step in building the DED was to critically examine current dictionaries in the field. An initial list was created of words that appeared in more than one of these dictionaries for the emotions 'anger' and 'anxiety'. The only dictionary offering additional emotion categories is the Linguistic Inquiry and Word Count, which includes optimism and sadness (Pennebaker et al., 2001). The content of all emotion dictionaries was examined by the authors, who also added words to each of the four emotion groupings that they thought deserved testing. The selection of these words was necessarily subjective, drawn from a thesaurus and from reading samples of political news content.

Fundamental to the development of these word lists was (1) a focus on *expression* of emotion and (2) a focus on public political content—namely the language that would be common in media and campaign rhetoric (as opposed to, for instance, everyday conversation). By focussing on the expression of emotion, we mean words that directly and clearly signal an emotion, not words that can be *interpreted* to evoke an emotion. For example, the word 'war' may be emotion-evoking, but it is unclear which emotion it might inspire depending on the person (e.g., anger, fear, and sadness). However, a phrase such as 'the congressman angrily disputed the corruption claims' directly points to the expression of anger with little ambiguity. These are the situations for which the dictionary was constructed.

The dictionary was pretested (Bachleda et al., 2021) using a sample of 40,000 *New York Times* front-page news articles from 2000 and 2001. First, the authors examined how often the word appeared in the corpus, and then they collected a random draw of 50 sentences in which each word occurred. Two human coders read the 50 sentences for each word, determining whether each sentence was accurately and appropriately expressing the emotion it was intended to measure, based on the dictionary (including negations such as 'not angry'), with little or no ambiguity. For example, words that potentially evoked an emotion but could be interpreted in multiple ways failed the validity test (as described previously). Furthermore, if the word represented a concept that was not an emotional expression, such as crimes, descriptions of weather patterns, official titles, and so on, it failed the coding test. If a word was deemed accurate by the two coders in 85% or more of the sentences, it was kept. All other words were removed for further analysis.

The DED is, in this way, the product of human-coded language in news content, with an eye toward being able to identify discrete emotions in large bodies of news content. We turn to that large body of news content here.

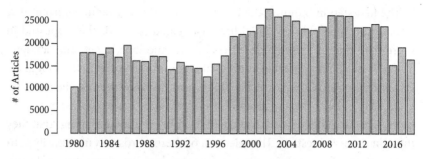

Figure 5.1 *The New York Times* front-section corpus.

We apply the DED to a large corpus of front-section news articles in *The New York Times*. Of course, we do not argue that *The New York Times* is representative of all newspapers in the United States or throughout the world. It is nevertheless a paper of record in the United States, and content from *The New York Times* is readily available over an extended period in several full-text news indices. Here, we rely on a database drawn from Lexis-Nexis using the Web Services Kit, which allowed for large-scale downloads. The database includes 785,321 stories in total, well over 10,000 articles per year. The distribution of stories by year is shown in Figure 5.1.

We implement the DED using the *quanteda* package in R (Benoit et al., 2018). Results are relatively straightforward to interpret and are shown in Figure 5.2. The figure shows the average frequency of each emotion in front-section news stories, based on the categories of the DED. We arrive at the estimations using ordinary least squares regression models of the number of words referencing each emotion, by story, as a function of year, which we include as a factor variable. Estimating this model for each of four emotions (anxiety, anger, optimism, and sadness) produces an estimate for each year, along with a margin of error. We use those results to graph 95% confidence intervals in Figure 5.2 for each of the four emotions over time.

What do results in Figure 5.2 tell us about the frequency of discrete emotions in news content? There quite clearly is a good deal of anxiety in *The New York Times* content. There is an average of roughly 0.7 anxiety words per article over the entire time period—and a marked increase in anxiety from roughly 2008 onwards. The frequency of other expressed emotions is lower. Anger and optimism words occur at roughly the same frequency, hovering at approximately 0.2 words per article during the time period. Sadness occurs at roughly half that frequency.

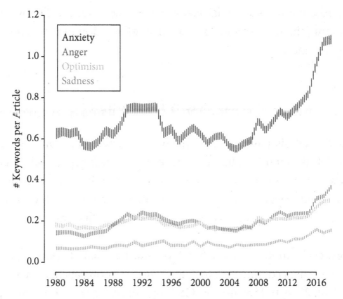

Figure 5.2 The frequency of expressed discrete emotions in *The New York Times*.

Do these results suggest a high or low frequency of expressed emotions in *The New York Times* content? Our inclination is to view these proportions as relatively high. Consider the following: On average, for every 10 front-section articles in *The New York Times*, roughly 7 of those articles include a word indicating expressed anxiety. This strikes us as a lot of anxiety. For every 10 articles, there are 2 with a word indicating expressed anger, 2 with a word indicating expressed optimism, and 1 with a word indicating expressed sadness. These need not all be different articles, of course: Emotions likely co-occur in a subset of articles, and some articles probably have many expressions of an emotion, whereas many have none. Even so, the frequency with which regular news readers will encounter expressed emotions seems to us to be relatively high. Based on the DED, it appears as though the frequency of discrete emotions has been increasing in *The New York Times* content during the past decade.

We thus take Figure 5.2 as an indication that (1) there is a good deal of expressed emotion in regular news content, especially anxiety, and (2) the frequency of emotion in news content has been increasing during the past decade. We take this as our starting point for a discussion of the relevance and impact of emotion in news content. Figure 5.2 makes clear that expressed emotion is a regular feature of news coverage. It follows that understanding the sources and consequences of emotion in news content is of real significance.

What Exactly Is 'Emotion'?

Our data analysis has focussed on several discrete emotions. Using a few clearly defined emotions has advantages for a quick explication of emotion in news content, of course, but definitions of emotion are nevertheless not at all straightforward. To consider the role that emotion plays in the production and influence of news content, we should first review what exactly 'emotion' is.

In general, emotions are defined as 'internal mental states representing evaluative valenced reactions to events, agents or objects that vary in intensity' (Nabi, 2010, p. 153; also see Cacioppo & Gardner, 1999). Conceptually, emotions differ from 'moods' in that they are responses, often uncontrollable, to the external environment that are relatively short in duration—a *reactive* state rather than an *enduring* one (Beedie et al., 2005). In the context of journalism, emotion is something that can be communicated, or invoked, through written, audio, or visual content.

There exists a robust and complex history of studying emotions in the field of journalism and political communication. Existing work considers both individual emotional states and emotion-evoking content. However, over decades of research, 'We have not yet converged on a singular theory of the role that emotions play in political thinking and behavior' (Neuman et al., 2007, p. 1); 'By our count, there are 23 named theories, models or central concepts used to explicate the interaction of affect and cognition' (p. 6). Why is this the case? On the one hand, the quantity of work dedicated to studying emotion is a signal of its importance and worthiness of study. On the other hand, a diversity of approaches reflects the immense complexity of human emotion itself, and hence the difficulty of measuring it.

There is compelling evidence (reviewed later) that emotions play a role in journalism and political communication. With more than 20 named approaches to research on emotionality, however, synthesizing the state of the literature defining 'emotion' is rather daunting. Fortunately, Neuman et al. (2007) suggest that most fall into one of the following four theoretical framework categories: valence, multidimensionality, discrete, and appraisal. The *valence* approach focusses on a unidimensional positive–negative continuum. Work that relies on this approach highlights, for instance, that people are drawn to negative news more than positive news, despite reporting preferences for positive (Trussler & Soroka, 2014). *Multidimensional* models consider not just valence but also the intensity of the emotion, via arousal (Russell, 1980). In this view, the strength of an emotion is of real importance; for instance, reported interest in photographs, and how long people view them, is correlated with levels of physiological arousal (Lang et al., 1993).

Some scholars argue that measuring valence and arousal is not sufficient for understanding the nature and impact of emotions on people's thoughts and behaviours. Nabi (2010) makes the case for *discrete* emotional models, arguing that there are unique patterns of cognition and action associated with specific emotion categories. She posits that two emotions can register the same in terms of negativity/positivity and intensity but lead to dramatically different outcomes. Research employing this perspective has found, for instance, that anxiety leads to information seeking, whereas anger suppresses it (Valentino et al., 2008); that anxiety leads to more openness to political compromise, whereas aversion leads to digging into prior attitudes (MacKuen et al., 2010); that anger, more than anxiety, mobilizes political participation (Valentino et al., 2011); that discrete emotional frames of political information lead to different causal attributions, information-seeking behaviour, and retribution policy preferences (Nabi, 2003); and that political persuasion is most effective when the discrete emotionality of the information matches the emotional state of the receiver (DeSteno et al., 2004). This body of work suggests that valence and arousal capture only a part of the emotional experience. Nabi (2010) states,

> The beauty of the discrete emotion view is that it in fact incorporates the dimensional perspective in that valence and intensity are assessed, but it goes much further by capturing the additional elements that provide nuance necessary to explain human action more fully. (p. 154)

Appraisal theories of emotion take an even more fluid approach. They argue that our emotional state is constantly changing and overlapping, contingent on thought processing and continuous assessment of our environment. As Ellsworth (2013) states, 'Emotional experience is an ever-changing process, like a river, rather than a collection of separate pools, or like the weather, rather than like sunlamps and refrigerators' (p. 125). In other words, emotion itself is a dynamic process of appraising stimulus as it affects our well-being, rather than a static 'state' (Moors et al., 2013). This process is complex—it is unique to every individual and the sensitivities or contextualities that shape each individual's view of the world.

For the purposes of understanding the role of emotion in journalism, we need not stake a claim on which approach is best. Of course, appraisal theories make the measurement of emotion very complex. But different applications of valence, dimensionality, or discrete approaches to emotion have led to different and valuable understandings of the nature of news content and to individual-level variation in communication effects. Using a simple valence approach, Soroka and McAdams (2015) find negative news provokes stronger and more sustained psychophysiological reactions compared with positive news, which may help us understand the old adage 'negative news sells'. Taking a more multidimensional approach to emotion, Berger and Milkman (2012) find that it is not just the positive or negative aspect of content that makes news stories go viral; it is also whether the content evokes high arousal (e.g., awe or anger) rather than deactivating emotional states (e.g., sadness). Nabi (2003), relying on a discrete approach to emotion, demonstrates that differing emotional categories, such as fear and anger, lead to different political information-seeking behaviour and policy preferences.

The discrete approach used by Nabi is obviously the one that motivates the preceding content analysis. Given that past work suggests different effects of fear and anger, it seems appropriate to build content-analytic tools that can distinguish these quantities—and the lack of tools with which to do so was the motivation for the development of the DED (Bachleda et al., 2021). The discrete approach, like the valence approach, is also readily applicable to an analysis of content rather than just to effects. Multidimensional and appraisal theories focus in part either on the intensity of felt emotion or on contextual differences between emotionally reacting message recipients. These are quantities that cannot be examined by looking at the content of journalism independent of its impact on audience members. And indeed, even in the case of valence or discrete emotions approaches, a content analysis captures expressed emotion independent of the fact that felt emotion may be just as relevant where media effects are concerned. We thus consider both in the following sections. We begin with a discussion of the sources of expressed emotion in news content. We then turn to the consequences of felt emotion, resulting from expressed emotion as well through emotional reactions to content more generally.

The Sources of Expressed Emotion in News Content

What accounts for the relatively high frequency of emotional keywords in news content? It is not entirely obvious that emotion-provoking events or information will transfer into emotional content in news coverage. There is, after all, a long-standing belief that fact-focussed, objective journalism requires that it is void of emotion. In fact, emotion in news is regularly conflated with sensationalism or bias, and it is often treated as a journalistic flaw (Peters, 2011).

The most prevalent counterargument is that objectivity does not require information to be sterile and dry; in fact, emotion *must* be a regular feature of news, just as it is a regular feature of the everyday life on which journalists aim to report (Pantti, 2010). When a tragedy occurs, such as the death of a public figure or an extreme weather event resulting in loss of life, the emotional impact of the event is in itself part of what makes it newsworthy to begin with.

Work in journalism suggests that emotion can also be an effective tool for journalists to involve their audience more directly, and that it helps audiences more effectively understand or experience the event (Peters, 2011; Pantti, 2010). This fits with psychological research focussed on the role of emotion—emotions have in that literature been shown to be central for information processing and 'rational' thinking (for a review, see Cacioppo & Gardner, 1999). It follows that emotion, expressed and/or felt, may be central rather than antithetical to good journalism, insofar as one aim of journalism is to engage and inform an audience. Stenvall (2014) makes the distinction between 'observed affect' and 'authorial affect', where the former describes the emotionality of the event or of a third party (good journalistic practice) and the latter is the individual journalist's own emotional feelings about the event (bad practice). Both may be beneficial under the right circumstances, however. We return to the potential benefits of emotion where engagement and interest are concerned in the final section of this chapter. For now, it is critical to recognize that we see expressed emotion in news content because it is a defining feature of newsworthiness, and quite likely central to good journalistic practice.

The Consequences of Felt Emotion and News Content

Emotions may be both an effect of consuming news and a mechanism through which news consumption matters for attitudes and behaviour. In other words, media effects research examines emotion as both a dependent variable and a moderating variable. The former approach focusses on how news content provokes emotions. The content of news, how that content is framed, the images or videos included, and of course the emotionality of those delivering the information all have the potential to evoke emotions among audience members, for instance. The latter approach focusses on the possibility that felt emotions, either provoked by the news or pre-existing at the time of consumption, influence the ways in which we interpret (and act upon) information. Examples of these two approaches are outlined next.

Felt Emotion as a Dependent Variable

To what extent are expressed emotions in news content transferred to felt emotions by news consumers? There is work suggesting that expressed emotions in news coverage, evidenced in the content analysis presented previously, can produce the same emotion among news consumers. For instance, Coleman and Banning (2006) exposed viewers to news videos of presidential candidates Al Gore and George W. Bush, recorded during the 2000 US election. Gore's coverage showed him expressing positivity in his language and demeanour, whereas Bush's coverage showed him expressing more negative affect. Results suggest that these emotional expressions by the candidates were transferred to viewers: Gore viewers reported higher positive emotional states of hope and pride, whereas Bush viewers reported elevated levels of fear and anger. The authors take these results as evidence of a mirroring connection between emotional content and the emotional states of viewers.

The connection between expressed and felt emotion need not be so clear, however. Bucy and Bradley (2004) find that when a president displays emotion incongruent with the situation or event the president is addressing, viewers do not mirror the emotion; indeed, viewers report elevated dislike toward the president. For example, when the participants were shown a news story covering an international crisis followed by images of President Clinton animated and smiling (incongruent behaviour), they were less physiologically activated (engaged in the material) and reacted in a way opposite of the president by frowning. It is only in cases of emotional congruence that these authors find evidence of emotional transfer. Expressed emotion can thus be transferred to news consumers, but this may be contingent on the context and evaluative processes at play.

News content may provoke emotions among consumers in other ways as well. News on any issue can provoke emotions: We may see a story about a sick child, for instance, and feel sadness; we may see a story about police violence and racism and feel a combination of anxiety and anger. Recent work highlights this dynamic, linked not just to current news stories but also to past news. For example, Wagner and Boczkowski (2019) measured people's emotional reactions as they reflected on news coverage of President Trump roughly 10 months after his inauguration. Respondents reported heightened emotional feelings of anger and anxiety when asked to reflect on news coverage during that time, and their emotional responses were elevated when asked to think about the coverage of a political issue they personally cared about, such as immigration, racism, or LGBTQ rights. These felt emotions need not be the product of emotional transfer; indeed, viewers likely do not remember the details of President Trump's inaugural speech 10 months later. Felt emotions in this instance are viewers' own emotional reactions to political issues. In short, news stories can produce felt emotions among consumers, even when the news stories themselves do not include expressed emotion.

Note that felt emotions may often reflect a complex interaction between text, photographs, and video in news coverage. Bucy (2003) exposed participants to varying images of the September 11, 2001, World Trade Center terrorist attacks in combination with coverage of President Bush's response to the event in order to gauge the effect of the emotionality of photos on the effectiveness of the president's address. He found that when exposed to low-intensity images of the trauma as a result of the attacks, President Bush's statements seemed to calm participants' anxiety. When exposed to high-intensity, more traumatic images of the attacks, President Bush's statements seemed to lose their influence (i.e., no effect on participants' anxiety). Pfau et al. (2006) similarly found that when news stories of war casualties were combined with a photograph and caption, people expressed more negative emotions (e.g., anger and sadness) than when reading the text of the story alone. These photographs had a high probability of provoking emotions because one depicted a solider saluting three coffins draped in the American flag and the other showed the dead bodies of four enemy insurgents killed by US troops.

In these different ways—be it through emotional transference or coverage of salient political issues, and via text, photographs, or video, independently or in combination—the content of news can provoke emotions in news consumers. Why might this matter? Felt emotions may matter for news selection. The considerable body of work on 'uses and gratifications' in media use (e.g., Blumler, 1979) suggests the possibility that consumers use media content in part to satisfy emotional needs—to seek out calming or provoking content, perhaps to help moderate or augment their own emotional state. This argument fits well with work suggesting that interest in negative content is driven not by negativity per se but, rather, outlyingness—we are most attentive to information that is at odds with our expectations, and those expectations (or interests in different types of news) vary systematically over time (Lamberson & Soroka, 2018). The nature of news consumption, in the moment and in the future, may depend in part on emotions felt as a consequence of news coverage.

Behaviours beyond news consumption may be affected by felt emotions provoked by news content as well. Consider the literature that highlights the mobilizing versus information-seeking consequences of anger versus anxiety. Valentino et al. (2011) found that political news content that inspired anger and enthusiasm could activate citizens, bolstering their intentions to participate in politics. On the other hand, when participants felt anxiety, they were less interested in participation and more focussed on seeking more information. MacKuen et al. (2010) also found that feelings of anger or aversion led people to further support already existing political beliefs, whereas general feelings of anxiety led to more openness to political compromise. If anxiety is provoked through activation of identity cues, it can make people more closed off to different groups (e.g., Brader et al., 2008). Yet if anxiety is felt more generally, it may lead people to seek out more news (e.g., Valentino et al., 2011) or become more open to political compromise (e.g., MacKuen et al., 2010). These findings are of some significance given the prevalence of anger and anxiety in news content, as demonstrated previously. We return to this issue in the concluding discussion.

Felt Emotion as a Moderating Variable

Information processing is affected by one's emotional state. There is a rich literature in psychology focussed on this fact—a literature that makes clear that anger or fear, or activation generally, changes the ways in which we focus on detail, or seek more information, or not (as highlighted by the work discussed in the next section). This moderating influence of emotion on news consumption may be a product of news consumption: News may make us angry, leading to anger-infused information processing. We might also simply arrive at news in an angry state, and that will matter with regard to how we select and process news content.

There is ample evidence of each of these dynamics. Consider work by Brosius (1993) suggesting that photographs can produce emotions that then draw readers' attention to specific elements of the story. For example, participants were asked to read a news story about the problems related to increased traffic. Two-thirds of the story focussed on noise and pollution issues, with the final section devoted to describing the danger for children. One version of the story was paired with a photograph of children playing, and another was paired with children running into the street in front of a car. Those who were exposed to the latter condition consistently and significantly reported children as the main issue of the story compared to the latter (who reported the other issues such as noise or pollution). Emotion, driven by photographs in this instance, affects the processing and interpretation of the information. There is also work suggesting that even as people are drawn to news stories eliciting feelings of disgust (Miller, 2006), viewing that disgust-evoking news content *limits* viewers' ability to process the information (Miller & Leshner, 2007). For example, across the board, participants were less accurate at recalling information about a story in which a dead body was involved (disgust) compared to a story about a tornado (fear). Because disgusting information requires more mental capacity to consume (compared to other stories that elicited fear, for example), Miller and Leshner (2007) argue, it leaves fewer resources to understand or remember the information.

There are two lessons to be drawn from the study by Miller and Leshner (2007). First, expressed-emotional content can be attention-grabbing, in part because it produces (or is noticed by audiences because it may potentially produce) felt emotions in news audiences. This account fits with the uses and gratifications account of emotionally laden news content, and it also helps account for the prevalence of emotion in news content that was identified in the content analysis discussed previously. News content is emotional in part because audiences seek emotional content. Second, felt emotions condition the ways in which we understand and process news content. Reading the news in an angry, or anxious, or happy state shifts the ways in which we encode the information. In other words, both our understanding and the consequences of news consumption depend in part on the emotional state we are in when we consume the news.

Consider the following examples. In an analysis of emotional framing of public policy, DeSteno et al. (2004) find that persuasion is more likely when the emotional frame of the story matches the emotional state of the receiver. If a news organization uses anxiety appeals to discuss issues about immigration, for instance, those appeals are more influential on people who already feel anxiety about that particular topic. In this instance, felt emotion augments the potential impact of expressed emotion in news content. Brader et al. (2008) found that when social group cues were emphasized by political elites while discussing their stance on immigration policy, respondents reported higher levels of anxiety, which in turn led to more anti-immigration policy attitudes post-exposure. Expressed emotion is not the critical factor here; rather, social group cues produce felt emotion, which has knock-on effects on information processing and attitudes.

It is this complex interaction between expressed and felt emotions, in which felt emotions are both an outcome and a moderating factor in news consumption, that produces some of the most interesting consequences of emotion in news content.

Conclusion: The Role of Emotion in News Consumption and Production

What are the normative implications of emotion in current affairs news coverage? The emphasis in the literature on either negativity generally or anxiety and anger specifically might lead one to conclude that news would be better off if emotion—expressed emotion at least—was less prevalent. We are not convinced that this is the case, however. Given that news consumers appear to be more activated and attentive to emotion-laden news content, engagement with political news may depend on a certain amount of emotion-laden or emotion-evoking content. This is the crux of the argument in Soroka (2014) where negativity is concerned: The positive consequences of negativity may well outweigh the negative ones. In short; if education, engagement, and mobilization are the primary objectives of political reporting, it is not at all clear that emotion, negative or positive, is a bad thing.

Indeed, there already is a small body of work emphasizing this point. Emotion can facilitate a more experiential connection between the reader and an event (Peters, 2011). Bas and Grabe (2015) found that when news content included more emotional appeal content (e.g., direct interviews with victims), it decreased the knowledge gap in understanding the information between high- and low-educated readers. Audiences are also not uncontrollably susceptible to emotional appeals. Vettehen et al. (2008) studied how emotional arousal affected whether or not readers liked a sensationalized news story. They found that if the story evoked small to moderate amounts of emotional arousal, readers liked the story more. (Although note that if the story evoked too much emotional intensity, it could decrease readers' enjoyment of the story.) Emotional appeals in journalism can in some conditions improve attention and learning.

This fact is of some significance given the apparent prevalence of expressed emotions in news content, as identified in the content analysis presented in this chapter. There clearly is a good deal of emotion in traditional newspaper content. There is likely even more given technological change and the consequent shifts in the news-making environment. The increased competition for attention that is the result of an unlimited amount of space for news content, ready access to a multitude of new sources on smartphones, and the redistribution through both social media contacts and algorithms of 'popular' news stories all point in the direction of more activating and attention-grabbing content. Whether this is a bad or good thing for the quality and impact of political journalism remains to be seen, however. Emotion is certainly a central element of news coverage and impact. There are risks to the use of emotion in news-making, but there are benefits as well.

References

Bachleda, S., Hasell, A., Soroka, S., & Weeks, B. (2021). *Constructing a dictionary for the automated identification of discrete emotions in news content*. Manuscript in preparation.

Back, M. D., Küfner, A. C. P., & Egloff, B. (2011). 'Automatic or the people?' Anger on September 11, 2001, and lessons learned for the analysis of large digital data sets. *Psychological Science, 22*(6), 837–838.

Bas, O., & Grabe, M. E. (2015). Emotion-provoking personalization of news: Informing citizens and closing the knowledge gap? *Communication Research, 42*(2), 159–185.

Beedie, C. J., Terry, P. C., & Lane, A. M. (2005). Distinctions between emotion and mood. *Cognition and Emotion, 19*(6), 847–878.

Benoit, K., Watanabe, K., Wang, H., Nulty, P., Obeng, A., Müller, S., & Matsuo, A. (2018). quanteda: An R package for the quantitative analysis of textual data. *Journal of Open Source Software, 3*(30), 774.

Berger, J., & Milkman, K. L. (2012). What makes online content viral? *Journal of Marketing Research, 49*(2), 192–205.

Blumler, J. G. (1979). The role of theory in uses and gratifications studies. *Communication Research, 6*(1), 9–36.

Brader, T., Valentino, N. A., & Suhay, E. (2008). What triggers public opposition to immigration? Anxiety, group cues and immigration threat. *American Journal of Political Science, 52*(4), 959–978.

Brosius, H. (1993). The effects of emotional pictures in television news. *Communication Research, 20*(1), 105–124.

Bucy, E. P. (2003). Emotion, presidential communication, and traumatic news: Processing the World Trade Center attacks. *Harvard International Journal of Press/Politics, 8*(4), 76–96.

Bucy, E. P., & Bradley, S. D. (2004). Presidential expressions and viewer emotion: Counterempathic responses to televised leader displays. *Social Science Information, 43*(1), 59–94.

Cacioppo, J. T., & Gardner, W. L. (1999). Emotion. *Annual Review of Psychology, 50*(1), 191–214.

Coleman, R., & Banning, S. (2006). Network TV news' affective framing of the presidential candidate: Evidence for a second-level agenda-setting effect through visual framing. *Journalism & Mass Communication Quarterly, 83*(2), 313–328.

DeSteno, D., Petty, R. E., Rucker, D. D., Wegener, D. T., & Braverman, J. (2004). Discrete emotions and persuasion: The role of emotion-induced expectancies. *Journal of Personality and Social Psychology, 86*(1), 43–56.

Ellsworth, P. C. (2013). Appraisal theory: Old and new questions. *Emotion Review, 5*(2), 125–131.

Lamberson, P. J., & Soroka, S. (2018). A model of attentiveness to outlying news. *Journal of Communication, 68*(5), 942–964.

Lang, P. J., Greenwald, M. K., Bradley, M. M., & Hamm, A. O. (1993). Looking at pictures: Affective facial, visceral and behavioral reactions. *Psychophysiology, 30*(3), 261–273.

MacKuen, M., Wolak, J., Keele, L., & Marcus, G. E. (2010). Civic engagements: Resolute partisanship or reflective deliberation. *American Journal of Political Science, 54*(2), 440–458.

Miller, A. (2006). Watching viewers watch TV: Processing live, breaking, and emotional news in a naturalistic setting. *Journalism & Mass Communication Quarterly, 83*(3), 511–529.

Miller, A., & Leshner, G. (2007). How viewers process live, breaking and emotional television news. *Media Psychology, 10*(1), 23–40.

Moors, A., Ellsworth, P. C., Scherer, K. R., & Frijda, N. H. (2013). Appraisal theories of emotion: State of the art and future development. *Emotion Review, 5*(2), 119–124.

Nabi, R. L. (2003). Exploring the framing effects of emotion. *Communication Research, 30*(2), 224–247.

Nabi, R. L. (2010). The case for emphasizing discrete emotions in communication research. *Communication Monographs, 77*(2), 153–159.

Neuman, W. R., Marcus, G. E., Crigler, A. N., & MacKuen, M. (2007). Theorizing affect's effects. In W. R. Neuman, G. E. Marcus, A. N. Crigler, & M. MacKuen (Eds.), *The affect effect: Dynamics of emotion in political thinking and behavior* (pp. 1–20). University of Chicago Press.

Pantti, M. (2010). The value of emotion: An examination of television journalists' notions on emotionality. *European Journal of Communication, 25*(2), 168–181.

Pennebaker, J. W., Francis, M. E., & Booth, R. J. (2001). *Linguistic inquiry and word count* [computer software]. Erlbaum.

Peters, C. (2011). Emotion aside or emotional side? Crafting an 'experience of involvement' in the news. *Journalism, 12*(3), 297–316.

Pfau, M., Haigh, M., Fifrick, A., Holl, D., Tedesco, A., Cope, J., Nunnally, D., Schiess, A., Preston, D., Roszkowski, P., & Martin, M. (2006). The effects of print news photographs on the casualties of war. *Journalism & Mass Communication Quarterly, 83*(1), 150–168.

Russell, J. A. (1980). The circumplex model of affect. *Journal of Personality and Social Psychology, 39*(6), 1161–1178.

Soroka, S. (2014). *Negativity in Democratic Politics: Causes and Consequences.* Cambridge University Press.

Soroka, S., & McAdams, S. (2015). News, politics and negativity. *Political Communication, 32*(1), 1–22.

Soroka, S., Young, L., & Balmas, M. (2015). Bad news or mad news? Sentiment scoring of negativity, fear and anger in news content. *Annals of the American Academy of Political and Social Science, 656*(1), 108–121.

Stenvall, M. (2014). Presenting and representing emotions in news agency reports. *Critical Discourse Studies, 11*(4), 461–481.

Strapparava, C., & Mihalcea, R. (2008). Learning to identify emotions in text. In *Proceedings of the 2008 ACM symposium on applied computing* (pp. 1556–1560). Association for Computing Machinery.

Trussler, M., & Soroka, S. (2014). Consumer demand for cynical and negative news frames. *International Journal of Press/Politics, 19*(3), 360–379.

Uribe, R., & Gunter, B. (2007). Are 'sensational' news stories more likely to trigger viewers' emotions than non-sensational news stories?: A content analysis of British TV news. *European Journal of Communication, 22*(2), 207–228.

Valentino, N. A., Brader, T., Groenendyk, E. W., Gregorowicz, K., & Hutchings, V. L. (2011). Election night's alright for fighting: The role of emotions in political participation. *Journal of Politics, 73*(1), 156–170.

Valentino, N. A., Hutchings, V. L., Banks, A. J., & Davis, A. K. (2008). Is a worried citizen a good citizen? Emotions, political information seeking, and learning via the internet. *Political Psychology, 29*(2), 247–273.

Vettehen, P. H., Nuijten, K., & Peeters, A. (2008). Explaining effects of sensationalism on liking of television news stories: The role of emotional arousal. *Communication Research, 35*(3), 319–338.

Wagner, M. C., & Boczkowski, P. (2019, September). Angry, frustrated and overwhelmed: The emotional experience of consuming news about President Trump. *Journalism.* doi:10.1177/1464884919878545

6

Norms and Roles

'Wale Oni

Norms and roles have been fascinating sociological and social psychological concepts for decades. They are often talked about in social science literature as playing a pivotal role in explaining human behaviour in virtually all circumstances. A norm is thought of as a powerful underlying force guiding how we should behave, which often goes 'underdetected' (Fiske et al., 2010). As individuals, we follow norms without conscious recognition of their undercurrent force, which we often deny. Therefore, a norm is a means of understanding human behaviour. Roles, on the other hand, are driven by norms, as they are often carried out under the guiding force of social norms—a term that describes human actions as a product of societal influences. Our existence as humans is realized in the multiple roles that we play in every sphere/stage of our lives. People secure and affirm their role within a group by holding consonant attitudes and engaging in socially accepted behaviours, with the hope that the likelihood of social sanctions brought about by social deviance is reduced. Therefore, what counts as our experience are stacked up learned behaviours associated with roles we have played and those we have observed others play too. Attunement to social norms becomes manifest at a very early age, long before language development in infants (Hamlin & Wynn, 2011). This means that we learn to internalize and perform certain roles through observing the behaviours of others. Our perceptions of roles and how we enact them are intricately tied to beliefs that we hold as individuals in a given society and members of certain groups.

Given the primacy of these two important concepts, this chapter provides an overview of literature on the function of social norms and roles in shaping emotions and beliefs about the world held by both individuals and groups. Although norms and roles are vast concepts to unpack within a chapter, our focus is on how norms and roles (as conceived in psychology) contribute to our understanding of journalism. The chapter covers social norms and their role in attitudes and persuasion and also how social norms

'Wale Oni, *Norms and Roles* In: *The Psychology of Journalism.* Edited by: Sharon Coen and Peter Bull, Oxford University Press. © Oxford University Press 2021. DOI: 10.1093/oso/9780190935856.003.0006

shape professional practice. Attention is paid to journalistic role conceptions as an offshoot of role theory, which has its roots in psychology. Finally, a case study is presented on journalists' acceptance and use of digital technology, thereby to buttress the primacy of social norms and role theory in journalism practice. Scholars have acknowledged that the occupation of journalism is typically technology-dependent and intricately 'woven into the fabric of society' (Tong & Lo, 2018, p. 6). Hence, in discussing the impact of social norms on journalism practice, the chapter reiterates the effects of sociocultural forces rooted in norms, roles, and individual characteristics—attitudes, perceptions, and persuasion (among other concepts in sociology and social psychology)—in understanding journalists' behavioural intentions and behaviours.

The Concept of Social Norms

Despite the popularity of work on norms, the concept still remains fluid because there is no general agreement as to how powerful norms are in shaping human actions. Norm has been operationally defined in so many ways that it has become difficult to draw conclusions from the vast body of research available on this construct. Some scholars, such as Cristina Bicchieri, have provided integrated accounts of how social norms emerge[1] and why and how we yield to them. They expressed their strong convictions concerning norms as a fundamental means of understanding human behaviour, while describing social norms as the unwritten social codes of conduct and the foundation of the world we live in (e.g., Bicchieri, 2006; Elster, 1992; Rimal & Real, 2003). However, scholars such as Campbell (1965) believe that norm is a vague concept with contradictory evidence of its influence on behaviour despite long-standing research on the concept. Therefore, an air of uncertainty still lingers over norm as a concept in social science, despite a thriving tradition of relevant social–psychological research. Social scientists (e.g., Shulman et al., 2017) have pointed to the cultural evolution of the norm as the basis for its uncertainty and multiple interpretations. But limiting norms to the realm of culture alone is also misleading, considering current

---

[1] Titlestad et al. (2019) explored how norms are formed in a recent study that investigated the development of cooperation norm in groups over time. The way in which groups are formed was found to affect norm development and norm adherence.

conceptual advancement in behavioural sciences (see McDonald & Crandall, 2015). Factors such as biological evolution, individual learning, and rational deliberation have all been proffered by social psychologists as playing important parts in understanding the 'dynamical processes' responsible for the formation, sustenance, transformation, and dissolution of norms (Bicchieri et al., 1997).

For the purpose of definition, *norm* is conceptualized in this chapter in relation to a variety of socially dependent behaviours (based on approval or disapproval of others) with accompanying expectations. This is what is meant by social norm. There are various definitions of social norms in the literature. Bicchieri (2006) defines social norms as 'informal understandings that govern the behaviour of members of a society' (p. 8). Morris et al. (2015) describe social norms as a navigation tool used in decision-making that guides individuals toward acting in socially appropriate ways. In social psychology, the social norms construct is defined as 'rules and standards that are understood by members of a group, and that guide and/or constrain social behaviour without the force of law' (Cialdini & Trost, 1998, p. 152). The social norm approach posits that people look to other people within their group or society—'the referent others'—before engaging in certain behaviours to ensure their behaviours are typical and will be met with social approval (Shulman et al., 2017; Shulman & Levine, 2012). Interpreted in line with the principle of 'social proof' (Cialdini, 1987), the concept of social norm is based on the assumption that people secure and affirm their role within a group by holding consonant attitudes and by engaging in socially accepted behaviours with the hope that the likelihood of ostracism or other social sanctions brought about by social deviance is reduced.

Recent attempts to explain the foundations and the status of social norms are marked by an important controversy: that between 'holism' and 'individualism' (Tutui, 2013). This also reflects the two prominent focal points being used in conceptualizing social norms between social psychologists and psychologists. In addition, it informs the distinction between the social norm and the personal norm. From the social psychology perspective, the proponents of the holistic approach posit that social norms derive from trans-individual and external social influences such as economic, judicial, or political structures, which exist and evolve independently over and above the individual characteristics. The individualistic approach expresses the view of researchers with a background in psychology, and it uses several psychosocial theoretical terms. Tutui (2013) notes that the key element in the individualistic approach is 'reason combined with the tendency to satisfy egoistic interests and desires' (i.e., intrinsic motivations), as well as the irrational dimensions of human nature such as emotional states of mind (p. 125). The argument is that if every behaviour is shaped by the dynamics of transindividual realities, how can we account for individual liberty, autonomy, and responsibility?

Given that social norms are *social* in that they are shared with other people and dependent on approval or disapproval (through social sanctions or ostracism), Jon Elster (1989) points to the emotive dimension of social norms in differentiating social norms from other normative behaviours driven by rationality and outcomes. Rationality, he explains, presupposes difficult mental calculations regarding the opportunity of a specific action. Elster (1990, p. 100) explains that the operation of norms is to a large extent blind, compulsive, mechanical, or even unconscious. Hence, social norms are compelled by emotions such as embarrassment, anxiety, guilt, and shame, which are experienced by the individuals when they are observed violating them, or by pride when people anticipate others' approval (e.g., Tangney & Fischer, 1995). It is important to bear in mind that norm violations may not necessarily be dysfunctional, as counternormative behaviour can benefit group functioning (Peters et al., 2017). Studies such as that by Gelfand et al. (2011) have demonstrated that people who deviate from group or societal norms often trigger negative emotions, which may later spur norm abidance.

Several other distinctions have been made by social psychologists in an attempt to provide appropriate construct definitions for social norms. Rimal and Lapinski (2015), for instance, provide a clear explanation by drawing on the distinction between collective norms and individual's perceived norms. Perceived norms operate at the individual level, which links a person's cognitions, beliefs, and behaviours with macro-level social contexts and determinants. This is based on the notion that an individual's beliefs about others' perceptions and behaviours in their social environment, pressures they perceive to conform, and their decisions to act in certain ways are shaped not only by factors impinging on them at the individual level but also by macro-level phenomena of which they may or may not be consciously aware. Collective norms, on the other hand, are based on a 'socioecological' perspective, which recognizes the place of social environment or social networks in shaping human behaviour (Sallis et al., 2008). How these social norms shape journalists' professional practice is discussed later.

To further refine the definition of social norms, it is important to consider the distinction between 'injunctive' and 'descriptive' norms as subcategories of the social norm construct. This distinction also supports the division between psychological/individualistic and sociological/social constructivist points of view. In contemporary literature, these meta-concepts—injunctive and descriptive norms—are regarded as explicit and implicit rules that inform individuals on what is deemed acceptable behaviour in a given social context (Cialdini & Trost, 1998). Operating at the individual level and in the context of self-expression, injunctive norms refer to the perception of what most people deem appropriate or inappropriate in certain situations—that is, other people's approval or disapproval (Bergquist et al., 2019; Waterloo et al., 2018). In other words, they address the perceptions of how strongly significant others approve or disapprove of a behaviour. Injunctive norms are dependent on the desire for social approval, the desire or motivation to 'do the right thing', based on the perceptions of others (Rimal & Real, 2005). Wombacher et al. (2017) explain that this category of social norms can be understood as the level of pressure one feels to engage in a specified behaviour. Therefore, injunctive norms are outcome-oriented and pressure-driven. Outcome expectations are beliefs that one's actions will lead to benefits or that not engaging in the behaviour will result in social disapproval. Outcome expectations may result as a fear of missing out (FOMO) or as a result of perceived benefits of the behaviour, such as being the first among peers or as an act of solidarity in group tasks (Rimal, 2008).

Descriptive norms, on the other hand, concern an individual's perceptions and beliefs about how prevalent a certain behaviour is among others in the group—that is, what other people do. For instance, those who believe a certain behaviour is highly prevalent within a group are most likely to believe that specific behaviour to be the norm and to be prescribed by their group (Wombacher et al., 2017). Furthermore, people who expect the behaviour to result in a positive outcome are more likely to engage in it compared to those who expect a negative outcome. Descriptive norms contrast in meaning with 'prescriptive' social norms as an indication of rule-governed behaviour—that is, what is approved or socially disapproved and which involves sanctions if they are not. This equally contrasts with what we do in uncertain situations. In this instance, what other people do is adaptive (Sevillano & Olivos, 2019).

The 'script' theory is also foregrounded in newer discussions on prescriptive social norms. Bosson and colleagues (2020) studied social scripts as a form of injunctive norm in their interesting study on gender equality norms (paternalism norm). In their work, script refers to such normative obligations as to protect and provide for women. It denotes heterosexual dating social norms, such as offering to pay when out to dinner with a woman, asking women for dates, and initiating sexual activity; all are quite common. There may be an implicit assumption (expectation) that a man who pays for a date is 'owed' sex. Research interest in this line of thought includes constructs such as 'benevolent sexism' and 'hostile sexism' that are used to test how misogyny is enhanced through exposure to 'paternalism norms', which emphasize men's obligation to protect and provide for women (Emmers-Sommer et al., 2010; Muehlenhard et al., 1985). Roles and statuses in occupational contexts are also script-based in that they follow from one's occupational code of conduct or rule-governed behaviour attached to an official status or role. For instance, teachers/lecturers are expected to be morally upright and work in line with some rule-governed ethos. Deviations from such role-/status-based rules often lead to reprimand by their professional bodies, such as the National Education Union in the United Kingdom.

Researchers have noted that the motivational antecedents and processes driving conformity to social norms differ between the injunctive and descriptive norms. Whereas conformity to injunctive norms fulfils the 'interpersonal goal' of making or gaining social approval, descriptive norms seek to fulfil the 'intrapersonal goal' of making accurate/effective decisions (Jacobson et al., 2011, 2015; Bergquist et al., 2019). With regard to discouraging undesirable behaviours, injunctive norms have been found to be more effective, whereas descriptive norms are more likely to encourage undesirable behaviour. One of the popular approaches to test the difference between injunctive and descriptive social norms is to evaluate the impact of norm-based information (messages) communicated explicitly versus implicitly. By explicit norms, psychologists assess the effect of openly communicated social norms that overtly detail other people's behaviours (approvals or disapprovals). In contrast, implicit normative information is communicated through subtle cues in the environment by indicating what other people have done or (dis)approve of.

Examples of the use of explicit and implicit normative information in field experiments abound in psychological research. In one instance, it was found that more participants took the stairs when prompted with the following normative message: 'More than 90 per cent of the time, people in this building use the stairs instead of the elevator'. But low participation was recorded when an implicit health-based prompt was used: 'Taking the stairs instead of the elevator is a good way to get some exercise' (Burger & Shelton, 2011). In promoting hotel linen reusage, Goldstein and colleagues (2007) found that prompts with normative information, such as 'Almost 75% of guests . . . use their towel more than once', were more effective than prompts with implicit pro-environmental information, such as 'Help save environment'.[2] Researchers working on persuasiveness of social norms note that dissatisfaction with the effectiveness of factual information and economic inducements has led to the use of normative information as a primary tool for changing a wide range of socially significant behaviours (Hang et al., 2020).[3]

Injunctive and descriptive norms have been found to be consistent predictors of intention and behaviour with unique variances explained (e.g., Manning, 2009; see also Bergquist et al., 2019). A study by Cialdini et al. (2006) found that preventive campaign messages constructed as injunctive norms successfully promoted 'good' behaviour such as using the staircase rather than the lift. However, messages with descriptive norms that alluded to the fact that everyone else was doing the negative behaviour (e.g., littering parks or leaving one's dog's poop on the pavement) had the tendency to encourage 'good' behaviour. Therefore, our behaviours are heavily influenced by others in terms of both what we think they do and what we think they want us to do (e.g., Goldstein et al., 2008; Nolan, 2008). Using the two meta-constructs together has been known to increase the predictive potential of intentions (e.g., Smith et al., 2012) and behaviours (e.g., Cialdini, 2003). Cialdini and Goldstein's (2004) theory of normative conduct suggests that conformity to injunctive norms can be driven by a goal of affiliation or by a goal of maintaining a positive self-image. Whereas the motive of affiliation reflects people's desire for social contact or belongingness, the motive of maintaining a positive self-image in public reflects people's use of injunctive norm conformity as an impression management tool for managing their image in public. A recent meta-analysis also reported a positive main effect of social norms on environmental behaviours (see Abrahamse & Steg, 2013; Bergquist et al., 2019). A preliminary systematic review of 8,204 published articles on norm-based research indexed in the Scopus electronic database revealed dominance of norm-related psychological research, with 38.2%

---

[2] Accounts of field experiments on explicit versus implicit normative information can be found in Nisa et al. (2017) and Scheibehenne et al. (2016).
[3] See McEachan and colleagues' (2011, 2016) systematic reviews on normative information.

representation over and above other academic disciplines in which the concept has been studied.[4]

There is growing interest in the deployment of theoretical approaches such as social norms, social learning, social comparison, leadership, and public commitment in norm research (e.g., Cinner, 2018; Sevillano & Olivos, 2019). Likewise, theories such as the model of personal normative influence (Schwartz, 1977), the theory of reasoned action (Fishbein & Ajzen, 1975), and the theory of planned behaviour (Ajzen, 1985, 1991) have witnessed increasing use of the concept of norms in the past 20 years. With a theoretical foundation in altruism, the model of personal normative influence has been employed consistently to explain prosocial behaviour such as helping. Normative propositions, such as the bystander effect, have been used to explain emerging social norms on human judgement and decision-making, such as using one's mobile phone to record crime rather than helping a victim or sharing an online crowdfunding Web link rather than donating. The bystander effect posits that people tend to be passive toward helping while in the presence of multiple other witnesses. Researchers usually include the normative components of a personal and interpersonal nature in this kind of study.

As the climate change debate and interest in the environment (proenvironmental behaviour) and public health awareness grow stronger, these psychosocial theories have gained more prominence (Stern et al., 1999; Sparkman & Walton, 2017). The boomerang effect and reciprocal effect are two of the norm-related notions under the theory of reactance (Brehm, 1966; Brehm & Brehm, 1981) that have been applied to interpret media messages and foreign policy. Reactance theory[5] is concerned with individuals' responses to coercion or influence attempts. Brehm and Brehm (1981) state,

---

[4] The following search string was used to arrive at this preliminary systematic review: ('social norms' OR 'norm' OR 'norms' OR 'injunctive norm' OR 'descriptive norms' OR 'prescriptive norms' OR 'implicit norms' OR 'explicit norms' OR 'personal norms' OR 'normative information' OR 'subjective norm' OR 'normative influence' AND 'psychology'). Scopus is the world's largest abstract and citation database of peer-reviewed research literature. It has more than 22,000 titles from more than 5,000 international publishers.

[5] According to reactance theory (Brehm, 1966), most people perceive themselves as having freedom over their beliefs and actions. But when feelings of personal freedom are threatened, they experience an unpleasant arousal that motivates efforts to reassert control (psychological reactance). Thus, when persuasion messages are perceived as overly coercive or heavy-handed, they can elicit efforts to re-establish personal freedom by increasing pursuit of the forbidden belief or behaviour. This counterreaction is called the boomerang effect. Descriptive norms provide a standard for people to follow with the possibility of leading to a boomerang effect [see Binder et al.'s (2019) study on children, peer cues, and food choices].

'The theory holds that a threat to or a loss of a freedom motivates the individual to restore that freedom' (p. 4). According to reactance theory, any persuasive communication can be expected to create two opposite reactions: a positive change reaction (i.e., in the direction advocated by the persuasive message) and a negative reaction leading to resistance (see Brehm & Brehm, 1981, p. 140). If a persuasive communication is worded strongly enough (and the freedom not to comply is sufficiently important to the target of the communication), reactance motivation, the force directed at noncompliance, may be triggered. An understanding of the dynamic relationship between compliance and resistance due to reactance is therefore necessary if one wishes to create persuasive communications of maximum effectiveness. The effects of multiple positive influence attempts, their specificity and strength, and the difficulty of complying have been systematically investigated in several field experiments (e.g., Mann & Hill, 1984). Relatedly, a nation's own conceptualization of interests and capabilities, as well as the role expectations of significant or generalized others that come about through social interaction between them, have found applications in understanding foreign policies (e.g., Chafetz et al., 1996; Nilsson, 2019). How this increasing popularity of psychological theories contributes to our understanding of journalism is examined next.

Social Norms and Professional Practice

Journalism is a profession rooted in cultural norms and practices. A number of studies have emerged in the past 10 years focussing on an examination of normative dimensions of journalistic practices, including professionalism, ethics, and moral development (e.g., Jenkins & Tandoc, 2019; Tandoc & Oh, 2017; Wasserman & Maweu, 2014). An example is Lee et al.'s (2016) study, which applied injunctive and descriptive norms to investigate the effects of social norms on ethical behaviour in journalism. It was found that individual journalists may be more prone to behave ethically if they perceive ethical behaviour as the norm in the field. Conversely, journalists appear to be more prone to act unethically if they perceive that unethical behaviour is approved in the field. The study showed that of the six unethical behaviours tested, 49.3% of respondents claimed to have used a press or video release without any editing, 42.3% said they had adjusted the image quality of a photograph or video, and 20.6% of respondents had done a story on an organization or club to which they or someone in their family belonged. Nearly all respondents claimed they had reported multiple perspectives in a story, with 87% claiming that they had separated analysis and commentary from news reporting. Overall, both injunctive and descriptive norms emerged as predictors of how journalists think and act. However, descriptive norms account for almost half of the variance in ethical journalistic behaviours. Injunctive norms account for slightly less than one-third of the variance. Although Lee et al.'s study is silent as to why descriptive norms have a stronger impact on ethical behaviour, existing research has shown that journalists, compared with other professionals such as medical doctors, are among the most capable of making good moral judgements (Coleman & Wilkins, 2009).

Journalism clearly does not possess all the attributes ordinarily associated with 'classical' professions, such as medicine or the church. However, despite the debate about declining professionalism in the field, with journalists' internal ideological conflicts constantly in crisis with external pressures, journalists have been found to have an edge in moral development over other professional groups, including nurses, orthopaedic surgeons, and dental and veterinary students[6] (Coleman & Wilkins, 2002, 2004, 2009; Rest et al., 1999). One of the reasons for this is traceable to journalists' individual intrinsic motivations (injunctive norms). Journalists' intrinsic motivators have been found to be stronger in predicting their behaviour compared to external forces (extrinsic influences), such as regulatory laws, organizational policies, market forces, newsroom environment codes of ethics, news subject and sources advertisers, and audiences (Singletary et al., 1990).

A way to enhance individuals' reliance on intrinsic motivations is to increase their feelings of autonomy (Kohlberg, 1969). Singer (2007) discusses the concept of journalists' autonomy in relation to the idea of journalists' public accountability, adding that journalists who have made independence a part of their ethical code constantly fight any attempts to encroach on this

[6] Coleman and Wilkins' (2004) large-scale sample study ($N = 249$) found that journalists scored fourth highest among professionals such as nurses, graduate students, undergraduate college students, veterinary students, business students, and adults in general, ranking only behind seminarians/philosophers, medical students, and physicians, but above dental students (see also Wesbrook, 1995). These studies draw upon Kohlberg's (1969, 1981, 1984) seminal work on moral development. Rest et al. (1999) developed the Defining Issues Test as a scale for measuring the percentage of time that people use universal principles when making decisions. Suffixes to add that while journalists always score highly on ethic tests, they do not always act ethically (Lee et al., 2016). The fact that Coleman and Wilkins' (2004) study compared journalists and student-professionals has also been largely criticized (Ferucci et al., 2019).

autonomy. Despite the diversity of journalistic practices and different ideo-logical orientations that shape news construction (Hanusch, 2015), journal-ists across national contexts do share certain universal ideals in constructing their professional identity. For instance, journalists in democratic societies are known to espouse the role of watchdog, which is anchored on the public's right to know, irrespective of cultural or national differences.

International studies have found remarkable similarities in journalists' professional role conceptions, editorial procedures, ethical views, and so-cialization processes in diverse countries. Values of objectivity and account-ability permeate many newsrooms throughout the world, through transfer or diffusion of occupational ideologies from the Global North to the Global South (Hanitzsch et al., 2011). Through accountability, an ethical precept that is shared by many journalists operating in democratic settings, journal-ists have been able to frame their stance in terms of the need to fulfil public obligations such as 'informing the citizenry, free from influences of govern-ment or obligations to any external force' (Singer, 2007, p. 81). Therefore, by identifying with public service, most journalists in different climes have at-tracted unto themselves the responsibility of investigating and disseminating news and of distinguishing the providers of fake information from sources of reliable information. The ethical precepts alluded to in the accountability claim are lofty, 'often too close to the ideal than to the reality', as Singer (2011, p. 3) rightly notes. Nevertheless, these ethical precepts are fundamental to most journalists' conceptions of their role in democratic society.

Accountability, together with openness, has been linked with another re-cently articulated concept of transparency and truth (Singer, 2007). Truth as a normative concept in journalism is defined as 'being honest about the na-ture of what is known and how that knowledge has been generated' (Kovach & Rosentiel, 2007). Transparency, on the other hand, is tied to the journal-ists' adversarial role: to speak truth to power, to be critical of government, and to scrutinize people in authority, thereby making them accountable to the public. Transparency also shares its normative interpretation with the broader notion of social responsibility. As an ethical theory, social respon-sibility addresses a situation in which individuals (e.g., journalists) are *ac-countable* for fulfilling their civic duty (e.g., creating opportunities that motivate ordinary people to get involved in decision-making on public is-sues). Thus, to be socially responsible will be to imbibe service to the public such that one's action is seen to be beneficial to the whole society.

The social responsibility norm in psychology describes a concept in which some individuals have a moral motivation to help and assist others. This is the situation with journalism. In journalism, social responsibility theory situates journalism strategically in the centre of political action and the public need for reliable information in order to call government to account. Journalists owe a duty to provide the public with 'a substantial and honest basis of fact for its judgements of public affairs' (Hocking, 1947, p. 169). Christians and Nordenstreng (2004) have argued for the centrality of social responsibility as a worldwide ethical commitment in journalism, adding that accountability becomes vital as the media become simultaneously more citizen-based and more globally oriented. Despite this interrelatedness among the aforementioned ideas, Singer (2007) draws our attention to the difference between accountability and responsibility, citing ethicist Lou Hodges' (1986) assertion that responsibility connotes 'proper conduct', whereas accountability is more about 'compelling' proper conduct.

Having established the importance of social norms in understanding journalists' behaviours and concepts of professionalism, we proceed to explore the relationship between social norms and roles. The task is to explore how the concepts of social norms and roles intertwine and how they have been adapted in journalism research, with particular reference to journalists' acceptance and use of new digital technologies.

Social Norms and Roles

There is no doubt that role as a sociological and social psychological concept has witnessed significant scholarly consultation across diverse fields with interest in the study of social patterns and structures. The term *role*, although it originates as a figurative expression in theatrical performance, has been used to explain how human beings are 'social actors' (Goffman, 1956). Human beings exhibit behaviours that appear scripted and predictable. We act based on our social identities and the situation at hand by observing others. When we act based on social influence, we are said to be performing social roles. Social roles are the parts people play as members of a social group. People are expected to behave in certain ways in particular situations, but not randomly. Every social situation entails its own particular set of expectations about the appropriate way to behave. With each social role an individual adopts, their behaviour changes to fit the expectations of both the role player and the expectancies of others. Apart from this, there are other ways whereby people can influence the behaviour of others. However, what is important to us in this chapter is that the presence of others does create expectations. Role is understood in relation to other sociological phenomena, such as 'status', 'rank', 'social role', and 'social circle'. All of these have been factored into what is known as social role (Fitcher, 1966; Linton, 1936; Parsons, 1937).

For instance, social role and social circle are interpreted in connection with how an individual is viewed not only in connection with their profession or occupational activities, such as a teacher, a priest, or a journalist, but also as a member of certain groups within their structure. These concepts also bring to the fore the concept of 'social personality', which is a synthesis of all the different roles that an individual performs simultaneously or successively in a lifetime. 'Social circle' relates to the performance of roles as influenced by the actor's social circle. Statuses as social positions are a function of the social categories that an individual belongs to in a society, often expressed as binomial categories such as child/parent, student/teacher, or audience/journalist. This also foregrounds the concept of 'relationship', which is often used in relation to status. Hence, one's social status is a function of one's relationship with others—for example, wife-husband and doctor–patient. Ranks, on the other hand, express a means of social evaluation, which enables people to be evaluated relative to social categories or positions—for example, wealthy or poor, and educated or uneducated. Other concepts that are associated with the structuralist theoretical paradigm of role theory include social networks, kinship, role sets, and exchange relationships including comparative analysis of forms of social systems and economic behaviours (Biddle, 1986).

In summary, whereas status is conceptualized as a social label, role is viewed as a cluster of norms—an activity-defined phenomenon, an activity expected of the people in certain specific roles. This can be further explained using other sociological terms, such as role behaviour, role performance, role conception, role orientation, and role enactment. Therefore, in any investigation into social behaviour (e.g., role enactment), it is always the case that the status of the actor, the visible output of the actor's performance, as well as demographic information must be considered [see Hanitzsch (2007) and his essay on 'role conceptions and professional values worldwide'].

Journalistic Role Conception Paradigm

A number of theoretical perspectives on role theory were summarized in Biddle's (1986) seminal article on the development of role theory. Journalism scholars have pointed to the influence of some of these perspectives on their concepts of the journalist's role. These perspectives include functional role theory, structural role theory, symbolic interactionist role theory, organizational role theory, and cognitive role theory. These theoretical perspectives form the basis of what is known as the journalistic role conception paradigm.[7]

The functionalist role theory, for instance, focusses on the behavioural characteristics of the individuals who occupy social positions within a stable social system. Roles within this theoretical paradigm are conceptualized as shared, normative expectations that prescribe and explain behaviour. Structuralist role theory focusses on the roles of sets of persons who hold positions or statuses within a social structure or an organization. These sets of persons are conceptualized as sharing the same patterned behaviours (roles) that are directed toward other sets of persons in the structure, as in social networks. The symbolic interactionist theory of role emphasizes the role of individual actors. It is also norm-oriented and assumes that shared norms are associated with social positions as understood by the role actors. This perspective prioritizes role enactment and the observation of the other role actors. It has contributed to discussions of self-presentation, impression, and identity management, including deviancy and social labelling. Organizational role theory, on the other hand, discusses role at the organizational level and in relation to social systems that are preplanned, task-oriented, and hierarchical. Roles in this context are assumed to associate with identified social positions and to be generated by normative expectations. However, it recognizes that norms may emanate from multiple sources and could vary among individuals within an organization, as dictated by the official demands and social pressures within and outside an organization. The role-taking model (Katz & Kahn, 1978) has been particularly useful in understanding role behaviour in work settings. This has become useful in assessing the impact of culture via cooperation norms and acculturation in role enactment in multicultural organizations (e.g., Berry, 1995).

This last theoretical paradigm of cognitive role theory is associated with cognitive social psychology, which focusses on social conditions that give rise

---

[7] See Biddle (1986) for a detailed historical account of these perspectives.

to expectations, as well as on the procedures for measuring expectations at the individual level. According to Biddle (1986), the bulk of cognitive role theory concerns the ways in which a person perceives the expectations of others and the effects of those perceptions on behaviour. This perspective discusses such concepts as role playing, role taking, role conception, and the effects of group norms and roles of leaders and followers. Whereas role playing has to do with an actor trying to imitate other role actors and functions as a measurable therapeutic and educative process, role taking refers to the degree to which persons attribute sophisticated thoughts to others.

A number of media researchers have turned to the previously named theoretical orientations for their sociology of journalism studies. Apart from the plethora of work on journalistic role conceptions, there has been sustained interest in understanding the intercultural dimensions of journalists' role orientations, role perceptions, and role enactment. This is in addition to long-standing issues on professionalism in journalism. Likewise, theories from psychology have for decades shaped studies of media use and media effect, with a particular timeline in the era of radio (Cantril & Allport, 1935). With the growing diffusion and adoption of digital innovations in journalism, scholars have found prospects in adapting models and theories from psychology to understand acceptance and use of newsroom technologies (Oni, 2018; Oni & Coen, 2015). For instance, the theories of reasoned action (Fishbein & Arjen, 1975) and planned behaviour (Arjen, 1991) are precursors to the technology acceptance model (Davis, 1989), the diffusion of innovation theory (1962), as well as the uses and gratification theory (Bulmer & Katz, 1974), all of which have been widely adopted and adapted to journalism research. These studies are predominantly in the area of technology adoption, news production, and news consumption behaviour of audiences in the digital era (e.g., Chan-Olmsted et al., 2012; Zhou, 2008).

Zhou (2008), for instance, studied Chinese journalists' ($N = 813$) adoption of the internet by combining the diffusion of innovation theory (DIT; Rogers, 1995) with the technology acceptance model (TAM; Davis, 1989). Their synthesized framework accounted for 30% of the total variance in Chinese journalists' internet adoption, which was statistically highly significant ($\chi^2 = 444.73$, $df = 32$, $p < .001$). Two DIT constructs (i.e., relative advantage and ease of use) turned out to be significantly positive predictors alike for both non-adopters and adopters (both voluntary and forced). Hence, Chinese journalists who think favourably about advantages and ease of using the internet are more likely to be voluntary adopters than forced adopters or non-adopters. The performance observability and image constructs in the model were reported as not satisfactory. However, journalists who observe good results from the internet tend to be forced adopters rather than voluntary adopters. A significantly positive relationship was found between perceived popularity of the internet and individual's (Chinese) internet adoption. Zhou also found that young journalists tend to be more likely to be voluntary adopters than forced adopters or non-adopters. In the Chinese context, forced adopters were reported to be high-ranking journalists who believe the internet can enhance their job performance and who work in large technologically oriented organizations.

Chan-Olmsted et al. (2012) also explored a combination of TAM and DIT in their examination of the predictors of mobile news consumption among young American adults. Their study was based on the assumption that the growth of mobile news would impact on the news consumption habit of youthful news users and, consequently, would have a considerable effect on the news business. As predicted, there was high mobile news consumption among the sampled young adults (84%), with 17% claiming they will use mobile news in the future. Data suggested that respondents would prefer to access the news on the internet over their mobile phones than from television. Still, television remains the preferred traditional source of news for young adults in the United States.

So far, we have been able to establish the strong link between a social norms and roles theoretical trajectory in psychology. We have also demonstrated how these psychological constructs have led to the development of popular models of technology adoption. In addition, we have demonstrated how they have been adapted to study journalists' behavioural intentions and their actual use of new technologies, with indications of new patterns of behaviour among journalists and audiences in multiple contexts. Now we move on to examine the development of role theory in journalism, with a view to balance our understanding of norms and roles as fundamental social psychological concepts underpinning journalism as a profession and as a field of enquiry.

Role Theory and Journalism

Historically, the notion of role conception took shape in journalism literature as a result of mass media scholars' discussions about the role of the media. The discussions were not originally targeted at defining the role of the journalist but, rather, that of the entire media industry. The earliest formulation in this regard is traceable to Harold Lasswell's (1948) and Charles Wright's (1959) media functions. However, the clearest reference to role theory in media studies is traceable to Bernard Cohen's (1963) work on the press and foreign policy. In this seminal work, Cohen refers to journalistic role conception as the 'reporter's formal ideology of the press' and as a 'conception the reporter has of his professional tasks' (p. 20). This was achieved by drawing on the functionalist perspective on role theory. In addition, there was Talcott Parsons' (1968) empiricist proposition that one can study institutions and cultures by investigating the roles played by people within. Thus, culture or institutions could only be studied as internalized elements of individuals (see DiMaggio & Powell, 1992). With this empiricist approach, role theory could be used to examine institutions by studying individuals who hold institutional roles.

Despite these classical theoretical contributions, there is a marked difference between the role theory of the 1960s and the more recent conceptions that were largely influenced by Biddle's (1986) landmark work. Biddle's central thesis was the idea that roles are patterned behaviours that create stability in an organization and society. Given this understanding, the role of journalists would constitute a set of behaviours that result in the orderly production of news and that which journalists owe as duty to fulfil their 'professional' roles. However, this notion has been contested by scholars in journalism due to divergent views of what really constitutes the exact role of journalists, especially between the traditional normative roles such as the disseminator role and the interpretive or investigative role, and how these have evolved across different cultures and in converged/multimedia newsrooms where journalists perform reportorial and editorial, as well as technical roles (Singer, 2007, 2011).

Also drawn from the literature on social norms with implications on role conceptions in journalism is the idea that role behaviour often takes place in a complementary or collaborative relationship (Coyne, 1984, p. 260). In other words, roles are interpreted as social phenomena that regulate human relationships on either an interpersonal or a societal level. Interpreting this view with the notion of 'functional' role theory would mean that journalists are bound to the larger society as a group of people with societal responsibility. From this viewpoint, roles are interpreted as normative because journalists derive their function and legitimacy from the expectations of the people they serve. Roles would function to regulate journalists' behaviour and to provide, as Coyne stated, a kind of template to be followed by journalists. In this way, to enact a role will be to wittingly or unwittingly invite expectations of further conformity (p. 260). Journalists are required to work with the mindset that they are bound to certain behaviours, where a perceived lapse or compromise is met with widespread public disapproval. An overriding difference in role theory even within a functionalist perspective was the determination of what spurs these roles: Do they emerge as norms based on social expectations or are they a set of beliefs formulated by the role actors?

One of the critiques of the functionalist perspective on which the early conceptualizations depend was its relative exclusion of the place of self in journalists' role enactment. This issue has been addressed by theorists who posit that role can reflect collective behavioural patterns and that an individual must embody a role before it can be enacted and for it to assume consensus among the expectant news audience. If an individual is ill-suited to a role, 'self-congruence'—the ability of an individual to fit into a role—can become a problem; hence, behaviour may not be properly enacted or regulated (Sarbin, 1982). Thus, for social psychological theorists, the process that leads to an individual taking up a role is of interest because it affirms that the notion of self is central to the researchers' explanation of role conception.

Other notable scholars associated with the development of theoretical orientations for analysing journalistic role conceptions include Johnstone et al. (1976), Stark and Soloski (1977), Culbertson (1983), Weaver and Wilhoit (1986, 1996), Kocher (1986), and Zhu et al. (1997). For instance, Johnstone et al. (1976) presented an idea of journalistic role conceptions that touches on some of the features of formal role theory. This is also in sync with the functionalist camp of role theorists: the idea that role must embrace the social responsibilities of journalists. The core tenet of Johnstone et al.'s position is that any studies on journalistic role conceptions should consider the self (i.e., the individual journalist) in role enactment. This could be done by observing either several journalists or one single journalist repeatedly (Johnstone et al., 1976, p. 120).

Other common terminologies in journalistic role conception research include Stark and Soloski's (1977) 'predisposition'. Culbertson (1983), Kocher (1986), and Dillon (1990) also make reference to 'viewpoints', 'ideologies', and 'professional identities' in relation to the functionalist role theorists' point of view. Culbertson's (1983) factor analysis of journalists' role conceptions also referenced an *institutional factor* that may shape role conceptions. His study suggested an institutionalization of role in something outside the individual journalist—a location different from the mental location, self, or the individual. This perspective was catered for in building the conceptual model that was used for the case study in this chapter.

Typologies of Journalistic Roles

Research on journalists' role conceptions is vast. By examining several contributions made by journalism scholars to research in this area, we can earmark some of the prominent categorizations that informed research in this direction. Cohen (1963) identified 'the neutral reporter' and 'the reporter as participant' in his operational definition of reporter roles. His contribution best places the role of a reporter partly in the reporter (self) and partly in the institution of the press. Likewise, Johnstone et al. (1976) suggest a dichotomy that expresses the 'neutral' and the 'participant' reporter role division. This category they later called the 'Whole Truthers' and the 'Nothing-but-the-Truthers' (p. 120), which conceptualized journalists' roles as located both in the journalists and in the institution of the press. Two-part role category was also espoused by Kocher (1986) in his study of German and British journalists. He labels role conceptions as 'bloodhounds' and 'missionaries' (Kocher, 1986, p. 43). However, underlining these catchy labels is the location of roles in individual reporter, rather than in the institution of the press.

In 1986, Weaver and Wilhoit introduced the popular three-part journalistic role conceptions in which roles are labelled: 'adversarial, interpretive, and disseminating'. This typifies journalists as people who speak truth to power, who interpret policies, and who disseminate information. These roles are distinct, so journalists are seen to have an 'orientation' to see their roles in distinct ways (p. 117). Likewise, role is conceived in relation to the American journalists' view of their responsibilities. Within this frame, there is no sense that the role is located in the press as an institution. It is either in reporters (cognitively based) or among reporters (shaped by referent others)—as a group-defined norm. Weaver and Wilhoit added the fourth dimension, the 'populist mobilizer role', a decade later (Weaver & Wilhoit, 1996, p. 140). By profiling journalists who embrace these different role typologies, they were able to place the majority of American journalists into the interpretative role. From this perspective, journalistic roles are located in the reporter because these reporters are assumed to be conscious of their roles. Culbertson (1983) also affirms a threefold role division, but these are labelled differently as '3 belief clusters'—interpretive, traditional, and activist (p. 1). A recent three-tiered role conception was introduced by Donsbach (2012). Roles are categorized as participant-observational, advocacy-neutral, and commercial-educational. Hanitzsch (2007) also identified three similar dimensions: journalists' relationship to those with power, journalists' intervention in political matters, and journalists' orientation to the economic marketplace rather than the political marketplace of ideas. Wolfgang et al. (2019) posit that roles identified in earlier research can be evaluated on the basis that the journalist performing the adversary role would be distant from those with political power, whereas the journalist in the collaborator role would be close to those with political power.

More typologies of journalistic role conceptions have emerged in recent times to explore how citizen journalists are able to articulate their roles in line with or different from mainstream professional journalists (e.g., Chung et al., 2013). Chung et al. introduced a five-construct typology with civic role added to the populist mobilizer role in the Weaver and Wilhoit (1996) and Weaver et al. (2007) typologies. Tandoc et al. (2013) and Mellado and Lagos (2014) identified six professional roles: disseminator–interventionist, watchdog, loyal–facilitator, service, infotainment, and civic role. More recent work has suggested a greater range of roles. Hanitzsch and Vos (2018) present six broad functions related to political matters, with an extra layer of subroles identified: informational–instructive (including disseminator, curator, and storyteller roles), analytical–deliberative (including analyst, access provider, and mobilize roles), critical–monitorial (including monitor, detective, and watchdog roles), advocative–radical (including adversary, advocate, and missionary roles), developmental–educative (including change agent, educator, and mediator), and collaborative–facilitative (including facilitator, collaborator, and mouthpiece roles).

Within the African contexts, a few studies have equally attempted to identify journalistic role conceptions using the existing theoretical paradigm from Western studies. For example, Ngomba (2010) observes that despite situational differences, similar conclusions have been made by Afro-centric journalism scholars in relation to journalists' conceptions of their roles. He notes that African journalists considered 'dissemination of information about development activities', promotion of national unity, or 'societal growth' to be the most important roles for the press (see also Wete, 1986). Ngomba cites the marked differences among English-speaking and French-speaking Cameroonian journalists in their role conceptions. He concludes that Cameroonian political journalists espouse roles that can be grouped into four categories: the teacher–educator–informant role, the watchdog–surveillance role, the agenda-setting role, and the social responsibility role (Ngomba, 2010, p. 14).

From our discussions so far, we have been able to map the trajectory and multidimensionality of the concepts of social norms and roles with journalistic role conceptions. The multidisciplinary perspectives from which the various authors and scholars mentioned in this chapter have drawn their common but divergent operational definitions and theoretical orientations have been highlighted and articulated. This approach has assisted us in unpacking the functionality of social norms and roles, and to understand how beliefs held by journalists in the examples presented could have shaped their intention and actual use of technology. Ultimately, this has helped us prepare the ground for a conceptual model on which our case study in this chapter is based.

Case Study: Technology Adoption and Journalistic Role Conceptions in Nigeria

In order to demonstrate the significance of social norms and role theory in journalistic practice, we rely on a hybrid model built on the principle of 'dynamic interactivity'. Dynamic interactivity represents a research framework that 'interconnects a number of reciprocal social, technological, and human communication factors' (Lin, 2003, p. 346). Our conceptual model was based on the theoretical propositions that support the primacy of the social norm approach which underpins theoretical development in technology acceptance and use research. Recent role conception typologies with five constructs (e.g., Chung et al., 2013) were combined to strengthen the predictive power of the norm-related constructs and to understand the dynamic nuances of journalism practice in the study context.

Suffice to add that the traditional approach in technology adoption research usually focusses on a single technological artefact. However, we examined an array of new digital technologies that are often appropriated together in the study context, Nigeria. We did take all the necessary contextualizing suggestions and precautions to validate the constructs and improve our scale's reliability.

The Constructs and Operationalisation

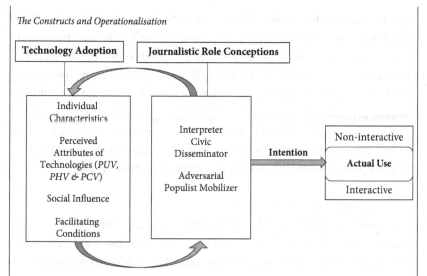

Figure 6.1 Anticipated mutual cyclical relationship between technology adoption and journalistic role conceptions as predictors of behavioural intention and actual use of digital technologies in broadcast journalism. PCV, perceived communication value; PHV, perceived hedonic value; PUV, perceived utilitarian value.

Source: Oni (2018).

The Constructs and Operationalization

The main constructs in the model are perceived utilitarian value, perceived hedonic value, and perceived communication value (Figure 6.1). These constructs were formulated to address the erstwhile perceived usefulness and perceived ease of use of the theory of planned behaviour in the first instance. They were revalidated in a meta-analysis study in which the unified theory of acceptance and use of technology (UTAUT) was introduced (Venkatesh et al., 2003). In addition, we operationalized two more constructs, perceived organizational support and agenda (POSA) and perceived institutional policy and regulatory control (PIPC), to evaluate the effects of media ownership/proprietor and a governmental regulatory agency such as the National Broadcasting Commission (NBC)[8]

---

[8] The National Broadcasting Commission is a parastatal of the Federal Government of Nigeria established by Section 1 of the National Broadcasting Commission Act, Cap. NII, laws of the Federation, 2004, and vested with the responsibilities of, among other things, regulating and controlling the broadcasting industry in Nigeria. The agency metes out punitive measures on erring broadcasters and stations, including revocation or suspension of broadcast license, fines, or an outright ban.

on the broadcast journalists. These constructs also capture the 'facilitating conditions' constructs of the UTAUT model, as well as the environmental forces or subjective norm or perceived behavioural control of the theory of planned behavior (Ajzen, 1991; Taylor & Todd, 1995a, 1995b; Thompson et al., 1991). PIPC as a construct captured the beliefs about power influence of professional bodies and institutional regulatory agencies in sanctioning erring professionals and regulating the media landscape. The POSA constructs specifically sought to evaluate the beliefs about the influential role of journalists' media organization on how they act.

Methods and Instruments

The study engaged mixed methods of surveys, with questionnaire and semistructured interviews as the instruments for data collection. Quantitative and qualitative data were collected in situ among broadcast journalists ($N = 149$) in Nigeria.

Sample

Participants were selected following a non-probability sampling (multistage, purposive, and snowball) technique. Berkowitz's (1993) definition of broadcast journalist as 'a list of all reporters, anchors, producers, editors, news directors, and other people working in a journalistic capacity' was used for sample selection. The questionnaire was distributed at 18 radio broadcast stations spread across urban areas of southwest Nigeria, where technology use is predominant and interactive programming frequent among broadcasters. Only four out of six southwest states were reached, given some peculiarities of broadcast station ownership in Nigeria. Participants' representation reflected a set of broadcast professionals, more male than female, who held various managerial and midlevel cadre roles across the '2.5 tiers' of broadcasting in Nigeria.[9]

Instrument Reliability and Validity

Apart from ensuring that validated scales were used, the adaptation of statements to suit the current scenario followed through a critical

---

[9] Media ownership is usually delineated into three tiers: public or state-owned, private/commercial media, and community media. However, in the Nigerian context, the governments have consistently failed to license a full-fledged community media. The term '2.5 tiers' is coined to reflect the partial license granted to some tertiary educational institutes to operate campus radio for teaching and learning purposes alone.

assessment process and evaluation. Cronbach's α helped establish that the items measuring the constructs were consistent and error-free in terms of what they measured, and Pearson's correlation was used to determine if there was a significant difference in the participants' perception of the constructs. All constructs yielded Cronbach's α of between .66 and .88, except for the adversary role construct, which had two items with an inter-item correlation score of .69.

Results

Multiple regression (stepwise) was performed to confirm the relationships among the variables and their potential as predictors of Nigerian journalists' behavioural intentions and actual use of non-interactive and interactive technologies. Analyses of results are presented in Tables 6.1 and 6.2.

Predictors of Intention and Actual Use of Non-Interactive Technologies

In relation to behavioural intention and actual use of non-interactive technologies, all the independent variables account for 31% of the total variance. Like Zhou's (2008) Chinese journalists' study, none of the demographic variables yielded a statistically significant model. However, role conceptions variables appeared significant, accounting for approximately 14% of variance. Two journalistic roles (disseminator and interpreter) approached significance as potential predictors of actual use of non-interactive technologies. On the other hand, technology adoption variables also appeared significant, contributing approximately 10% of the total variance. PIPC as normative influence emerged as a strong positive significant predictor ($\beta = .23$, $p < .05$), and PCV was also significant as a positive predictor ($\beta = .23$, $p < .05$). A combination of role conceptions and technology adoption variables, even though they appeared not to have been moderated by participants' individual characteristics (e.g., age, experience, and job status), proved to be strong predictors of actual use of non-interactive technologies, with approximately 25% of variance explained. Overall evaluation of results also showed that there was a marginal moderating effect of gender on technology adoption ($\beta = -.15$, $p < .05$) and intention to use non-interactive technologies ($\beta = -.15$, $p < .05$). Media ownership types did emerge significant with a slight improvement to the regression model ($R^2 = .259$, $p < .05$). However, none of the tiers of media ownership (state-owned, private/commercial, or campus radio) surfaced as a significant predictor.

Table 6.1 Summary of Hierarchical Regression Analysis for Variables Predicting Actual Use of Non-Interactive Technologies

Variable	Model 1			Model 2			Model 3			Model 4			Model 5		
	B	SE B	β	B	SE B	β	B	SE B	β	B	SE B	β	B	SE B	β
Gender	0.03	0.22	.01	0.05	0.21	.02	0.16	0.21	.06	0.20	0.21	.08	0.29	0.20	.12
Age	-0.05	0.27	-.02	-0.07	0.26	-.03	-0.23	0.25	-.09	-0.13	0.26	-.05	-0.09	0.25	-.03
Experience	0.02	0.02	.11	0.01	0.02	.07	0.03	0.23	.20#	0.03	0.02	.21#	0.04	0.02	.22#
Job status	0.18	0.32	.06	0.14	0.30	.05	-0.01	0.30	-.04	-0.19	0.30	-.06	-0.20	0.29	-.07
Disseminator				0.24	0.12	.19*	0.08	0.12	.06	0.06	0.12	.05	0.02	0.12	.01
Interpreter				0.20	0.12	.19*	0.14	0.12	.13	0.16	0.12	.15	0.12	0.11	.11
Adversary				-0.08	0.07	-.11	-0.11	0.06	-.14	-0.11	0.06	-.14	-0.09	0.06	-.12
Mobilizer				-0.03	0.07	-.04	0.00	0.07	.00	-0.01	0.07	.02	0.01	0.07	.01
Civic				0.12	0.09	.12	0.03	0.95	.03	0.00	0.09	.00	0.02	0.09	-.024
PUV							-0.15	0.14	-.12	-0.15	0.14	-.12	-0.19	0.14	-.15
PHV							-0.28	0.14	-.02	-0.13	0.14	-.01	0.04	0.14	.03
PCV							0.28	0.13	.23**	0.27	0.13	.22*	0.15	0.13	.12
PIPC							0.23	0.08	.23**	0.23	0.08	.23**	0.22	0.08	.22**
POSA							0.18	0.12	.14	0.16	0.12	.12	0.19	0.12	.14
Ownership (broadcast tiers)										0.21	0.15	.12	0.17	0.14	.09

Intention to use						
Incremental R^2	.02	.12	.09	.01	.05	
R^2	.02	.14	.24	.25	.31	
R	.14	.38	.49	.50	56	
Adjusted R^2	-.00	.09	.16	.17	.22	
F	0.74	2.56*	2.97**	2.92**	3.57***	
F change	0.74	3.94**	3.30*	2.01	10.08**	

0.34 0.10 .28**

Note: $*p < .10$, $**p < .05$, $***p < .001$, $\#p$ value above .05 for marginally significant coefficients.

PCV, perceived communication value; PHV, perceived hedonic value; PIPC, perceived institutional policy and regulatory control; POSA, perceived organizational support and agenda; PUV, perceived utilitarian value.

Source: Oni (2018).

Table 6.2 Summary of Hierarchical Regression Analysis for Variables Predicting Actual Use of Interactive Technologies

Variable	Model 1			Model 2			Model 3			Model 4			Model 5		
	B	SE B	β	B	SE B	β	B	SE B	β	B	SE B	β	B	SE B	β
Gender	0.01	0.17	.00	0.03	0.16	.01	0.13	0.17	.06	0.13	0.17	.06	0.12	0.16	.06
Age	-0.20	0.22	-.10	-0.24	0.21	-.12	-0.34	0.20	-.17	-0.35	0.21	-.17	-0.30	0.20	-.15
Experience	0.03	0.19	.20	0.02	0.01	.16	0.03	0.01	.26*	0.03	0.01	.26*	0.04	0.01	.28*
Job status	0.15	0.25	.06	0.11	0.24	.05	-0.08	0.24	-.03	-0.08	0.25	-.03	-0.13	0.23	-.05
Disseminator				0.20	0.17	.19*	0.08	0.10	.08	0.08	0.10	.08	0.01	0.10	.01
Interpreter				0.12	0.20	.14	0.07	0.09	.08	0.07	0.10	.08	0.09	0.09	.10
Adversary				-0.7	0.05	-.11	-0.08	0.05	-.13	-0.08	0.05	-.13	-0.04	0.54	-.07
Mobilizer				-0.00	0.05	-.00	0.02	0.58	.04	0.02	0.05	.03	0.02	0.56	.03
Civic				0.11	0.07	.14	0.03	0.07	.04	0.03	0.07	.04	-0.03	0.07	-.04
PUV							0.10	0.11	.10	0.10	0.11	.10	0.08	0.11	.08
PHV							-0.12	0.11	-.12	-0.12	0.12	-.12	-0.10	0.11	-.10
PCV							0.17	0.10	.17	0.17	0.11	.17	0.04	0.11	.04
PIPC							0.14	0.07	.17#	0.14	0.07	.17#	0.13	0.06	.16#
POSA							0.14	0.10	.13	0.14	0.10	.13	0.16	0.09	.15

Ownership (broadcast tiers)			−0.00	0.11	−.00
Intention to use			0.35	0.09	.35***
Incremental R^2	.04	.12**	.08**	.00	.08***
R^2	.04	.16	.24	.24	.32
Total R^2	.20	.40	.49	.49	.57
Adjusted R^2	.01	.10	.16	.15	.24
F	1.44	2.85**	2.46**	2.30**	3.80***
F change	1.44	3.86**	2.71*	0.00	15.54***

Note: $*p < .10$, $**p < .05$, $***p < .001$, $^{\#}p$ value above .05 for marginally significant coefficients.

PCV, perceived communication value; PHV, perceived hedonic value; PIPC, perceived institutional policy and regulatory control; POSA, perceived organizational support and agenda; PUV, perceived utilitarian value.

Source: Oni (2018).

Predictors of Intention and Actual Use of Interactive Technologies
Another series of models were tested in a stepwise regression to explore the predictors of actual use of interactive technologies—namely social media, email, mobile phone calls, and text messaging. Demographic variables as a measure of individual characteristics proved not to be significant predictors of actual use of interactive technologies. However, role conception variables surfaced as significant predictors, accounting for 12% of variance in explaining actual use of interactive technologies over and above demographic variables. Disseminator role was highly significant as a positive predictor ($\beta = .19$, $p < .05$). Likewise, there was significant improvement when technology adoption variables were added to the regression equations, with 24% of total variance in actual use of interactive explained. Technology adoption variables independently contributed 8% of the total variance in the regression model. Again, PIPC) emerged as a marginally significant predictor ($\beta = .17$, $p < .05$), with job experience surfacing as a strong positive moderating variable ($\beta = .26$, $p < .05$). Perceived communication value has been suppressed.

The emergence of PIPC in the regression models highlights the significance of pressures from the government through the broadcast regulatory agency on the use of digital technologies in the context of interactive programming, although there was a slight improvement with the addition of media ownership types as variables, ($R^2 = .244$, $p < .05$). However, the model failed to yield a significant predictor to prove the effect of media ownership in the use of interactive technologies. Job experience surfaced twice as a moderating variable, pointing to the effect of individual journalists' experience in deploying interactive technologies ($\beta = .26$, $p < .05$). There seems not to be a strong association between job experience, age, or job status. The effect of gender is marginal. Ultimately, these results re-established the linear positive relationship between intention and actual use of technology. Behavioural intention surfaced as a strong positive predictor of participants' actual use of interactive technologies ($\beta = .35$, $p < .001$) and independently contributed 8% to the total variance.

Discussion and Implications
The conceptual framework in the case study presupposes that journalists' behaviour is shaped by their conceptions of normative roles and values embedded in the digital tools being used in the context of interactive programming. Variables adapted to test this assumption accounted for

significant amounts of variance that explained intention and actual use of both non-interactive and interactive digital technologies popularly deployed by broadcast journalists in areas of Nigeria. The findings show that 31% to 32% variance in digital technology-use behaviour is explained by a combination of subjective norms and perceived values inherent in the technological tools in focus. Specific technology adoption variables point to the presence of social influences such as the pressures from the government regulatory agency, the NBC. Journalists' roles, such as the civic role, disseminator role, and interpreter role, surfaced alongside perceived communication and utilitarian value to predict behavioural intention and actual use of digital technologies. The most significant effect is in relation to journalists' perceived institutional policy control and perceived support of media proprietor toward adopting the interactive technologies. These variables are marginally moderated by the journalists' job experience and gender only. Thus, male journalists appeared more likely to be adopters of non-interactive technologies. Given these findings, the functionality of social norms has been established in the way some Nigerian broadcast journalists conceive their roles and also in their appropriation of new digital technologies in the context of interactive programming.

The study's qualitative findings through thematic analysis (Clarke & Braun, 2013) of the participants' interview transcripts further lend credence to how these normative influences shape broadcast journalists' perceptions of roles and adoption of new digital technologies. Participants relayed their experiences as regards new digital technologies use in relation to three main themes. Their responses validated the primacy of perceived utilitarian and communication values as well as 'environmental factors' (also called facilitating conditions). These themes captured the significance of new digital technologies and how the participants respond to internal and external sources of influence that drive adoption of technology and perception of roles. Apart from the confirmation of traditional normative roles (e.g., agenda-setting and gate-watching), there are indications of the emergence of new journalistic roles. This is an attempt to ensure that journalists' old traditional practices fit the evolving new media environment (for a similar trend, see Hedman & Djerf-Pierre, 2013). The qualitative data established how new digital technologies engender the reconstruction and enhancement of participants' normative roles, such as agenda-setting and gate-keeping. Consequently, it re-establishes the notion that journalists have learned to re-navigate old routes and evolve new roles using new digital technologies. This reaffirms the presence and effect of 'normalization' in the Nigerian journalists' use of new digital technologies (Singer, 2005; see also Hedman, 2015; Lasorsa et al., 2012). As new digital technologies serve new newsgathering and sourcing approaches to the practice of journalism, the real motivations derived from use (according to the participants in the interview data) are in relation to the speed of production, perceived ease of use of the digital tools, and their cost-effectiveness. Perceived utilitarian value also extends to the use of technologies for social interactions within the journalists' own network of other users and for collaborative reportorial roles and practices. In this regard, the digital tools serve to maintain social contact within and outside the newsroom (or belongingness), for professional branding (e.g., maintaining a positive self-image in public) and moonlighting (e.g., paid private practice as masters of ceremonies) at private events, and for receiving feedback. These are in addition to other functional uses, such as for content dissemination as reported by Singer (2011) and a host of other 'digital journalism' scholars (e.g., Mabweazara, 2014).

More importantly, participants mentioned their perceptions of new digital technologies as a double-edged sword. This alludes to the duality of purpose that defines the negative and positive perceptions of the impact of new communication technologies. It also buttresses the attributive reference to digital technologies in newsrooms as 'equivocal and indeterminate' innovations (Lyntinen & Yoo, 2002, p. 384). For example, one of the participants remarked that

it [technology] has done very well in boosting information gathering and as such people have access to information. But herein lies the challenge; do they [journalists] have access to the right information? By the same social media which is supposed to be an advantage, now you see what is called a highly indolent broadcasting practice whereby one broadcaster simply see one of the research someone may have done and the next thing you see everybody just making adaptation of that. As such we can't have the core investigative journalism when you get information in that way. What you see on social media most times is just a replication . . . a duplication or a watered down or exaggerated version of an original story.

This response attests to the centrality of the dual attributes of new communication technologies even in the Nigerian setting. It indicates that although broadcast journalists are significantly empowered by these tools, there is the perceived dumbing down effect of digital technology on the professional practice of broadcast journalists in such a way that certain normative roles (e.g., sourcing information and experts) are jeopardized and professional ethics violated. Some of the peculiar role-inhibiting factors mentioned by participants include poor funding, infrastructural decay, overcommercialization of airtime, political/ownership interference, and strict institutional policy control with regard to the use of social media and user-generated content. Other issues raised include incessant technical glitches from poor telecommunication network service providers and incompetent use of digital technology among some broadcast journalists who produce local content.

Conclusion

This chapter provided an overview of the literature on the function of social norms and role conceptions and on how the concepts can be used to understand beliefs about the world held by individuals and groups. The scope covered has aided our understanding of how these foremost social science concepts have helped in building several theories and models for interpreting human behaviour across settings. The chapter buttressed the effect of sociocultural forces rooted in norms, roles, and individual characteristics, among other sociological and social psychological concepts, in understanding journalists' behavioural intentions and behaviours in relation to new digital technology use. We established the functionality of norm and role by reducing the concepts to the realm of social norms and social roles, the popularity and fluidity of the terms and how they are interpreted in existing literature.

The bottom line is that the journalism profession, especially in a democratic environment, is anchored on popular ideological claims that have diffused from the Global North to the Global South (Hanitzsch et al., 2011). Through accountability, transparency, truth, and the broader notion of social responsibility, journalism is presented as a norm-driven socially constructed profession with universal and context-specific contingencies. The social responsibility norm, with its roots in psychology, describes a situation in which some individuals have a moral motivation to help and assist others. This, to some extent, is true of the journalism profession in certain contexts. Using a recent case, we further established the functionality of norms and roles.

The chapter also presented results from an exploratory study of Nigerian broadcast journalists' beliefs about normative influences and perceived attributes of new digital technologies and how these shape the adoption of technologies. It was found that Nigerian broadcast journalists are motivated to adopt interactive technologies, following Kelman's (1958) sociocognitive model of compliance and identification. Compliance emerged as a result of the journalists' perceived expectations or benefits that are tied to the public perception of the journalists' roles. An identification process is established through the journalists' perceptions that interactive technologies could be used to build and maintain a satisfying self-defining relationship with expert sources, co-journalists, as well as a new breed of online but not on-air audience. There is the 'bandwagon effect' in the perceptions of some broadcast journalists, which suggested that they are more motivated to adopt interactive technologies on account of not wanting to be left behind (FOMO) in the competitive business environment. Thus, there seems to be a hint of market-driven intention or competitiveness over professional value creation in the interpretation of normative influences on Nigerian broadcast journalists, based on the findings from the case study. It is hoped that further studies on factual role performance in relation to technology adoption may help throw some light on this grey area. It will also be useful to balance journalists' role conceptions with audience perceptions of what roles they think journalists play.

In summary, in using the case study presented in this chapter, I recognize the variegated nature of journalism practice, as widely acknowledged in journalism literature (see Hallin & Mancini, 2004). I also acknowledge the shortcomings in using individual-level perceived norms as the operational basis of collective norms. However, support was found for the social epistemological idea that an aggregation of individuals' behaviours, following a systematic sampling of participants, can serve as a proxy for collective norms.

References

Abrahamse, W., & Steg, L. (2013). Social influence approaches to encourage resource conservation: A meta-analysis. *Global Environmental Change, 23*(6), 1773–1785.

Ajzen, I. (1985). From intentions to action: A theory of planned behaviour. In J. Huhl & J. Beckman (Eds.), *Action control: From cognition to behavior* (pp. 11–39). Springer-Verlag.

Ajzen, I. (1991). The theory of planned behavior. *Organizational Behavior and Human Decision Processes, 50*, 179–211. doi:10.1016/0749-5978(91)90020-T

Bergquist, M., Nilsson, A., & Schultz, W. P. (2019). A meta-analysis of field-experiments using social norms to promote pro-environmental behaviours. *Global Environmental Change, 59*, 1–18.

Berkowitz, D. (1993). Work roles and news selection in local TV: Examining the business–journalism dialectic. *Journal of Broadcasting & Electronic Media, 37*(1), 67–81. doi:10.1080/08838159309364204

Berry, J. W. (1995). Psychology of acculturation. In N. R. Goldberger & J. B. Veroff (Eds.), *The culture and psychology reader* (pp. 457–488). New York University Press.

Bicchieri, C. (2006). *The grammar of society: The nature and dynamics of social norms.* Cambridge University Press.

Bicchieri, C., Jeffrey, R., & Skyrms, B. (Eds.). (1997). *The dynamics of norms.* Cambridge University Press.

Biddle, B. J. (1986). Recent developments in role theory. *Annual Review of Sociology, 12*, 67–92.

Bosson, J. K., Kuchynka, S. L., Parrot, D. J., Swan, S. C., & Schramm, A. T. (2020). *Psychology of Men & Masculinities, 21*(1), 124–138.

Brehm, J. W. (1966). *A theory of psychological reactance.* Academic Press.

Brehm, S. S., & Brehm, J. W. (1981). *Psychological reactance: A theory of freedom and control.* Academic: Press.

Burger, J., & Shelton, M. (2011). Changing everyday health behaviors through descriptive norm manipulations. *Social Influence, 6*(2), 69–77.

Campbell, D. T. (1965). Variation and selective retention in sociocultural evolution. In H. R. Barringer, G. I. Blanksten, & R.W. Mack (Eds.), *Social change in developing areas: A reinterpretation of evolutionary theory* (pp. 14–99). Schenkman.

Cantril, H. & Allport, G. W. (1935). Psychology of radio. Harper and Brothers.

Chafetz, G., Abramson, H., & Grillot, S. (1996). Role theory and foreign policy: Belarussian and Ukrainian compliance with the nuclear nonproliferation regime. *Political Psychology, 17*(4), 727–757.

Chan-Olmsted, S., Rim, H. & Zerba, A. (2012). Mobile news adoption among young adults: Examine the roles perceptions, news, consumption, and media usage. *Journalism & Mass Communication Quarterly, 90*(1), 126–147. DOI: 10.1177/1077699012468742.

Christians, C., & Nordenstreng, K. (2004). Social responsibility worldwide. *Journal of Mass Media Ethics, 19*(1), 3–28.

Chung, D. S., Nah, S., & Carpenter, S. (2013). Journalistic role conceptions and sourcing practices—A study of U.S. citizen journalists. *Ewha Journal of Social Sciences, 29*(1), 65–99.

Cialdini, R. B. (1987). *Influence.* HarperCollins.

Cialdini, R. B. (2003). Crafting normative messages to protect the environment. *Current Directions in Psychological Science, 12*(4), 105ñ109. Retrieved from https://doi.org/10.1111/1467-8721.01242.

Cialdini, R. B., Demaine, L. J., Sagarin, B. J., Barrett, D. W., Rhoads, K., & Winter, P. L. (2006). Managing social norms for persuasive impact. *Social Influence, 1*(1), 3–15. doi:10.1080/15534510500181459

Cialdini, R. B., & Goldstein, N. J. (2004). Social influence: Compliance and conformity. *Annual Review of Psychology, 55*, 591–621.

Cialdini, R. B., & Trost, M. R. (1998). *Social influence: Social norms, conformity and compliance* (4th ed.). Oxford University Press.

Cinner, J. (2018). How behavioral science can help conservation. *Science*, *362*(6417), 889–890. doi:10.1126/science.aau6028

Clarke, V., & Braun, V. (2013). Teaching thematic analysis: Overcoming challenges and developing strategies for effective learning. *The Psychologist*, *26*(2), 120–123.

Cohen, B. C. (1963). *The press and foreign policy*. Princeton University Press.

Coleman, R., & Wilkins, L. (2002). Searching for the ethical journalists: An exploratory study of the ethical development of news workers. *Journal of Mass Media Ethics: Exploring Questions of Media Morality*, *17*(3), 209–225.

Coleman, R., & Wilkins, L. (2004). The moral development of journalists: A comparison with other professions and a model for predicting high quality ethical reasoning. *Journalism & Mass Communication Quarterly*, *81*(3), 511–527.

Coleman, R., & Wilkins, L. (2009). The moral development of journalists: A psychological approach to understanding ethical judgments. In L. Wilkins & C. G. Christians (Eds.), *The handbook of mass media ethics*. (pp. 40–54). Taylor & Francis.

Coyne, M. (1984). Role and rational action. *Journal for the Theory of Social Behaviour*, *14*(3), 259–270.

Culbertson, H. M. (1983). Three perspectives on American journalism. *Journalism Monographs*, *83*, 1–33.

Davis, F. D. (1989). Perceived usefulness, perceived ease of use, and user acceptance of information technology. *MIS Quarterly*, *13*(3), 319–340.

Deuze, M., & Dimoudi, C. (2002). Online journalists in the Netherlands: Towards a profile of a new profession. *Journalism, Theory, Practice & Criticism*, *3*(1), 85–100.

Dillon, J. (1990). Career values as predictor of the perceived role of media. *Journalism Quarterly*, *67*(2), 369–376.

DiMaggio, P., & Powell, W. (1992). Introduction. In W. Powell & P. DiMaggio (Eds.), *The new institutionalism in organisational analysis* (pp. 1–38). University of Chicago Press.

Donsbach, W. (2012). Journalists' role perception. In W. Donsbach (Ed.), *The international encyclopedia of communication*. Blackwell. (pp. 1–6). Reference Online. Retrieved https://onlinelibrary.wiley.com/doi/book/10.1002/9781405186407?id=g9781405131995_yr2013_chunk_g978140513199515_ss10-1.

Elster, J. (1989). *The cement of society: A study of social order*. Cambridge University Press.

Elster, J. (1992). *The Cement of Society: A Study of Social Order*. Cambridge University Press.

Elster, J. (2007). *Explaining social behavior: More nuts and bolts for the social sciences*. Cambridge University Press.

Emmers-Sommer, T. M., Farrell, J., Gentry, A., Stevens, S., Eckstein, J., Battocletti, J., & Gardener, C. (2010). First date sexual expectations, sexual- and gender-related attitudes: The effects of who asked, who paid, date location, and gender. *Communication Studies*, *61*, 339–355. http://dx.doi.org/10.1080/10510971003752676

Fishbein, M., & Ajzen, I. (1975). *Belief, attitude, intention, and behavior: An introduction to theory and research*. Addison-Wesley.

Fiske, S. T., Gilbert, D. T., & Lindzey, G. (2010). *Handbook of social psychology* (5th ed., Vol. 2). Wiley.

Fitcher, J. (1966). Sociological Aspects of the Role Authority in the Adaptation of the Religious Community for the Apostolate in Dimensions of Authority in Religious Life, University of Notre Dame.

Gelfand, M. J., Raver, J. L., Nishii, L., Leslie, L. M., Lun, J., Lim, B. C., Duan, L., Almaliach, A., Ang, S., Arnadottir, J., Aycan, Z., Boehnke, K., Boski, P., Cabecinhas, R., Chan, D., Chhokar, J., D'Amato, A., Ferrer, M., Fischlmayr, I. C., Fischer, R., et al.. (2011).

Differences between tight and loose cultures: A 33-nation study. *Science, 332,* 1100–1104.

Goffman, E. (1956). *The presentation of self in everyday life.* Doubleday.

Goldstein, N. J., Cialdini, R. B., & Griskevicius, V. (2008). A room with a viewpoint: Using social norms to motivate environmental conservation in hotels. *Journal of Consumer Research, 35*(3), 472–482.

Goldstein, N. J., Griskevicius, V., & Cialdini, R. B. (2007). Invoking social norms: A social psychology perspective on improving hotels' linen-reuse programs. *Hotel Management, 48*(2), 145–150.

Hallin, D. C., & Mancini, P. (2004). *Comparing media systems.* Cambridge University Press.

Hamlin, J. K., & Wynn, K. (2011). Young infants prefer prosocial to antisocial others. *Cognitive Development, 26,* 30–39.

Hang, H., Davies, I., & Schüring, J. (2020). Children's conformity to social norms to eat healthy: A developmental perspective. *Social Science & Medicine, 244,* 1–9.

Hanitzsch, T. (2007). Deconstructing journalism culture: Toward a universal theory. *Communication Theory, 17*(4), 367–385.

Hanitzsch, T., Hanusch, F., Mellado, C., Anikina, M., Berganza, R. Cangoz, I., Coman, M., Hamada, B., Hernandez-Ramirez, M.-E., Karadjov, C. D., Moreira, S. V., Mwesige, P. G., Plaisance, P. L., Reich, Z., Seethaler, J., Skewes, E. A., Vardiansyah, D., Yuen, E. K. W. (2011). Mapping journalism cultures across nations. *Journalism Studies, 12*(3), 273–293.

Hanitzsch, T., & Vos, T. P. (2018). Journalism beyond democracy: A new look into journalistic roles in political and everyday life. *Journalism: Theory, Practice & Criticism, 19*(2), 146–164.

Hanusch, F. (2015). Cultural forces in journalism: The impact of cultural values on Maori journalists' professional views. *Journalism Studies, 16*(2), 191–206.

Hedman, U. (2015). J-tweeters. *Digital Journalism, 3*(2), 279–297. doi:10.1080/21670811.2014.897833

Hedman, U. & Djerf-Pierre, M. (2013). The social journalist: Embracing the social media life or creating a new digital divide?, *Digital Journalism,* DOI:10.1080/21670811.2013.776804.

Hocking, W. E. (1947). *Freedom of the press: A framework of principle.* University of Chicago Press.

Hodges, L. W. (1986). The journalist and professionalism. *Journal of Mass Media Ethics, 1*(2), 32–36.

Jacobson, R. P., Mortensen, C. R., & Cialdini, R. B. (2011). Bodies obliged and unbound: Differentiated response tendencies for injunctive and descriptive social norms. *Journal of Personality and Social Psychology, 100*(3), 433–448.

Jacobson, R. P., Mortensen, C. R., Jacobson, K. L. J., & Cialdini, R. B. (2015). Self-control moderates the effectiveness of influence attempts highlighting injunctive social norms. *Social Psychological and Personality Science, 6*(6), 718–726.

Jenkins, J., & Tandoc, E. C. (2019). Journalism under attack: The *Charlie Hebdo* covers and reconsiderations of journalism norms. *Journalism, 20*(9), 1165–1182.

Johnstone, J. W. C., Slawski, E. J., & Bowman, W. W. (1976). *The news people.* University of Illinois Press.

Katz, D., & Kahn, R. (1978). *The social psychology of organizations* (2nd ed.). Wiley.

Kelman, H. C. (1958). Compliance, identification, and internalisation: Three processes of attitude change. *Journal of Conflict Resolution, 2*(1), 51–60.

Kocher, R. (1986). Bloodhounds and missionaries: Role definitions of German and British journalists. *European Journal of Communication, 1,* 43–64.

Kohlberg, L. (1969). Stage and sequence: The cognitive development approach to socialization. In D. A. Goslin (Ed.), *Handbook of socialization theory* (pp. 347–480). Rand McNally.

Kohlberg, L. (1981). *The philosophy of moral development: Moral stages and the idea of justice.* Harper & Row.

Kohlberg, L. (1984). *The philosophy of moral development: The nature and validity of moral stages.* Harper & Row.

Kovach, B., & Rosenstiel, T., (2007). The elements of journalism: What newspeople should know and the public should expect. New York: Crown.

Lasorsa, D., Lewis, S. and Holton, A. (2012). "Normalizing Twitter". *Journalism Studies, 13*(1): 19–36.

Lasswell, H. (1948). The structure and function of communication in society. In L. Bryson (Ed.), *The communication of ideas* (pp. 37–51). Harper & Row.

Lee, A. M., Coleman, R., & Molyneux, L. (2016). From thinking to doing: Effects of different social norms on ethical behaviour in journalism. *Journal of Media Ethics, 31*(2), 72–85. http://dx.doi.org/10.1080/23736992.2016.1152898

Lin, C. A. (2003). An interactive communication technology adoption model. *Communication Theory, 13*(4), 345–365.

Linton, R. (1936). *The study of man.* Appleton Century Crofts.

Mabweazara, H. M. (2014). Introduction: Digital technologies and the evolving African newsroom: Towards an African digital journalism epistemology. *Digital Journalism, 2*(1), 2–11. doi:10.1080/21670811.2013.850195

Mann, M. F., & Hill, T. (1984). Persuasive communications and the boomerang effect: Some limiting conditions to the effectiveness of positive influence attempts. *Advances in Consumer Research, 11,* 66–70.

Manning, M. (2009). The effects of subjective norms on behaviour in the theory of planned behaviour: A meta-analysis. *British Journal of Social Psychology, 48*(4), 649–705.

McDonald, R. I., & Crandall, C. S. (2015). Social norms and social influence. *Current Opinion in Behavioral Sciences, 3,* 147–151.

McEachan, R., Conner, M., Taylor, N., & Lawton, R. J. (2011). Prospective prediction of health-related behaviors with the theory of planned behavior: A meta-analysis. *Health Psychology Review, 5,* 97–144. https://doi.org/10.1080/17437199.2010.521684

McEachan, R., Taylor, N., Harrison, R., Lawton, R., Gardner, P., & Conner, M. (2016). Meta-analysis of the reasoned action approach (RAA) to understanding health behaviors. *Annals of Behavioral Medicine, 50,* 592–612.

Morris, M. W., Hong, Y., Chiu, C., & Liu, Z. (2015). Normology: Integrating insights about social norms to understand cultural dynamics. *Organizational Behavior and Human Decision Processes, 129,* 1–13.

Muehlenhard, C. L., Friedman, D. E., & Thomas, C. M. (1985). Is date rape justifiable? The effects of dating activity, who initiated, who paid, and men's attitudes toward women. *Psychology of Women Quarterly, 9,* 297–310. http://dx.doi.org/10.1111/j.1471-6402.1985.tb00882.x

Ngomba, T. (2010). Journalists' role conceptions and the democratisation of contemporary Cameroon. *Cameroon Journal on Democracy and Human Rights, 4*(2), 36–63.

Nilsson, N. (2019). Role conceptions, crises, and Georgia's foreign policy. *Cooperation & Conflict, 54*(4), 445–465.

Nisa, C., Varum, C., & Botelho, A. (2017). Promoting sustainable hotel guest behaviour: A systematic and meta-analysis. *Cornell Hospitality Quarterly*, 58(4), 354–363.

Nolan, D. (2008). Journalism, education and the formation of 'public subjects'. *Journalism*, 9, 733–749.

Oni, 'W. (2018). *An exploratory study of new media adoption for participatory programming in southwest Nigeria's radio station*. PhD thesis, University of Salford.

Oni, 'W., & Coen, S. (2015). Technology adoption and journalistic role conceptions: A conceptual review and operational model. *African Notes*, 39(1 2), 02–95.

Parsons, T. (1937). *The structure of social action*. McGraw-Hill.

Parsons, T. (1968). The structure of social action: A study in social theory with special reference to a group of recent European Writers. McGraw Hill.

Peters, K., Jetten, J., Radova, D., & Austin, K. (2017). Gossiping about deviance: Evidence that deviance spurs the gossip that builds bonds. *Psychological Science, 28*, 1610–1619.

Rest, J. R., Narvaez, D., Bebeau, M. J., & Thomas, S. J. (1999). *Postconventional moral thinking: A neo-Kohlberian approach*. Psychology Press.

Rimal, R. (2008). Modeling the relationship between descriptive norms and behaviors: A test and extension of the theory of normative social behavior (TNSB). *Health Communication, 23*, 103–116. doi:10.1080/10410230801967791

Rimal, R. N., & Lapinski, M. K. (2015). A re-explication of social norms, ten years later. *Communication Theory, 25*, 393–409. doi:10.1111/comt.12080

Rimal, R. N., & Real, K. (2003). Understanding the influence of perceived norms on behaviours. *Communication Theory, 13*, 184–203. doi:10.1093/ct/13.2.184

Rimal, R. N., & Real, K. (2005). How behaviours are influenced by perceived norms: A test of the theory of normative social behavior. *Communication Research, 32*, 389–414. doi:10.1177/0093650205275385

Rogers, E. (1995). *Diffusion of innovations* (4th ed.). Free Press.

Sallis, J. F., Owen, N., & Fisher, E. B. (2008). Ecological models of health behavior. *Health Behavior and Health Education, 4*, 465–485.

Sarbin, T. R. (1982). A preface to a psychological theory of metaphor. In V. L. Allen & K. E. Scheibe (Eds.), *The social context of conduct: Psychological writings* of T. R. Sarbin (pp. 233–249). Praeger.

Scheibehenne, B., Jamil, T., & Wagenmakers, E. J. (2016). Bayesian evidence synthesis can reconcile seemingly inconsistent results the case of hotel towel reuse. *Psychological Science, 27*(7), 1043–1046.

Schwartz, S. H. (1977). Normative influences on altruism. *Advances in Experimental Social Psychology, 10*, 221–279.

Sevillano, V., & Olivos, P. (2019). Social behaviour and environment: The influence of social norms on environmental behaviour. *Psychologist Papers, 4*(40), 182–189.

Shulman, H. C., & Levine, T. R. (2012). Exploring social norms as a group-level phenomenon: Do political participation norms exist and influence political participation on college campuses? *Journal of Communication, 62*, 532–552. doi:10.1111/j.1460-2466.2012.01642.x

Shulman, H. C., Rhodes, N., Davidson, E., Ralston, R., Borghetti, L., & Morr, L. (2017). The state of the field of social norms research. *International Journal of Communication, 11*, 1192–1213.

Singer, J. B. (2005). The political J-blogger: 'Normalizing' a new media form to fit old norms and practices. *Journalism: Theory, Practice and Criticism, 6*(2), 173–198.

Singer, J. B. (2007). Contested autonomy: Professional and popular claims on journalistic norms. *Journalism Studies, 8*(1), 79–95, DOI: 10.1080/14616700601056866.

Singer, J. B. (2011). Journalism and digital technologies. In W. Lowry & P. Gade (Eds.), *Changing the news: Forces shaping journalism in uncertain times* (pp. 213–229). Routledge.

Singletary, M. W., Caudill, S., Caudill, E., & White, A. (1990). Motives for ethical decision-making. *Journalism Quarterly, 67*(4), 964–972.

Smith, J. R., Louis, W. R., Terry, D. J., Greenaway, K. H., Clarke, M. R., & Cheng, X. (2012). Congruent or conflicted? The impact of injunctive and descriptive norms on environmental intentions. *Journal of Environmental Psychology, 32,* 353–361.

Sparkman, G., & Walton, G. M. (2017). Dynamic norms promote sustainable behavior, even if it is counternormative. *Psychological Science, 28*(11), 1663–1674. doi:10.1177/0956797617719950

Tandoc, C. E., Hellmueller, L., & Vos, T. P. (2013). Mind the gap: Between journalistic role conception and role enactment. *Journalism Practice, 7*(5), 539–554. doi:10.1080/17512786.2012.726503

Tandoc, E. C., & Oh, S. K. (2017). Small departures, big continuities? Norms, values, and routines in the *Guardian*'s big data journalism. *Journalism Studies, 18*(8), 997–1015.

Tangney, J. P., & Fischer, K. W. (1995). Self-conscious emotions: The psychology of shame, guilt, embarrassment, and pride. Guilford.

Taylor, S., & Todd, P. A. (1995a). Assessing IT usage: The role of prior experience. *MIS Quarterly, 19*(2), 561–570.

Taylor, S., & Todd, P. A. (1995b). Understanding information technology usage: A test of competing models. *Information Systems Research, 6*(4), 144–176.

Thompson, R. L., Higgins, C. A., & Howell, J. M. (1991). Personal computing: Toward a conceptual model of utilization. *MIS Quarterly, 15*(1), 124–143.

Titlestad, K., Snijders, T. A. B., Quayle, M., Durrheim, K., & Postmes, T. (2019). The dynamic emergence of cooperative norms in a social dilemma. *Journal of Experimental Social Psychology, 84,* 103799. https://doi.org/10.1016/j.jesp.2019.03.010

Tong, J., & Lo, S. (2018). *Digital technology and journalism: An international comparative perspective.* Palgrave Macmillan.

Tutui, V. (2013). Emotions versus reasons: A critical analysis of Jon Elster's view about social norms. Retrieved from https://www.fssp.uaic.ro/argumentum/Numarul%2013%20issue%201/08_Tutui_tehno.pdf

Venkatesh, V., Morris, M. G., Davis, G. B., & Davis, F. D. (2003). User acceptance of information technology: Toward a unified view. *MIS Quarterly, 27*(3), 425–478.

Wasserman, H., & Maweu, J. M. (2014). The freedom to be silent? Market pressures on journalistic normative ideal at the Nation Media Group in Kenya. *Review of African Political Economy, 41*(142), 623–633.

Waterloo, S. F., Baumgartner, S. E., Peter, J., & Valkenburg, P. M. (2018). Norms of online expressions of emotion: Comparing Facebook, Twitter, Instagram, and WhatsApp. *New Media & Society, 20*(5), 1813–1831. doi:10.1177/1461444817707349

Weaver, D. H., Beam, R. A., Brownlee, B. J., Voakes, P. S., & Wilhoit, G. C. (2007). *The American journalist in the 21st century: U.S. news people at the dawn of a new millennium.* Erlbaum.

Weaver, D. H., & Wilhoit, G. C. (1986). *The American journalist: A portrait of US newspeople and their work.* Indiana University Press.

Weaver, D. H., & Wilhoit, G. C. (1996). *The American journalist in the 1990s: U.S. news-people at the end of an era.* Erlbaum.

Wete, F. (1986). *Development journalism: Philosophy and practice in Cameroon.* Unpublished PhD dissertation, University of Missouri, Columbia, MO.

Wolfgang, J. D., Vos, T. P., & Kelling, K. (2019). Journalism's relationship to democracy: Role, attitudes, and practices. *Journalism Studies, 20*(14), 1977–1994.

Wombacher, K., Reno, J. E., & Veil, S. R. (2017). NekNominate: Social norms, social media, and binge drinking. *Health Communication, 32*(5), 596–602.

Wright, C. M. (1959). *The sociological imagination.* Oxford University Press.

Zhou, Y. (2008). Voluntary adopters versus forced adopters: Integrating the diffusion of innovation theory and the technology acceptance model to study intra-organisational adoption. *New Media and Society, 10*(3), 475–496. doi:10.1177/1461444807085382

Zhu, J.-H., Weaver, D. H., Lo, V.-H., Chen, C., & Wu, W. (1997). Individual, organizational, and societal influences on media role perceptions: A comparative study of journalists in China, Taiwan, and the United States. *Journalism & Mass Communication Quarterly, 74*(1), 84–96.

7

Social Psychology of Identity and Stereotyping in the Media

The Case of Refugee Media Bias

Catherine Lido, Ariel Swyer, and Leyla De Amicis

The field of social psychology emerged around the dawn of the 19th century with the work of Triplett (1898) on social facilitation, although human social behaviour has been of interest to social philosophers for millennia before, from Plato and Miletus to Comte and Kant (Nisbet, 1973). The field exploded post World War II, led by Lewin (1951). He moved the discipline away from the dominant paradigm of behaviourist thought, based on the study of the human mind through observing human and animal behaviours (for the roots of social psychology see Farr 1996), and toward an exploration of the human mind through self-reflection on the nature of self-hood and how the self is affected by one's context. This shift led to a closer relationship with the more established field of sociology, arguing that behaviour is context-specific and our behaviour when alone is very different from that when in the company of even one other person (for a full review of social psychology see Hogg & Vaughan, 1995). The focus of social psychology is thus on how the social world impacts upon our thoughts, feelings, and behaviours, as well as how we impact upon the world around us (Hogg & Vaughan, 1995). Sherif's (1948) outline of the discipline is centred on motivations, social change, and social reactions, but the largest section is devoted to social norms and social group interactions. Given the ubiquity of media—and the rise of social media use in particular—our engagement with others online and in the real world has strengthened the urgency for an applied social psychology of media and journalism. Hence, this chapter is crucial to understanding how the media influences societal attitudes (and even behaviours, such as voting and charitable giving), but also how our individual brains respond even to short-term media exposure.

Catherine Lido, Ariel Swyer, and Leyla De Amicis, *Social Psychology of Identity and Stereotyping in the Media* In: *The Psychology of Journalism*. Edited by: Sharon Coen and Peter Bull, Oxford University Press. © Oxford University Press 2021. DOI: 10.1093/oso/9780190935856.003.0007

In 1954, Allport published the first book on prejudice, and social psychology took a crucial turn toward its core concepts of identity, categorization, and prejudice (for a 50-year review of the field's progress see Dovidio et al., 2008). Therefore, we begin with this chapter with an overview of traditional social psychological work on normative influence, and as it has been applied to the media in general, and then move on to the core social psychological area of identity and categorization, with implications for stereotyping and prejudice in the media. We then proceed to more modern theoretical frames for bias and emotions in the field, which can be applied to a case study on media bias regarding refugees, with practical guidance for avoiding such unintentional bias in journalism and media outputs more widely.

Media as Social Influence

Social psychology has a wealth of theory and research on the nature of media as an entity for social influence; for instance, Chamberlain and Hodgetts (2008) review traditional social psychological approaches to media research, highlighting a need for a more critical review of media consumption as social practice, and not simply a direct and explicit relationship. Although a full review of how the media, and increasingly social media, act as a significant influence on human attitudes, behaviours, and development is beyond the scope of this chapter, we must at least signpost social psychology's contributions to such debates on the media as a force for pro- and antisocial outcomes, such as aggression (e.g., L'Engle et al., 2006; Anderson et al., 2003), health behaviours (e.g., L'Engle et al., 2006), in addition to attitudes toward women (e.g., Trolan, 2013) and marginalized groups. Slater (2007) presents the social influence of media as broadly reinforcing spirals, whereby resulting attitudes and behaviours from consuming media direct future media attention, selection, and consumption.

According to social psychology, the presence of real or implied others, including the media, may have positive effects on one's thoughts and behaviours—for example, mobilizing, facilitating, or group cohesion effects (e.g., Zajonc, 1965; Drury et al., 2009). However, initial forays of social psychology into the world of media influence stemmed from traditional social influence research, which largely concluded that groups sway our opinions and behaviours—for example, extensive social psychology research in the area of conformity and even obedience to group norms (e.g., Asch, 1951;

Milgram, 1963; Moghaddam, 2013). Recently, social influence research on conformity and obedience has stressed divergent outcomes for individuals, including reactance to social norms (for recent debate in this area, see Haslam & Reicher, 2003, 2012; Haslam et al., 2010).

Scholars initially classified the type of influence exerted by media as either normative or informational (McDavid & Sistrunk, 1964; Price et al., 2006). The former consists of bringing the individual's opinion in line with what is expected of the social or cultural group—for instance, family or peers (Price et al., 2006). We may think of this as peer pressure or 'media pressure' to fit in with others whose opinions matter to us. On the other hand, informational influence consists of the individual's desire to be in line with factual or legitimate arguments or to bring their opinion more in line with factual reality (as they perceive it). These two spheres of influence are not unavoidable, nor are they distinct; however, it has been put forth that there may be additional types of social influence which the media may exert, termed 'referent informational influence' (Turner, 1982). According to this perspective, the most likely influence will come from groups to which we identify and that best represent our social norms rather than those that are more accurate, or even more personally valued (Turner, 1982). This referent informational influence explains the power over which some politically leaning media might have over and above the influence of our friends and family (Price et al., 2006). It becomes clear, therefore, that the processes of selection and interpretation of news can be influenced by how we view ourselves (i.e., our sense of identity), as well as the relative importance we place on the groups to which we belong. In fact, the effect of news on our thoughts and behaviours may even depend on the specific group we are presently thinking about (e.g., our home nation).

Social Psychology of Identity and Belonging

Identity is a key area of theory and research for social psychologists. For many decades, psychologists have sought to outline stages in the development of our sense of self (e.g., classical stage development theories by Erikson, 1968; Maslow, 1943; and Freud, 1953). Social psychology concerns not only the introspective aspect of our identity (our 'personal' self-perception) but also our social identity, which is the aspect of our self derived from belonging to groups which are important to us (see Brown, 1988; Brewer et al., 1998; Brown & Pehrson, 2019). These may be groups into which we are born (ascribed groups such as one's family or national group) or groups we acquire and choose to join (based on interests, such as clubs, or peer groups).

According to social identity theory (SIT) (Tajfel & Turner, 1979, 1986), individuals will categorize themselves as being members of many different demographic and social groups in society. This categorization helps humans to function because it provides access to previously experienced 'social scripts', to better understand our social environment, and, more important, to offer us the feeling of belonging to wider communities. Such categorization leads to a sense of 'social identification' (Tajfel et al., 1971; Tajfel & Turner, 1979). Social identification is a mental process we employ to determine the extent to which we belong within a particular group, and this subsequent belonging may then directly affect our self-esteem (Gailliot & Baumeister, 2007). SIT is concerned not only with the cognitive processes linked with categorization but also with (1) the consequences of such categorization for our interactions with others and (2) the motivations driving these inter-actions (Hogg & Abrams, 1988). For instance, experiencing affiliation to a group may help us meet our needs for individual belonging, but equally it may lead us to prioritize the needs of our group over others (in-group bias), as well as protect the needs of our group if threatened, potentially even dero-gating an out-group as a result. In this way, SIT explains many prosocial be-haviours stemming from a group-based identity (e.g., positive outcomes of national pride), as well as negative outcomes stemming from derogation of out-groups (e.g., prejudice stemming from nationalism).

In addition to needs of belonging, SIT highlights the relevance of iden-tity needs on self-esteem and one's sense of positive distinctiveness in the world around us (Tajfel & Turner, 1986). Authors have expanded the range of needs that underlie social identity processes, including belonging (Brewer, 1991) and subjective meaning (Hogg, 2000). Most recently, some researchers have integrated in a unified model different identity needs, the so-called mo-tivated identity construction theory (Vignoles, 2011). This theoretical ap-proach states that people are motivated to belong to groups when the social identities derived from these memberships enable them to fulfil the needs of self-esteem, distinctiveness, belonging, efficacy, meaning, and continuity. This means that people would value social identities that would make them feel (1) positive about themselves compared with others (self-esteem need), (2) unique (distinctiveness need), (3) as belonging to a group (belonging need), (4) capable and influential for their environment (efficacy need), (5) as having a purpose in life, and (6) a sense of continuity over time (continuity need). Empirical evidence has shown that satisfaction of needs for self-esteem, efficacy, and meaning predicts higher positive affect (Vignoles et al., 2006), whereas satisfaction of needs for distinctiveness, belongingness, and continuity predicts greater in-group bias (Smeekes & Verkuyten, 2014; Vignoles & Moncaster, 2007). Some researchers have shown that with real groups, these values can be clustered in fewer groups (e.g., Çelebi et al., 2017). Scholars have shown how identity-related models can drive media consumption and use, particularly in the case of social media (Manzi et al., 2018).

A theory emerging from SIT is self-categorization theory (SCT) (Turner et al., 1987), according to which our identity can be collocated along a continuum from individual to collective (group-level) categorization. Certain aspects of the situations we encounter might lead us to act on a more individualized level, whereas others might lead us to act on a higher group-based level. Both SIT and SCT emphasize the complexity of social identities in how they may influence pro- and antisocial behaviour. Trepte and Loy (2017) illustrate how these theories can be usefully applied to explore and understand media effects—for example, by interpreting the 'hostile media effect' as an intergroup phenomenon based on social identity-related processes. It is worth noting that other theorists have further explored our overlapping social identities from social psychological, sociological, and intersectional lenses (Deaux, 1991; Markus & Nurius,1986; Crenshaw, 1990). They highlight how social context dictates which aspects of our social identity may become 'salient' and how such dynamic identity shifting may affect our attitudes and behaviours.

Belonging is the key driving factor behind most theories of social categorization, social identification, and developmental stage theories. Relevant to the context of this book, scholars have fruitfully applied the constructs of identity and belonging to country affiliations and the implications of an 'us versus them' approach for deploying nationalism and xenophobia in media discourse. Paasi (2003) argues that identity discourses are becoming increasingly personalized in the Western world and that movements away from larger, more collective identities are leading to a resurgence in national identification. Moreover, Paasi (2009) highlights the need for re-examining and redefining the nature of regions and regional identities in the changing context of the European Union (EU). In the world of journalism, this is mirrored by a growing tendency toward personalization in news reporting and the way in which journalists (and their 'followers') talk about domestic versus EU-related issues on social media (Barberá et al., 2017).

Categorization and Stereotypes

A core component of the identity processes described previously stems from our need to categorize ourselves and the world around us in order to make sense of the massive amount of stimuli we encounter in our daily lives (e.g., Fiske & Taylor, 1991). We describe this process in social psychology broadly as 'social categorization', and we often do it automatically, particularly when we encounter other people—ascribing them to groups based on gender, race, ethnicity, social roles or social status, and other (mainly demographic) criteria (Crisp & Hewstone, 2007).

Once we categorize someone (including ourselves) to a particular social group, we are likely also to assign that person a series of personal characteristics which we often associate with members of that group. This process is called stereotyping. Stereotypes are viewed in social psychology mainly as cognitive structures, or 'schemata', consisting of mental associations between concepts (e.g., a demographic group of people) and their associations (e.g., traits). For example, a stereotype may consist of the mental association between asylum seekers and terrorism, crime, and/or victimization highlighted previously (see further details in Dovidio et al., 1986; Perdue et al., 1990).

Once a stereotype or concept has been activated, other related stereotypes may also be activated, theorized as the process of *spreading activation*, whereby the activation of one concept leads to the activation of related 'nodes' or associations presumed to be stored in long-term memory (Collins & Loftus, 1975; Domke et al., 1999; Valentino, 1999). Therefore, from a journalistic perspective, it is important to consider not only the extent to which certain groups are present (or represented in news) but also the contexts in which they are represented. For example, Chiricos and Eschlnoz (2002) conducted a study on the representation of minority ethnic persons (MEPs) in crime news in Orlando, Florida, and showed how ethnic minorities were more likely to appear as criminal suspects than as victims or positive role models. Moreover, MEPs seemed in general to appear in more threatening contexts than White persons. Why is this problematic? According to theories of associative learning, the more often these associated nodes are activated in conjunction with each other, the deeper the association and the likelihood that the activation of one will trigger the activation of the others in future (Dixon & Azocar, 2007). With regard to journalism, therefore, one would expect that the frequent exposure to news in which a particular group is presented in association with particular attributes or in particular contexts will mean that whenever that particular group is activated, people will be more likely to think about those attributes or contexts.

Research has traditionally been focussed on the activation of a stereotype and the application of the stereotype (through one's judgements and behaviour) as separate processes; research suggests that the first step does not necessarily lead to the second (Lido et al., 2005; Kawakami et al., 2007). Once a stereotype has been activated, its application may be prevented if one has the motivation, cognitive resources, and time in which to do so (Moskowitz, 2005; 2012; Dixon & Azocar, 2007; Arendt, 2013a; 2013b). For instance, if one reflects on values such as equality, one may be able to prevent the activation of negative stereotypes (Devine, 1989; Shrum, 2002). In addition, if someone's goals are fundamentally egalitarian, possibly chronically egalitarian, then unintentional stereotype activation may be avoided (Moskowitz & Stone, 2012). However, if one does not have the motivation or ability to prevent the activation of the stereotype, then it is likely to occur automatically, and stereotype congruent judgements may then be applied to tasks following the stereotype activation. Although recent research suggests that even the first step—stereotype activation—may be automatically inhibited by personal beliefs (e.g., Moskowitz et al.,1999; Moskowitz & Stone, 2012), there still remains the risk that cognitive stereotypes, activated by exposure to the media, may automatically bias judgements in everyday life without our intention or awareness, even when we are low in explicit prejudice.

Traditional approaches as to how social psychologists perceive identity processes, social categorization (leading to stereotypes), and biased judgements in everyday life have been outlined previously. Before we apply these approaches more fully to the journalistic context and specifically to bias in the media regarding refugees, we must visit more recent frameworks to assess how such categorization and stereotypes may affect our thoughts and behaviours in the real world—posing questions such as To what extent does exposure to stereotypes affect the thoughts and behaviours toward a specific cultural group? and What are other components are relevant for predicting such bias, particularly in the media?'

Current Models of Intergroup Bias

A growing body of research, begun in the 1990s, has been focussed on intergroup emotions as an essential connector between stereotypes and specific types of behaviour toward different groups (for reviews, see Giner-Sorolla et al., 2007; Mackie & Smith, 2017). Intergroup emotions can be defined as specific emotional responses that people experience toward in-group and out-group members because of their respective group member-ships. As Parkinson et al. (2005) noted, intergroup emotions need to have their basis in an individual's membership of a group and also take another group as a target. In other words, intergroup emotions are experienced by individuals when both the subject and the object of the emotions are groups rather than individuals, as it is perceived to have been done 'to them' or 'by them' as members of social groups.

What are the advantages of studying intergroup emotions? According to intergroup emotion researchers, specific emotional prejudices can more accurately predict differentiated types of group behaviour and are a better predictor than general prejudice, which is defined as a negative attitude experienced undistinguishably toward out-groups (Dijker, 1987; Islam & Hewstone, 1993; Ray et al., 2012). Although stereotypes are associated with intergroup discrimination, the relationship between specific intergroup emotions, such as intergroup anger or fear, and different types of intergroup behaviour, such as harm or avoidance, has been found to be well supported by evidence (Frijda et al., 1989). Importantly, intergroup theoretical models have shown that specific stereotypes generate differentiated intergroup emotions toward particular out-groups, which in turn leads to particular action tendencies toward them (Fiske & Taylor, 1991; Parkinson et al., 2005). For instance, if one endorses a stereotype of immigrants as contributors to a mul-ticultural society, then one would feel admiration and respect toward them, perhaps supporting their inclusion within the community. However, if one associates immigrants with negative stereotypes, and potentially as a threat, then one may feel annoyed or angry with their participation in the commu-nity. These core assumptions have been supported by many researchers, and different theoretical approaches have been proposed and tested, three of which are reported here.

Intergroup Emotion Theory

Smith (E.R.) (1993, 1999) and colleagues (Mackie et al., 2000) proposed the intergroup emotions theory (IET), stemming from SCT described previously (Turner et al., 1987). IET expands upon how people experience different emotions depending on their self-categorizations and group identification in intergroup contexts. According to IET (for reviews, see Moons et al., 2017; Giner-Sorolla, 2019), people emotionally react and consequently behave toward others dependent upon on whether they perceive themselves as individuals or as group members in specific situations. Research has shown that people report their emotions differently when asked to view themselves with a group affiliation, such as a university student or national citizen, when compared with report their emotions as an individual. Thus, when their group identity was subtly activated with songs or symbols, they shifted away from their personal sense of self (Seger et al., 2009; Moons et al., 2009). As Parkinson et al. (2005) stated, among the factors that increase the salience of social identity are actual or imagined presence of an out-group, competition with that out-group, and perception that characteristics (e.g., views, values, and behaviour) co-vary with group membership. Hence, if personal or social identities are salient, the outcomes are very different. For example, if a British person is in an elevator with three people speaking a foreign language, that person's national or cultural identity is likely to be made salient; however, if an encounter with a foreign stranger happens as a one-to-one conversation, then personal identities are likely be more prominent, with less automatic activation of conceptions of intergroup differences.

According to IET, self-categorization and in-group identification affect the degree and the type of intergroup emotions that people experience in intergroup contexts (Devos et al., 2002; Mackie, 2017). For example, the activation of specific social memberships changes how one feels toward a group. Ray et al. (2008) demonstrated that participants reported different emotions toward Muslims and the police when they were asked to think of themselves as either 'an American' or 'a student'. Social identification also changes the way in which people appraise intergroup situations. For example, participants reported feeling more unjust and more anger toward a proposal to increase tuition fees for non-residents at the University of Colorado when they identified as students rather than as Colorado residents (Gordijn et al., 2006). Last, in-group identification also affects the extent to which group members experience intergroup emotions. As Mackie (2000; Moons et al., 2017) notes, high rather than low identifiers experience more intensive intergroup emotions that support rather than negate their in-group. Thus, with a positive image of the in-group, emotions such as pride and anger are felt more intensely (Combs et al., 2009; Maitner et al., 2007), whereas emotions that reflect negativity toward their in-group (e.g., guilt) are felt less intensely

(Kuppens & Yzerbyt, 2014; Maitner et al., 2007). Empirical evidence indicates how group membership and identification affect the way in which people emotionally react and behave toward others in face-to-face contact, but this can also be abstracted to intergroup contexts that are perceived or implied (such as by the media). For example, the more people identify with being British, the angrier they may feel reading online newspaper coverage that a national charity cannot respond to local needs because of its international aid expenses, and perhaps then the more they will respond with negative posts and tweets about this issue.

IET has conceptualized how group-based or stereotypical appraisals play a relevant role in generating intergroup emotions and intergroup behaviour in intergroup situations (Mackie et al., 2000). By combining appraisal theories of emotion (for a review, see Scherer et al., 2001) with the principles of SCT (Turner et al., 1987) and then applying this to the intergroup sphere, IET researchers transpose the question, Does this situation affect me personally? to the intergroup context question, Does this situation affect my group? In this way, IET may predict the specific emotions that members of a group are likely to experience in intergroup emotion-eliciting situations (e.g., successes, threats, or injustices). Fiske and Taylor (1991; Fiske, 1998) explained how appraisals in intergroup contexts are stereotypes that entail dimensions of perceived responsibility, fairness, and certainty.

Smith (1993) offered the applied example of emotional intergroup reactance, whereby Western industrialized citizens might be more likely to perceive asylum seekers as unfairly taking money from the in-group's public money, thereby limiting the money available for the in-group. This intergroup situation, involving perceived resource competition with an out-group over limited resources, may lead citizens to experience anger against weaker out-groups (in line with realistic conflict theory; Campbell, 1965). This intergroup anger is, in turn, associated with action tendencies associated with this emotion—for example, manifesting in aggressive actions against asylum seekers within one's community. Following the review of recent theoretical models, this chapter will illustrate how identity processes, categorization, stereotypes, and intergroup emotions can be deployed by news media, in short- and long-term strategies, to (intentionally or unintentionally) trigger intergroup emotions and stereotypical appraisals in society.

The Stereotype Content Model and BIAS Map

According to the stereotype content model (SCM) (Fiske et al., 2002; for a review, see Fiske et al., 2007), to understand intergroup emotions and consequent action tendencies, it is important to analyse two social structural variables: perceived relative status and perceived competition with one's own group. These social structure components are associated with how people perceive out-groups on two fundamental social judgement dimensions, namely *competence* and *warmth*. According to SCM, the combinations of these two dimensions generate four types of stereotypes: two ambivalent ones, such as high on one dimension and low on another one, and two univalent ones, namely low or high on both dimensions.

The BIAS map (Behaviours from Intergroup Affect and Stereotypes) offers an extension of SCM, predicting how these stereotype-based clusters may be associated with specific intergroup emotions (Fiske et al., 2002) and intergroup behaviours (Cuddy et al., 2007). More precisely, groups stereotyped as capable but not warm—for example, Asian American people—may be targeted with envy and resentment, and their behaviours may be perceived as passive accommodation or potentially even active harm (see also Salovey, 1991; E. E. Smith, 2000). Social groups stereotyped as incapable but warm and trustworthy, such as elderly adults, may trigger pity, an emotion that involves unequal status, undermining autonomy, perhaps leading to active helping or social neglect (E. E. Smith, 2000; Weiner, 2005). Groups stereotyped as low in warmth and competence, such as homeless people, are likely to elicit emotions such as contempt and disgust, which in turn may lead to passive neglect and active attack (Rozin & Fallon, 1987). Groups associated with both high competence (namely in-group members) and high warmth are likely to elicit pride and admiration, likely leading to positive associations and behaviours (Cuddy et al., 2007).

Cultural variations and historical changes affect the stereotypes associated with various social groups (Cuddy et al., 2009; Durante et al., 2018). According to the SCM and BIAS map (Fiske, 2015), changes of the social structure variables (increased perceived cooperation and competence of out-groups) can lead to improving intergroup perceptions, emotions, and derived behavioural tendencies. It might be expected that if refugees were framed in the news as future citizens, not stealing jobs but rather supporting the countries in which they reside, doing necessary jobs and vital in the creation of new employment avenues, thus contributing to national economic growth, they would be associated with more warmth (Fiske, 2015). If refugees are described not as a drain on societies, unable to navigate job markets, but rather resilient humans, able to overcome adverse circumstances, then their associations with competence will also grow (in line with Cikara & Fiske, 2013). Such new frames offered in journalistic discourse would shift affective associations of refugees and asylum seekers.

The Threat Model

The integrated threat theory (ITT) (Stephan et al., 2002) attempts to integrate sociological and psychological frameworks to explain when prejudice might arise between groups, under various conditions of perceived 'threat' from the out-group (often minority or marginalized groups). This theory identifies several antecedents of perceived intergroup threat, including intergroup relations (e.g., conflict and/or unequal status), individual differences (e.g., in-group identity and/or contact experience), cultural dimensions (e.g., collectivism), and intergroup context. These precursors are thought to predict how some out-groups are perceived as being a *realistic threat* (e.g.,) (bringing tangible harm to the in-group, stealing resources, damaging the economy, and/or bringing criminality and diseases) and/or a *symbolic threat* (eroding socio-moral-cultural in-group values). Hence, out-groups perceived as realistic and/or symbolic threats will elicit intergroup anxiety, which strengthens stereotypical views and results in greater out-group prejudice (Stephan & Stephan, 2000).

These theoretical assumptions have been supported by a range of empirical evidence, which has also led to suggestions on how to improve intergroup relations (Stephan et al., 2000, 2005). More recent empirical work has also shown how specific threats lead to differentiated emotional reactions and consequent action tendencies (Abeywickrama et al., 2018). This theory well represents how prejudice and anxiety against refugees, asylum seekers, and migrants in the UK can be related to the stereotypical representations of these social groups as both realistic and symbolic threats to British values in the UK mass media (Arif, 2018; Innes, 2010; Kale & Hart, 2017; Looney, 2017). According to ITT theorists, the general public should be encouraged to experience empathy to contrast intergroup anxiety felt toward out-groups (Stephan & Stephan, 2000). Abeywickrama et al. (2018) have shown that threat to in-group morality (an in-group is experienced as immoral) is associated with positive emotions toward out-groups, and this result should be replicated and explored further. Research evidence discussed previously implicates a need for clear and factual information about demographic groups, particularly those marginalized within society, in order to reframe social representations of such stigmatized groups (Johnson et al., 2009; Finlay & Stephan, 2000; Stephan & Finlay, 1999). Journalism plays a crucial role in shifting cultural perceptions of refugees and asylum seekers from active threats to recipients of empathy, as knowledge about out-groups helps decrease prejudice and increase familiarity (Berry et al., 2016); however, as discussed previously, warmth alone is not enough to activate conceptions of equality and inclusion.

Summary

In sum, Intergroup emotion frameworks encourage us to change how social groups are appraised and associated with threat, relative competition, and unequal status (for a study on for perception change, see Gaucher et al., 2018). The theories and frameworks we have reviewed all emphasize the role of emotional reactions as key predictors of intergroup behaviour. This suggests the need for a change in media messages, moving away from emotion-provoking material, such as wave metaphors (for association of metaphors and emotions, see Citron et al., 2016), and toward individual perceptions of warmth, competence, and contribution toward societies. Increasing actual contact between groups has consistently been shown to positively change both cognitive and emotional associations involved in contact with out-groups (Allport, 1954; Pettigrew & Tropp, 2008). Therefore, changing journalistic coverage of migration issues can promote meaningful and positive social relations among people from different groups (Briant, 2016). Thus, journalists may be the most powerful weapon society has for prejudice reduction.

Direct Effects of Stereotype Exposure from Media

McQuail's (1987) model of media effects places theoretical findings of media bias from intention to unintentional and long to short term. This section discusses the unintentional and short-term effects of media exposure on one's thoughts and behaviours due to so-called priming or 'framing' effects. The media has been shown to effectively activate stereotypes in the short term in prior empirical studies (e.g., Lido et al., 2005; Dixon & Azocar, 2007; Mastro & Tukachinsky, 2012; Esses et al., 2013; Arendt & Marquart, 2015), including meta-analytic evidence of media exposure as a replicable short-term effect (Roskos-Ewoldsen et al., 2007). For instance, recent research has shown that short-term media exposure to stories of Black criminals in news media can increase the perceived culpability of a Black suspect, and this is moderated by longer term news exposure, whereby heavy TV news viewers were more susceptible to this effect, illustrating a chronic activation of a Black criminal stereotype (Dixon & Azocar, 2007).

In addition to effectively activating stereotypes, the media, in the first instance, contribute to the formation (content) and maintenance of stereotypes themselves. When significant portions of the news media consistently put forward the same idea about a group of people, such as asylum seekers, the information will begin to hold 'reiteration bias' (e.g., Hertwig et al., 1997). According to reiteration bias, the more one hears a piece of information repeated from a number of sources, the more likely one is to believe it as factual (Hertwig et al., 1997). In addition, these stereotypes become chronically accessible because the more stereotype-consistent information is absorbed, the stronger the cognitive connections become (Dixon & Azocar, 2007; Devine, 1989; Domke et al., 1999; Fiske & Taylor, 1991).

The more that stereotype-consistent information is activated in regard to a particular group, the stronger the cognitive connections between the stereotypical characteristics and the group to which the stereotypes are applied (Devine, 1989; Domke et al., 1999; Fiske & Taylor, 1991). The biased information which has been put forward about the group in question quickly becomes part of the schemata used to understand that group (Ramasubramanian, 2007). One experiment demonstrated the cumulative effects of news viewing by directly comparing heavy news viewers to light news viewers, showing that the concept of crime was more likely to prime anti-Black racism in the former than the latter. In other words, in a context in which the media consistently links blackness and criminality, the association was stronger in those who had had greater exposure to the news (Dixon & Azocar, 2007). Another study showed that with regard to several stereotype priming paradigms such as race and gender, co-occurrence of the stereotyped group and the stereotype in culture can almost completely explain the effect of priming (Verhaeghen et al., 2011). This further implicates the media, which is a key source of the formation of cultural attitudes in stereotype formation (Verhaeghen et al., 2011).

For example, the negative news portrayal of asylum seekers may constitute chronic activation of stereotypes about asylum seekers. The portrayals of asylum seekers as criminal, a threat to security, and a strain on the system (Greussing & Boomgaarden, 2017) may consistently strengthen the associations between these concepts and asylum seekers. This chronic exposure to negative stereotypes may in turn lead to the formation of attitudes which can influence behaviour (Appel, 2011; Arendt, 2013a; 2013b). It is therefore important to investigate the ways in which media portrayals of asylum seekers affect perceptions of them so that we may understand how these portrayals may influence behaviour toward asylum seekers and asylum policy.

A few studies have examined portrayals of asylum seekers in the media in the wake of the 2015 refugee influx, due largely to the Syrian conflict (Goodman et al., 2017; Greussing & Boomgaarden, 2017). Prior research revealed it is possible to activate both positive and negative attitudes toward asylum seekers. Pedersen and Thomas (2013), for instance, primed differing attitudes toward asylum seekers and then assessed prejudiced attitudes. In this study, participants were primed to think of asylum seekers as either similar to or different from themselves, and the results showed that when thinking of asylum seekers as similar, participants showed higher prejudice—presumably in an attempt at social distance, although this effect was moderated by the subjective importance participants placed on identity. Yet few studies have explored the potential for media coverage to directly activate attitudes toward asylum seekers after the 2015 refugee influx, which potentially offers a crucial turning point in the media coverage and public opinion about the refugee crisis. The case study presented next addresses this gap in the literature by presenting the work of Lido et al. (2005) and its partial replication in 2015, which examined whether newspaper article exposure could directly affect attitudes toward asylum seekers in the UK.

Case Study: Direct Effects of Media Refugee Bias on Stereotypes

In 2005, Lido et al. conducted a series of studies aimed at examining the impact of the British media on attitudes toward asylum seekers. In these studies, participants were divided into three groups and exposed to a negative article about asylum seekers, a positive article about asylum seekers, or an unrelated control article. The negative article associated asylum seekers with criminality and suggested that they were an economic burden. The positive article described an incident in which an asylum seeker exhibited exceptional honesty, and the control article discussed trains and was unrelated to asylum seekers. Participants read the article assigned to them and were then asked to make judgements on mock asylum applications. They also filled out a measure of explicit prejudice that was composed of items adapted from a measure of subtle and blatant prejudice (Pettigrew & Meertens, 1995) and a measure of in-group favouritism (Calitri, 2005). These studies found that exposure not only to the negative article but also to the positive article led to significantly higher levels of explicit prejudice toward foreigners compared to exposure to the control article. The studies also found that participants in both the positive and negative news groups were less likely to believe that asylum applications were legitimate and less likely to want to grant them asylum compared to those exposed to the control article.

In 2017, these studies were replicated. Many of the themes and stereotypes about asylum seekers appearing in news coverage remained the same as when the original studies were carried out, with an emphasis on invasion, criminality, and being a threat to social and economic stability. The context, however, had changed between 2005 and 2017. The increase in number of refugees arriving in Europe in 2015 brought on by the Syrian civil war and the increase in traffic through the Mediterranean route had complicated the narratives surrounding asylum seekers, or at least added new ones. There was also an increased emphasis on the threat of terrorism, in addition to an emerging political landscape publicly opposed to migration, immigration, and acceptance of refugees. Therefore, the replication employed articles that had been updated to reflect changes in public perception of refugees. For instance, the negative news article was based on the idea of refugees as terrorists rather than as criminals. It also tested prejudice using the same measure of explicit prejudice and similar mock asylum applications (with names changed to sound more Syrian in origin).

Like the original studies, this replication found that exposure to a negative article about asylum seekers led to higher levels of prejudice on an explicit prejudice scale. However, unlike in the original studies, the negative article was not associated with more negative assessments of individuals in mock asylum applications. Furthermore, unlike the original studies, the replication did not find higher levels of prejudice in those who had read a positive article compared to those who had read the control article. This could be due to increased accessibility of warmer stereotypes of asylum seekers than when the original studies were conducted, such as the notion of asylum seekers as in need of help.

Among the narratives about asylum seekers, compared to 2005, there was a greater emphasis on humanitarianism in 2017, which had begun with the publication of the photograph in 2015 of a drowned child, Aylan Kurdi, who had washed up on a beach in Turkey. The photograph appeared on the front pages of newspapers throughout the world, regardless of their political leaning. The *Daily Mail*, which had previously been very aggressive in tone toward refugees, ran the photograph with the headline, 'Tiny Victim of a Human Catastrophe' (Berry et al., 2016). However, these warmer narratives (which could also be viewed as another form of stereotype; see Fiske et al., 2002) were not sufficient to activate attitudes which were more positive than those seen in the control condition.

The most consistent finding across both series of studies was that exposure to negative news media content activated stereotyped associations of asylum seekers and produced negative outcomes (attitudinal and even behavioural, in the form of dishonest behaviours such as accepting a second payment when given the opportunity or lying on a lie scale; see Lido et al., 2005). However, positive news media exposure did not activate any positive associations, attitudes, or outcomes. These findings may be explained by the chronic accessibility of negative stereotypes of asylum seekers due to the prevalence of negative content of the news media. If negative views of asylum seekers are more easily accessible than positive ones, then it may be that the very mention of asylum seekers, regardless of the context, may be enough to activate negative associations, leading to more negative judgements on mock asylum applications and explicit measures of prejudice (even for those low in prejudice). In the 10 years between the series of studies, there was reportedly a surge in far-right-wing political parties, which often base much of their traction on anti-refugee rhetoric and appeal to nationalistic identities and xenophobia (Berry et al., 2016; Vieten & Poynting, 2016). There has also been media coverage which has periodically increased support for refugees, such as the Aylan Kurdi coverage described previously (de-Andrés-del-Campo et al., 2016; Berry, et al., 2016).

Some of this coverage may feed into what may be construed as a positive stereotype: the representation of refugees as victims. Although this stereotype is still negative in that it ties into the notion of refugees as lacking in agency and their dependence on others (Greussing & Boomgaarden, 2017), it may simply produce a subtyping stereotype, leading to higher warmth toward refugees but not competence, nor contribution to citizen ship (as described in the BIAS map).

Strategies for Reducing Media Stereotype Reliance: What Could Work?

Media-biased information can have a real impact on prejudice toward refugees, as illustrated by our case study presentation. Media reporting has even been tied to hate crimes (e.g., Githens-Mazer & Lambert, 2010). It appears urgent to propose strategies for responsible journalism and for audiences to be more overtly aware of misleading bias, particularly within written (often newsprint) media—given the direct effects illustrated by Lido (2003, 2005) and other social psychologists. Here, we list some useful tips for (1) supporting journalists to be more factually accurate in reporting about migration and (2) guiding UK (and global) audiences to critically evaluate mass media information to which they are exposed. The following points are the result of discussions among academics, journalists, and the public attending a symposium on media and migration in 2018. We have grounded these suggestions in a social psychological evidence base and integrated them with suggestions elaborated by the authors of this chapter, drawn from current theoretical knowledge and research findings on this topic across different disciplines.

Avoid reification of authorities' opinions: Consistent research has shown that claims by politicians and other authorities about migration are overreported in media outlets (Briant, 2016; Coen, 2018; Mongtomery et al., 2018; Migrant Voice, 2014). It is important, for conceptual honesty, that authorities' speeches (which often embed stereotypical views about refugees, asylum seekers, and migrants more widely) are clearly presented as quotes rather than facts, enabling people to shape their own opinions regarding migration, consider different perspectives, question others' opinions, and simultaneously become informed on facts.

Report the correct numbers: Journalists should report figures, statistics, and the results of polls about migration in the UK, retrieving them from official and reliable sources of information and checking for consistency across reliable sources. Numbers and percentages about migration should be explained and contextualized, providing some points of reference to interpret them (Ford, 2011; Philo et al., 2013). Information reported with accurate numbers and clear graphs will contrast the stereotypical view of refugees and asylum seekers as an unmanageable mass of people invading the country.

Deconstruct the 'migration' threat: As Migrant Voice (2014) and Simon Goodman (2018) have emphasized, news should also be reported with some historical, economic, and geographical information to contextualize the facts—for instance, the role of the countries such as the UK in modern international relations and conflicts. This additional information could be useful, if repeated consistently across different channels, to change the stereotypical image of asylum seekers, refugees, and migrants as a physical, economic, and symbolic threat to the country (for techniques of stereotype change, see Rothbart, 2004). This message is also supported by intergroup emotion researchers; changing emotional appraisals of intergroup situations involving refugees, as well as their perceived social status and competition, will affect attitudes toward such stigmatized out-groups (Fiske, 2013; Mackie, 2017). Some authors have also emphasized the importance of eliciting empathy toward refugees (e.g., Finlay & Stephan, 2000), and photographs of individual refugees have helped with this (de-Andrés-del-Campo et al., 2016). Publishing children's photographs and stories has also been considered a strategy to implement and also empower minority status groups, but ethical issues need to be considered, given the vulnerable nature of refugee groups and children in particular (Sime, 2018).

Disconfirm junk news: Nowadays, social media are used as a primary source of information by significant percentages of populations, particularly among younger people throughout the world (Reuters Institute, 2017). A vast amount of nonfactual, unreliable 'junk news' is spread throughout the world via these channels. A report focussing on Twitter accounts and Facebook pages illustrates how far-right-wing users provided the majority of news, including misleading, deceptive, or incorrect information, as if it was real news about politics, economics, or culture (Bradshaw et al., 2019). Although people tend to believe and defend information that supports their views, even if it is provably untrue, some authors have shown that critical skills reduce this tendency (Pennycook & Rand, 2019; Wood & Porter, 2019). Hence, training to uncover so-called fake news and develop critical media literacy skills is needed.

Report positive news (but not only) about integrated communities: As highlighted by the journalist Catriona Stewart and by academics during the Media and Migration symposium (see also Briant, 2016), regional coverages can provide a multifaceted and more realistic perspective on refugees' reality and their integration in communities. Providing voice to people affected by forced migration can also identify problems and potential solutions to these difficulties, particularly when attempting to promote positive intergroup relations in communities with recent demographic population change. Including in the news stories that highlight good relations between refugees and local people—for instance, reporting intergroup helping and friendships—may also be likely to change intragroup norms (De Amicis & Rahim, 2019, n.d.; Paluck, 2009).

Conclusions and Recommendations

This chapter began with an overview of social psychology, identity, stereotyping, prejudice, and the role of emotions in such processes. We then explored how notions of social identity are affected by stereotype content manufactured and activated by media in terms of development of stereotype content and direct activation of stereotypes. Such consumption, particularly of negatively biased news media regarding refugees, can directly impact upon people's beliefs, feelings, and behaviours.

We highlighted how the field of social psychology, and specifically social cognition, has offered theoretical approaches and research methods to understand and investigate how media can affect attitudes and behaviours through the formation of stereotype content and direct activation of such content, such as through exposure to print or social media. Moreover, we presented our own and others' experimental work, which highlighted how negative news may affect the general public, but we concluded that there is not a similar effect for positive news in the area of migration and refugees. We offered conclusions from a symposium making use of such academic findings, and sharing them with journalists and the public alike, to gather multiple stakeholder views on media bias of refugee and migration issues in the UK. We offered recommendations based on a triangulated analysis of historical social psychological theory, current empirical evidence, and views of journalists to explore how news and media information can become more accurate, less misleading, and present a more mindful migration discourse, offering strategies to improve news to reduce audience's stereotypical perceptions and to shift the valence of media content to be more positive.

Traditional and social media also offer the possibility of positive use/outcomes for refugees, with a global reach. It is important to note that to date, the effects of media have been explored only with the majority groups to check their relations with their prejudice. In the future, investigation of self-perception of news coverage by targeted minority group members, embedded in national and cultural contexts, is urgently needed.

In light of the current replication crisis in the wider field of psychology, in which there may be a dearth of successful replications of accepted research findings (see Maxwell et al., 2015), we strongly encourage further replications of direct asylum seeker news exposure effects, both short and long term. We also advocate further studies employing varied version of 'positive news coverage' to contribute to stereotype change and, eventually, prejudice reduction. Our research is in line with previous research, which has successfully primed negative attitudes but failed to prime positive ones (Arendt, 2016), yet it remains possible that effective positive news has simply not been developed or longitudinally tested. Discovering which types of coverage might lead to the development of more positive attitudes toward refugees and foreigners would be invaluable in providing practical advice for media reporting on issues concerning refugees and asylum seekers.

It would also be of value to explore more direct effects of specific vocabulary deployed in refugee news coverage. Much of the literature researching representations of refugees and asylum seekers in news coverage has included analyses of metaphorical language, such as comparisons of asylum seekers to waves or catastrophes (El Rafaie, 2001; Greussing & Boomgaarden, 2017). Other research has included analyses of the ways in which different metaphorical framings of a problem may prime different responses about the best solution to that problem (Thibodeau & Boroditsky, 2011), supporting our recommendations for deconstructing 'migrant threat' news coverage, and the power of the media in re-shaping valanced content of stereotypes.

The recommendations we have offered—*Avoid reification of authorities' opinions, Report the correct numbers, Deconstruct the 'migration' threat and Disconfirm junk news*—stem from theoretical and empirical developments in social psychology over decades, as well as discussions with diverse stakeholders—psychologists, sociologists, journalists, media information experts, and the general public. We believe that such interdisciplinary dialogue is necessary to address unintended effects of media identity discourse and stereotype activation. Politicians and decision-makers are exposed to the same media narratives as the general population. As such, we argued that addressing media bias overtly with journalists and publishers is essential for prejudice reduction strategies. Furthermore, public opinion can influence policy (de-Andrés-del-Campo, 2016), and the media directly and indirectly influences public attitudes—particularly toward marginalized out-groups. Therefore, we offer our chapter—of social psychological theory, empirical evidence, case study and recommendations—for press agencies and journalists, as well as those responsible for policy decisions in areas affected by implicit and explicit bias. We hope it can help us all to be more conscious of how the media we produce and consume may directly affect our stereotypes and judgements. We therefore conclude this chapter with a call for journalists, policy-makers, and public audiences to engage with the field of social psychology, and sub-field of social cognition, to become more mindful of the effects of news representations in society, particularly with regard to coverage of migration, refugee and asylum-seeker issues.

References

Abeywickrama, R. S., Laham, S. M., & Crone, D. L. (2018). Immigration and receiving communities: The utility of threats and emotions in predicting action tendencies toward refugees, asylum-seekers and economic migrants. *Journal of Social Issues, 74*(4), 756–773.

Allport, G. W. (1954). *The nature of prejudice*. Addison-Wesley.

Anderson, C. A., Berkowitz, L., Donnerstein, E., Huesmann, L. R., Johnson, J. D., Linz, D., Malamuth, N. M., & Wartella, E. (2003). The influence of media violence on youth. *Psychological Science in the Public Interest, 4*(3), 81–110.

Appel, M. (2011). A story about a stupid person can make you act stupid (or smart): Behavioral assimilation (and contrast) as narrative impact. *Media Psychology*, 14(2), 144–167. doi:10.1080/15213269.2011.573461

Arendt, F. (2013a). Dose-dependent media priming effects of stereotypic newspaper articles on implicit and explicit stereotypes: Dose-dependent media priming effects. *Journal of Communication*, 63(5), 830–851. doi:10.1111/jcom.12056

Arendt, F. (2013b). News stereotypes, time, and fading priming effects. *Journalism & Mass Communication Quarterly*, 90(2), 347–362. doi:10.1177/1077699013482907

Arendt, F. (2016). Disposition-content congruency and the negation of media stereotypes. *Communication Research Reports*, 33(1), 74–80. doi:10.1080/08824096.2015.1117446

Arendt, F., & Marquart, F. (2015). Corrupt politicians? Media priming effects on overtly expressed stereotypes toward politicians. *Communications*, 40(2), 185–197. doi:10.1515/commun-2015-0003

Arif, N. (2018). Consenting to Orientalism when covering migration: How the British media dehumanises migrants in the context of the Syrian civil war. *Critical Hermeneutics*, 2(1), 27–54.

Asch, S. E. (1951). Effects of group pressure upon the modification and distortion of judgments. In H. Guetzkow (ed.) *Groups, leadership and men*. Pittsburgh, PA: Carnegie Press.

Banaji, M. R., & Hardin, C. D. (1996). Automatic stereotyping. *Psychological Science*, 7(3), 136–141.

Barberá, P., Vaccari, C., & Valeriani, A. (2017). Social media, personalisation of news reporting, and media systems' polarisation in Europe. In M. Barisione & A. Michailidou (Eds.), *Social media and European politics* (pp. 25–52). Palgrave Macmillan.

Bauer, N. M. (2015). Emotional, sensitive, and unfit for office? Gender stereotype activation and support female candidates. *Political Psychology*, 36(6), 691–708.

Berry, M., Garcia-Blanco, I, Moore, K. (2015). Press coverage of the refugee and migrant crisis in the EU: A content analysis of five European countries (Report for the UNHCR). Available at: http://www.unhcr.org/protection/operations/56bb369c9/press-coverage-refugee-migrant-crisis-eu-content-analysis-five-european.html (accessed 16 April 2021)

Bradshaw, S., Howard, P. N., Kollanyi, B., & Neudert, L. (2019). Sourcing and automation of political news and information over social media in the United States, 2016–2018. *Political Communication*, 37, 173–193. doi:10.1080/10584609.2019.1663322

Brewer, M. B. (1991). The social self: On being the same and different at the same time. *Personality and Social Psychology Bulletin*, 17(5), 475–482.

Brewer, M. B., Brown, R. J., Gilbert, D. T., Fiske, S. T., & Lindzey, G. (1998). *Handbook of social psychology*. Wadsworth.

Briant, E. (2016). Language, empathy and reflection: Teaching journalists about the refugee crisis. *Journal of Narrative Studies*, 3, 49–71.

British Psychological Society. (2014). Code of human research ethics. https://www.bps.org.uk/sites/www.bps.org.uk/files/Policy/Policy%20-%20Files/BPS%20Code%20of%20Human%20Research%20Ethics.pdf

Brown, R., & Pehrson, S. (2019). *Group processes: Dynamics within and between groups*. Wiley.

Calitri, R. (2005). Nationalism and patriotism: The effects of national identification on implicit and explicit in-group bias. Doctoral dissertation, University of Kent.

Campbell, D. T. (1965). Ethnocentric and other altruistic motives. *Nebraska Symposium on Motivation, 13*, 283–311.

Çelebi, E., Verkuyten, M., & Bagci, S. C. (2017). Ethnic identification, discrimination, and physical health among Syrian refugees: The moderating role of identity needs. *European Journal of Social Psychology, 47*(7), 832–843.

Chamberlain, K., & Hodgetts, D. (2008). Social psychology and media: Critical considerations. *Social and Personality Psychology Compass, 2*(3), 1109–1125.

Chiricos, T., & Eshholz, S. (2002). The racial and ethnic typification of crime and the criminal typification of race and ethnicity in local television news. *Journal of Research in Crime and Delinquency, 39*(4), 400–442.

Chouliaraki, L. (2012). *Between pity and irony: Paradigms of refugee representation in humanitarian discourse.* Lang.

Cikara, M., & Fiske, S. T. (2013). Their pain, our pleasure: Stereotype content and schadenfreude. *Annals of the New York Academy of Sciences, 1299*, 52.

Citron, F. M., Güsten, J., Michaelis, N., & Goldberg, A. E. (2016). Conventional metaphors in longer passages evoke affective brain response. *NeuroImage, 139*, 218–230.

Collins, A. M., & Loftus, E. F. (1975). A spreading-activation theory of semantic processing. *Psychological Review, 82*(6), 407.

Combs, D. J., Powell, C. A., Schurtz, D. R., & Smith, R. H. (2009). Politics, schadenfreude, and ingroup identification: The sometimes happy thing about a poor economy and death. *Journal of Experimental Social Psychology, 45*(4), 635–646.

Condor, S., & Brown, R. (1988). Psychological processes in intergroup conflict. In W. Stroebe, A. W. Kruglanski, D. Bar-Tal, & M. Hewstone (Eds.), *The social psychology of intergroup conflict* (pp. 3–26). Springer.

Convention Relating to the Status of Refugees, July 28, 1951, 189 U.N.T.S. 150.

Crenshaw, K. (1990). Mapping the margins: Intersectionality, identity politics, and violence against women of color. *Stanford Law Review, 43*, 1241.

Crisp, R. J., & Hewstone, M. (2007). Multiple social categorization. *Advances in Experimental Social Psychology, 39*, 163–254.

Cuddy, A. J., Fiske, S. T., & Glick, P. (2007). The BIAS map: Behaviors from intergroup affect and stereotypes. *Journal of Personality and Social Psychology, 92*(4), 631.

Cuddy, A. J., Fiske, S. T., Kwan, V. S., Glick, P., Demoulin, S., Leyens, J. P., Bond, M. H., Croizet, J.-C., Ellemers, N., Sleebos, E., Htun, T. T., Kim, H.-J., Maio, G., Perry, J., Petkova, K., Todorov, V., Rodriguez-Bailon, R., Morales, E., Moya, M., Palacios, M., et al. (2009). Stereotype content model across cultures: Towards universal similarities and some differences. *British Journal of Social Psychology, 48*(1), 1–33.

Curtice, J. (2016). Scottish *social attitudes.* http://natcen.ac.uk/media/1361407/ssa16-2fr8m-1ndyref-2-1ndyr8f-tw0-two.pdf

De Amicis, L., & Rahim, E. A. (n.d.). *How religious communities can help: how inter- and intra-group helping affects interreligious attitudes and policies.* Manuscript in preparation.

de-Andrés-del-Campo, S., Nos-Aldas, E., & García-Matilla, A. (2016). The transformative image: The power of a photograph for social change: The death of Aylan. *Comunicar, 24*(1), 29–37.

Deaux, K. (1991). Social identities: Thoughts on structure and change. In R. C. Curtis (Ed.), *The relational self: Theoretical convergences in psychoanalysis and social psychology* (pp. 77–93). Guilford.

Devine, P. G. (1989). Stereotypes and prejudice: Their automatic and controlled components. *Journal of Personality and Social Psychology, 56*(1), 5.

Devos, T., Silver, L., Mackie, D. M., & Smith, E. R. (2002). Experiencing emotion on behalf of a group: Intergroup anger, fear, and contempt. In D. M. Mackie & E. R. Smith (Ed.), *From prejudice to intergroup emotions: Differentiated reactions to social groups* (pp. 111–134). Psychology Press.

Dixon, T. L., & Azocar, C. L. (2007). Priming crime and activating blackness: Understanding the psychological impact of the overrepresentation of Blacks as lawbreakers on television news. *Journal of Communication, 57*(2), 229–253. doi:10.1111/j.1460-2466.2007.00341.x

Dijker, A. J. (1987). Emotional reactions to ethnic minorities. *European Journal of Social Psychology, 17*(3), 305–325.

Dodd, V., & Booth, R. (2017, June 6). *London Bridge attack: Terror threat in UK now at 'completely different' level.* https://www.theguardian.com/uk-news/2017/jun/05/britain-faces-different-level-ofterror-threat-after-london-bridge-attacks

Domke, D., McCoy, K., & Torres, M. (1999). News media, racial perceptions, and political cognition. *Communication Research, 26*(5), 570–607.

Dovidio, J. F., Evans, N., & Tyler, R. B. (1986). Racial stereotypes: The contents of their cognitive representations. *Journal of Experimental Social Psychology, 22*(1), 22–37.

Dovidio, J. F., Glick, P., & Rudman, L. A. (Eds.). (2008). *On the nature of prejudice: Fifty years after Allport.* Wiley.

Drury, J., Cocking, C., & Reicher, S. (2009). Everyone for themselves? A comparative study of crowd solidarity among emergency survivors. *British Journal of Social Psychology, 48*(3), 487–506.

Durante, F., Fiske, S. T., Kervyn, N., Cuddy, A. J., Akande, A. D., Adetoun, B. E., Adewuyi, M. F., Tserere, M. M., Ramiah, A., Mastor, K. A., Barlow, F. K., Bonn, G., Tafarodi, R. W., Bosak, J., Cairns, E., Doherty, C., Capozza, D., Chandran, A., Chryssochoou, X., Latridis, T., Contreras, J. M., Costa-Lopes, R., González, R., Lewis, J. I., Tushabe, G., Leyens, P. J., Mayorga, R., Rouhana, N. N., Castro, V. S., Perez, R., Rodríguez-Bailón, R., Moya, M., Marente, E. M., Gálvez, M. P., Sibley, C. G., Asbrock, F., & Storari, C. C. (2018). Nations' income inequality predicts ambivalence in stereotype content: How societies mind the gap. In *Social cognition* (pp. 246–268). Routledge.

El-Enany, N. (2016). Aylan Kurdi: The human refugee. *Law and Critique, 27*(1), 13–15. doi:10.1007/s10978-015-9175-7

El Refaie, E. (2001). Metaphors we discriminate by: Naturalized themes in Austrian newspaper articles about asylum seekers. *Journal of Sociolinguistics, 5*(3), 352–371. doi:10.1111/1467-9481.00154

Erikson, E. H. (1968). *Identity: Youth and crisis* (No. 7). Norton.

Esses, V. M., Medianu, S., & Lawson, A. S. (2013). Uncertainty, threat, and the role of the media in promoting the dehumanization of immigrants and refugees. *Journal of Social Issues, 69*(3), 518–536. doi:10.1111/josi.12027

Eysenck, S. B. G., Eysenck, H. J., & Barrett P. (1985). A revised version of the Psychoticism Scale. *Personality and Individual Differences, 6*, 21–29.

Farr, R. M. (1996). *The roots of modern social psychology, 1872–1954.* Blackwell.

Finlay, K. A., & Stephan, W. G. (2000). Improving intergroup relations: The effects of empathy on racial attitudes 1. *Journal of Applied Social Psychology, 30*(8), 1720–1737.

Fiske, S. T. (1998). Stereotyping, prejudice, and discrimination. In D. T. Gilbert, S. T. Fiske, & G. Lindzey (Eds.), *The handbook of social psychology* (4th ed., Vol. 2, pp. 357–411). McGraw-Hill.

Fiske, S. T. (2015). Intergroup biases: A focus on stereotype content. *Current opinion in behavioral sciences, 3*, 45–50.

Fiske, S. T., Cuddy, A. J., & Glick, P. (2007). Universal dimensions of social cognition: Warmth and competence. *Trends in Cognitive Sciences, 11*(2), 77–83.

Fiske, S. T., Cuddy, A. J., Glick, P., & Xu, J. (2002). A model of stereotype content as often mixed: Separate dimensions of competence and warmth respectively follow from status and competition. *Journal of Personality and Social Psychology, 82*(6), 878–902.

Fiske, S. T., & Taylor, S. E. (1991). *Social cognition* (2nd ed.). McGraw-Hill.

Ford, R. (2011). Acceptable and unacceptable immigrants: How opposition to immigration in Britain is affected by migrants' region of origin. *Journal of Ethnic and Migration Studies, 37*(7), 1017–1037.

Freud, S. (1953). On psychotherapy (1905 [1904]). In *The Standard edition of the complete psychological works of Sigmund Freud, Volume VII (1901–1905): A case of hysteria, three essays on sexuality and other works* (pp. 255–268). Hogarth.

Frijda, N. H., Kuipers, P., & Ter Schure, E. (1989). Relations among emotion, appraisal, and emotional action readiness. *Journal of Personality and Social Psychology, 57*(2), 212.

Gailliot, M. T., & Baumeister, R. F. (2007). Self-esteem, belongingness, and worldview validation: Does belongingness exert a unique influence upon self-esteem? *Journal of Research in Personality, 41*(2), 327–345.

Gaucher, D., Friesen, J. P., Neufeld, K. H., & Esses, V. M. (2018). Changes in the positivity of migrant stereotype content: How system-sanctioned pro-migrant ideology can affect public opinions of migrants. *Social Psychological and Personality Science, 9*(2), 223–233.

Gemi, E., Ulasiuk, I., & Triandafyllidou, A. (2013). Migrants and media newsmaking practices. *Journalism Practice, 7*(3), 266–281.

Gilliam, F. D., Jr., & Iyengar, S. (1998). The superpredator script. *Nieman Reports, 52*(4), 45.

Giner-Sorolla, R. (2019). The past thirty years of emotion research: Appraisal and beyond. *Cognition and Emotion, 33*(1), 48–54.

Giner-Sorolla, R., Mackie, D. M., & Smith, E. R. (2007). Special issue on intergroup emotions: Introduction. *Group Processes & Intergroup Relations, 10*(1), 5–8.

Githens-Mazer, J., & Lambert, R. (2010). *Islamophobia and anti-Muslim hate crime: A London case study.* European Muslim Research Centre, University of Exeter, Exeter, UK.

Goodman, S., Sirriyeh, A., & McMahon, S. (2017). The evolving (re)categorisations of refugees throughout the 'refugee/migrant crisis'. *Journal of Community & Applied Social Psychology, 27*(2), 105–114. doi:10.1002/casp.2302

Gordijn, E. H., Yzerbyt, V., Wigboldus, D., & Dumont, M. (2006). Emotional reactions to harmful intergroup behavior. *European Journal of Social Psychology, 36*(1), 15–30.

Greussing, E., & Boomgaarden, H. G. (2017). Shifting the refugee narrative? An automated frame analysis of Europe's 2015 refugee crisis. *Journal of Ethnic and Migration Studies, 43*, 1749–1774.

Hafez, F. (2015). The refugee crisis and Islamophobia. *Insight Turkey, 17*(4), 19.

Haslam, S. A., & Reicher, S. (2003). Beyond Stanford: Questioning a role-based explanation of tyranny. *Dialogue, 18*, 22–25.

Haslam, S. A., & Reicher, S. D. (2012). Contesting the 'nature' of conformity: What Milgram and Zimbardo's studies really show. *PLoS Biology, 10*(11), e1001426.

Haslam, S. A., Reicher, S. D., & Platow, M. J. (2010). *The new psychology of leadership: Identity, influence and power*. Psychology Press.

Hertwig, R., Gigerenzer, G., & Hoffrage, U. (1997). The reiteration effect in hindsight bias. *Psychological Review, 104*(1), 194.

Hogg, M. A. (2000). Subjective uncertainty reduction through self-categorization: A motivational theory of social identity processes. *European Review of Social Psychology, 11*(1), 223–255.

Hogg, M. A., & Vaughan, G. M. (1995). *Social psychology: An introduction*. London: Harvester Wheatsheaf.

Home Office. (2016, August 25). *National statistics: Asylum*. https://www.gov.uk/government/publications/immigration-statistics-april-to-june-2016/asylum

Innes, A. J. (2010). When the threatened become the threat: The construction of asylum seekers in British media narratives. *International Relations, 24*(4), 456–477.

Islam, M. R., & Hewstone, M. (1993). Dimensions of contact as predictors of intergroup anxiety, perceived out-group variability, and out-group attitude: An integrative model. *Personality and Social Psychology Bulletin, 19*(6), 700–710.

Johnson, J. D., Olivo, N., Gibson, N., Reed, W., & Ashburn-Nardo, L. (2009). Priming media stereotypes reduces support for social welfare policies: The mediating role of empathy. *Personality and Social Psychology Bulletin, 35*(4), 463–476.

Kale, K., & Hart, R. (2017). *Faith will move mountains: A qualitative exploration of veiled British Muslim women's experiences in the UK following the Brexit referendum*.

Kawakami, K., Dovidio, J. F., & Van Kamp, S. (2007). The impact of counterstereotypic training and related correction processes on the application of stereotypes. *Group Processes & Intergroup Relations, 10*(2), 139–156.

Kuppens, T., & Yzerbyt, V. Y. (2014). When are emotions related to group-based appraisals? A comparison between group-based emotions and general group emotions. *Personality and Social Psychology Bulletin, 40*(12), 1574–1588.

L'Engle, K. L., Brown, J. D., & Kenneavy, K. (2006). The mass media are an important context for adolescents' sexual behavior. *Journal of Adolescent Health, 38*(3), 186–192.

Lewin, K. (1939, May). Field Theory and Experiment in Social Psychology. *American Journal of Sociology. 44*(6): 868–896. doi:10.1086/218177

Lido, C. (2003). *The cognitive and behavioural effects of facilitating and inhibiting gender stereotypes*. [Unpublished doctoral dissertation]. University of Sussex.

Lido, C., Brown, R., Calitri, R., & Samson, A. (2005). *The effects of the media priming positive and negative asylum-seeker stereotypes*. Economic and Social Research Council, Swindon, UK.

Looney, S. (2017, April 28). Breaking point? An examination of the politics of othering in Brexit Britain. *TLI Think*.

Mackie, D. M., Devos, T., & Smith, E. R. (2000). Intergroup emotions: Explaining offensive action tendencies in an intergroup context. *Journal of Personality and Social Psychology, 79*(4), 602.

Mackie, D. M., & Smith, E. R. (2017). Group-based emotion in group processes and intergroup relations. *Group Processes & Intergroup Relations, 20*(5), 658–668.

Mahtani, M. (2001). Representing minorities: Canadian media and minority identities. *Canadian Ethnic Studies Journal, 33*(3), 99.

Maitner, A. T., Mackie, D. M., & Smith, E. R. (2006). Evidence for the regulatory function of intergroup emotion: Emotional consequences of implemented or impeded intergroup action tendencies. *Journal of Experimental Social Psychology, 42*(6), 720–728.

Maitner, A. T., Mackie, D. M., & Smith, E. R. (2007). Antecedents and consequences of satisfaction and guilt following ingroup aggression. *Group Processes & Intergroup Relations, 10*(2), 223–237.

Mange, J., Chun, W. Y., Sharvit, K., & Belanger, J. J. (2012). Thinking about Arabs and Muslims makes Americans shoot faster: Effects of category accessibility on aggressive responses in a shooter paradigm. *European Journal of Social Psychology, 42*(5), 552–556. doi:10.1002/ejsp.1883

Manzi, C., Coen, S., Regalia, C., Yévenes, A. M., Giuliani, C., & Vignoles, V. L. (2018). Being in the social: A cross-cultural and cross-generational study on identity processes related to Facebook use. *Computers in Human Behavior, 80*, 81–87.

Markus, H., & Nurius, P. (1986). Possible selves. *American Psychologist, 41*(9), 954.

Maslow, A. H. (1943). A theory of human motivation. *Psychological Review, 50*(4), 370.

Mason, V., & Poynting, S. (2007). The resistible rise of Islamophobia: Anti-Muslim racism in the UK and Australia before 11 September 2001. *Journal of Sociology, 43*(1), 61–86. doi:10.1177/1440783307073935

Mastro, D., & Tukachinsky, R. (2012). The influence of media exposure on the formation, activation, and application of racial/ethnic stereotypes. In E. Scharrer (Ed.), *The International Encyclopedia of Media Studies, Media effects/Media psychology*, Vol. 5. (A. Valdivia, Gen Ed). (pp. 295–315). Boston, MA: Wiley-Blackwell.

Maxwell, S. E., Lau, M. Y., & Howard, G. S. (2015). Is psychology suffering from a replication crisis? What does 'failure to replicate' really mean? *American Psychologist, 70*(6), 487.

McDavid, J. W., & Sistrunk, F. (1964). Personality correlates of two kinds of conforming behavior. *Journal of Personality, 32*(3), 420–435. https://doi.org/10.1111/j.1467-6494.1964.tb01350.x

McHugh-Dillon, H. (2015, April). 'If they are genuine refugees, why?' Public attitude unauthorised arrivals in Australia. Victorian Foundation for Survivors of Torture, Brunswick, Australia.

McLaren, L., & Johnson, M. (2007). Resources, group conflict and symbols: Explaining anti-immigration hostility in Britain. *Political Studies, 55*(4), 709–732.

McQuail, D. (1987). *Mass communication theory: An introduction.* Sage.

Meisner, B. A. (2011). A meta-analysis of positive and negative age stereotype priming effects on behavior among older adults. *Journals of Gerontology Series B: Psychological Sciences and Social Sciences, 67*(1), 13–17.

Micceri, T. (1989). The unicorn, the normal curve, and other improbable creatures. *Psychological Bulletin, 105*(1), 156.

Milgram, S. (1963). Behavioral study of obedience. *Journal of Abnormal and Social Psychology, 67*(4), 371.

Moghaddam, F. M. (2013). *The psychology of dictatorship.* American Psychological Association.

Moons, W. G., Leonard, D. J., Mackie, D. M., & Smith, E. R. (2009). I feel our pain: Antecedents and consequences of emotional self-stereotyping. *Journal of Experimental Social Psychology, 45*(4), 760–769.

Moons, W. G., Chen, J. M., & Mackie, D. M. (2017). Stereotypes: A source of bias in affective and empathic forecasting. *Group Processes & Intergroup Relations, 20*(2), 139–152.

Moskowitz, G. B. (2005). *Social cognition: Understanding self and others.* Guilford.

Moskowitz, G. B. (2012). *The representation and regulation of goals*. In H. Aarts & A. J. Elliot (Eds.), *Frontiers of social psychology. Goal-directed behavior*. (p. 1–47). Psychology Press.

Moskowitz, G. B., Gollwitzer, P. M., Wasel, W., & Schaal, B. (1999). Preconscious control of stereotype activation through chronic egalitarian goals. *Journal of Personality and Social Psychology, 77*, 167–184.

Moskowitz, G. B., & Stone, J. (2012). The proactive control of stereotype activation: Implicit goals to not stereotype. *Zeitschrift für Psychologie, 220*(3), 172–179. doi:10.1027/2151-2604/a000110

Nisbet, R. A. (1973). *The social philosophers: Community and conflict in Western thought*. Crowell.

Norman, G. (2010). Likert scales, levels of measurement and the 'laws' of statistics. *Advances in Health Sciences Education, 15*(5), 625–632.

Oliver, M. B., & Fonash, D. (2002). Race and crime in the news: Whites' identification and misidentification of violent and nonviolent criminal suspects. *Media Psychology, 4*(2), 137–156.

Paasi, A. (2003). Boundaries in a globalizing world. In K. Anderson, M. Domosh, S. Pile, & N. Thrift (Eds.), *Handbook of cultural geography* (pp. 462–472). Sage.

Paasi, A. (2009). The resurgence of the 'region' and 'regional identity': Theoretical perspectives and empirical observations on regional dynamics in Europe. *Review of International Studies, 35*(S1), 121–146.

Paluck, E. L. (2009). Reducing intergroup prejudice and conflict using the media: A field experiment in Rwanda. *Journal of Personality and Social Psychology, 96*(3), 574.

Parkinson, B., Fischer, A. H., & Manstead, A. S. (2005). *Emotion in social relations: Cultural, group, and interpersonal processes*. Psychology Press.

Pedersen, A., & Thomas, E. F. (2013). 'There but for the grace of God go we': Prejudice toward asylum seekers. *Peace and Conflict, 19*(3), 253.

Pennycook, G., & Rand, D. G. (2019). Lazy, not biased: Susceptibility to partisan fake news is better explained by lack of reasoning than by motivated reasoning. *Cognition, 188*, 38–50.

Perdue, C. W., Dovidio, J. F., Gurtman, M. B., & Tyler, R. B. (1990). Us and them: Social categorization and the process of intergroup bias. *Journal of Personality and Social Psychology, 59*(3), 475.

Pettigrew, T. F., & Meertens, R. W. (1995). Subtle and blatant prejudice in Western Europe. *European Journal of Social Psychology, 25*(1), 57–75.

Pettigrew, T. F., & Tropp, L. R. (2008). How does intergroup contact reduce prejudice? Meta-analytic tests of three mediators. *European Journal of Social Psychology, 38*(6), 922–934.

Philo, G., Briant, E., & Donald, P. (2013). *Bad news for refugees*. Pluto Press.

Power, J. G., Murphy, S. T., & Coover, G. (1996). Priming prejudice: How stereotypes and counter-stereotypes influence attribution of responsibility and credibility among ingroups and outgroups. *Human Communication Research, 23*(1), 36–58.

Price, V., Nir, L., & Cappella, J. N. (2006). Normative and informational influences in online political discussions. *Communication Theory, 16*(1), 47–74.

Radvansky, G. A., Copeland, D. E., & von Hippel, W. (2010). Stereotype activation, inhibition, and aging. *Journal of Experimental Social Psychology, 46*(1), 51–60. doi:10.1016/j.jesp.2009.09.010

Ramasubramanian, S. (2007). Media-based strategies to reduce racial stereotypes activated by news stories. *Journalism & Mass Communication Quarterly, 84*(2), 249–264.

Ray, D. G., Mackie, D. M., Rydell, R. J., & Smith, E. R. (2008). Changing categorization of self can change emotions about outgroups. *Journal of Experimental Social Psychology, 44*(4), 1210–1213.

Ray, D. G., Mackie, D. M., & Smith, E. R. (2014). Intergroup emotion: Self-categorization, emotion, and the regulation of intergroup conflict. In C. von Scheve & M. Salmella (Eds.), *Collective emotions: Perspectives from psychology, philosophy, and sociology* (pp. 235–250). Oxford University Press.

Ray, D. G., Mackie, D. M., Smith, E. R., & Terman, A. W. (2012). Discrete emotions elucidate the effects of crossed-categorization on prejudice. *Journal of Experimental Social Psychology, 48*(1), 55–69.

Reuters Institute. (2017). *Digital news report 2017.* https://reutersinstitute.politics.ox.ac.uk/sites/default/files/Digital%20News%20Report%202017%20web_0.pdf

Roskos-Ewoldsen, D. R., Klinger, M. R., & Roskos-Ewoldsen, B. (2007). Media priming: A meta-analysis. In R. W. Preiss, B. M. Gayle, N. Burrell, M. Allen, & J. Bryant (Eds.), *Mass media effects research: Advances through meta-analysis* (pp. 53–80). Routledge.

Rozin, P., & Fallon, A. E. (1987). A perspective on disgust. *Psychological Review, 94*(1), 23.

Rudman, L. A., & Borgida, E. (1995). The afterglow of construct accessibility: The behavioral consequences of priming men to view women as sexual objects. *Journal of Experimental Social Psychology, 31*(6), 493–517.

Salovey, P. (Ed.). (1991). *The psychology of jealousy and envy.* Guilford.

Schemer, C. (2012). The influence of news media on stereotypic attitudes toward immigrants in a political campaign. *Journal of Communication, 62*(5), 739–757. doi:10.1111/j.1460-2466.2012.01672.x

Scherer, K. R., Schorr, A., & Johnstone, T. (Eds.). (2001). *Appraisal processes in emotion: Theory, methods, research.* Oxford University Press.

Schneider, D. J. (2004). *The psychology of stereotyping.* Guilford.

Seger, C. R., Smith, E. R., & Mackie, D. M. (2009). Subtle activation of a social categorization triggers group-level emotions. *Journal of Experimental Social Psychology, 45*(3), 460–467.

Sherif, M. (1948). *An outline of social psychology.* Harper.

Shire, W. (2009). Home. In A. Triulzi & R. McKenzie (Eds.), *Long journeys: African migrants on the road.* Brill.

Shrum, L. J. (2002). Media consumption and perceptions of social reality: Effects and underlying processes. *Media Effects: Advances in Theory and Research, 2,* 69–95.

Sime, D. (2018). *Educating migrant and refugee pupils.* In T. G. K. Bryce, W. M. Humes, A. Kennedy, & D. Gillies (Eds.), *Scottish education.* (pp. 768–779). Edinburgh University Press.

Slater, M. D. (2007). Reinforcing spirals: The mutual influence of media selectivity and media effects and their impact on individual behavior and social identity. *Communication Theory, 17*(3), 281–303.

Smeekes, A., & Verkuyten, M. (2013). Collective self-continuity, group identification and in-group defense. *Journal of Experimental Social Psychology, 49*(6), 984–994.

Smeekes, A., & Verkuyten, M. (2014). When national culture is disrupted: Cultural continuity and resistance to Muslim immigrants. *Group Processes & Intergroup Relations, 17*(1), 45–66.

Smith, E. E. (2000). Neural bases of human working memory. *Current Directions in Psychological Science*, *9*(2), 45–49.

Smith, E. R. (1993). Social identity and social emotions: Toward new conceptualizations of prejudice. In D. M. Mackie & D. L. Hamilton (Eds.), *Affect, cognition and stereotyping* (pp. 297–315). Academic Press.

Smith, E. R. (1999). Affective and cognitive implications of a group becoming a part of the self: New models of prejudice and of the self-concept. In D. Abrams & M. A. Hogg (Eds.), *Social identity and social cognition* (pp. 183–196). Blackwell.

Stangor, C. (2000). *Stereotypes and prejudice: Essential readings*. Psychology Press.

Stephan, W. G., & Finlay, K. (1999). Reducing racial prejudice, discrimination, and stereotyping: Translating research into programs—The role of empathy in improving intergroup relations. *Journal of Social Issues*, *55*(4), 729.

Stephan, W. G., Boniecki, K. A., Ybarra, O., Bettencourt, A., Ervin, K. S., Jackson, L. A., ... & Renfro, C. L. (2002). The role of threats in the racial attitudes of Blacks and Whites. *Personality and Social Psychology Bulletin*, *28*(9), 1242–1254.

Stephan, W. G., Renfro, C. L., Esses, V. M., Stephan, C. W., & Martin, T. (2005). The effects of feeling threatened on attitudes toward immigrants. *International Journal of Intercultural Relations*, *29*(1), 1–19.

Stephan, W. G., & Stephan, C. W. (2000). An integrated threat theory of prejudice. *Reducing prejudice and discrimination*, 23–45.

Tajfel, H., Flament, C., Billig, M., & Bundy, R. (1971). Social categorization and intergorup behavior. *European Journal of Social Psychology*, *1*, 149–178.

Tajfel, H., & Turner, J. C. (1979). An integrative theory of inter-group conflict. In W. G. Austin & S. Worchel (Eds.), *The social psychology of inter-group relations*. (pp. 33–47). Monterey, CA: Brooks/Cole.

Tajfel, H., & Turner, J. (1986). The social identity theory of intergroup behaviour. In S. Worchel & W. G. Austin (Eds.), *Psychology of intergroup relations* (pp. 7–24). Nelson Hall.

Thibodeau, P., & Boroditsky, L. (2011). Metaphors we think with: The role of metaphor in reasoning. *PLoS One*, *6*(2), e16782. doi:10.1371/journal.pone.0016782

Trepte, S., & Loy, L. S. (2017). Social identity theory and self-categorization theory. In P. Rossler (Ed.), *The international encyclopedia of media effects* (pp. 1–13). Wiley-Blackwell.

Triplett, N. (1898). The dynamogenic factors in pacemaking and competition. *American Journal of Psychology*, *9*(4), 507–533.

Trolan, E. J. (2013). The impact of the media on gender inequality within sport. *Social and Behavioral Sciences*, *91*, 215–227.

Turner, J. C. (1982). Towards a cognitive redefinition of the social group. In H. Tajfel (Ed.), *Social identity and intergroup relations* (pp. 15–40). Cambridge University Press.

Turner, J. C., Hogg, M. A., Oakes, P. J., Reicher, S. D., & Wetherell, M. S. (1987). *Rediscovering the social group: A self-categorization theory*. Basil Blackwell.

United Nations High Commissioner for Refugees. (2016, July 16). UNHCR viewpoint: 'Refugee' or 'migrant'—Which is right? http://www.unhcr.org/uk/news/latest/2016/7/55df0e556/unhcr-viewpoint-refugee-migrant-right.html

United Nations High Commissioner for Refugees. (n.d.). Asylum-seekers. http://www.unhcr.org/uk/asylum-seekers.html

Valentino, N. A. (1999). Crime news and the priming of racial attitudes during evaluations of the president. *Public Opinion Quarterly*, *63*, 293–320.

Verhaeghen, P., Aikman, S. N., & Van Gulick, A. E. (2011). Prime and prejudice: Co-occurrence in the culture as a source of automatic stereotype priming. *British Journal of Social Psychology, 50*, 501–518.

Verkuyten, M. (2004). Emotional reactions to and support for immigrant policies: Attributed responsibilities to categories of asylum seekers. *Social Justice Research, 17*(3), 293–314.

Verkuyten, M., Mepham, K., & Kros, M. (2018). Public attitudes towards support for migrants: The importance of perceived voluntary and involuntary migration. *Ethnic and Racial Studies, 41*(5), 901–918.

Vieten, U. M., & Poynting, S. (2016). Contemporary far-right racist populism in Europe. *Journal of Intercultural Studies, 37*(6), 533–540.

Vignoles, V. L. (2011). Identity motives. In S. J. Schwartz, K. Luyckx, & V. L. Vignoles (Eds.), *Handbook of identity theory and research* (pp. 403–432). Springer.

Vignoles, V. L., & Moncaster, N. J. (2007). Identity motives and in-group favouritism: A new approach to individual differences in intergroup discrimination. *British Journal of Social Psychology, 46*, 91–113.

Vignoles, V. L., Regalia, C., Manzi, C., Golledge, J., & Scabini, E. (2006). Beyond self-esteem: Influence of multiple motives on identity construction. *Journal of Personality and Social Psychology, 90*(2), 308.

Wang, P., Yang, Y., Tan, C., Zhao, X., Liu, Y., & Lin, C. (2016). Stereotype activation is unintentional: Behavioural and event-related potentials evidence. *International Journal of Psychology, 51*(2), 156–162. doi:10.1002/ijop.12135

Weiner, B. (2005). Motivation from an attribution perspective and the social psychology of perceived competence. In A. J. Elliot & C. S. Dweck (Eds.), *Handbook of competence and motivation* (pp. 73–84). Guilford.

Wood, T., & Porter, E. (2019). The elusive backfire effect: Mass attitudes' steadfast factual adherence. *Political Behavior, 41*, 135–163.

Zajonc, R. B. (1965). Social facilitation. *Science, 149*(3681), 269–274.

8

Ideology and Culture

Nathalie Van Meurs, Sharon Coen, and Peter Bull

Journalists cannot ignore that they are not operating in a vacuum, immune to environmental influences. 'The social environment—consisting of a specific national setting as well as a certain type of media system—has an influence on journalists' professional ideology, which in turn affects journalists' behaviour' (Ginosar, 2015, p. 290). Moreover, the interpretations of any investigation require a self-awareness in terms of ideological, culturally biased, perspectives. The coronavirus disease 2019 (COVID-19) crisis has highlighted the importance of transparent knowledge sharing across countries and how this may be limited by ideological motivations. In a study of 1,800 journalists across 18 nations, Hanitzsch et al. (2011) concluded that 'traditional western ideals of detachment and being a watchdog of the government flourish among the standards accepted by journalists around the world' (p. 8). But what is 'western' or any cultural influence, and how does one measure it?

Starting with a case study on comparative approaches to media, in this chapter we propose potential theoretical and methodological approaches from the field of cross-cultural psychology that may extend and complement our current understanding of the impact of ideology and culture in journalism. We start by describing extant comparative research on media systems to relate it to ideology and culture. We then suggest that cross-cultural psychology can give both theoretical and methodological contributions to the field and help us design and interpret more effectively studies aimed at understanding the role of ideology and culture in journalism. In order to achieve that, we first define ideology in relation to social psychological research and news values. The chapter then focusses on social identity theory (SIT) (Tajfel, 1981) and explores a specific 'value' within group dynamics— that is, tolerance—as an example. The section on culture reviews the historical conceptualization of this 'system of shared meaning' and how it differs

Nathalie Van Meurs, Sharon Coen, and Peter Bull, *Ideology and Culture* In: *The Psychology of Journalism.* Edited by: Sharon Coen and Peter Bull, Oxford University Press. © Oxford University Press 2021. DOI: 10.1093/oso/9780190935856.003.0008 from ideology. This leads to the development of the importance of cultural values as a 'currency' for measurement in comparative research. As people, organizations, and nations evolve over time, the aim of a cross-cultural psychologist is to compare and contrast across-cultural contexts.

Case Study: Comparing Media Systems in Search for Universality and Specificity in News Practices Throughout the World

Scholars interested in news media and their role in democratic societies now recognize the important role played by culture in influencing the way in which news is provided, accessed, and interpreted by the public. Although the vast majority of studies on news environments generally focus on a single country (Aalberg & Curran, 2012; Hallin, 2015), there is a growing awareness that in order to understand news and journalism, and their role in society, it is important to recognize that these do not exist in isolation and are shaped by the social structures within which they exist (in line with what is suggested by Siebert et al., 1956). From this perspective, comparative research—that is, cross-cultural research within psychology—becomes an important tool. Hallin and Mancini (2019) stress that comparative research allows us to refine our understanding of media and their influence by rendering us more sensitive to universal and culture-specific aspects of news production and provision. In particular, these authors state that 'important aspects of media are assumed to be "natural", or in some cases are not perceived at all' (p. 168).

A comparative approach helps us move away from this perspective and 'denaturalize' our understanding of the phenomenon in which we are interested (e.g., how news media talk about politics) and identify its culture-universal and culture-specific aspects, while also allowing us to 'test hypotheses about the interrelationships among social phenomena' (Hallin & Mancini, 2019, p. 168). Similarly, Tiffen and Gittins (2009) argue that cross-country comparisons allow us to see the phenomenon we are interested in ('ourselves' in the case of reflections concerning one's country) and to 'expand our universe of possibilities' (p. 2). At the same time, they argue that comparative research is the 'social scientists' substitute for the experiment' (p. 2) because it allows researchers to assess differences on factors they cannot really manipulate by comparing countries that differ along those dimensions.

There are, however, important obstacles to conducting comparative research. As Tiffen and Gittins (2009) state, one of the main difficulties is that much of what we understand as culture defies quantification. We offer in this chapter some potential solutions to this issue in the section dedicated to measuring culture. Moreover (and in line with what is discussed later in this chapter), issues of reliability and equivalence of measures are quite significant when trying to draw comparisons between countries. Furthermore, scholars have recognized the dangers of making sweeping generalizations in classifying countries along the Western/non-Western dimension and that this does not account for fundamental differences in the media environment between countries.

Particularly successful in this field in terms of its rigour, systematicity, and influence in the more general field is the model developed by Hallin and Mancini (2004). In their work, Hallin and Mancini were interested in identifying different types of 'media systems' within 'Western' media. A media system is defined by Stonczyk (2009) as

> an internally complex, autonomous entity being part of a greater whole, such as a country, also treated as a system. The media system is comprised of institutional structures and final products which recipients use directly and frequently as they are addressed to them (newspapers, journals, radio and TV programmes), as well as entities (such as press agencies, distributors) with which people are less familiar with but which, nevertheless, are crucial to the functioning of the media system. (p. 1)

Hallin and Mancini (2004) operationalized media systems along four dimensions: the history of the development of the media market, the relationship between the media and the political system (in terms of the extent to which there are clear parallels between the media and the political system in the country), the extent to which journalism is professionalized, and the role of state in regulating media content and outputs. Adopting these criteria, the authors identified three broad models of media systems that could be applied to the 18 countries across Europe and North America considered in their work. First is a liberal model, characterized by a wide development of a media market with a strong dominance of commercial media, relatively (but varied) small political parallels, and a strong tradition of journalistic professionalism. A second model is particularly characteristic of Northern European countries. This model, called democratic corporatist, is characterized by a strong circulation of both commercial and party newspapers, a long tradition of political parallelism between press and political parties, stronger state intervention in the media, and a strong journalistic professionalism. The third model—found more frequently in Mediterranean countries—is the polarized pluralist model, which is characterized by a closer connection of media to political (as opposed to market) forces, a high political parallelism, a relatively interventionist role of the state, and a lower level of journalistic professionalism (Hallin, 2015).

Scholars have drawn on this classification to explore the extent to which the classification of countries along the dimensions identified in these models resulted in differences across countries in the amount and quality of information provided, as well as in patterns of media use, knowledge, and political engagement in the population. For example, a series of studies (Curran et al., 2009, 2012, 2014) were conducted in 4, 6, and 11 nations in which content features of the news (press, television, and websites in the latter study) were considered alongside survey measures on representative samples of the population. In the development and completion of these studies, it was interesting to notice the emergence of many of the issues to be discussed in this chapter.

For example, initially assumptions were made on the universality of the concepts of *hard news* (i.e., that which plays an important role in providing the audience with information that is relevant to their role as citizens in a society) and *soft news* (i.e., information not directly related to citizenry issues). In other words, researchers made the assumption that these labels (hard and soft news) meant the same for everyone. However, this had to be reappraised when, in the first study (Curran et al., 2009), it emerged that, for example, news concerning culture in certain countries was considered hard, whereas in others it was considered soft. After consultation with all researchers and coders involved across the four nations, it was decided that in order to allow for comparison there should have been a multistep classification whereby the topic of the news item had to be combined with the extent to which the item was contextualized within social and/or political debates before it would be classified as hard or soft. Cross-cultural differences emerged throughout the studies and were addressed in a way that recognized different approaches to the issue, while also attempting to collect some information on the culture-universal features of content that we could usefully adopt for comparison.

Hallin and Mancini's (2011) proposed classification overall did find some support in that, by and large, countries with a stronger 'public service' tradition (i.e., democratic corporatist) usually provided higher quality news (in terms of the proportion of hard versus soft news), accompanied by higher levels of knowledge in the citizens, compared to countries that more closely matched the liberal model. However, the studies (in line with Hallin & Mancini, 2011) highlighted how the models can be better understood as broad interpretative frameworks as opposed to rigid classifications. Indeed, Hallin and Mancini (2019) explain how the proposed models do not fit perfectly to any particular country, but they constitute 'ideal types' that can be useful analytical tools to understand the development of *media ecosystems*[1] within and across nations.

At the same time, Hallin and Mancini (2011) acknowledge the fact that media systems are not static but, rather, in constant flux, so although it is useful to have guiding dimensions along which these can be identified and classified, the typologies and classifications derived can and do change across time and space. Moreover, the proposed model seems to be less effective in accounting for media systems as identified by Hallin and Mancini (2011) as 'beyond the Western world'. In subsequent years, there have been attempts to extend the 2004 model, for example, by proposing a classification of six media systems (the Atlantic–Pacific liberal model, the Southern European clientelism model, the Northern European public service model, the Eastern European shock model, the Arab–Asian patriot model, and the Asia–Caribbean command model) (for a detailed explanation of the models and different accounts of media system classification, see Cushion, 2012). In general, cross-national research seems to suggest that in countries in which media have a strong public service mandate and public broadcasting systems, research tends to find better quality news provision and a corresponding higher level of informed and engaged citizenry (Cushion, 2012).

What is important, however, is to query the underlying values that drive such cultural differences and to consider how journalists can delineate their own value-based practice to be aware of the cultural lenses with which they observe the world while not falling into the trap of relativism. In other words, a journalist may want to consider what values drive their

---

[1] We define the term media ecosystems as the combination and interaction between people, information, and technologies within a particular (physical and social) environment.

interest in their work, such as the search for truth, liberalism, entertainment, conservatism, political support, and so on. These values and ideological positions and their correlates with the way we think about—and act within—our social context have been extensively explored in psychology.

The Role of Cross-Cultural Psychology

Psychology is a science that is rooted in Western culture, and its theories and practices have spread widely throughout the world, sometimes without the necessary regard for local cultural circumstances or needs (Berry et al., 2002). Journalism is not dissimilar, and it may serve any field of research to be critical of both from where ideas originated and how they are disseminated. When considering the range of psychological processes affecting journalistic practice in the modern era, it is important to think of the role played by ideology and culture. Indeed, both these concepts have been explored widely in psychology, and this chapter reviews the literature by linking it to journalistic practice. The key message is that because ideology and culture influence the ways in which news is provided, a psychological perspective may help shed light on the processes underpinning media communication. Moreover, whereas ideological thinking is often viewed in a negative light, and the link to culture is easily made, in psychology, cross-cultural theories and methods are important tools to differentiate between universal and subjective norms that explain the thinking and behaviours of groups in specific contexts without prejudice (see Chapter 6 for a discussion of norms and roles in journalism).

As described in Chapter 2, journalism is in flux, with new types of independent media platforms such as MediaPart, De Correspondent, Tortoise, and NewsHero espousing beliefs that are not bound by national borders, launching throughout the world. This kind of entrepreneurial, citizens-of-the-world journalism goes hand in hand with technological developments, with democratic and positive results such as Wikipedia and Bellingcat, but also with negative ones framed as 'surveillance capitalism' (e.g., McNamee, 2019). Deuze (2005) distinguishes micro-level challenges, such as the role of the journalist, from macro-level challenges. The latter he further defines as multiculturalism and new media (social); corporate colonization of the newsroom and media concentration (economic); and localization versus globalization, press freedom, and media law (political). Micro-level and macro-level challenges are linked to individual norms and organizational and national ideologies. Psychology can provide some clarification by delineating values underlying existing differences throughout the world that may cause some of the complexities currently faced by media communication. In other words, a psychological perspective may identify commonalities and differences not only in the structure, forms, and content of news provision (as illustrated in the previously presented case study) but also in how these translate into differences in the ways in which news producers and news recipients construct their profession and the world around them. We argue that ideology and culture play an important role in the construction process and can help bridge the gap between structural differences and professional practice.

Ideology

It is of little surprise that journalism is strongly linked to ideology—readers often know the political leaning of the source they consult for information. Many individual journalists and, moreover, the media companies for which they work are accused of biased reporting by each other, government leaders, and readers. Still, organizations such as the Nieman Foundation in association with Harvard University profess to elevate standards of journalism, and a recent study in the United States claims that there is no 'liberal media bias' in what journalists choose to cover as they aim to avoid ideological bias (Hassell et al., 2020). The key here is to engage in critical thought and to query such studies because, as will become evident later, ideological thinking is closely linked to cultural upbringing, which is deeply embedded in the self and difficult objectively to control.

Ideology in journalism is linked to journalists' vocational devotion and can be defined by how journalists give meaning to their work (Deuze, 2005). In Deuze's view, ideology is 'a collection of values, strategies and formal codes characterising professional journalism and shared more widely by its members' (p. 444). This definition is similar to the way in which psychologists would understand and explore culture. The key element here is the incorporation of aspects of practice, which is noticeably absent in psychological approaches to ideology.

Ideology in mainstream psychological research is often assumed, and rarely defined, perhaps because it is deemed more suitable for sociology or politics. For example, Gordon Allport in *The Nature of Prejudice* (1956) discusses ideologies and research methods to explore their role in prejudice but does not seem to attempt to provide a definition. However, ideology has been defined as a set of persistent and pervasive belief systems (Jost & Amodio, 2012) and mostly explored in political and religious contexts. Hogg and Vaughn (2008) further clarify the relationship, function, and purpose of these beliefs by adding that ideology concerns 'a systematically interrelated set of beliefs whose primary function is explanation. It circumscribes thinking, making it difficult for the holder to escape from its mould' (p. 578). It is interesting to notice the negative slant adopted by the authors with their use of the 'mould' metaphor. This might point to the work of Augoustinos and Walker (1998) and their critique of mainstream social psychology as an approach that has scientifically tried—at least in the case of stereotypes and stereotyping—to disentangle itself from the 'mouldy' study of ideology by focussing on the cognitive aspects of the phenomenon, without taking into account the broader context in which the phenomenon takes place.

As Tajfel (1979) noted in his review of Eysenck and Wilson's (1978) book on ideology, most social psychologists treat ideology as an individual difference variable that is predicted by or can predict other psychological factors, but very few actually consider ideology as a superordinate factor that shapes and informs the (physical and social) environment within which we live, as well as a way in which we interact with and within it (see also Weiss & Miller, 1987). Although there have been attempts (described later) to move away from this approach, we argue that this still applies to a significant portion of the literature. An attempt to provide a psychological definition of ideology that acknowledges its social nature is provided by Homer-Dixon et al. (2013), who define ideology as 'systems of socially shared ideas, beliefs, and values used to understand, justify, or challenge a particular political, economic, or social order' (p. 337). The authors provide a comprehensive review of the ideology literature in the social and political sciences, highlighting the complexity of theoretical and methodological approaches to the study of ideology within psychological and political science.

Within psychology, Homer-Dixon et al. (2013) argue that biological approaches attempt to explain individuals' tendency to adhere to a particular ideology in terms of genetic or neurophysiological factors. Similarly, other researchers, such as Pratto et al. (1994), have examined ideology as a personality type (e.g., in relation to authoritarianism), which implies that it is an unconscious cognitive bias and difficult to eradicate. Within social cognition, researchers have examined the antecedents and consequences of ideology, whereas discursive analysts have viewed ideology as a 'filter' through which we understand and relate to the world, or rather a tool we use in constructing our understanding of reality. Cross-cultural psychologists, as discussed later, alerted psychologists to their own ideological positions in conducting research whereby they imposed certain values on the people they evaluated (e.g., Berry et al., 2002). Not dissimilarly, journalism too is subject to specific values that form a socially desirable journalism culture (see also Chapter 6 on norms and roles). BBC journalist Rajan (2020) argues that journalism has three main functions: to inform a citizenry, to apply scrutiny to power, and to enlighten a culture through the editing of events (making decisions regarding what is newsworthy). This links to cognitive biases such as the availability heuristic—people remember more what they see everywhere, and it colours their version of reality (e.g., Thomas & Peterson, 2018).

Ideology and News Values

Researchers in the area of journalism have explored the ways in which ideology relates to journalists' and audiences' attention to news and events. In the research literature, the criteria adopted by journalists in order to select particular events as newsworthy are often called news values. According to Stuart Hall (1973),

> 'News values' are one of the most opaque structures of meaning in modern society. . . . Journalists speak of 'the news' as if events select themselves. Further, they speak as if which is the 'most significant' news story, and which 'news angles' are most salient are divinely inspired. Yet of the millions of events which occur daily in the world, only a tiny proportion ever become visible as 'potential news stories': and of this proportion, only a small fraction are actually produced as the day's news in the news media. We appear to be dealing, then, with a 'deep structure' whose function as a selective device is un-transparent even to those who professionally most know how to operate it. (p. 181)

News values can be summarized as the set of criteria used by journalists to select news to be covered (see, e.g., O'Neill & Harcup, 2009; Deuze, 2005). It is not surprising, therefore, that ideology can play an important role in shaping news values. If we understand ideology as a set of beliefs used to interpret, understand, and explain reality, then this may have an impact on decisions about what is important and what is not, as well as on our understanding and interpretation of the events (e.g., see Hall, 1973).

Deuze's (2005) work in general illustrates an important point about the complexity of ideology as a structure of beliefs about one's professional identity. Thus, studying ideology does not only mean studying the dimensions along which journalists evaluate an event in order to determine its 'newsworthiness' but also entails considering why those choices are made. In other words, it becomes important to understand how journalists (and their audiences) answer the questions What is journalism? and What values drive news communication? (for a more in-depth discussion, see Chapter 6 and the section on culture later in this chapter).

If we assume that ideology provides a framework on the basis of which we evaluate reality, it becomes apparent how different ideological positions will guide us in the way in which we answer the previously presented questions and how we attend to, perceive, and evaluate events. Thus, in line with literature on motivated cognition (see Chapter 3 on perception and attention), we can expect people who uphold a certain ideology to be motivated to scan the environment differently than people upholding a different ideological position. Moreover, we can expect them to interpret stimuli in the environment differently. For example, it is likely that journalists who report on tragic events (e.g., a shooting of young people at protests, riots, or on street corners by police) or an ongoing crisis (e.g., the war in Syria) have not visited, let alone lived in, such environments, yet they have to report on these events. They can do this, of course, but they must be aware of their ways of viewing the world. The reasoning in this case is similar to that underlying the use of projective tests in therapeutic settings: Human perception of ambiguous/unfamiliar stimuli will be driven by interpretative frameworks in our minds, with ideology being one of these frameworks.

But although ideology is mostly defined in terms of systems of beliefs, it is also important to explore how these beliefs are translated into practice. The behavioural element, in our mind, is an important distinction between studying ideology and studying culture. Culture provides behavioural scripts by which to regulate one's relation with the outside world. Cross-cultural psychology is primarily concerned with the question of whether psychological findings have universal validity and what aspects of thinking and behaving vary across cultures. So, in the case of journalism, a cross-cultural approach will explore similarities and differences in journalistic practices across cultures. Journalists too may want to consider their methods of investigation. As much as they may report on unfamiliar environments, as described previously, they may ask questions that the interviewee does not understand or misinterprets, in a similar manner to the distinction between hard and soft news for the researchers in the case study reported previously. Journalist Luyendijk (2010) cautions journalists against the pressures of speed and word limits, as they do not allow for contextualizing complicated cultural differences (see Chapter 2). In psychology, methods that were viewed as unambiguous were questioned by cross-cultural psychologists for their evident cultural bias. For example, if a psychologist uses the Christmas story to measure children's ability to recall details, is it not unfair to apply this to children in a country in which Christmas is not celebrated? Furthermore, are we comparing apples with oranges if we measure the spatial awareness of two groups when, for example, one group, as Segall and colleagues (1999) described so well, grew up in a 'carpentered world' and the other in round huts in the Kalahari desert? In fact, Ruparelia et al. (2016) argue that the use of tests can have dire consequences for a child or adult, depending on the cultural context, and journalists may need to evaluate their own methods of enquiry:

> Previous research in cross-cultural assessment clearly shows that stimulus unfamiliarity is likely to contribute to poor performance in tests. Reading is yet another example of task that may lead to bias. Some cultures such as the African cultures are largely oral. Therefore children may grow up with very limited access or familiarity to picture books; if requested to participate in this task and they perform poorly, teachers may not be sure if the poor performance reflects their ability levels or their lack of familiarity with the task. (p. 1024)

Culture

In general, psychology adheres to the Platonic assumption sometimes referred to as the principle of 'psychic unity'. This implies that all mental functioning can be attributed to a 'presupposed... processing mechanism inherent ... in human beings, which enables them to think ... experience ... act ... and learn' (Shweder, 1990, p. 4). This mechanism is believed to be fixed and universal because it exists within each individual. However, once one commences to learn, cultural issues come into play, even in cognitive psychology (D. Miller & Prentice, 1994):

> Traditionally, culture was defined behaviourally, in terms of actions, rituals, and customs. One imagined people in a culture; culture (like the group) was something out there. [Researchers] have become to conceive of culture more in cognitive terms, as a [cognitive structure] in people's heads. (p. 451)

Fiske et al. (1998) argue that social psychology cannot ignore culture in its analyses due to the fact that 'basic' psychological processes, such as self-enhancing biases characterizing the self, the 'fundamental attribution error', intrinsic motivation and extrinsic rewards, avoidance of cognitive dissonance, and moral development, 'depend substantially on cultural meanings and practices' (p. 915). They conclude that cultural differences effectively may make psychological generalizations void, or at least applicable only in the region of social research: 'Social psychology must consider the idea that psyche and social relations are culturally contingent' (p. 963). To ignore culture empirically when performing social research and then treat the outcomes as conclusive universal evidence is to omit an essential variable, which subsequently affects the generalizations of the results. Culture is thus a crucial component of the psychology of human behaviour.

However, in order to understand culture as a concept and ensure it is not a tautology, capturing everything, it is necessary to define it in a way that is useful for comparative analysis. The work of Hofstede (e.g., Hofstede, 2001; Hofstede et al., 2010) has been paramount in this context through the identification of six dimensions, whereby cultures can be compared and contrasted. This work is ongoing, and two more dimensions (long-term orientation and indulgence) have been added to the original four (power distance, uncertainty avoidance, individualism, and masculinity).[2] Hofstede's dimension scores (available online) may be used like economic indicators such as gross domestic product (GDP).

The original four dimensions enabled researchers to map cultures and categorize them to facilitate the understanding of differences. For example, North America was found to be highly individualist, just like most of Western Europe and Australia, whereas Guatemala, Ecuador, and Panama were the most collectivist. Furthermore, Greece, Portugal, and Guatemala were the most uncertainty avoidant cultures, whereas Denmark, Jamaica, and Singapore were the least uncertainty avoidant. One conclusion from this brief analysis could be that Guatemala is thus a highly group-oriented country with a need to plan ahead. Hofstede's work has been replicated, adapted, and reviewed to the extent that he is one of the most cited non-American researchers in the field of social sciences (De Volkskrant, 2020). His dimensions have been used to explain phenomena not only in the field of cross-cultural psychology but also in management, economics, and politics.

Like any tool, the Hofstede dimensions are useful up to a point. As mentioned previously, they can be used to compare countries at a macrolevel, much like GDP (wealth) or other economic indices, but one cannot use them to make inferences about individuals. Just because America is a wealthy nation does not mean every American is rich. Similarly, just because America is an individualistic nation does not mean every American holds that value strongly; some may, in fact, be collectivistic. Therefore, the models of cultural values are not suitable for understanding the personal values of individuals.

Furthermore, it must be acknowledged cross-cultural comparative research, of which Hofstede's work is one example, has frequently been

---

[2] As per the official website, Hofstede Insights, the dimensions are defined as follows: Power distance is 'the degree to which the less powerful members of a society accept and expect that power is distributed unequally'. Individualism/collectivism is 'a preference for a loosely-knit social framework in which individuals are expected to take care of only themselves and their immediate families versus a preference for a tightly-knit framework in society in which individuals can expect their relatives or members of a particular in-group to look after them in exchange for unquestioning loyalty'. Masculinity/femininity is 'a preference in society for achievement, heroism, assertiveness, and material rewards for success versus a preference for cooperation, modesty, caring for the weak, and quality of life. Uncertainty avoidance is 'the degree to which the members of a society feel uncomfortable with uncertainty and ambiguity'. Long-term orientation is a preference for 'a pragmatic approach . . . [to] encourage thrift and efforts in modern education as a way to prepare for the future'. Indulgence 'stands for a society that allows relatively free gratification of basic and natural human drives related to enjoying life and having fun' (https://www.hofstede-insights.com/models/national-culture).

criticized (Bull, 2015; McSweeney, 2002). The unit of analysis is the nation state, but cultures may be fragmented across groups and national boundaries. A further criticism is that the research work cannot be effectively implemented in an era of a rapidly changing environment, international convergence, and globalization. Still, the COVID-19 pandemic shows that cultural divergence still exists when it comes to the response to and reporting on this global crisis by governments and the media.

A Brief Historical Reflection

At the onset of the development of cross-cultural psychology as a field, two anthropologists argued that 'in explanatory importance and generality of application it [culture] is comparable to such categories as gravity in physics, disease in medicine, evolution in biology' (Kroeber & Kluckhohn, 1952, p. 3). Organized and cooperative research on cultures started to take shape only in the mid-1960s (Berry, 1969), and (cross-) cultural perspectives became a visible force in psychology both conceptually and methodologically (Lonner, 1999). The main difference between general and (cross-) cultural psychology is that in the latter's 'process of extending the range of variation as far as possible, researchers are confronted with differences in behaviour patterns that fit neither Western "common sense" notions about behaviour nor their formal and almost entirely Western theories' (Lonner & Adamopoulos, 1997, p. 53). A major limitation of social psychological research was that it was conducted in North America, potentially making many of the findings valid for that culture only. However, in order to facilitate more universally valid comparisons, an agreement on its conceptualization as a tool became a much-debated issue.

Culture contains man-made objects (e.g., different types of houses) and social institutions (e.g., marriage), but researchers in cross-cultural psychology focus mainly on the symbolic meaning associated with the artefacts and social institutions and how this is translated into messages between people, which result in certain types of behaviour (Smith & Bond, 1998). Similarly, in the field of journalism, after World War II, it was deemed appropriate to expand value-based notions of journalism beyond the West European and North American region: 'Independent media was understood as integral for the development of democracy . . . it was expected to produce better journalists, organisations, and media systems which were supposed to contribute to the development of democracy'

(Higgins, 2014, p. 2). However, this was not a view supported across the field of journalism, and it may be considered in terms of a distinction between so-called *emic* and *etic* approaches. Whereas an emic approach refers to research conducted from within a social group (from the perspective of the participant/participants), an etic approach refers to research conducted from outside that group (from the perspective of the observer).

In this context, based on the replication of (mainly) North American studies in other countries, Berry (1969) coined the term *imposed etic* with regard to methodologies and/or analyses where one assumes similarity in meaning of the measures (items) across nations. Over time, the so-called imposed etic of a Western type of journalism has been disputed: 'You can't drive at a speed of 100 miles an hour on a rocky road. Likewise, you can't take the media in the West and place them in Ethiopia and expect them to function properly. You need to adjust' (Skjerdal, 2011, p. 44). Now, within journalism that may be viewed as an ideological debate: Are Western journalism norms better than others? Within psychology, it is viewed as a methodological faux pas of general, ethical, and professional conduct.

Thus, imposed etic analyses may be a starting point for comparative research, but in order to avoid making assumptions, it is important to develop measures in an emic fashion to capture the local interpretations of knowledge. Instead, according to Berry (1969), 'ideally each behaviour system should be understood in its own terms; each aspect of behaviour must be viewed in relation to its behaviour setting (ecological, cultural and social background). Failing to do so would be "comparing incomparables"' (p. 122).

Hence, due to the complex nature of measure development in each culture separately, the *derived etic* method was proposed, which involved the extensive use of emic approaches in a number of cultures so that psychological universals may emerge (Berry, 1989, 1999). Because the measures are constructed separately, no metric equivalence is enforced. Any convergence found is an indication of equivalent processes to be used for derived etic generalizations. By moving from emic to derived etic methods, it becomes clear that 'indigenous psychologies, while valuable in their own right, serve an equally important function as useful steps on the way to achieving a universal psychology' (Berry, 1999, p. 10). The derived etic method is important especially because it defines a core difference between general and (cross-) cultural psychology. Furthermore, it unveiled the need for a framework to measure culture, using items that have been universally validated, refraining from relying on nationality as a distinguishing label when examining psychological constructs comparing cultures.

Whereas ideology was defined previously as 'systems of socially shared ideas, beliefs, and values *used to understand, justify, or challenge a particular political, economic, or social order*' (Homer-Dixon et al., 2013, p. 337, emphasis added), culture may be viewed as a system of shared meanings without any purpose per se, although Schwartz (1994) argues that cultural values are guiding principles. People have a culture, just like they have a language, but are part of a group, be it racial, national, or other (Rohner, 1984). The reason some researchers steer clear of cross-cultural research is because the terms culture and society are often used interchangeably, incorporating everything from 'arts' to 'language' and 'habits'. This may confuse developing theories and conducting research: 'Most contemporary theorists of culture . . . agree that one must distinguish the cultural realm . . . from the social realm . . . if we are to unwrap and refine the concept of culture . . . sufficiently to make [it] useful for research' (Rohner, 1984, p. 114). Cross-cultural psychology aims to understand shared systems of belief, but it steers clear from justifying or challenging a specific phenomenon.

When we make an argument or premise, we must be aware of our own perspective. The lenses with which we observe the world and create our hypotheses are not free from biased perceptions. Second, we need to ensure that our methods are cross-culturally valid and not an assumed neutral design (Berry, 1969). Third, we need to ensure that we cross-check our findings to be sure the results are valid across cultures. Finally, when we draw our conclusions, we need to be willing to consider alternative hypotheses.

The focus in cross-cultural psychology is on values because regardless of differences in individual behaviour within national boundaries, there appears to be a deeper level of functions and generalizations that remain constant across cultures (Kagitçibasi & Berry, 1989; Smith, 1997). In order to achieve the first step mentioned previously, one must assess one's own lenses (Smith & Bond, 1998):

> Values are universalistic statements about what we think is desirable or attractive. Values do not ordinarily contain statements about how they are to

be realised. Behaviours are specific actions, which occur in a particular setting at a particular time and the difference between the two can be compared to the etic–emic distinction. (p. 65)

The review provided here may seem archaic, yet only in recent years have
critical voices within the social sciences crept up about imposed theories and methodologies. As discussed in the remainder of this chapter,
within journalism, multicountry studies exploring the role of journalists,
for example, still use nationality as an explanatory factor for differences
observed and do not actually measure the antecedents of variance. The
following section explores cross-cultural psychological considerations in
designing one's research.

Cross-Cultural Psychology as a Methodology

Culture acts as a basis for forming groups and constructing intergroup relations. With this in mind, it is necessary to define the concept of culture
and assess a means of its application to research. Unlike society, culture is
not an entity to which one becomes a member but, rather, a relatively organized system of shared meanings that involves 'the internal constraints
of genetic and cultural transmission and the external constraints of ecological, socioeconomical, historical, and situational contexts, with a range
of distal to proximal effects within each type of constraint' (Bond & Smith,
1996, p. 209).

These internal cultural constraints termed *boundary conditions for behaviour* (Poortinga, 1992, p. 13) 'limit and shape the behavioural expression of the universal process' (Bond & Smith, 1996, p. 209). Thus, unlike
general psychology, (cross-) cultural psychology concerns the notion that
behaviours vary across cultures due to generations of people living in
proximity to each other, sharing and communicating symbolic meanings.
Nations are particular groups with shared symbols, which can be represented by values that act as guiding principles in life that subsequently
affect behaviour.

Media organizations also have a responsibility in how they deal with culture and identity in terms of their reporting. Depending on the status of
a cultural group, certain values (e.g., security and uncertainty avoidance)
will be more important to a group when it is under threat or when the nation is in political turmoil. If this difference in status pertains to different
cultural groups within a nation, conflict arises and requires management.

Furthermore, when group cultures within a nation differ on one particular aspect in terms of their values, and this, rather than the similarity, is constantly highlighted, the divide may continue to grow. For example, this can result in amplified dissonance of faith and feelings about homosexuality or gender about which the media either warns the community (e.g., Carlo, 2019) or causes to flare up (e.g., Bracchi, 2019). In the United Kingdom, for example, underneath the blanket of the overarching national identity (e.g., British), there are other, non-passported groups that are continuously confronted with their differing to the perceived national norm (e.g., Muslim). Chapter 7 explores these processes in more detail.

For the purpose of the current chapter, it suffices to consider that people, media, and government have a power and responsibility to maintain the psychological peace of a nation collectively. Still, defining people in the media or in government speeches by their social identity or ideology simplifies a complex issue. Furthermore, when politicians and their supportive media claim socially desirable values as their own, or even when tax money is spent on researching relationships between culture, values, and behaviour as part of policymakers' agendas, it may be time for cross-cultural researchers to step in.

Groupthink is also important when considering SIT (e.g., Tajfel, 1981) and how our behaviour is determined by the social identities we have, which vary in salience depending on the context. SIT includes three key elements: (1) the psychological analysis of the cognitive–motivational processes producing a need for positive social identity, (2) the elaboration of this analysis in its application to real-world intergroup relationships, and (3) the hypothesis of an interpersonal–intergroup continuum (Tajfel, 1981, 1982; Hogg, 2001; see also Chapter 7, this volume). The media has a powerful hand in creating 'teams' that each have their say from their own corner. The phenomenon of the 'minimal group paradigm' (us versus them) in social psychology explains how easy it is to create divisive feelings among people by simply assigning them to meaningless so-called minimal groups—for example, people who prefer a painting by Klee versus those who prefer a painting by Kandinsky (Tajfel, 1970). In essence, in order for there to be favouritism toward one's own group and prejudice against another group, simply belonging to a group may suffice.

If this theory is accepted, then fitting in for someone may be far more basic than we think. Asking about value congruence—Are you with us or against us?—may activate this sense of belonging or, in fact, wanting to rebel. It highlights the importance of misfit, in the sense of whose side one is on. The media can also use a celebrity's or figurehead's actions as an example of socially undesirable behaviour as a way to fuel underlying racial or immigrant tensions. In Britain, the continuous disparagement of Meghan Markle in comparison to Kate Middleton[3] is a prime example (as analysed by Duncan & Bindman, 2020). The consequences for journalism that is steeped in ethnocentrism, racism, or stereotyping may be that reporters are viewed as entertainers or gossip columnists and no longer as professional, detached purveyors of truth. Humphreys (2020) of the *Irish Times*, in a discussion with Rolf Dobelli [the Swiss author of *The Art of Thinking Clearly* (2013)], called for turning off the news but acknowledged that the 'entertainment' culture is systemic and individual journalists are frustrated.

A refinement of SIT led to the development of self-categorization theory (SCT), through which the conceptualization of personal and social identity as a bipolar continuum was replaced by the notion that these identities represent different levels (of inclusiveness) of self-categorization (Turner, 1987). This theoretical development thus shifted the predominant focus on the person–group dichotomy toward a more refined investigation of both the person and the group. According to SCT, categorizations of the self are formed by the cognitive processes, behaviours, and emotions of the self (Turner, 1987). Group identity enables the emergent group processes and products of social life, whereas the personal identity functions as the conduit by which these group processes, relations, and products mediate human cognition (Turner et al., 1994). From the perspective of SCT, culture was not perceived as an expression of behaviour (e.g., the arts) but, rather, as a group identity to which one can belong.

Much of the SCT work in relation to the self and the collective with regard to culture was based on Markus and Kitayama's (1991) independent versus interdependent self, which has been linked back to Hofstede's concepts of individualism and collectivism (e.g., Hofstede, 2001; Hofstede et al., 2010). Research has shown that the concept of the self contributes to that which we know as culture (e.g., Adamopoulos & Kashima, 1999). It is reasonable to assume that the way structures are construed in one cultural setting would differ from the way they are construed in another. Hence,

---

[3] Spouses of Prince Harry and Prince William, respectively, who are the sons of Prince Charles, the next in line for the British Monarchy. Meghan Markle is a dual-heritage Afro-American, who as such was the target of a campaign of sustained disparagement from the British press.

through the processes of social categorization theory, that which is considered beneficial to one particular in-group may not be perceived as such in another due to cultural differences. It may be that for a group of journalists in a certain national context—for example, Pakistan—their faith and nationality are important drivers in their professional role (e.g., Pintak & Nazir, 2013). The national as well as the faith culture may be defined by group belonging (i.e., collectivist) as opposed to working independently (i.e., driven by individualist norms) (e.g., Islam, 2004). The challenge for a journalism scholar, however, is to link the two: What norms have predictive validity with regard to specific behaviours?

This can be complex. In a 13-nation study that explored the impact of national-level uncertainty on organizations and individual employees, Fischer et al. (2019) found that in countries in which people perceived the national situation to be uncertain, employees would engage in more collaborative behaviour (helping others and voicing ideas) if the organizations had plans and procedures in place (formalization). According to conventional organizational psychology theory, in our complex, global environment, organizations would do better to be organic and flexible and to avoid bureaucracy; however, that theory was developed at a time when the United States was relatively stable.

Similarly, then, depending on the national context of where journalism is practised, news media organizations may have to decide what organizational approach to embrace in order for individual journalists to engage in behaviour that is conducive to the aims of the profession, be it reporting facts, campaigning, or making money, depending on the state of the nation. This links back to Deuze's (2005) work: What level of culture is of influence in which way if we review journalism as a vocation, driven by certain norms? In other words, there is a global culture of journalism that is bound by national norms related to freedom of speech, for example, and by journalists' individual cultural values.

For example, some generally accepted psychological findings need a more nuanced perspective. For instance, Asch's (1956) famous experiment on 'conformity' found that 67% of the respondents went along with the opinion of a group that deliberately gives the wrong answer. Replications show that people outside of Europe and America are 'guilty' of this more often (and so, theoretically, do not think for themselves) and that this may be due to the importance of collectivistic values that prompt normative behaviour (e.g., avoiding loss of face) as being more important than being correct (Bond & Smith, 1996). This does not invalidate Asch's findings about group conformity, but it does affect the interpretation of whether conformity is desirable or not (in that specific context).

Finding out the Why

Research in journalism often uses multicountry designs to ensure incorporation of various 'cultures' when exploring the role of journalists and how they practise. Ginosar (2015) juxtaposes patriotic journalism, biased toward the nation (e.g., during the Vietnam War or after the September, 11, 2001, terrorist attack in the United States) with a type that is not so much 'liberal' or 'Western' as it is focussed on 'global patriotism', where 'journalists take a normative position in favour of universal values; they prefer expressing solidarity with the whole human society rather than with their own national or ethnic community' (p. 295). Ginosar concludes that a journalist needs to consider their stance to balance their personal and professional values (see also Chapter 6, this volume).

As mentioned previously, Hanitzsch et al. (2011) found universals, in that surveyed journalists throughout the world agreed that 'reliability and factualness of information as well as the strict adherence to impartiality and neutrality belong to the highly esteemed professional standards of journalism' (pp. 286–287). This means that the beliefs in detachment and to be a watchdog of governments was found to be present across countries and across different types of media, media ownership, in people working for national versus local media, and independently from editorial ranks. Hanitzsch et al. thus found similarities across cultures in terms of role perception, but they also observed distinct cultural differences in terms of normative orientations with regard to the acceptance of harmful consequences. In order to explain cultural differences in relation to journalism's institutional roles, Hanitzsch et al. focussed not on interventionism and market orientation as explanations but, rather, on what they termed *power distance*. Although this is the same term as that used by Hofstede (Hofstede, 2001; Hofstede et al., 2010), it is defined differently; Hanitzsch et al. define power distance as

> the journalist's position towards loci of power in society. The adversary pole
> of the continuum captures a kind of journalism that, in its capacity as the
> 'Fourth Estate', openly challenges those in power. 'Loyal' or opportunist

journalists, on the other hand, tend to see themselves more in a collabora-tive role, as 'partners' of the ruling elites in political processes. (p. 3)

This role in society is linked to the values and norms that drive the news source (e.g., newspapers and television). The 18-nation study by Hanitzsch et al. also identified cultural variation with regard to inter-ventionist aspects of journalism, which they connect to subjectivity and objectivism.

Although Hanitzsch et al. (2011) do not mention it, there seems to be a fault line between journalists from different cultures with regard to rule-based versus consequence-based decision-making, in terms of whether harm is (n)ever justifiable.[4] Hanitzsch et al. link this to a key divide: jour-nalists who favour a subjective reasoning about ethical dilemmas and those who prefer a situational approach (p. 15). The authors argue that although developing nations are playing catch-up, and in some countries journalists are in genuine danger if they report against the sitting govern-ment, the old bastions of objectivity are also changing. They give as an example the national context of the United States, now no longer viewed as a prime example of objective journalism. Still, they acknowledge that cultural differences are not clear-cut and only occur to a degree and that any proposal that journalism culture can be divided as 'the West and the rest' is denying within-group variation.

There are examples of studies that explore the underlying, ideological reasons for cultural differences. In their seven-nation survey of jour-nalism students, Mellado et al. (2013) argued that

in line with assumptions about the increasing consumer-orientation in Western developed societies, students from Australia, Switzerland, and the United States favour addressing audiences as consumers, while still living up to their respective countries' traditions of watchdog journalism despite the finding that US journalism students do not display that much support for it. Chilean and Brazilian students show strong support for the watchdog

---

[4] If the aim of journalism is to work toward a democratic framework of universally desirable prac-tices, an obvious difficulty with rule-based normative approaches is achieving wide consensus on which rules (whose values) this will be based. The Organisation for Economic Co-operation and Development (OECD) publicizes policies and principles that member governments agree to take to their national legislative governing bodies for approval and implementation. The OECD website also features articles for journalists on protection and their role to combat corruption, among others (http://www.oecd.org).

role as well as for addressing audiences as citizens, both traditional ideals associated with Western journalism. The reason for this strong support arguably lies in the recent history of democratization in both countries and corresponding notions of journalism's role in supporting this process. Mexico and Spain similarly support a citizen-orientation, but both display much less support for watchdog journalism, again, it was argued, due to specific national contexts. (p. 15)

In another example, Zhong (2008) presented several ethical scenarios to American and Chinese journalism students and found similarities in the way in which they defined journalistic values and norms. Chinese students, contrary to expectations, also did not prioritize the views of the editor over and above colleagues' views. Moreover, the American students thought more about the needs of the organization, which, the author argued, is unexpected for an individualistic culture. However, Chinese students did consult others more when deciding on ethical dilemmas, which Zhong linked to collectivism. The author concluded that

the differences detected in this study should be introduced to students for a greater understanding of the ethical decisions by their colleagues from different cultures. This may help them appreciate the concept of the 'global journalist' and the media globalization as a whole. (p. 120)

Although Zhong (2008) and other researchers cited previously support a cross-cultural psychology approach, a critical point is paramount here. Mellado et al. (2013), Zhong (2008), and Hanitzsch et al. (2011) did not measure *why* they found cultural differences and thus did not use a cross-cultural *methodology*. Journalism research may need to incorporate value measures to acquire data that explain variations in comparative studies.

How to Measure Culture
Initially, the introduction of values as a currency to measure cultural profiles was welcomed as an alternative to the mere categorization by group (e.g., nationality, ethnic group, or socioeconomic status). Researchers who compare national groups have been criticized for using nations in the same way as sex (male/female) is used as a variable—that is, without measuring the level of 'Britishness' or 'Chineseness'—although it is now noted that sex and gender are equally nonbinary and, if relevant for the

hypothesis, should be measured on a Likert scale. Furthermore, criticism levelled at country-level cross-cultural research focussed on its treatment of culture like another macroeconomic index, such as GDP, because the within-nation differences may be larger than the between-nation differences, depending on which dependent variable is explored [e.g., see Graham et al. (2016) on morality]. Still, Hofstede (1980) argues that although within-nation variety exists, ultimately citizens are subject to the political, legal, economic, and social system of a country. There are values and norms particular to being a citizen of a certain country.

As mentioned previously, in order to make valid cross-cultural comparisons, it is necessary to have a measure of culture that can be used universally and will not result in researchers (and others) making tautological inferences. 'One cannot describe the cultural profile of a sample of respondents until an agreed set of concepts and measures is available for the purpose' (Smith & Bond, 1998, p. 40). A key issue here, however, is that the meaning of the value must be agreed upon before establishing levels of endorsement. The meaning of values is a precarious issue: Researchers have explored the existence of a cross-cultural equivalence in meaning because the use of any value becomes ambiguous and meaningless without this (e.g., Schwartz & Sagie, 2000).

It may appear that research on culture is supportive of the ideological idea that value consensus is the way forward to a peaceful society; however, the main premise of cross-cultural psychologists is that no one value is preferable over another. It is just a value; thus, culture can be perceived as positive or negative, depending on one's ideological beliefs. For example, 'tolerance' is a much used, socially desirable value. A noble cry for a need for tolerance may obtain the agreement from many of us who hear it initially. Yet, tolerance as a value can be interpreted in at least two different ways, possibly explaining why its political usage is so attractive. Tolerance can indicate a power relationship, with those who tolerate as the more powerful. For instance, to say 'I will tolerate you' at a personal level reflects this power difference clearly. Yet, it seems an acceptable rhetoric at the national level, even if the meaning is the same and is not, as also commonly thought, an issue of liberalism. Wemyss (2006) argues that tolerance is not a positive national aspiration as it is in fact 'the conditional withholding of force by those at the top of a "hierarchy of belonging"' (p. 215).

Of course, tolerance also indicates acceptance and benevolence for the greater good, which, throughout the years, has become synonymized with a social and liberal political view. Thus, using the word 'tolerance' can be indicative of an implied power relationship as much as it is supportive of the idea of a multicultural society. The meaning of any espoused value is a complex issue, which is a function of history, language, and the current socioeconomic status of the community, among others. Cross-cultural researchers have done extensive research in finding value dimensions with universal meaning (e.g., Schwartz, 1994; House et al., 2002), and their findings show that most people throughout the world value security, happiness, and benevolence, which is neither an ideological mould nor a Western gospel.

In order to apply culture as a variable in research, it was necessary to define a framework that is universal and organized in such a way that it is applicable to most countries but simple enough for interpretation and ease of use. Hofstede's dimensions (Hofstede, 2001; Hofstede et al., 2010) are a useful tool but only work at the national or macro level.

As the most quoted researcher in economics, Hofstede put a forcible mark on the map of cultural research (Hofstede, 2001; Hofstede et al., 2010). However, since Hofstede's work, it has been acknowledged that non-Western values need to be included to yield a more universal measure. Furthermore, differentiation between culture level and individual level was required because societal phenomena cannot explain individual-level behaviour and vice versa.

A more robust and reliable method to measure culture for individuals, somewhat like a personality profile, was devised by Schwartz (the Value Survey; Schwartz, 1992, 1994). He presented a tightly argued theoretical basis for a universal structure of individual values, supported by data from more than 60 nations, proposing that values are organized according to a circumplex model. For example, the values of self-enhancement (i.e., the extent to which one values individual goals and one's status within society, including the value categories of power and achievement) are opposed to self-transcendence (i.e., the extent to which one values things that benefit the collective above the single individual's interest, including the value categories of benevolence and universalism). Values and conservation (i.e., the extent to which one values the preservation of the status quo, including the value categories of security, conformity, and tradition) are opposed to openness to change (i.e., the extent to which one values the challenge of the status quo, including the value categories of self-direction, stimulation, and hedonism). Measures of these values can be used to determine the dominant guiding principles of an individual's behaviour.

Schwartz (1996) linked these values to, for instance, interpersonal co-operation and preference for out-group contact by correlating values with the type of choice one would make during a version of the prisoner's dilemma[5] negotiation game (Luce & Raiffa, 1957) and with the type of contact in which people in intergroup conflict would be willing to engage. Results showed that respondents endorsing conservation values would engage in noncooperative behaviour and were less ready for social contact with an out-group, whereas those endorsing openness to change values would opt for cooperative behaviour and were more ready for out-group contact. Schwartz's values profile may be used to explore a person's cultural profile.

At a macro level, the Hofstede framework (or later variations and augmentations thereof) suffices (Hofstede, 2001; Hofstede et al., 2010). Consider again the example of journalism in Pakistan mentioned previously. One of the most studied dichotomies in cultural studies is that between individualistic and collectivistic cultures (e.g., Triandis, 1988). The main difference between individualistic and collectivistic cultures seems to be the emphasis that is given in the definition of an individual on their personal goals, choices, and achievements rather than on the set of groups and collective organizations to which the individual belongs (e.g., Markus & Kitayama, 1991). One of the major factors that differentiate individualism and collectivism is the relative importance of the in-group. Individualists have many specific in-groups that may influence behaviour in any particular social situation. Because there are many, they exert little influence on behaviour.

For journalism scholars, the relationship of values with communication is particularly important. According to Ting-Toomey (1999), the communication process in individualistic cultures focusses on inter-individual levels, whereas collective cultures focus on the group base [whether you are in-group (one of us), or out-group (one of them)]. Ting-Toomey argues that this results in individualistic people tending to be verbally direct: They value communication straightforwardness and like to be direct,

---

[5] The prisoner's dilemma is a game utilized in game theory that concerns two players, both suspects in a crime. The dilemma faced by the prisoners is that each is better off confessing rather than remaining silent, but if both confess, then the outcome is worse than the outcome they would have obtained if both remained silent.

whereas in collectivistic group–oriented cultures, indirect communication is preferred because group harmony is essential. For example, it is rare in Asian cultures to have open conflict within the in-group because it appears to disrupt group harmony. However, collectivists are more stringent in treating the in-group differently from the out-group (Triandis, 1988). The fundamental difference in interaction behaviour between collectivists and individualists is thus a concern for harmony, whereby collectivists are more concerned with maintaining harmony, particularly with in-group members, than are individualists (e.g., Brown & Levinson, 1987; Ting-Toomey, 1999).

This may explain why it is a surprise to some Western governments, media, and people that foreign intervention is not welcomed, even if the leadership is corrupt or oppressive. The outraged Iraqi reaction to the Americans' capture of Iraq's former leader (the dictator Saddam Hussein) during the Iraq War of 2003 is an interesting example. If through military action a foreign government engages in 'freeing a nation', this may rid a people of perceived oppression, but it may cause unrest or outrage at the interference. Moreover, one must be 'seen' to protest, to be faithful to the in-group. If even it is welcomed, it still strips a population from one particular social identity, allowing others to rise to the surface; the complexity of post-colonialism is a case in point. Cultural groups (be they national, team, or religious) are socially constructed and have value systems that are created through communication, artefacts, and a general way of life. Because value systems usually change slowly and often from within the group, a quick fix value change is unlikely to succeed; any intervention in another state's affairs is a strong case in point.

Note, however, that such correlations are complicated. Simplistic bipolar or even orthogonal dimensions give us some insight, but more often than not, the research needs deeper analysis. For example, in a study comparing seven nations regarding the link between individualism/collectivism and orientations toward authority, the results showed that 'vertical' (hierarchical) individualism and collectivism (I/C) was linked to authoritarianism but 'horizontal' I/C was not, unless it concerned former Soviet states (Kemmelmeier et al., 2003).

As another example, in an essay on the return of ideology to China's journalism education, Xu (2018), a scholar resident in Australia (and therefore, presumably, with freedom of press), notes that China's leader Xi launched an ideological campaign to curb the perceived pernicious influence of Western values and to seek ideological consistency. This thinking, the author argues, also reflects 'collectivism'—to put the interest of the group before oneself and to align with the group norm. Yet, Xu acknowledges, 'the adherence to party ideology by educators and students appears to be more on the surface than in substance' (p. 8). Such debates require more data to know and understand the nuances of cultural differences. Theoretically, differences may be explained by I/C, but this needs to be measured, preferably using a framework that taps into the cultural specifications of the sample, while being aware of one's own current situation, employment context, and adherence to (vocational) ideology.

Implications for Journalistic Communication

The number of interactions between people from different cultures has greatly increased due to the increase in world population and advances in technology. The fact that technological developments and the world population have grown at an exponential rate implies that related aspects, such as the number of personal interactions, have also increased in frequency, even despite the COVID-19 crisis rendering such interactions online. This, of course, is paramount to journalism. Carey (2008) argues that 'the ritual view of communication' is not so much about the transmission but about the representation of shared beliefs, whereby reality is produced, maintained, and transformed. Zelizer (2004) adds that journalists are then the spokespeople for events in the public domain, and they maintain their cultural authority through this ritual way of communication.

More generally, communication between people varies on a number of contextual dimensions: the length, the nature of the relationships between people, the topic, and the way people speak, among others. Argyle (1982) states,

> Difficulties of social interaction and communication arise in several main areas: (1) language use, including forms of polite usage; (2) non-verbal communication: uses of facial expressions, gesture proximity, touch, etc.; (3) rules of social situations, e.g., for bribing, gifts and eating; (4) social relationships, within the family, at work, between members of different groups; (5) motivation, e.g., achievement motivation and for face-saving; (6) concepts and ideology, e.g., ideas derived from religion and politics. (p. 76)

Added to this, of course, are the exponential advances within information technology, artificial intelligence, and (social) media, but also the changes with regard to advertising revenue (and also how it has transferred to Facebook and Google), which have changed the journalism landscape in terms of business models and how journalists fulfil their role. Therefore, developing competence in everyday use of effective verbal and nonverbal codes can be a major challenge to intercultural communicators, including the professional media (see Chapter 2).

The culture of a person influences communication style; however, to an equal degree, 'communication behaviour is the primary vehicle for the active creation and maintenance of cultures' (Davenport Sypher et al., 1985, p. 17). As Gudykunst (1998) notes,

> The relationship between culture and communication . . . is reciprocal. . . . Understanding communication on any culture . . . requires culture general information (i.e., where the culture falls on the various dimensions of cultural variability) and culture specific information (i.e., the specific cultural constructs associated with the dimension of cultural variability). (pp. 44–45)

For example, two cultures can both be qualified as 'collectivist', but one may emphasize the family, whereas the other may focus on groups that are not family related (e.g., professional groups, those associated with hobbies, and political groups) (Gudykunst, 1998). Again, as noted previously, one is related to hierarchy and status, whereas in another form it is related to equality (Singelis et al., 1995). Communication between people can be regarded as the user interface or front end of culture, which, according to Hofstede (1991), is 'the software of the mind' (p. 4). Cultures can be viewed as dynamic, meaning systems, and people help construct their culture through the communication and negotiation of meanings of their experiences (van Meurs & Spencer-Oatey, 2010). Through increased interaction between people from different cultures, cultural universals and differences as a focus of psychological research have develop quickly: 'In the West, the crisis of confidence in Western media has created confusion in media assistance. The traditional business model in newspapers and broadcasting in the West no longer seems to be working' (Higgins, 2014, p. 9).

People use sociological, psychological, and cultural information to make predictions of their communication behaviours—that is, they 'choose among various communicative strategies on the basis of the predictions about how the person receiving the message will respond' (G. Miller & Steinberg, 1975, p. 7). Sociological information helps predict behaviour in an intracultural context, as it involves group membership such as gender or social class and roles such as student or journalist. Similarly, intercultural information provides the person with some clues to their likely responses based on common knowledge about the person's culture or knowledge acquired during the interaction (G. Miller & Sunnafrank, 1982):

> Knowledge about another person's culture—its language, beliefs, and prevailing ideology—often permits predictions of the person's probable response to messages. . . . Upon first encountering . . . [another person], cultural information provides the only grounds for communicative predictions. (p. 226)

Psychological information involves personal knowledge of the person with whom one is communicating. However, it is impossible to get to know each person we communicate with well; therefore, people rely mostly on cultural and sociological information during interactions (G. Miller & Steinberg, 1975). This can be complex, as Van Meurs and Spencer-Oatey (2010) argue: Communication, culture, and conflict are like the Bermuda Triangle.[6] As much as globalization is a fact, and we may all seem to be citizens of the world, recent research shows that, for example, language barriers affect international teams in that language diversity is perceived to imply deep-level cultural differences (Tenzer et al., 2014).

In an extensive review of intercultural communication research, Ting-Toomey and Dorjee (2017) conclude that

> more and more individuals in the global world have mosaic oppositional or compatible cultural identities . . . the more . . . researchers attune to the dynamic interplay of multiple sociocultural identity and personal identity issues within hybrid individuals (and in conjunction with situational dynamic issues), the more likely we can catch up to the cultural frame-switching cognition and emotion that drive such individuals to form and shape their close relationships. (p. 168)

---

[6] The Bermuda Triangle is a geographical location between Bermuda, Florida, and Puerto Rico in the North Atlantic Ocean that is well known because ships supposedly disappear under mysterious circumstances.

If the art of communication is your business, then it pays to know what drives people to buy into your media delivery. Moreover, if the buying public does not want to be the product, then they too have the responsibility to support a different kind of culture-aware, investigative journalism (e.g., Humphreys, 2020).

Conclusion

In many respects, social groups are the outcome of history and specific circumstances. However, they are sustained by human volition, and the media has a powerful role in this. We need to become aware of the perspective that we ourselves are not normal or the norm, and the other is not the problem for being different, as they see themselves as normal. This does not legitimize relativism; the previous review shows that a simple 'when in Rome do as the Romans do' approach does not suffice, and a culturally intelligent approach is to ensure journalists focus on investigating facts while being aware that there is no 'absolute truth'. For example, there are scientific facts about climate change, and 'alternative facts' in this scenario can be equated to opinions with dangerous consequences. This also highlights the responsibility of media organizations and why new media platforms have been gaining momentum. In summary, a 'Western' (or any ideological) approach to journalism is not a neutral norm to which others need to adhere. Journalists can keep themselves and each other in check by questioning the approach taken to a story and identifying the lens they employ. Second, diverse recruitment within media organizations is key, not just in terms of ethnic, gender, or national backgrounds but also in terms of value profiles. There is no one nation that holds the gold standard for journalism and can be used as a reference point for all others. In other words, there is no such thing as Greenwich Mean Time[7] journalism.

References

Aalberg, T., & Curran, J. (Eds.). (2012). How media inform democracy: Central debates. In *How media inform democracy* (pp. 3–14). Routledge.

[7] Greenwich Mean Time is the clock time at the Royal Observatory Greenwich; it has been widely used as an international standard time.

Adamopoulos, J., & Kashima, Y. (Eds.). (1999). *Cross-cultural psychology series: Social psychology and cultural context*. Sage. doi:10.4135/9781452220550

Allport, G. (1956). *The nature of prejudice*. Harvard University Press.

Argyle, M. (1982). Inter-cultural communication. In S. Bochner (Ed.), *International series in experimental social psychology, Vol. 1: Cultures in contact: Studies in cross-cultural interaction* (pp. 61–80). Pergamon.

Augoustinos, M., & Walker, I. (1998). The construction of stereotypes within social psychology. From social cognition to ideology. *Theory & Psychology, 8*(5), 629–652.

Berry, J. W. (1969). On cross-cultural comparability. *International Journal of Psychology, 4*(2), 119–128. doi:10.1080/00207596908247261

Berry, J. W. (1989). Psychology of acculturation. In R. A. Dientsbier & J. J. Berman (Eds.), *Nebraska Symposium on Motivation Vol. 38: Perspectives on motivation* (pp. 201–234). University of Nebraska Press.

Berry, J. W. (1999). Subjective culture as a research tradition. In J. Adamopoulos & Y. Kashima (Eds.), *Cross-cultural psychology series: Social psychology and cultural context* (pp. 7–15). Sage.

Berry, J. W., Poortinga, Y. H., Segall, M. H., & Dasen, P. R. (2002). *Cross-cultural psychology: Research and applications* (2nd ed.). Cambridge University Press.

Bond, M. H., & Smith, P. B. (1996). Cross-cultural social and organisational psychology. *Annual Review of Psychology, 47*, 205–235.

Bracchi, P. (2019). *Across the country, fundamentalist Muslims are protesting over LGBT lessons in class*. Retrieved January 2020 from https://www.dailymail.co.uk/news/article-7089099/Across-country-fundamentalist-Muslims-protesting-LGBT-lessons-class.html

Brown, P., & Levinson, S. (Eds.). (1987). *Politeness: Some universals in language use*. Cambridge University Press.

Bull, P. (2015). Collectivism and individualism in political speeches from the UK, Japan and the USA: A cross-cultural analysis. *Politics, Culture & Socialisation, 6*(1–2), 71–84.

Carey, J. W. (2008). *Communication as culture: Essays on media and society* (rev. ed.). Routledge.

Carlo, A. (2019). *The far right paint Muslims as the enemy of the LGBT+ community—but they are the real danger*. Retrieved January 2020 from https://www.independent.co.uk/voices/farright-lgbt-muslims-christchurch-shooter-salvini-le-pen-a8846031.html

Curran, J., Coen, S., Aalberg, T., & Iyengar, S. (2012). News content, media consumption, and current affairs knowledge. In T. Aalberg & J. Curran (Eds.), *How media inform democracy* (pp. 81–96). Routledge.

Curran, J., Coen, S., Soroka, S., Aalberg, T., Hayashi, K., Hichy, Z., Hichy, Z., Iyengar, S., Jones, P., Mazzoleni, G., Papathanassopoulos, S., Rhee, J. W., Rojas, H., Rowe, D., & Tiffen, R. (2014). Reconsidering 'virtuous circle' and 'media malaise' theories of the media: An 11-nation study. *Journalism, 15*(7), 815–833.

Curran, J., Iyengar, S., Brink Lund, A., & Salovaara-Moring, I. (2009). Media system, public knowledge and democracy: A comparative study. *European Journal of Communication, 24*(1), 5–26.

Davenport Sypher, B., Applegate, J. L., & Sypher, H. E. (1985). Culture and communication in organizational contexts. In W. B. Gudykunst, L. Stewart, & S. Ting-Toomey (Eds.), *Communication, culture, and organizational processes* (pp. 13–29). Sage.

Deuze, M. (2005). What is journalism? Professional identity and ideology of journalists reconsidered. *Journalism, 6*(4), 442–464.

De Volkskrant (2020). Geert Hofstede meest geciteerde Nederlander onder Europese Sociale Wetenschappers. Retrieved 28 April 2021 from https://www.volkskrant.nl/mensen/geert-hofstede-meest-geciteerde-nederlander-onder-europese-sociale-wetenschappers-onze-cultuur-is-extreem-feminien~bf20de97/?referrer=https%3A%2F%2Ft.co%2F

Dixon, T., Leader Maynard, J., Mildenberger, M., Milkoreit, M., Mock, S., Quilley, S., Schroder, T., & Thagard, P. (2013). A complex systems approach to the study of ideology: Cognitive affective structures and the dynamics of belief systems. *Journal of Social and Political Psychology, 1*(1), 337–363. doi:10.5964/jspp.v1i1.36

Dobelli, R. (2013). *The art of thinking clearly.* Sceptre.

Duncan, P., & Bindman, P. (2020). Meghan gets twice as many negative headlines as positive, analysis finds. *The Guardian.* Retrieved January 2020 from https://www.theguardian.com/global/2020/jan/18/meghan-gets-more-than-twice-as-many-negative-headlines-as-positive

Eysenck, H. J., & Wilson, G. D. (1978). *The psychological basis of ideology.* University Park Press.

Fischer, R., Ferreira, M. C., Van Meurs, N., Gok, K., Jiang, D.-Y., Fontaine, J. R. J., Harb, C., Cieciuch, J., Achoui, M., Mendoza, M. S. D., Hassan, A., Achmadi, D., Mogaji, A. A., & Abubakar, A. (2019). Does organizational formalization facilitate voice and helping organizational citizenship behaviors? It depends on (national) uncertainty norms. *Journal of International Business Studies, 50,* 125–134. doi:10.1057/s41267-017-0132-6

Fiske, A. P., Kitayama, S., Markus, H. R., & Nisbett, R. E. (1998). The cultural matrix of social psychology. In D. Gilbert, S. Fiske, & G. Lindzey (Eds.), *Handbook of social psychology* (4th ed., 915–981). McGraw-Hill.

Ginosar, A. (2015). Understanding patriotic journalism: Culture, ideology and professional behavior. *Journal of Media Ethics, 30*(4), 289–301. doi:10.1080/23736992.2015.1082915

Graham, J., Meindl, P., Beall, E., Johnson, K. M., & Zhang, L. (2016). Cultural differences in moral judgment and behavior, across and within societies. *Current Opinion in Psychology, 8,* 125–130. https://doi.org/10.1016/j.copsyc.2015.09.007

Gudykunst, W. B. (1998). *Bridging differences. Effective intergroup communication* (3rd ed.). Sage.

Hall, S. (1973). The Determinations of News Photographs. In S. Cohen & J. Young (Eds), *The Manufacture of News, Social Problems, Deviance and The Mass Media.* London: Constable. Hallin, D. C. (2015). Media systems. In G. Mazzoleni (Ed.), *The international encyclopedia of political communication.* Wiley.

Hallin, D. C., & Mancini, P. (2004). *Comparing media systems: Three models of media and politics.* Cambridge University Press.

Hallin, D. C., & Mancini, P. (Eds.). (2011). *Comparing media systems beyond the Western world.* Cambridge University Press.

Hallin, D. C., & Mancini, P. (2012). Comparing media systems: A response to critics. *Handbook of comparative communication research* (pp. 207–220).

Hallin, D. C., & Mancini, P. (2019). Western media systems in a comparative perspective. In J. Curran & D. Hesmondhalgh (Eds.), *Media and society.* Bloomsbury Academic.

Hanitzsch, T., Hanusch, F., Mellado, C., Anikina, M., Berganza, R., Cangoz, I., Coman, M., Hamada, B., Hernández, M. E., Karadjov, C. D., Moreira, S. V., Mwesige, P. G., Plaisance, P. L, Reich, Z., Seethaler, J., Skewes, E. A., Vardiansyah Noor, D., & Kee Wang Yuen, E. (2011). Mapping journalism cultures across countries. *Journalism Studies, 12*(3), 273–293. doi:10.1080/1461670X.2010.512502

Hassell, H. J. G., Holbein, J. B., & Miles, M. R. (2020). There is no liberal media bias in which news stories political journalists choose to cover. *Science Advances, 6*(14), eaay9344. doi:10.1126/sciadv.aay9344. PMID: 32270038; PMCID: PMC7112764.

Higgins, D. (2014). The Western way: Democracy and the media assistance model. *Global Media Journal, 4*(2), 1–15.

Hofstede, G. (1980). *Culture's consequences: International differences in work-related values*. Sage.

Hofstede, G. (2001). *Culture's concoquonooot Comparing values, behaviors, institutions, and organizations across nations* (2nd ed.). Sage.

Hofstede, G., Hofstede, G. J., & Minkov, M. (2010). *Cultures and organizations: Software of the mind* (3rd ed.). McGraw-Hill.

Hogg, M. A. (2001). A social identity theory of leadership. *Personality and Social Psychology Review, 5*, 184–200.

Hogg, M. A., & Vaughan, G. M. (2008). *Socialpsychology* (5th ed). London: Prentice Hall.

House, R., Javidan, M., Hanges, P., & Dorfman, P. (2002). Understanding cultures and implicit leadership theories across the globe: An introduction to project GLOBE. *Journal of World Business, 37*, 2–10.

Humphreys, J. (2020). *Journalism has become ridiculous: The case for turning off the news*. https://www.irishtimes.com/culture/journalism-has-become-ridiculous-the-case-for-turning-off-the-news-1.4131646

Jost, J. T., & Amodio, D. M. (2012). Political ideology as motivated social cognition: Behavioral and neuroscientific evidence. *Motivation and Emotion, 36*(1), 55–64.

Kagitçibasi, C., & Berry, J. W. (1989). Cross-cultural psychology: Current research and trends. *Annual Review of Psychology, 40*, 493–531.

Kemmelmeier, M., Burnstein, E., Krumov, K., Genkova, P., Kanagawa, C., Hirshberg, M. S., Herb, H. P., Wieczorkowska, G., & Noels, K. A. (2003). Individualism, collectivism, and authoritarianism in seven societies. *Journal of Cross-Cultural Psychology, 34*(3), 304–322. https://doi.org/10.1177/0022022103034003005

Kroeber, A. L., & Kluckhohn, C. (1952). *Culture: A critical review of concepts and definitions* (Papers of the Peabody Museum of American Archaeology and Ethnology, Harvard University, Vol. XLVII, No. 1). Harvard University Press.

Lonner, W. (1999). Foreword. In J. Adamopoulos & Y. Kashima (Eds.), *Cross-cultural psychology series: Social psychology and cultural context* (pp. ix–xii). Sage. doi:10.4135/9781452220550

Lonner, W. J., & Adamopoulos, J. (1997). Culture as antecedent to behavior. In J. W. Berry, Y. H. Poortinga, & J. Pandey (Eds.), *Handbook of cross-cultural psychology* (2nd ed., Vol. 1, pp. 43–83). Allyn & Bacon.

Luce, R. D., & Raiffa, H. (1957). *Games and decisions: Introduction and critical survey*. Wiley.

Luyendijk, J. (2010). *Hello everybody!* Profile Books.

Markus, H. R., & Kitayama, S. (1991). Culture and the self: Implications for cognition, emotion, and motivation. *Psychological Review, 98*, 224–253.

McNamee, R. (2019). *Zucked: Waking up to the Facebook catastrophe*. HarperCollins.

McSweeney, B. (2002). Hofstede's model of national cultural differences and consequences: A triumph of faith—a failure of analysis. *Human Relations, 55*, 89–118.

Mellado, C., Hanusch, F., Humanes, M. L., Roses, S., Pereira, F., Yez, L., De León, S., Márquez, M., Subervi, F., & Wyss, V. (2013). The pre-socialization of future journalists. *Journalism Studies, 14*(6), 857–874. doi:10.1080/1461670X.2012.746006

Miller, D. T., & Prentice, D. A. (1994). Collective errors and errors about the collective. *Personality and Social Psychology Bulletin, 20,* 541–550.

Miller, G., & Steinberg, M. (1975). *Between people.* Science Research Associates.

Miller, G., & Sunnafrank, M. (1982). All is for one but one is not for all. In F. Dance (Ed.), *Human communication theory.* (pp. 220–242). Harper & Row.

O'Neill, D., & Harcup, T. (2009). News values and selectivity. In K. Wahl-Jorgensen & T. Hanitzsch (Eds.), *The handbook of journalism studies* (pp. 181–194). Routledge.

Poortinga, Y. (1992). Towards a conceptualisation of culture for psychology. In S. Iwaki, Y. Kashima, & K. Leung (Eds.), *Innovations in cross-cultural psychology* (pp. 3–17). Swets & Zeitlinger.

Pratto, F., Sidanius, J., Stallworth, L. M., & Malle, B. F. (1994). Social dominance orientation: A personality variable predicting social and political attitudes. *Journal of Personality and Social Psychology, 67*(4), 741–763. https://doi.org/10.1037/0022-3514.67.4.741

Rajan, A. (2020). Trends vs events in news coverage. Retrieved January 2020 from https://www.bbc.co.uk/news/entertainment-arts-51038695

Rohner, R. (1984). Toward a conception of culture for cross-cultural psychology. *Journal of Cross-Cultural Psychology, 15,* 111–138.

Ruparelia, K., Abubakar, A., Badoe, E., Bakare, M., Visser, K., Chugani, D. C., Chugani, H. T., Donald, K. A., Wilmshurst, J. M., Shih, A., Skuse, D., & Newton, C. R. (2016). Autism spectrum disorders in Africa: Current challenges in identification, assessment, and treatment: A report on the International Child Neurology Association meeting on ASD in Africa, Ghana, April 3–5, 2014. *Journal of Child Neurology, 31*(8), 1018–1026. https://doi.org/10.1177/0883073816635748

Schwartz, S. H. (1992). Universals in the content and structure of values: Theoretical advances and empirical tests in 20 countries. *Advances in Experimental Social Psychology, 25* 1–65.

Schwartz, S. H. (1994). Beyond individualism/collectivism: New cultural dimensions of values. In U. Kim, H. C. Triandis, & G. Yoon (Eds.), *Individualism and collectivism: Theory, method, and applications* (pp. 85–119). Sage.

Schwartz, S. H. (1996). Value priorities and behavior: Applying a theory of integrated value systems. In C. Seligman, J. M. Olson, & M. P. Zanna (Eds.), *The psychology of values: The Ontario Symposium* (Vol. 8, pp. 1–24). Erlbaum.

Schwartz, S. H., & Sagie, G. (2000). Value consensus and importance: A cross-national study. *Journal of Cross-Cultural Psychology, 31,* 465–497.

Segall, M. H., Dasen, P. R., Bery, J. W., & Poortinga, Y. H. (1999). *Human behavior in global perspective: An introduction to cross-cultural psychology* (2nd ed.). Allyn & Bacon.

Shweder, R. A. (1990). Cultural psychology: What is it? In J. W. Stigler, R. A. Shweder, & G. Herdt (Eds.), *Cultural psychology: Essays on comparative human development* (pp. 1–43). Cambridge University Press.

Siebert, F., Siebert, F. T., Peterson, T., Peterson, T. B., & Schramm, W. (1956). *Four theories of the press: The authoritarian, libertarian, social responsibility, and Soviet communist concepts of what the press should be and do* (Vol. 10). University of Illinois Press.

Singelis, T. M., Triandis, H. C., Bhawuk, D. P. S., & Gelfand, M. J. (1995). Horizontal and vertical dimensions of individualism and collectivism: A theoretical and measurement refinement. *Cross-Cultural Research, 29*(3), 240–275. doi:10.1177/106939719502900302

Skjerdal, T. (2011). Teaching journalism or teaching African journalism? Experiences from foreign involvement in a journalism programme in Ethiopia. *Global Media Journal, 5*(1), 24–51.

Smith, P. B. (1997). Cross-cultural leadership: A path to the goal? In P. C. Earley & M. Erez (Eds.), *New perspectives on international industrial/organisational psychology* (pp. 626–639). New Lexington Press.

Smith, P. B., & Bond, M. H. (1998). *Social psychology across cultures.* Prentice Hall Europe.

Tajfel, H. (1970). Experiments in intergroup discrimination. *Scientific American, 223*(5), 96–103.

Tajfel, H. (1979). *The psychological basis of ideology.* Edited by H. J. Eysenck and G. D. Wilson. Lancaster: MTP Press. 1978. Pp 312. £12.95. *British Journal of Psychiatry, 134*(4), 443. doi:10.1017/S0007125000058670

Tajfel, H. (1981). *Human groups and social categories.* Cambridge University Press.

Tajfel, H. (1982). *Social identity and intergroup relations.* Cambridge University Press.

Tenzer, H., Pudelko, M., & Harzing, A. (2014). The impact of language barriers on trust formation in multinational teams. *Journal of International Business Studies, 45*, 508–535. doi:10.1057/jibs.2013.64

Thomas, D., & Peterson, M. (2018). *Cross-cultural management: Essential concepts* (4th ed.). Sage.

Tiffen, R., & Gittins, R. (2009). *How Australia compares* (2nd ed.). Cambridge University Press.

Ting-Toomey, S. (1999). *Communicating across cultures.* Guildford.

Ting-Toomey, S., & Dorje, T. (2017). Multifaceted identity approaches and cross-cultural communication styles: Selective overview and future directions. In L. Chen (Ed.), *Intercultural communication* (Handbooks of Communication Science, Vol. 9, pp. 141–178). de Gruyter.

Triandis, H. C. (1988). Collectivism vs. individualism. In G. Verma & C. Bagley (Eds.), *Cross cultural studies of personality, attitudes, and cognition* (pp. 60–95). Macmillan.

Turner, J. C. (1987). *Rediscovering the social group: A self-categorization theory.* Basil Blackwell.

Turner, J. C., Oakes, P. J., Haslam, S. A., & McGarty, C. (1994). Self and collective: Cognition and social context. *Personality and Social Psychology Bulletin, 20*, 445–463.

Van Meurs, N., & Spencer-Oatey, H. (2010). Multidisciplinary perspectives on intercultural conflict: The 'Bermuda Triangle' of conflict, culture, and communication. In D. Matsumoto (Ed.), *APA intercultural handbook of communication* (pp. 59–78). American Psychological Association.

Weiss, R. M., & Miller, L. E. (1987). The concept of ideology in organizational analysis: The sociology of knowledge or the social psychology of beliefs? *Academy of Management Review, 12*(1), 104–116.

Wemys, G. (2006). The power to tolerate: Contests over Britishness and belonging in East London. *Patterns of Prejudice, 40*(3), 215–236.

Xu, J. (2018). The return of ideology to China's journalism education: The 'joint model' campaign between propaganda departments and journalism schools. *Asia Pacific Media Educator, 28*(2), 176–185. https://doi.org/10.1177/1326365X18799134

Zelizer, B. (2004). When facts, truth, and reality are God-terms: On journalism's uneasy place in cultural studies. *Communication and Critical/Cultural Studies, 1*(1), 100–119.

Zhong, B. (2008). Thinking along the cultural line: A cross-cultural inquiry of ethical decision making among U.S. and Chinese journalism students. *Journalism & Mass Communication Educator, 63*(2), 110–126. https://doi.org/10.1177/107769580806300202

9

Language and Categorization

Zira Hichy and Graziella Di Marco

Language is a tool that people use for transferring information about themselves and their world. However, the way in which language is used can generate different inferences. For example, referring to a running person, we can say 'he/she is running', 'he/she is a runner', or 'he/she is a cheetah'. In each of the three cases, we have transferred different information: In the first case, we only said what he/she is doing at a certain moment; in the second case, we simply said that he/she usually runs and, therefore, this characteristic is part of him/her; finally, in the third case, using a metaphor, we are saying not only that he/she runs habitually but also that he/she does so very quickly.

In this chapter, we analyse the various linguistic biases, with particular reference to biases involved in intergroup relations; indeed, language can be a useful clue of intergroup relations. Once established that language used by people is an expression of their attitudes, we discuss the effect of biased language use on recipients. Finally, we discuss use of biased language in mass communication, especially how such communication is affected by linguistic biases and how these biases can affect the audience.

Linguistic Category Model

The linguistic category model (LCM) (Semin, 2012; Semin & Fiedler, 1988, 1991) considers language as an expression of cognitive processes; it asserts that the language that people use to describe an event depends on cognitive processes involved in the representation of the event itself. In order to provide a systematic model of the linguistic terms used by people in communicating about social events and their actors, the LCM makes a distinction between five different categories (four verb categories and one adjective category) of interpersonal terms: descriptive action verbs (DAVs), interpretative action verbs (IAVs), state action verbs (SAVs), state verbs (SVs), and

Zira Hichy and Graziella Di Marco, *Language and Categorization* In: *The Psychology of Journalism.*
Edited by: Sharon Coen and Peter Bull, Oxford University Press. © Oxford University Press 2021.
DOI: 10.1093/oso/9780190935856.003.0009

adjectives (ADJs) (Semin & Fiedler, 1991). This distinction was made on the basis of a number of converging grammatical tests and semantic contrasts (Brown & Fish, 1983; G. Miller & Johnson-Laird, 1976),

The first category consists of DAVs. These are the most concrete terms, and they represent an objective description of a single behavioural event, preserving its perceptual features. These verbs are specific and related to a particular object, situation, and context; moreover, in general they do not have in themselves positive or negative valence (e.g., 'A punches B').

The second category is represented by IAVs, which add to the description of a specific observable event its interpretation. These verbs are more abstract and refer to a general class of behaviours, without preserving the perceptual features of an action, and have positive or negative valence (e.g., 'A hurts B').

The next two categories are represented by SAVs and SVs, both referring to psychological states. SAVs refer to the states caused by observable action of subject and describe emotional consequences of this action for the object (e.g., 'A thrills B'), whereas SVs refer to a mental or emotional state already existent for the subject (e.g., 'A hates B'). The last category is represented by adjectives (e.g., 'A is aggressive') that imply a generalization across specific events and objects and describe a disposition of the subject.

All these categories can be placed along a continuum of concreteness–abstractness: DAVs (kick, kiss) are the most concrete category, followed by IAVs (help, cheat), SVs (like, abhor), and finally ADJs (friendly, impulsive)—the most abstract category. As can be seen, at the concreteness end, terms retain a reference to the contextual and situated features of an event, whereas at the abstractness end, there are no references to situation or context, and the terms are highly interpretative and detached from specific behaviours (Semin & Fiedler, 1988; Semin & Greenslade, 1985). In other words, the use of adjectives is governed by abstract, semantic relations rather than by the contingencies of contextual factors. This concreteness–abstractness dimension has psychological implications: The more a term is abstract, the less it refers to specific situations and the more it refers to general and stable characteristics of a person.

In addition to four levels of abstractness proposed initially by the LCM, Semin et al. (2002) added nouns because nouns may describe characteristics of a person in the same way as adjectives. Moreover, some authors suggest that the noun level is more abstract and more strongly indicates group membership (Carnaghi et al., 2008) and that it enhances stereotypic inferences and ingroup bias at the adjective level (Graf et al., 2012). At least in

Indo-European languages, nouns and adjectives are very similar, differing only in suffix (flower vs. floral), or being distinguishable only by the article ('Jack is an American' vs. 'Jack is American'), and they seem to play almost the same role in personality description (Saucier, 2003).

However, Carnaghi et al. (2008) affirm that nouns differ from adjectives in various ways. Nouns categorize objects identifying the class to which they belong ('Victoria is an athlete' means that Victoria belongs to the category of athletes); on the other hand, adjectives denote qualities that objects possess ('Victoria is athletic' means that Victoria has this quality). Nouns imply multiple qualities ('Mary is a blond' implies multiple characteristics owned by Mary—that is, sexy, glamorous, and not particularly intelligent), whereas adjectives identify a single quality ('Mary is blonde' refers to a single quality of Mary—that is, her hair colour, see Wierzbicka, 1986). Moreover, nouns have an either–or quality ('Victoria is an athlete' means that Victoria either is or is not an athlete); on the contrary, adjectives permit distinctions of degree ('Victoria is athletic' means that Victoria may be more or less athletic). Finally, nouns are semantically superordinate, whereas adjective plays a subordinate role (the word 'Englishman' focusses attention on the gender, qualified by nationality, whereas the words 'male English' focusses attention on the nationality qualified by gender) (Wierzbicka, 1986).

As discussed previously, LCM explains the linguistic choices made by people when describing an event, but what effect do these choices have on people who listen or read the description? It is proposed that the more abstract is the description of the behaviour, the stronger the audience will attribute the behaviour to the actor rather than to the situation (Wigboldus & Douglas, 2007; Wigboldus et al., 2006). Abstract sentences lead people to perceive that they are gaining more information about the subject of the sentence (Maass et al., 1989) and give the impression that the behaviour is more likely to be repeated (Semin & Fiedler, 1991; Wigboldus et al., 2000). Thus, the more abstract is a message, the more likely recipients will attribute the behaviour of the subject to dispositional causes and, as a result, the more they will think this behaviour will be repeated in the future.

Moreover, there is evidence that level of abstractness can also affect the inclusiveness or globality of categorization. Stapel and Semin (2007) conducted an experiment using nonsocial categories, in which participants first were primed, using the scrambled-sentence test (see Stapel et al., 1998), with sentences that contained either action verbs or adjectives. Then, in an apparently unrelated task, participants completed a measure of inclusiveness of categorization, in which they had to indicate to what degree atypical exemplars (e.g., camel) were good members of a given category (e.g., vehicle). Results showed that participants in the adjective condition were more inclusive than participants in the action verb condition; that is, in the adjective condition, atypical exemplars were assigned to an abstract category, whereas in the action verb condition they were not.

Linguistic Intergroup Bias

Based on Semin and Fiedler's (1988, 1991) LCM, the linguistic intergroup bias model (LIB) (Maass et al., 1989) states that verbs and adjectives used to describe action and people may have a different level of abstractness: Adjectives and state verbs are the most abstract terms carrying more stable and global information than interpretative and descriptive action verbs, which are the most concrete terms. According to the LIB, people use different words describing people and their behaviour on the basis of their membership (ingroup vs. outgroup), resulting in a systematic intergroup bias. In particular, when describing positive behaviours of ingroup members and negative behaviours of outgroup members, people tend to use abstract terms ('helpful', 'aggressive'); while describing negative behaviours of ingroup members and positive behaviours of outgroup members, people tend to use concrete terms ('hit', 'help'). In other words, the positive behaviours of the ingroup and the negative behaviours of the outgroup are described with reference to stable characteristics; conversely, the negative behaviours of the ingroup and the positive behaviours of the outgroup are described with reference to transitory characteristics that depend on situation or context.

Thus, the LIB works as postulated by the fundamental attribution error (Heider, 1958), whereby people who observe a person performing a negative behaviour will attribute that behaviour to dispositional (internal) causes if the person is a member of the outgroup; on the other hand, they will attribute that same negative behaviour to situational (external) factors if the person is a member of the ingroup. At the same time, positive behaviours will be attributed to situational causes when made by a member of the outgroup and dispositional causes when made by a member of the ingroup.

Various studies, using different groups (ethnic, gender, regional, etc.) and different response formats (free verbalization or multiple choice), have confirmed the LIB model (Maass, 1999; Maass et al., 1995, 1996; Moscatelli et al.,

2008; Rubini & Semin, 1994; Wigboldus et al., 2000; Werkman et al., 1999). For example, Maass et al. (1996) conducted an experiment with hunters and environmentalists from northern Italy. Participants were presented with eight single-frame cartoons, four depicting hunters and four depicting environmentalists engaging in either positive (e.g., study) or negative (e.g., smoking) behaviours. For each cartoon, participants were asked to choose among four sentences the ones that described the scene best. The sentences were devised according to the four levels of abstraction (Semin & Fiedler, 1988)—for example, 'picks up paper' (DAV), 'cleans up the wood' (IAV), 'respects nature' (SV), and 'is conscientious' (ADJ). Results showed that positive behaviours were described more abstractly when performed by an ingroup rather than an outgroup member; on the other hand, negative behaviours were described more abstractly when performed by an outgroup rather than an ingroup member.

Regarding psychological processes responsible for linguistic intergroup bias, there are two possible explanations. The first one draws on social identity theory (Tajfel & Turner, 1979, 1986), whereby to maintain a positive social identity people will strive to create favourable comparisons between ingroup and outgroup, for example, by denigrating the outgroup. From this perspective, the LIB serves to maintain a positive ingroup image (Maass, 1999; Maass et al., 1989). The second explanation utilizes a cognitive process based on expectations (Hamilton et al., 1992; Wigboldus et al., 2000). From this point of view, unexpected behaviours (positive ones of the outgroup and negative ones of the ingroup) are described more concretely, whereas expected behaviours (negative ones of the outgroup and positive ones of the ingroup) are described more abstractly. Evidence from research is equivocal; indeed, there is evidence for both cognitive and motivational explanations (Arcuri et al., 1993; Fiedler et al., 1993; Karpinski & von Hippel, 1996; Maass et al., 1994; Rubini & Semin, 1994; von Hippel et al., 1997).

Linguistic intergroup bias is present not only in informal communication but also in the news. Maass et al. (1994) analysed the reports in Italian newspapers (both Jewish and non-Jewish) of an anti-Semitic incident that took place during a basketball game between an Italian team and an Israeli team. The results showed that there were no differences in the abstractness when Jewish and non-Jewish newspapers described the victims, but there were differences when they described assaulters: The Jewish newspapers used more abstract terms describing assaulters compared to the non-Jewish newspapers. The same results were found in a study that analysed U.S. newspaper articles concerning immigration to the United States from Mexico. It was found that positive ingroup and negative outgroup statements were encoded using more abstract language than were negative ingroup and positive outgroup statements (Dragojevic et al., 2017). Moreover, LIB seemed to increase when a newspaper had a right-wing political orientation, as was shown in a study conducted on three Italian newspapers investigating the description of rapists on the basis of their nationality. The results showed that when describing a rape perpetrated by an immigrant versus an Italian, the right-wing politically oriented newspaper (*Il Giornale*) presented the assaulter in a more abstract way compared to the other newspapers (*La Repubblica* and *Il Corriere della Sera*) (D'Andrea et al., 2016).

Many studies on intergroup biases in language have been focussed typically on words that denote specific groups or identities (e.g., immigrants, African American). However, following Gustafsson Sendøn et al. (2013), the pronouns (we, they, I, he/she) may also be viewed as markers of social categories. In one study, Gustafsson Sendøn et al. tested whether in a large amount of media news, pronouns occur in contexts of different valence reflecting a systematic self- or group-serving bias. In this study, researchers took into account two dimensions of pronouns. The first one was the inclusiveness dimension, which categorized first personal pronouns (I, we) as self-inclusive and third-person pronouns (he, she, they) as self-exclusive. The second dimension was the individuals versus collectives dimension, which categorized singular pronouns (I, he, she) to individual levels and plural pronouns (we, they) to collective levels (see also Gustafsson Sendøn et al., 2014). Results showed that self-inclusive pronouns were associated with more positive contexts compared to self-exclusive pronouns and that individual pronouns appeared in more positive contexts compared to collective pronouns. Thus, this study showed that the semantic context of pronouns in news media varies systematically in valence, in order to reflect self- and group-serving biases.

In another study, Gustafsson Sendøn et al. (2015) tested whether there is a male bias in the media by examining how the pronouns she and he are used in news media. To do this, approximately 800,000 Reuters news messages published in 1996 and 1997 were examined. The results showed not only that the he pronoun was used more frequently than the she pronoun but also that the he pronoun appeared in more positive semantic contexts than the she pronoun. Furthermore, sentences utilizing the she pronoun contained more words representing gender and were more homogeneous than the words related to the he pronoun, indicating that women were described as more similar to one another than were men.

At this point, it is natural to wonder what might be the effect of LIB on news audiences. So, in the case of negative behaviour of an outgroup, an abstract sentence might lead the recipients to believe that behaviour depends on personal disposition, thereby perpetuating stereotypes and prejudice. For example, in a study conducted in the United States, Gorham (2006) examined LIB shown by television viewers after watching news about a crime. Results showed that participants (White Americans) who viewed an outgroup member (Afro-American) as a suspect in a television news story about a crime chose more abstract language to describe the suspect's role in the story compared to participants who viewed a White suspect. Similarly, Geschke et al. (2010) analysed the effects of LIB in newspaper articles on German readers' attitudes toward migrants. They found that abstract language in news articles led to higher estimates of criminal behaviour compared to concrete language; moreover, participants showed higher levels of subtle prejudice [as measured by Pettigrew and Meertens' (1995) Subtle and Blatant Prejudice Scale] after reading linguistically abstract articles than after reading linguistically concrete articles.

Similar results were also found among television viewers by Gilliam et al. (1996), who conducted an experiment to investigate effects of race manipulation of a suspect (Afro-American vs. White) in a crime story. Participants were White and Asian Americans employed as administrative and clerical staff at the University of California, Los Angeles. Results showed that when the suspect was Afro-American, participants were more likely to attribute the causes of crime to group characteristics and expressed more concern for the crime.

From the studies so far reviewed, it appears that the recipient reaction to the source messages can be seen to reflect similar levels of LIB—that is, when the outgroup behaviours are described using an abstract language, receivers tend to believe that behaviours depend on personal disposition. However, a series of studies conducted by Porter et al. (2016) indicate that the recipients are not as naive as one might think. They conducted four studies to investigate the effect of LIB on social category inferences. Participants first read a text that began as follows: 'Imagine that someone is communicating with you about a man named Peter. Peter is American, has an interest in politics, and voted for Barack Obama' (this information was given to all participants to inform them that the subject was a Democrat). Following these sentences, participants read a description of Peter using a positive LIB (positive behaviour described abstractly and negative behaviour described concretely) or a negative LIB (positive behaviour described concretely and negative behaviour described abstractly). Subsequently, participants were asked to determinate the social category to which the source of the message belonged (e.g., Democrat vs. Republican). Results showed that participants were able to infer the social category to which the source belonged, regardless of their own political affiliation; moreover, they evaluated more positively the source when its LIB agreed with their own social identity (e.g., Democrat participants preferred the source who used the favourable LIB when describing a Democrat subject).

As demonstrated by the previous discussion, the concept of LIB has received support in both laboratory and field studies; however, some points need further investigation. The first point regards what drives LIB, whether be it cognitive (expectations) or motivational (ingroup protection) processes; indeed, studies have found evidence for both. As argued by Maass et al. (1996), it is possible that the two processes may work together in a complex and circular way: Ingroup protection can lead people to have negative expectations about the outgroup, but at the same time negative expectations about the outgroup can lead to ingroup protection. Another point concerns the generalization of LIB across different societies. Following Hofstede's (1980) model, culture and societies can be placed along a continuum from individualistic to collectivistic. Individualistic cultures have loose ties between people and give priority to the self over the group; on the other hand, collectivistic cultures stress the cohesion among individuals and give priority to the group over the self. It is possible that, as for the fundamental attribution error (J. Miller, 1984), LIB can vary between individualistic cultures (that more probably make dispositional attributions) and collectivistic cultures (that more probably make situational attributions).

Linguistic Expectancy Bias

As discussed previously, a possible explanation of LIB refers to a cognitive process based on expectations—that is, when behaviour is consistent with expectations, people choose more abstract terms, whereas when behaviour is inconsistent with expectations, people choose more concrete terms. For example, Maass et al. (1995) induced an expectation about a target person (e.g., 'This person has been described by parents and friends as sociable and friendly') and then showed participants pictures of the target person, representing either an expectancy consistent behaviour (e.g., going out with friends) or an expectancy inconsistent behaviour (e.g., refusing the invitation of a friend). Subsequently, they asked participants to choose between four descriptions (devised according to the four levels of abstraction of the LCM; Semin & Fiedler, 1988) which one best described the pictures. Results showed that participants chose more abstract terms for expectancy consistent pictures (e.g., the picture showed the person going out with friends when the person was described as sociable and friendly) than for expectancy inconsistent pictures. From this example, it can be seen that biased language use can also be found outside an intergroup context; for this reason, it has recently been proposed to refer to this more general linguistic bias as linguistic expectancy bias (LEB) (Wigboldus et al., 2000).

Similar results were found in an experiment conducted by Wigboldus et al. (2006) using free verbalization. In their study, participants were first asked to think of a friend whom they knew well and then asked to describe one event in which their friend demonstrated an expected behaviour and another event in which the same friend demonstrated an unexpected behaviour. Results showed that expected behaviours were communicated at a higher level of linguistic abstraction compared to unexpected behaviours. These results were also found using stereotypes as the source of expectancy consistent behaviour. In another experiment conducted by Wigboldus et al. (2000), the experimenter asked Dutch participants to report in their own words a stereotype-relevant story received from an unknown source. The story described either a Dutch or a Flemish subject who behaved in either a stereotypically Dutch or a stereotypically Flemish way that could be desirable or undesirable. Results showed that the stereotype-consistent information (a Flemish subject behaving in a stereotypically Flemish way) was reported in a more abstract way than the stereotype-inconsistent information (a Flemish subject behaving in a stereotypically Dutch way), regardless of the desirability of the behaviour.

The study conducted by Wigboldus et al. (2000) showed that transmitters refer messages at a higher level of linguistic abstraction for stereotype-consistent information than for stereotype-inconsistent information. When these messages were referred to other Dutch participants, the results showed that their pattern almost exactly mirrored the results obtained for the linguistic abstraction information provided by transmitters. Information about the Flemish protagonist behaving in a stereotypically Flemish way led to more dispositional inferences than did information about the Flemish protagonist behaving in a stereotypically Dutch way. These results showed that the use of biased language influenced recipients' judgements in order to confirm the stereotype, demonstrating that biased language might by responsible for the transmission and maintenance of stereotypes (see also Wenneker et al., 2005). Other studies obtained the same results, showing that when recipients were presented with messages that were consistent with expectation, the behaviours were attributed more strongly to dispositional factors; moreover, these effects were mediated by linguistic abstraction of the stories (Wigboldus et al., 2006).

Currently, to our knowledge, no studies have investigated the effects of LEB on the news; however, LEB may contribute to explaining the relationship between news exposure and stereotypes. It is possible to hypothesize that LEB effects will be similar to, if not stronger than, LIB effects. As demonstrated previously, LIB tended to affect receivers with a high level of prejudice when a negative behaviour of the outgroup was described in an abstract way. In the case of LEB, it might be expected that the effect should be the same when a negative outgroup behaviour confirms expectations.

The Induction–Deduction Asymmetry

The induction–deduction asymmetry refers to a phenomenon whereby inductive inferences from behaviours to traits occur more frequently than deductive inferences from traits to behaviours (Maass et al., 2001). Inductive inference occurs when people infer traits from behaviours; for example, if we see a person hit someone (behaviour), we will deduce that this person is aggressive (trait). On the basis of this process, people tend to infer a general disposition (trait) from a specific occurrence (behaviour). On the other hand, deductive inference occurs when people infer specific behaviours from general traits; for example, if we know that a person is aggressive (trait), we might deduce that this person may be likely to hit someone (behaviour). Various studies have focussed on inductive inference (e.g., Carlston & Skowronski, 1994; Carlston et al., 1995, Uleman, 1987; Uleman et al., 1996), but only a few studies have focussed on deductive inference or have compared the two processes (but see Maass et al., 2001, 2006).

The first studies investigating inductive and deductive inferences simultaneously and within the same experimental paradigm were performed by Maass et al. (2001). In the first study, participants first received descriptions of a target person, presented in trait form (e.g., 'superstitious') or in behaviour form (e.g., 'makes gestures to ward off bad luck'). Then they completed a recognition task comprising traits and behaviours already seen in the first part and new traits and behaviours not seen in the first part, which might be inferred from the information given (i.e., traits from behaviours or behaviours from traits). Results showed that participants frequently wrongly recognized traits as already seen if they could be inferred from behaviours (i.e., they frequently made mistakes by indicating that they had seen a trait when, in fact, they had seen only the implied behaviour) but rarely wrongly recognized behaviours as already seen if they could be inferred from traits.

In the second study, Maass et al. (2001) measured response times in the recognition task and found that participants responded with the same speed in the case of inferred and actually seen traits; however, in the case of behaviours, response time to inferred behaviours was slower than response time to actually seen behaviours. Thus, the results from both studies suggested that people frequently made inductive inferences but rarely deductive inferences, confirming the induction–deduction asymmetry. Similar results were also found in a series of experiments using both recognition and free recall tests, which showed that these biases appear also when adjectives and verbs share the same word stem (e.g., 'aggressive' vs. 'aggress') (Maass et al., 2006).

Taken together, the results from these studies suggest that people made spontaneous and unconscious inductive inferences but not deductive inferences, thereby confirming that people tend toward abstraction when processing social information (Fiedler et al., 1989; Semin & Fiedler, 1988). Moreover, it seems that induction–deduction asymmetry is specific to person perception; indeed, it appears only when the information refers to a person but not when it refers to a nonhuman or is provided as a simple word list (Maass et al., 2006). This suggests that induction–deduction asymmetry is quite similar to the correspondence bias (Gilbert, 1998), whereby when accounting for the behaviour of others, people tend to emphasize internal characteristics rather than external situational factors.

The effect of induction–deduction asymmetry varies when considering stereotypic expectancies. Maass et al. (2005) performed an experiment whereby participants (male and female) were asked to read a letter of recommendation for a male or a female job applicant. Each letter presented the candidate using gender-neutral characteristics (e.g., 'precise') and stereotype-congruent or stereotype-incongruent characteristics. For example, 'dominant' was regarded as stereotype congruent in the case of a male candidate but incongruent in the case of a female candidate; on the other hand, 'intuitive' was regarded as stereotype congruent in the case of a female candidate but incongruent in the case of a male candidate. Moreover, half of the characteristics were provided in trait form (e.g., 'dominant') and half in behavioural form (e.g., 'expects to be obeyed'). Subsequently, participants completed a recognition task. Results showed that inductive inferences increased when the behaviour corresponded to stereotypic expectancies and decreased when the behaviour was inconsistent with stereotypic expectancies, whereas deductive inferences were unaffected by stereotypic expectancies. These results suggest that the transformation of verbs (and behaviours) into adjectives (and traits) is facilitated when behaviour is expectancy consistent and inhibited when behaviour is expectancy inconsistent, showing that induction–deduction asymmetry works in memory just as LIB works in communication. Indeed, in both cases, people enhance the level of abstraction when the information is congruent with expectations.

Even in the case of induction–deduction asymmetry, there are no studies, to our knowledge, investigating its effects on the news. However, just as for LEB, it is possible to formulate some hypotheses about possible effects of induction–deduction asymmetry on news receivers. In particular, induction–deduction asymmetry should work transforming and memorizing the original message in line with expectancies: for example, a prejudiced receiver that reads news about an outgroup member who 'hits' an ingroup member may store in memory that the outgroup member is 'violent'.

The Use of Metaphors

According to conceptual metaphor theory (Lakoff & Johnson, 1980), a metaphor is a cognitive tool that people use to understand abstract concepts, called a target (e.g., social hierarchy, lawyers) through more concrete concepts, called a source (e.g., ladder, sharks) (see also Gibbs, 2008; Kövecses, 2010). For example, considering the phrase 'lawyers are sharks', 'lawyers' are the abstract target concept, and 'sharks' are the concrete source concept. Although target and source are not related to each other, they have some common characteristic (e.g., lawyers and sharks are both vicious, aggressive, and merciless) for which they are matched and inserted in the same category (Glucksberg & Haught, 2006).

Another approach to the study of metaphors is the Metaphor Power Index (MPI) method, proposed by De Landtsheer (2009), specifically created for political discourse. This method combines the metaphor identification procedure proposed by the Pragglejaz group (Steen et al., 2010) and conceptual metaphor theory as proposed by Lakoff and Johnson (1980). The MPI method allows a quantitative representation of the metaphorical power of a text, distinguishing emotional or 'metaphorical style' from an actual substantive or 'content style'. The MPI is calculated by multiplying metaphor frequencies, metaphor intensity, and metaphor content (De Landtsheer, 2009). The metaphor frequencies take into account the number of metaphors used in the text (number of metaphors per 100 words) or in speech (number of metaphors per minute). Metaphor intensity relates to the novel and original character of the metaphor. A metaphor is strong if its words cannot be substituted because they are particularly expressive (e.g., the 1991 Iraq War was called Desert Storm). Finally, with regard to metaphor content, the semantic field from which the metaphor meaning is derived is grouped into categories differing in metaphor power. De Landtsheer found that the weakest category was 'every-day life and reality' (e.g., putting the problem into a refrigerator), followed by 'nature' (e.g., blowing with the wind), 'politics, intellect, technology' (e.g., being a locomotive), 'violence and disaster' (e.g., exploding a bomb), 'sports, games and drama' (e.g., scoring a goal), and finally 'body, disease, medical, and death' (e.g., catching a virus), the strongest category. When metaphor content is high, the metaphor elicits stronger emotion. As asserted by De Landtsheer, during periods of crisis, politicians and political journalists use language with stronger metaphor power.

By linking a concept with another that stands in for it, metaphors are effectively transferring a series of characteristics associated with that object to the construct for which they stand in. In this way, the representation of the target construct becomes associated with a concrete, vivid, and familiar object to which people already associate a series of characteristics (Rakic & Maass, 2019). Various studies have demonstrated that the activation of metaphors influences the way in which people understand their social world (Landau et al., 2010, 2014). For example, Thibodeau and Boroditsky (2011) found that the use of different metaphors influences the way in which people face a problem. In their study, participants (students from Stanford University and the University of California) were provided with different metaphorical descriptions of rising crime: a preying beast versus an infecting virus. Results showed that participants in the beast metaphor condition were more likely to suggest catching and caging the criminals; on the other hand, participants in the virus metaphor condition were more likely to suggest investigating the root causes of crime. Thus, the particular metaphor utilized may influence thoughts to the extent that solutions proposed by participants reflect the metaphor itself.

Moreover, the exposure to metaphors affects person perception and attitude change (Landau & Keefer, 2014; Meier et al., 2014; Ottati & Renstrom, 2010). For example, Morris et al. (2007) asked participants (undergraduate students from Cornell University) to read stock market commentaries describing a price trend as a living agent—that is, as something moving with intention (e.g., 'the NASDAQ starting climbing upward')—or as an inanimate object—that is, as something that does not move with intention (e.g., 'the NASDAQ was swept upward'). After reading the commentary, participants were asked for their expectations about price trends for the next day. Results showed that participants in the first condition were more likely than participants in the second condition to expect that price trends would continue along their current trajectory.

The previous discussion indicates that metaphors can be a valuable aid in understanding the world, but not always a valid one. Indeed, metaphors may draw attention to specific characteristics of the concept (e.g., defining lawyers as sharks draws attention to characteristics such as their aggressiveness and mercilessness). Furthermore, when used habitually, metaphors may become literal (White & Landau, 2016); for example, referring to immigration as 'invasion' makes the immigration perceived to all effects as an invasion, hence as a wilful threat posed by immigrants to one's group. For all these reasons, metaphors are very powerful in communicating about groups but at the same time might enhance prejudice.

In the intergroup domain, metaphors that often appear are tied to non-human entities, such as food or animals (Haslam et al., 2016; Maass et al., 2014). For example, in various cultures, men refer to women using metaphor such as geese, hens, and kittens (Kövecses, 2005). Maass and colleagues (2014) have argued that the use of this kind of metaphoric language may guide categorization, enhance group homogeneity, facilitate inferences of stereotype-congruent information, and favour the dehumanization of the outgroup. For example, a study performed by Loughnan et al. (2009)

showed that when participants were led to believe that a novel group was like an animal (labelling the group as animal-like), they viewed its members as less human.

Metaphors may also be used to shape public attitudes toward specific topics or groups. For example, Woods et al. (2012) found that British newspapers used religious metaphor to denigrate the concept climate change (describing it as creed, cult, or myth), especially when the newspapers had a conservative rather than liberal orientation; in the same way, environmentalists were presented in a negative way as extremists, describing them as fundamentalists or zealots.

Another example can be seen in Hitler's *Mein Kampf* (1925), in addition to other kinds of Nazi propaganda during World War II, that portrayed the European Jewish people as 'subhuman', using metaphors of rats or parasites (Capozza & Volpato, 2004). Similar results were found in Western media descriptions after the terrorist attacks of September 11, 2001, with the Islamists characterized as animals or vermin (Steuter & Wills, 2010). Thereby, the use of animal metaphors may be seen to increase intergroup prejudice and discrimination. This was also confirmed in a series of studies by Marshall and Shapiro (2018), who investigated the effects of using vermin metaphors to represent unauthorized immigrants from Latin America to the United States. Results indicated that the presence of vermin metaphors in an American news article led to a disgust reaction and to support for more stringent immigration policies.

Metaphors have the advantage of reducing complexity and thereby may enhance the understanding of complex issues. However, metaphorical language may also affect receivers' perception of the news, and hence their attitudes. In particular, the use of particularly negative metaphors (e.g., virus, vermin) may generate correspondingly negative attitudes in receivers of the news.

Conclusion

In this chapter, we analysed various linguistic biases affecting intergroup relations. As discussed previously, people may express their attitudes using different kinds of language, and media communication can also be affected by comparable linguistic biases. Thus, when people refer to categorized people and their behaviours, their attitudes and their stereotypes about that group are often reflected in the language use. At the same time, other people who received these kinds of biased messages may be influenced by them, thereby shaping their attitudes.

The use of linguistic bias in mediated communication can be very dangerous because of its impact on people's perception of the reported topics and the large audience reached by media. Indeed, media communication may work to promote certain views of the world, shaping people's attitudes and consequent behaviours according to the message conveyed. Moreover, considering that most people consult just a few sources for news, which may also reflect their established attitudes (Frey, 1986), it is easy to understand how the aforementioned effects may become amplified, making the sources of news a kind of flywheel for negative attitudes and stereotype perpetuation. All this makes people unable to view different perspectives of the same topic and consequently unable to have unbiased opinions.

As discussed in this chapter, various studies have been carried out on linguistic biases and their effects. However, despite evidence, relatively few studies have investigated the effect of linguistic biases in the field of journalism, which suggests that linguistic biases need more attention in media communication research, particularly with regard to how audiences react to the use of language in media content. Indeed, because the media may shape people's attitudes toward social groups, it is important to better understand the subtle ways in which the media can influence people's attitudes. Thereby, the mass media might not only prevent the perpetuation of negative stereotypes and consequent negative intergroup relations but also favour the reduction of discrimination and social tolerance. Recognizing and limiting the use of biased language is an important component of producing quality journalism.

References

Arcuri, L., Maass, A., & Portelli, G. (1993). Linguistic intergroup bias and implicit attributions. *British Journal of Social Psychology, 32*, 277–285.

Brown, R., & Fish, D. (1983). The psychological causality implicit in language. *Cognition, 14*, 233–274.

Capozza, D., & Volpato, C. (2004). *Le intuizioni psicosociali di Hitler: Un'analisi del Mein Kampf* [Hitler's psychosocial intuitions: An analysis of the *Mein Kampf*]. Pàtron Editore.

Carlston, D. E., & Skowronski, J. J. (1994). Savings in the relearning paradigm of trait information as evidence for spontaneous inference generation. *Journal of Personality and Social Psychology, 66*, 840–856.

Carlston, D. E., Skowronski, J. J., & Sparks, C. (1995). Savings in relearning: II. On the formation of the behavior-based trait associations and inferences. *Journal of Personality and Social Psychology, 69*, 420–436.

Carnaghi, A., Maass, A., Gresta, S., Bianchi, M., Cadinu, M., & Arcuri, L. (2008). Nomina sunt omina: On the inductive potential of nouns and adjectives in person perception. *Journal of Personality and Social Psychology, 94*(5), 839–859.

D'Andrea, S., Roccato, M., Russo, S., & Serafin, F. (2016). Mass media, linguistic intergroup bias, and fear of crime. In D. Chadee (Ed.), *Psychology of fear, crime, and the media: International perspectives* (pp. 194–210). Routledge.

De Landtsheer, C. (2009). Collecting political meaning from the count of metaphor. In A. Musolff & J. Zink (Eds.), *Metaphor and discourses* (pp. 73–96). Palgrave Macmillan.

Dragojevic, M., Sink, A., & Mastro, D. (2017). Evidence of linguistic intergroup bias in US print news coverage of immigration. *Journal of Language and Social Psychology, 36*(4), 462–472.

Fiedler, K., Semin, G. R., & Bolten, S. (1989). Language use and reification of social information: Top-down and bottom-up processing in person cognition. *European Journal of Social Psychology, 19*, 271–295.

Fiedler, K., Semin, G. R., & Finkenauer, C. (1993). The battle of words between gender groups: A language-based approach to intergroup processes. *Human Communication Research, 19*, 409–441.

Frey, D. (1986). Recent research on selective exposure to information. *Advances in Experimental Social Psychology, 19*, 41–80.

Geschke, D., Sassenberg, K., Ruhrmann, G., & Sommer, D. (2010). Effects of linguistic abstractness in the mass media: How newspaper articles shape readers' attitudes toward migrants. *Journal of Media Psychology: Theories, Methods, and Applications, 22*, 99–104.

Gibbs, R. W., Jr. (2008). *The Cambridge handbook of metaphor and thought*. Cambridge University Press.

Gilbert, D. T. (1998). Speeding with Ned: A personal view of the correspondence bias. In J. M. Darley & J. Cooper (Eds.), *Attribution and social interaction: The legacy of E. E. Jones*. American Psychological Association.

Gilliam, D. F., Iyengar, S., Simon, A., & Wright, O. (1996). Crime in black and white: The violent, scary world of local news. *Harvard International Journal of Press/Politics, 1*, 6–23.

Glucksberg, S., & Haught, C. (2006). Can Florida become like the next Florida? When metaphoric comparisons fail. *Psychological Science, 17*, 935–938.

Gorham, B. W. (2006). News media's relationship with stereotyping: The linguistic intergroup bias in response to crime news. *Journal of Communication, 56*, 289–308.

Graf, S., Bilewicz, M., Finell, E., & Geschke, D. (2012). Nouns cut slices: Effects of linguistic forms on intergroup bias. *Journal of Language and Social Psychology, 32*, 62–83.

Gustafsson Sendøn, M., Lindholm, T., & Sikstrom, S. (2013). Biases in news media as reflected by personal pronouns in evaluative contexts. *Social Psychology, 45*, 103–111.

Gustafsson Sendøn, M., Lindholm, T., & Sikstrom, S. (2014). Selection bias as reflected by choice of words: The evaluations of 'I' and 'We' differ between communication contexts but 'They' are always worse. *Journal of Language and Social Psychology, 33*, 49–67.

Gustafsson Sendøn, M., Lindholm, T., & Sikstrom, S. (2015). 'She' and 'he' in news media messages: Pronoun use reflects gender biases in semantic contexts. *Sex Roles, 72,* 40–49.

Hamilton, D. L., Gibbons, P. A., Stroessner, S. J., & Sherman, J. W. (1992). Language, intergroup relations and stereotypes. In K. Fiedler & G. R. Semin (Eds.), *Language, interaction and social cognition* (pp. 102–128). Sage.

Haslam, N., Holland, E., & Stratemeyer, M. (2016). Intergroup metaphors. In H. Giles & A. Maass (Eds.), *Language as social action: Vol. 21. Advances in intergroup communication* (pp. 103–117). Lang

Heider, F. (1958). *The psychology of interpersonal relations.* Wiley.

Hitler, H. (1925). *Mein kampf.* Verlag Franz Eher Nachfahren.

Hofstede, G. (1980). *Culture's consequences: International differences in work-related values.* Sage.

Karpinski, A., & von Hippel, W. (1996). The role of the linguistic inter-group bias in expectancy maintenance. *Social Cognition, 14,* 141–163.

Kövecses, Z. (2005). *Metaphor in culture: Universality and variation.* Cambridge University Press.

Kövecses, Z. (2010). *Metaphor: A practical introduction.* Oxford University Press.

Lakoff, G., & Johnson, M. (1980). *Metaphors we live by.* University of Chicago Press.

Landau, M. J., & Keefer, L. A. (2014). This is like that: Metaphors in public discourse shape attitudes. *Social and Personality Psychology Compass, 8,* 463–473.

Landau, M. J., Meier, B. P., & Keefer, L. A. (2010). A metaphor-enriched social cognition. *Psychological Bulletin, 136,* 1045–1067.

Landau, M. J., Robinson, M. D., & Meier, B. P. (2014). *The power of metaphor: Examining its influence on social life.* American Psychological Association.

Loughnan, S., Haslam, N., & Kashima, Y. (2009). Understanding the relationship between attributed-based and metaphor-based dehumanization. *Group Processes & Intergroup Relations, 12,* 747–762.

Maass, A. (1999). Linguistic intergroup bias: Stereotype perpetuation through language. *Advances in Experimental Social Psychology, 31,* 79–121.

Maass, A., Cadinu, M., Boni, M., & Borini, C. (2005). Converting verbs into adjectives: Asymmetrical memory distortions for stereotypic and counterstereotypic information. *Group Processes & Intergroup Relations, 8,* 271–290.

Maass, A., Cadinu, M., Taroni, M., & Masserini, M. (2006). The induction–deduction asymmetry: Fact or artifact? *Social Cognition, 24,* 74–109.

Maass, A., Ceccarelli, R., & Rudin, S. (1996). Linguistic intergroup bias: Evidence for in-group-protective motivation. *Journal of Personality and Social Psychology, 71*(3), 512–526.

Maass, A., Colombo, A., Colombo, A., & Sherman, S. J. (2001). Inferring traits from behaviors versus behaviors from traits: The induction–deduction asymmetry. *Journal of Personality and Social Psychology, 81*(3), 391–404.

Maass, A., Corvino, P., & Arcuri, L. (1994). Linguistic intergroup bias and the mass media. *Revue de Psychologie Social, 1,* 31–43.

Maass, A., Milesi, A., Zabbini, S., & Stahlberg, D. (1995). Linguistic intergroup bias: Differential expectancies or in-group protection? *Journal of Personality and Social Psychology, 68,* 116–126.

Maass, A., Salvi, D., Arcuri, L., & Semin, G. (1989). Language use in intergroup contexts: The linguistic intergroup bias. *Journal of Personality and Social Psychology, 57,* 981–993.

Maass, A., Suitner, C., & Arcuri, L. (2014). The role of metaphors in intergroup relations. In M. Landau, M. D. Robinson, & B. P. Meier (Eds.), *The power of metaphor: Examining its influence on social life* (pp. 153–177). American Psychological Association.

Marshall, S. R., & Shapiro, J. R. (2018). When 'scurry' vs. 'hurry' makes the difference: Vermin metaphors, disgust, and anti-immigrant attitudes. *Journal of Social Issues, 74,* 774–789.

Meier, B. P., Scholer, A., & Fincher-Kiefer, R. (2014). Conceptual metaphor theory and person perception. In M. Landau, M. Robinson, & B. Meier (Eds.), *The power of metaphor: Examining its influence on social life* (pp. 43–64). American Psychological Association.

Miller, G. A., & Johnson-Laird, P. (1976). *Language and perception.* Cambridge University Press.

Miller, J. G. (1984). Culture and development of everyday social explanations. *Journal of Personality and Social Psychology, 46*(5), 961–978.

Morris, M. W., Sheldon, O. J., Ames, D. R., & Young, M. J. (2007). Metaphors and the market: Consequences and preconditions of agent and object metaphors in stock market commentary. *Organizational Behavior and Human Decision Processes, 102,* 174–192.

Moscatelli, S., Albarello, F., & Rubini, M. (2008). Linguistic discrimination in minimal groups: The impact of status differentials. *Journal of Language and Social Psychology, 27,* 140–154.

Ottati, V. C., & Renstrom, R. A. (2010). Metaphor and persuasive communication: A multifunctional approach. *Social and Personality Psychology Compass, 4,* 783–794.

Pettigrew, T. F., & Meertens, R. W. (1995). Subtle and blatant prejudice in Western Europe. *European Journal of Social Psychology, 25,* 57–75.

Porter, S. C., Rhineschmidt-Same, M., & Richeson, J. A. (2016). Inferring identity from language: Linguistic intergroup bias informs social categorization. *Psychological Science, 27,* 94–102.

Rakic, T., & Maass, A. (2019). Communication between and about groups. In J. Harwood, J. Nussbaum, C. Gallois, H. Pierson, & J. Gasiorek (Eds.), *Language, communication, and intergroup relations* (pp. 66–97). Routledge.

Rubini, M., & Semin, G. R. (1994). Language use in the context of congruent and incongruent ingroup behaviors. *British Journal of Social Psychology, 33,* 355–362.

Saucier, G. (2003). Factor structure of English-language personality type nouns. *Journal of Personality and Social Psychology, 85,* 695–708.

Semin, G. R. (2012). The linguistic category model. In P. A. M. Van Lange, A. Kruglanski, & E. T. Higgins (Eds.), *Handbook of theories of social psychology* (pp. 309–326). Sage.

Semin, G. R., & Fiedler, K. (1988). The cognitive functions of linguistic categories in describing persons: Social cognition and language. *Journal of Personality and Social Psychology, 54,* 558–568.

Semin, G. R., & Fiedler, K. (1991). The linguistic category model, its bases, applications and range. *European Review of Social Psychology, 2,* 1–30.

Semin, G. R., Görts, C., Nandram, S., & Semin-Goossens, A. (2002). Cultural perspectives on the linguistic representation of emotion and emotion events. *Cognition and Emotion, 16,* 11–28.

Semin, G. R., & Greenslade, L. (1985). Differential contributions of linguistic factors to memory based ratings: Systematizing the systematic distortion hypothesis. *Journal of Personality and Social Psychology, 49,* 1713–1723.

Stapel, D. A., Koomen, W., & Zeelenberg, M. (1998). The impact of accuracy motivation on interpretation, comparison, and correction processes: Accuracy knowledge accessibility effects. *Journal of Personality and Social Psychology*, *74*, 878–893.

Stapel, D. A., & Semin, G. R. (2007). The magic spell of language: Linguistic categories and their perceptual consequences. *Journal of Personality and Social Psychology*, *93*, 34–48.

Steuter, E., & Wills, D. (2010). 'The vermin have struck again': Dehumanizing the enemy in post 9/11 media representations. *Media, War & Conflict*, *3*, 152–167.

Tajfel, H., & Turner, J. C. (1979). An integrative theory of inter group conflict. In W. G. Austin & S. Worchel Eds.), *The social psychology of inter-group relations* (pp. 33–47). Brooks/Cole.

Tajfel, H., & Turner, J. C. (1986). The social identity theory of intergroup behavior. In S. Worchel & W. G. Austin (Eds.), *The psychology of intergroup relations* (pp. 7–24). Nelson-Hall.

Thibodeau, P. H., & Boroditsky, L. (2011). Metaphors we think with: The role of metaphor in reasoning. *PLoS One*, *6*(2), e16782.

Uleman, J. S. (1987). Consciousness and control: The case of spontaneous inferences. *Personality and Social Psychology Bulletin*, *13*, 337–354.

Uleman, J. S., Hon, A., Roman, R. J., & Moskowitz, G. B. (1996). On-line evidence for spontaneous trait inferences at encoding. *Personality and Social Psychology Bulletin*, *22*, 377–394.

Vargas, P., Sekaquaptewa, D., & von Hippel, W. (2007). Armed only with paper and pencil: 'Low-tech' measures of implicit attitudes. In B. Wittenbrink & N. Schwarz (Eds.), *Implicit measures of attitudes: Procedures and controversies* (pp. 103–124). Guilford.

Von Hippel, W., Sekaquaptewa, D., & Vargas, P. (1997). The linguistic intergroup bias as an implicit indicator of prejudice. Journal of Experimental Social Psychology, 33(5), 490–509.

Wenneker, C. P. J., Wigboldus, D. H. J., & Spears, R. (2005). Biased language use in stereotype maintenance: The role of encoding and goals. *Journal of Personality and Social Psychology*, *89*, 504–516.

Werkman, W. M., Wigboldus, D. H. J., & Semin, G. R. (1999). Children's communication of the linguistic intergroup bias and its impact upon cognitive inferences. *European Journal of Social Psychology*, *29*, 95–104.

White, M. H., & Landau, M. J. (2016). Metaphor in intergroup relations. *Social and Personality Psychology Compass*, *10*, 707–721.

Wierzbicka, A. (1986). What's in a noun? (Or: How do nouns differ in meaning from adjectives?) *Studies in Language*, *10*, 353–389.

Wigboldus, D. H. J., & Douglas, K. (2007). Language, stereotypes, and intergroup relations. In K. Fiedler (Ed.), *Social communication* (pp. 79–106). Psychology Press.

Wigboldus, D. H. J., Semin, G. R., & Spears, R. (2000). How do we communicate stereotypes? Linguistic bases and inferential consequences. *Journal of Personality and Social Psychology*, *78*, 5–18.

Wigboldus, D. H. J., Semin, G. R., & Spears, R. (2006). Communicating expectancies about others. *European Journal of Social Psychology*, *36*, 815–824.

Woods, R., Fernández, A., & Coen, S. (2012). The use of religious metaphors by UK newspapers to describe and denigrate climate change. *Public Understanding of Science*, *21*, 323–339.

10

Discursive Psychology and Journalism

Joanne Meredith

In an era of news reporting in which 'fake news' is a pressing concern (e.g., Ball, 2017; Corner, 2017), the potential bias of media organizations and reporting is debated (e.g., Deacon et al., 2019), and citizen journalism or 'non-mainstream media' is becoming more commonplace (Atton, 2009), the role that journalism plays in reporting and interpreting the news is of great importance. As Bull (2019) notes, there is a widespread consensus that television news has moved away from simply reporting facts to now offering an interpretation of those facts for viewers. Journalism can be viewed as performing a particular social function, in that it is produced in a particular local and political context. Journalists in all contexts have varying power relations with the machinery of government and with the public as a whole (Richardson, 2008). It is within this context that we can see how language can be so important for understanding the impact of journalism. Language in the media has been the focus of study for a number of years, across disciplines from media studies, linguistics, sociology, and discourse studies (e.g., Fowler, 1991; Cotter, 2010; Richardson, 2008). Journalistic language can be viewed as a form of text that can be analysed using the same tools and techniques as those used to analyse other texts. However, the language used in news stories and reporting can be said to be 'doing' certain things or fulfilling particular social roles in terms of how events are presented, and consequently understood, by the readers. Such an interest lends itself strongly to the analysis of media texts using discursive psychology (DP) (Edwards & Potter, 1992). This chapter first describes discursive approaches to psychology and their value, before moving on to discuss DP in detail. It then provides a demonstration of this type of analysis through an analysis of newspaper headlines related to Brexit. Overall, this chapter shows that taking a discursive psychological approach to understanding journalism can highlight how media texts perform certain social actions.

Joanne Meredith, *Discursive Psychology and Journalism* In: *The Psychology of Journalism*. Edited by: Sharon Coen and Peter Bull, Oxford University Press. © Oxford University Press 2021. DOI: 10.1093/oso/9780190935856.003.0010

The History of Discursive Approaches to Psychology

In the late 1980s and early 1990s, there was what has been termed the 'discursive turn' in psychology, which particularly took root in social psychology (Augoustinos, 2017). Potter and Wetherell's (1987) work *Discourse and Social Psychology* outlined how key psychological concepts could be understood through language rather than through exploration of the mind. Subsequent texts (e.g., Edwards & Potter, 1992; Edwards, 1997; Billig, 1996) furthered this research area and drove a change in how we understand psychological ideas and concepts. The core idea of a discursive approach is that we use language 'to understand and make sense of everyday life' (Augoustinos, 2017, p. 213). For discourse analysts, examining language is not a way to understand the inner workings of someone's mind but, instead, is an object of interest in its own right. Discourse analysis is firmly grounded within social constructionism (see Burr & Dick, 2017); that is, it presumes that the language we use constructs the world around us and our own identities. In examining language, discourse analysts seek to uncover the practices that people use. or the discourses that are being drawn upon in order to do particular actions.

Discourse analysis is not one single method. Wiggins (2017) identifies five different types of discourse analyses. Wiggins makes a broad distinction between micro-level approaches (e.g., discursive psychology and conversation analysis) and macro-level approaches (e.g., critical discourse analysis and Foucauldian discourse analysis). Macro-level approaches tend to focus on the ideological grounding and sociohistorical contexts of discourse. In Foucauldian discourse analysis, discourses are understood as not only constructing reality but also impacting upon the ways in which we think and behave. Discourses can produce power relations and social structures, which themselves validate the discourses being used. Discourses can change over time, which is why Foucauldian discourse analysis is also focussed on ideology and context. This form of discourse analysis is most commonly used to examine how a discourse 'makes available different ways of being and speaking in the world' (Wiggins, 2017, p. 50).

Another macro-level approach is critical discourse analysis (CDA). CDA takes an explicitly political stance, in that it argues that we can see the machinery of power and oppression in language. From this perspective, discourses and language draw on the sociopolitical context but also impact upon that broader context. CDA most often focusses on specific social issues such as gender inequality, racism, immigration, and so on. From the perspective of studies of journalism, the focus is on how journalistic texts might draw upon and reproduce those specific power inequalities.

Microanalytic approaches focus on the fine details of social interaction (e.g., Bull, 2019; Wiggins, 2017). A variety of different microanalytic approaches can be taken. Bull (2019) highlights how microanalysis can be used to understand more general theories of interaction and communication, such as face-work (Goffman, 1955). Critical discursive psychology (CDP) also uses a fine-grained approach, but it is also focussed on broader social issues (Edley, 2001). CDP takes a micro approach in terms of analysing everyday interaction, but it situates that interaction within broader ideological and cultural issues.

Membership categorization analysis (MCA) and conversation analysis (CA) (Sacks, 1992) are microanalytic methods that are strongly related and that have influenced DP. MCA examines how the deployment of categories in talk can invoke and infer certain understandings of behaviours and characteristics of those being described. For example, we can use many different words to describe a woman (girl, mother, sister, daughter, wife, teacher, doctor, whore, slut, etc.), and the word used will impact upon the inferences we make about that person. CA focusses on the organization of talk-in-interaction and how it is that we maintain social order and understanding in a variety of contexts. Ekström (2007) argues that CA can make a unique contribution to the study of journalism, in that it is a cohesive approach to studying interaction. He focusses predominantly on broadcast journalism, such as news interviews, because this is where much CA research has been focussed (Hutchby, 2005; Clayman & Heritage, 2002). CA can be applied to journalistic practices to investigate a number of key features of news interviews, such as interruptions (Bull & Mayer, 1988), asking questions (Clayman & Heritage, 2002), and neutrality (Clayman, 1988). However, CA is predominantly focussed on spoken interaction, and Ekström (2007) notes that there is a need to engage with discourse analysis when investigating text-based journalism.

Discursive Psychology

Discursive psychology was developed by Derek Edwards and Jonathan Potter in their 1992 book *Discursive Psychology*. DP re-specified psychology by focussing on how psychological concepts (memory, thought, emotion, attitudes, etc.) could be understood through talk. There was a shift in understanding psychological states as things that were operating behind talk to instead studying how these psychological states are constructed, deployed, and utilized in talk itself. DP treats interaction as 'a domain of situated social action, rather than a set of conventions for the expression of intended messages' (Edwards, 2004, p. 41). This approach moves away from treating lan guage as a system of rules and categories, or as a 'set of signs for transporting thoughts from one mind to another' (Edwards et al., 2009, p. 1). Its aim is not to understand talk by reference to 'underlying cognitive structures, mental processes or neuronal objects' (Potter & Edwards, 2013, p. 704) but, rather, to analyse 'what people *treat as* meaningful, publicly and for each other' (Potter & Edwards, 2013, p. 703). DP also engages with CA, merging an interest in how facts are constructed and how actions are made accountable, with an interest in interaction (Potter, 2012, p. 122).

Potter (2012) notes that DP starts with discourse because discourse is 'the primary arena for human action, understanding and intersubjectivity' (p. 120). Four key characteristics are highlighted by DP. The first of these is that discourse is *action-oriented*, meaning that discourse is studied for the potential actions that are being done, such as complaining, offering, joking, teasing, and so on. The second characteristic is that discourse is *situated*, in the sense that it is situated in a particular sequence (e.g., an answer to a question) or in a particular context (e.g., a news interview or a newspaper headline), and it is situated rhetorically; for example, a description may be built to counter any potential counterarguments (Billig, 1996). Discourse is also viewed as both *constructed* and *constructive*. It is constructed in the sense that it uses a range of resources (e.g., grammar, words, categories, and idioms) to build descriptions and accounts. It is constructive in the sense that it is used to build a version of the world, such as particular events. Finally, discourse is produced as *psychological*; in other words, DP is interested in how participants construct psychological categories and notions, such as personality, disposition, assessments, descriptions, and so on. Edwards (2007) distinguished between the subject side of descriptions, which is how the speaker might be viewed through a particular description or account, and the object side, which is how a description is built. It is this interest in the resources used for building descriptions and factual accounts that is relevant for the analysis of journalism. In building descriptions, participants may use a variety of rhetorical devices, including extreme case formulations (Edwards,

2000), category entitlement, stake inoculation, claiming corroboration for their version, and so on (Potter, 1996).

In terms of its methods, DP is not a universal approach to discourse (Tileaga & Stokoe, 2016). As previously noted, one branch is strongly influenced by CA in that it is interested in how psychological concepts are used in the unfolding context of an interaction. There is also a branch that is focussed on texts, such as online texts (Meredith & Richardson, 2019) and newspaper articles (MacMillan & Edwards, 1999). Unlike some other forms of micro-analytic research (e.g., Elliot & Bull, 1996), DP does not tend to use coding schemes or provide counts of specific features but, rather, focusses on taking an inductive approach to addressing how specific features occur in particular contexts. The aim of DP is, therefore, to understand how media texts 'operate within wider social, cultural and political concerns' (Tileaga & Stokoe, 2016, p. 4). Based on the influence of CA, there is a strong emphasis on using naturally-occurring data (Wiggins, 2017), which is described as data that have not been engendered by a researcher, although DP analyses have been conducted on generated data, such as interviews (e.g., Goodman & Walker, 2016). DP researchers have been interested in media texts and journalism from the outset, with Edwards and Potter's (1992) text including the analysis of a number of extracts from newspaper articles and broadcast interviews. Such texts can be considered naturally occurring data because they would have happened whether or not the researcher had been there. The following section explores some of the studies that use DP for media texts and demonstrates how these studies might help with understanding aspects of journalism.

Discursive Psychology and Studies of Journalism

One of the key studies that applied DP to media interactions was by Abell and Stokoe (1999), in which they analysed Princess Diana's *Panorama* interview. Princess Diana had been married to Prince Charles (Prince of Wales and heir to the British throne) until 1992, when they officially separated. There were multiple newspaper reports of infidelity on both sides of the marriage, as well as various other issues in their marriage. Diana appeared on *Panorama* in November 1995 in an interview with the journalist Martin Bashir. The interview was an opportunity for her to put 'on the record' her version of the story and to address the various rumours surrounding the state of her marriage to a television (TV) audience. In the interview, Diana admitted to infidelity and addressed her husband's extramarital affair; the couple subsequently filed for divorce the following year. Abell and Stokoe's paper showed, through the analysis of three extracts from the interview, how blame and accountability were ascribed—by both interviewer and interviewee—without the speaker being seen as in some way biased. They noted the various ways in which this was achieved by the speakers 'attending to issues such as the management of stake and interest using strategies of fact construction, active voicing, extreme-case formulation, narrative and script design' (p. 315). They highlighted how Diana blamed the media, the Royal household, and her ex-husband, Prince Charles, for the break-up of her marriage, while also managing the possibility that she could in some way be seen as to blame. This paper, therefore, highlights the variety of practices that interviewers and interviewees use to construct issues such as blame and accountability in a broadcast interview.

In another paper focussed on Princess Diana, media descriptions of Diana's death in newspaper articles were examined (MacMillan &Edwards, 1999). Princess Diana died in Paris in August 1997 following an accident in which the car she was riding was being pursued by paparazzi who wanted to take photographs of her with her boyfriend at the time, Dodi Fayed. The main focus of the paper was to explore how the media dealt with their own potential culpability for Diana's death. For example, in refuting the notion that her pursuit by press photographers led to the car accident, the press used different terms to describe the photographers who were involved, including 'yobs with cameras masquerading as photo-journalists' and 'foreign celebrity-snappers'. They also noted that the paparazzi were often described in terms of being foreign, with the implication that British photographers would not have behaved in this way. In highlighting this, MacMillan and Edwards showed how the British press were portrayed as moral and trustworthy, in comparison to the foreign, unprincipled paparazzi. Their analysis also demonstrated how the press constructed arguments to defy calls for legislation or privacy laws, by showing that those who wanted them were either biased or irrational. Finally, they showed how the media, through talking about 'the public' or 'the marketplace', blamed the public for wanting to see photographs of Princess Diana. Overall, MacMillan and Edwards concluded that in the reporting of Princess Diana's death, category distinctions were made by the press so that they developed a narrative of 'us versus them'. This highlights how a particular narrative can be developed by the press while they present themselves as sympathetic and unbiased in their reporting. In his re-reading of this paper, Attenborough (2016) noted how MacMillan and Edwards' analysis highlighted the ways in which the press often recontextualized a speaker's words so that they presented a specific understanding of those words. For example, he noted how the words of Earl Spencer, Princess Diana's brother who gave a eulogy at her funeral criticizing the press ('I always believed the press would kill her in the end'), were recontextualized by the *Daily Star* as a premonition of her death rather than as him blaming the press directly.

Studying these kinds of media texts using DP allows for an understanding to develop of how terms are used in specific contexts to do specific actions. In other words, it allows for an analysis of how one single term, such as 'joke', performs a particular social action in the context in which it is used. For example, in a headline such as 'Man prosecuted for a "joke" on Twitter', the term 'joke' has a different contextual meaning from that of a headline such as 'British prime minister is "a joke" says foreign secretary'. In the former meaning, the term 'joke' presents something that is intended to be laughable or funny. In the latter meaning, 'a joke' refers to someone as an object of ridicule rather than as someone who is particularly funny. A discursive psychological analysis of the media, therefore, allows for an understanding of how descriptions presented are social actions (Attenborough, 2016). Although this is also the case for ordinary descriptions, Attenborough highlights that with regard to the media, the audience is much larger, and the way in which descriptions are presented can have real-world consequences.

Since the research by Abell and Stokoe (1999) and MacMillan and Edwards (1999), studies that have used DP to analyse media texts have been relatively rare. Simmons and LeCouteur (2008) analysed a number of newspaper articles and television and radio interviews to explore how two different 'riots' were reported in the Australian media: one that involved Indigenous community members and one that involved non-Indigenous peoples. Their analysis highlighted how the cause of the conflict in each case was constructed; whether the group or the individual was attributed blame; and how a distinction was made between whether the cause was due to the inherent personality type of those involved or whether this was a more transient state. Overall, they concluded that in the case of the Indigenous riots, the media portrayed their desire for change as unattainable. However, in the case of the non-Indigenous riots, the media suggested that change was possible. In this way, the media constructed and perpetuated a form of modern racism, with potentially real-world consequences.

A more recent paper by Johnson and Goodman (2013) focussed on broadcast media only and analysed the discursive strategies used by Nick Griffin, the leader of the British National Party (BNP), in media appearances to respond to criticism of the extremist nature of the party. Johnson and Goodman focussed on three high-profile BBC appearances (Radio 4's *Today* programme; BBC 1's *Question Time*, and Five Live's *Breakfast* programme), which included political interviews as well as a debate on *Question Time*. They highlight two interconnected strategies that Griffin used: (1) that 'indigenous British' people are portrayed as victims of racism, and (2) that Griffin blames this issue on the elite rather than on immigrants or ethnic minorities. They also note how much of Griffin's talk was designed to avoid the suggestion that the BNP could be perceived as racist.

A final paper to highlight that has taken a discursive psychological approach to media texts is that of Goodman et al.'s (2017) research which examines how the media presented the migrant crisis in 2015. During 2015, there was a perceived crisis when more than 1 million refugees crossed into Europe, predominantly via the Mediterranean Sea, most often fleeing conflict situations in Syria, Libya, Iraq, and Afghanistan. There were multiple reports of boats sinking on their way to Europe, with more than 3,500 migrants dying during that year. Through in-depth analysis of media headlines and subheadings, Goodman et al. demonstrated how this crisis was first portrayed as a 'Mediterranean migrant crisis', followed by a 'Calais migrant crisis' and then 'Europe's migrant crisis'. After a particular newsworthy event, in which a small child who had washed up on a beach after drowning while he and his family attempted to cross from Turkey and Greece, the crisis then changed to a 'refugee crisis', before reverting to a migrant crisis. They noted that initially the key changes in the headlines concerned where the crisis was taking place, and this highlighted the proximity of the potential threat to their readers in the United Kingdom. However, the subsequent change to 'refugee' shifted the focus to who was a part of the crisis. Refugee is viewed as a more positive category, which suggests that there is a need for them to be supported. However, the shift back to a migrant crisis returned to the notion of a potential threat.

The previously discussed papers show how DP can be utilized to analyse media texts in general and how, through this analysis, we can start to see the potential impact that the terms and practices used might have on readers. The readership is an important aspect to consider, and we might consider how journalistic tests are 'recipient designed' (Sacks et al., 1974). Recipient design refers to the ways in which talk is designed to display an orientation to others involved in the interaction. In the case of media texts, we can consider how they might be written for those who view them and how the practices employed may help construct a particular political or ideological viewpoint.

Case Study: Brexit

This case study focusses on analysing the headlines of a number of articles about Brexit. *Brexit* refers to Britain leaving the European Union (EU); it is a portmanteau of the words 'Britain' and 'exit'. The referendum on the UK's membership of the EU was held in June 2016 after an extensive period of campaigning by the formal campaign groups, supported by other political, industrial, and civil society stakeholders. The campaign was incredibly bitter at times, with Moore and Ramsey (2017) suggesting that it was the 'most divisive, hostile, negative and fear-provoking of the 21st century'. More than 45 million people voted, with a turnout of 72%—the highest for any vote in more than 20 years in the United Kingdom. The final result (52% to leave the EU and 48% to remain) highlighted a stark political division in the country, which still resonated as the United Kingdom negotiated leaving the EU. The headlines analysed here were collected as part of a wider project on discourses of Brexit. For this project, the focus was on a well-publicized claim that 'We send £350m a week to the EU. Let's fund our NHS [National Health Service] instead'. This slogan was written on the side of the Leave campaign 'battle bus', and it became a particularly contested claim both during and after the referendum.

Four newspapers were chosen from which to collect data: *Daily Mail/Mail on Sunday*, *Daily Express/Sunday Express*, *Independent*, and *Guardian/Observer*. Data were collected in October 2016 and comprised articles from any time after the date that the referendum was announced until the date of data collection, resulting in a total of 34 newspaper articles being collected (for more detail, see Meredith & Richardson, 2019). The focus of this analysis is divided into two particular aspects: (1) how the £350m claim was described both before and after the referendum and (2) how persons and campaigns were referred to in the headlines.

Descriptions of the £350m Claim
In this section, the analysis focusses on how the '£350m a week to the NHS' campaign slogan was described in various newspaper headlines

over the course of the referendum campaign. It is first interesting to note an initial headline that referred to the NHS receiving money from *before* the bus was unveiled:

> Boris Johnson: Cash-starved NHS will receive BILLIONS if Britain leaves the European Union (*Daily Express*, 15 April, 2016)

Here, we can notice a few features that are relevant. First, this is directly attributed to a particular person, Boris Johnson, as if this is a quotation. The use of reported speech is a way of building an account so that it appears more factual (Potter, 1996). The person to whom this claim is attributed was one of the most prominent Leave politicians, and so in that sense his role in the category of 'persons involved in the Leave campaign' or 'prominent UK politicians' entitled him to have the right to make such claims (Potter & Hepburn, 2008). In terms of building the description of how the NHS would receive money if the United Kingdom left the EU, the imperative term 'will' is used. This is an expression of an intention; we could consider the other words that might be used here, such as 'might' or 'may' or 'could', which would make this a more conditional result of leaving the EU. However, using the term 'will' suggests that it is a definite event. There is also the implication in the headline that the NHS is 'cash-starved' *because* of Britain's membership of the EU, and therefore presents a description of what Johnson has said as a justification for leaving the EU.

The next headline is from a few weeks before the referendum, approximately a month after the bus with the slogan was unveiled:

> Nigel Farage: £350 million pledge to fund the NHS was a 'big mistake' (*Daily Express*, 4 June 2016)

As with the previous example, this headline presents the report of a statement by a specific person, in this case the leader of the UK Independence Party (UKIP), Nigel Farage. Farage was also one of the key figures on the Leave side during the referendum, but he was not part of the 'official' Leave campaign. In the headline, the term 'pledge' is used to refer to the £350 million slogan, and this suggests a promise is being made. We could consider the fact that we use the term 'pledge' in the context of, for example, pledging money to a charity and that this is a positive thing to do, but it may be seen as more negative if it does not eventually happen. The upshot of the headline is that the pledge itself has been called a 'big mistake', and through the use of quotation marks this is presented as Farage's direct words. It is important to remember that a newspaper report of someone's reported words is also recontextualizing that talk (Leudar & Antaki, 1996). Therefore, through the use of quote marks around the term 'big mistake', the potential veracity of Farage's claim is minimized. It is important to note that Farage was criticizing the pledge itself, which was made by the official Leave campaign in which he was not involved, and therefore his entitlement to make such claims might be limited. Therefore, in introducing a note of ambiguity into the headline, it potentially indicates doubt about the extent to which the pledge actually was a 'big mistake'. In addition, including the quotation marks might also be a way of mitigating Farage's quote, potentially providing implicit support for the £350m claim.

To show a brief example of a very different type of reporting of this slogan from before the referendum, consider the following headline from a 'fact-checking' piece from *The Guardian*:

> Why Vote Leave's £350m weekly EU cost claim is wrong (*The Guardian*, 10 June 2016)

The headline does not aim to report the news but, rather, to contradict a particular assertion. In contrast to the previous two headlines, this claim is attributed to a particular group (Vote Leave) rather than to an individual, suggesting that the group as a whole has responsibility for it. Here, the term 'claim' rather than 'pledge' is used, which might be because the aim of the article is to refute the underlying facts behind the slogan, and use of the term 'claim' provides an indication that it is inaccurate. It is worth noting that the headline is also presenting the fact that this piece will explain 'why' it is wrong; in other words, there is no ambiguity in this headline. A final point of interest is that this is very clearly labelled as 'fact-checking', and as such there is the recruitment of the notion that 'facts' themselves are unambiguous and can claim something as right or wrong. The ways in which facts are constructed for the reader to understand them *as* factual is of importance for journalism. The presentation of 'facts' can also do social actions; for example, presenting a 'fact' may be an argumentative move in a political debate and can therefore be doing disagreement (Demasi, 2019).

After the referendum, Nigel Farage went on TV and stated that the NHS would not receive £350 million a week as the slogan seemed to imply (although it was also contested as to whether this is actually what the slogan implied):

Video evidence emerges of Nigel Farage pledging EU millions for NHS weeks before Brexit vote (*The Independent*, 25 June 2016)

In this headline, we again see the term pledge referred to, although this time as a verb. As was commented on previously, pledging something can be seen as making a promise, and as such breaking that promise can be seen as negative. As this is attached to Farage, it is attributed to him as an individual rather than to the group Vote Leave. It is worth noting that in the previously discussed *Daily Express* headline in which Farage is mentioned, he is simply presented as referring to the slogan, but the slogan itself it not attributed to any particular person or group. In this case, however, the underlying action of the headline is to refute Farage's claim that he never made this pledge (which he had stated in the interview). In other words, by reporting about this video emerging, the action is not just to report the news but also to present evidence that Nigel Farage is lying.

Brexit: Vote Leave camp abandon £350m-a-week NHS vows in Change Britain Plans (*The Independent*, 27 June 2016)

In this headline, the term claim is changed to 'vows', which potentially seems to be a more permanent type of promise to a pledge. The 'vow' is also attributed to the 'Vote Leave camp' rather than to any specific person such as Farage or Johnson. In this sense, it is again the responsibility of the entire group to ensure this 'vow' is abided by. In comparison to the previous headline, the action of this is not to contradict a particular person but, instead, to underline the potential breaking of this vow by the whole campaign.

In contrast, consider the final extract in this section:

Brexit: £350 million a week extra for the NHS only 'an aspiration'—says Vote Leave campaigner Chris Grayling (*The Independent*, 27 June 2016)

The term used for the slogan is explicitly stated as 'an aspiration' rather than a 'pledge' or 'vow' or 'claim'. The term 'only' is also used to mitigate the strength of the claim itself, and quotation marks are placed around the term 'an aspiration' to show that this is a quote rather than simply the term the paper is using. The term is attributed to a particular person—Chris Grayling, a prominent Conservative politician—who is placed within the category of a 'Vote Leave campaigner', so in contrast to, for example, Johnson or Farage, he is seen as belonging to that particular campaign.

In this section, then, we have seen that the terms used in newspaper headlines to describe the £350 million claim, which was placed on a side of a bus during the campaign, changed over the course of the referendum campaign. We also saw that the ways in which the slogan was attributed to different individuals and groups also changed. The following section focusses in more detail on the ways in which persons and categories are referred to in headlines.

Referring to Persons and Categories in Newspaper Headlines

There are different ways in which people and organizations are referred to in headlines, including as individuals or categories. There are two preferences for references to persons (Sacks & Schegloff, 1979). The first is a preference for a recognitional reference; in other words, to maintain common understanding, there is a preference for using a name that all recipients will recognize (Heritage, 2007). The second preference is for a minimized reference form; in other words, a single reference form should be used (Sacks & Schegloff, 1979). For example, saying 'The President of the United States, Donald Trump' would breach the second preference because either name (The President of the United States or Donald Trump) would be recognized by recipients.

In the following instance, the two persons in the headline are referred to just by their surname:

> EU referendum: Sturgeon accuses Johnson of telling £350m 'whopper' (*The Guardian*, 9 June 2016)

Because there is a preference for a recognitional reference, the implication is that the recipients will recognize these individuals just by their surnames in this context. This also, then, meets the preference for only using one reference form, in that they are not also referred to by their roles (e.g.,

Nicola Sturgeon as the Scottish first minister and Boris Johnson as former London mayor), although these are used in the standfirst. In the context of making an accusation, an accusation coming from the officer of the Scottish first minister rather than an individual may sound more serious. Therefore, in using the individuals' names, it downgrades the severity of the accusation; in other words, it makes it an accusation by an individual toward another individual rather than an office of power.

The following headline comes from the *Daily Mail* following a TV debate about the issue of Britain leaving the EU. The debate included Amber Rudd, who at the time was the Conservative Home Secretary and a member of the Remain campaign, as well as Boris Johnson, who was a prominent Leave campaigner:

> 'He's not the man you want to drive you home at the end of the evening': Tory minister's extraordinary jibe at Boris in nastiest TV referendum debate yet (*Daily Mail*, 9 June 2016)

Here, the category term 'Tory minister' is used instead of the name (Amber Rudd). It is notable that this may well breach the preference for a recognitional reference, in that it is not clear precisely who is being referred to here. It is, then, interesting to analyse what using a category does in terms of how recipients might read this headline. When categories are used, it makes particular category-bound activities available, which are associated with someone who belongs to that category (Stokoe, 2012). Therefore, when the category 'Tory Minister' is used, the category-bound activities might be someone who makes laws, who represents the country, and so on. The category-bound activity of a minister is *not* to make jibes at another person, and therefore we can read this as a potential breach of their role, more so than if just a person reference were used. The recipient of the jibe is referred to as Boris, and as such this meets the preference for a single recognitional term; there is a presumption that readers will recognize this as referring to Boris Johnson. However, by the recipient being referred to simply by their first name compared to the category of the person doing the jibe, it implies a power imbalance between the two. In other words, one person is a minister who, by virtue of their category predicates or characteristics (Stokoe, 2012), has power, but by using a simple first name term, it seems that they have less power. We could imagine that this headline would read quite differently if it were 'Amber Rudd's extraordinary jibe at the former mayor of London' or 'Tory minister's extraordinary jibe at fellow Tory MP'.

The following headline shows a similar use of categories and person reference:

Senior Tory MP accuses Boris Johnson of trying to 'bribe' voters with his 'corrosive' claims about NHS funding during EU referendum as he declares for Remain (*Daily Mail*, 13 June 2016)

The accuser here is a 'senior Tory MP'; they are not referred to by name, and no information about them is given. One reason for this is that if there is a preference for a single recognitional term, then the name of the Tory MP may not be recognizable to the wider readership, and so the use of the category term is more appropriate here. The category term does, however, have some potential predicates, in that we might expect a senior MP to have experience and knowledge that gives them some category entitlement to make claims against Johnson. However, there is also the implication that the senior Tory MP is biased in their claims because they have declared for Remain, and so they have a specific interest in making such negative claims about Johnson. Boris Johnson is referred to by his full name, which is a recognizable reference term. However, note that Johnson could also be described as a 'senior Tory MP', but the use of his name provides readers with a recognitional reference term so a broader category term is not needed. As with the previous headline, using the category term for the accuser but just a person reference term for the recipient suggests a particular power imbalance between the two persons referenced in the headline.

In the following headline, a number of category terms are utilized:

'Doctor knows best': Don't trust Brexiteers to do what is best for NHS, top doctors warn as they claim leaving the EU will make it 'impossible' to care for ageing population (*Daily Mail*, 14 June 2016)

Before analysing the category terms in detail, it is worth discussing the idiom that is used at the start of the headline: 'Doctor knows best'. This phrase refers to the notion that doctors, as a category of persons, have the knowledge to be able to tell their patients what to do and how to behave. However, over time, this has become a somewhat ironic phrase that can potentially be used as a way of subverting the idea of a doctor knowing best. The use of the quotation marks also suggests that the term is being used ironically.

The first category term used after the idiomatic phrase is 'Brexiteers'. This category term does not, as with previous headlines, refer to the Brexit or Vote Leave *campaign* but instead to Brexiteers as a general category. This category could be understood as referring to anyone who is in support of Brexit rather than just to the politicians or public figures leading the campaign. The use of this particular category term implies that it is anyone who votes to leave the EU who does not care about the NHS, rather than just the category itself. In this way, it defines the potential category predicates of a Brexit voter (Meredith & Richardson, 2019). Those making the claim are also referred to, based on their category 'top doctors', which suggests that due to their category entitlement they have the right to make this claim. However, the category entitlement that these 'top doctors' might have has been mitigated by using the ironic idiom at the start of the headline, which perhaps suggests a more sceptical approach should be taken to the claims. In using the term Brexiteers, rather than Brexit campaign, the headline implies that the doctors are saying that Brexit voters more generally would not do the best for the NHS. However, in using the idiom at the start of the headline, a note of scepticism is introduced into the category-based entitlement that doctors have to make these claims.

The following headline was published after an appearance on the BBC programme *Question Time* by Diane Abbott, who at the time was Labour Shadow Secretary of State of International Development and a Remain campaigner:

> *Question Time* audience member puts down Diane Abbott as she attacks Farage for NHS 'lies' (*Daily Express*, 22 June 2016)

A category reference is used at the start of the headline when describing the agent of the behaviour as a '*Question Time* audience member'. The use of this category term fits with the preference for a recognizable form of reference because the name of the audience member would not be recognizable to readers. The politicians, on the other hand, are referred to by their names, which suggests that this would be a recognizable reference for readers. Interestingly, Farage is only referred to by his surname, which would imply that—like Sturgeon and Johnson—his name is recognizable enough without needing to include his forename. It could also be that the use of the surname alone could be viewed as a derogatory reference, although in this particular context that interpretation is less likely. In using a category to describe the question asker, the headline draws upon the category predicates of an audience member who we might expect to be less knowledgeable or less able to 'put down' experienced politicians such as Diane Abbott. It also draws on the notion that an audience member is someone who has a certain role, so potentially being somewhat passive in an interaction. We could consider the other terms that could be used here, such as '*Question Time* question asker', which as a category would suggest that one of the category-bound activities is to ask questions and challenge the politicians, rather than a passive audience member. In using the category terms here, then, the headline constructs a particular description of the event, with a passive, inexperienced audience member being able to effectively challenge Diane Abbott, an experienced politician.

The following two headlines both relate to the same event—an MP changing from Leave to Remain—and they show how the same person and event can be described in slightly different ways:

> Tory MP Sarah Wollaston switches from Leave to Remain over NHS claims (*Daily Express*, 9 June 2016)

> EU referendum: Respected Tory MP Sarah Wollaston quits Leave campaign over 'false' NHS claims (*The Independent*, 9 June 2016)

In the *Daily Express*, Sarah Wollaston is referred to by her category 'Tory MP' and also by her name. This potentially breaches the preference for a single recognizable term, but it is arguable that simply saying Tory MP would be too broad here because her name is not recognizable enough. There is one notable difference between the two headlines, in that the *Independent* headline adds the adjective 'respected'. The fact that she can be described as 'respected' invokes the notion that her switching sides should be treated as an important issue. We can also note that in the *Daily Express* headline, the word 'false' is omitted when referring to the claims about the NHS. In other words, from the headline in the *Daily Express*, the switching of sides has occurred merely due to some unspecified NHS claims, whereas in the *Independent*, the change of sides has happened specifically because Leave campaign has been making 'false' claims.

In the final headline, we again see a category and a person reference term used:

Ex-health secretary Andrew Lansley demands £5bn-a-year 'Brexit bonus' for NHS (*Daily Express*, 22 September 2016)

This headline, again, breaches the preference for a single recognizable reference, although it could be argued that 'ex-health secretary' would not have been specific enough, but the name Andrew Lansley might not have been recognizable. In using the category term 'ex-health secretary', there are particular category predicates that can be invoked, particularly that a health secretary would be expected to be knowledgeable about the NHS. It also provides for a higher category entitlement to be able to make such claims rather than other categories that could have been used, such as 'ex Tory Minister' or 'Tory MP'. In using this particular category, then, the claims of this individual can be read as having more weight than those of other MPs or campaigners.

Conclusion

The analysis of the Brexit headlines has shown how psychological issues are referred to and used in these media texts. The first section of the analysis demonstrated the way in which intention was at issue in the headlines. For example, using the term 'will' compared with the word 'pledge' implies different things about the intention of the actor(s) to deliver on the slogan. The use of terms such as 'aspiration' and 'claim' provides a particular context for the recipients' understandings of the expectations around the slogan. In other words, the use of different intention words creates an understanding for the recipients (the readers) of these terms of the context of the article, as well as potentially the broader context. The second section of the analysis demonstrates how identities and categories are invoked to do particular actions. The use of categories makes available category-bound activities and predicates which can be inferred about the people in the headlines. In addition, invoking someone's group identity can imply that they have category entitlements to make certain claims. In using individual person references, as opposed to categories, inferences can be made about aspects such as power and competencies.

Although there are many ways in which discourse analysis can be applied to media texts, discursive psychology focusses on the microanalysis of the language. In doing so, it analyses how specific words and practices can perform specific actions and how alternate ways of describing the situation are omitted. Thus, although the focus is on the fine-grained analysis, this can open up an enormous amount of information about how the texts are shaping an overall narrative—not just in one particular story but, rather, across the media as a whole (Goodman et al., 2017). In an era of 'post-truth' news (Demasi, 2019) and with concerns regarding media bias, journalists need to understand and appreciate the importance of the language that is used when reporting the news. For journalists, approaching their own and others' articles and reports through a microanalytic lens can assist in understanding how readers might interpret their words and what inferences may be drawn from this. Equally, analysing news reports and articles using DP can help readers explore how particular events, people, and texts are constructed. DP can explore how psychological concerns, such as identities, intentions, categories, and behaviours, are made relevant in these media texts and, as a result, can help with understanding how texts are understood and interpreted.

References

Abell, J., & Stokoe, E. H. (1999). 'I take full responsibility, I take some responsibility, I'll take half of it but no more than that': Princess Diana and the negotiation of blame in the 'Panorama' interview. *Discourse Studies, 1*(3), 297–319.

Attenborough, F. T. (2016). A forgotten legacy? Towards a discursive psychology of the media. In C. Tileagă & E. Stokoe (Eds.), *Discursive psychology: Classic and contemporary issues* (pp. 224–240). Routledge.

Atton, C. (2009). Alternative and citizen journalism. In K. Wahl-Jorgensen & T. Hanitzsch (Eds.), *The handbook of journalism studies* (pp. 265–278). Routledge.

Augoustinos, M. (2017). Discourse analysis. In B. Gough (Ed.), *The Palgrave handbook of critical social psychology* (pp. 205–224). Palgrave Macmillan.

Ball, J. (2017). *Post-truth: How bullshit conquered the world*. Biteback Publishing.

Billig, M. (1996). *Arguing and thinking: A rhetorical approach to social psychology* (2nd ed.). Cambridge University Press.

Bull, P. (2019). The construction of political journalism: A microanalytic approach. *Discourse, Context and Media, 27*, 7–14.

Bull, P., & Mayer, K. (1988). Interruptions in political interviews: A study of Margaret Thatcher and Neil Kinnock. *Journal of Language and Social Psychology, 7*(1), 35–46.

Burr, V., & Dick, P. (2017). Social constructionism. In B. Gough (Ed.), *The Palgrave handbook of critical social psychology* (pp. 59–80). Palgrave Macmillan.

Clayman, S. E. (1988). Displaying neutrality in television news interviews. *Social Problems, 35*(4), 474–492.

Clayman, S. E., & Heritage, J. (2002). *The news interview: Journalists and public figures on the air.* Cambridge University Press.

Corner, J. (2017). Fake news, post-truth and media–political change. *Media, Culture & Society, 39*(7), 1100–1107.

Cotter, C. (2010). *News talk: Investigating the language of journalism.* Cambridge University Press.

Deacon, D., Goode, J., Smith, D., Wring, D., Downey, J., & Vaccari, C. (2019). General election report 1-5. Retrieved 3 January, 2020, from https://www.lboro.ac.uk/news-events/general-election

Demasi, M. A. (2019). Facts as social action in political debates about the European Union. *Political Psychology, 40*(1), 3–20.

Edley, N. (2001). Conversation analysis, discursive psychology and the study of ideology: A response to Susan Speer. *Feminism & Psychology, 11*(1), 136–140.

Edwards, D. (1997). *Discourse and cognition.* Sage.

Edwards, D. (2000). Extreme case formulations: Softeners, investment, and doing nonliteral. *Research on Language and Social Interaction, 33*(4), 347–373.

Edwards, D. (2004). Shared knowledge as a performative category in conversation. *Rivista Di Psicololinguistica Applicata, 4*(2-3), 41–53

Edwards, D. (2007). Managing subjectivity in talk. In A. Hepburn & S. Wiggins (Eds.), *Discursive research in practice: New approaches to psychology and interaction* (pp. 31–49). Cambridge University Press.

Edwards, D., Hepburn, A., & Potter, J. (2009). Psychology, sociology and interaction: Disciplinary allegiance or analytic quality? A response to Housley and Fitzgerald. *Qualitative Research, 9*(1), 119–128.

Edwards, D., & Potter, J. (1992). *Discursive psychology.* Sage.

Ekström, M. (2007). Conversation analysis in journalism studies. *Journalism Studies, 8*(6), 964–973..

Fowler, R. (1991). *Language in the news: Discourse and ideology in the press.* Routledge.

Goffman, E. (1955). On face-work: An analysis of ritual elements in social interaction. *Psychiatry, 18*(3), 213–231.

Goodman, S., Sirriyeh, A., & McMahon, S. (2017). The evolving (re)categorisations of refugees throughout the 'refugee/migrant crisis'. *Journal of Community and Applied Social Psychology, 27*, 105–114.

Goodman, S., & Walker, K. (2016). 'Some I don't remember and some I do': Memory talk in accounts of intimate partner violence. *Discourse Studies, 18*(4), 375–392.

Heritage, J. (2007). Intersubjectivity and progressivity in references to persons (and places). In N. J. Enfield & T. Stivers (Eds.), *Person reference in interaction: Linguistic, cultural and social perspectives* (pp. 255–280). Cambridge University Press.

Hutchby, I. (2005). *Media talk: Conversation analysis and the study of broadcasting.* McGraw-Hill.

Johnson, A. J., & Goodman, S. (2013). Reversing racism and the elite conspiracy: Strategies used by the British National Party leader in response to hostile media appearances. *Discourse, Context and Media, 2*, 156–164.

Leudar, I., & Antaki, C. (1996). Discourse participation, reported speech and research practices in social psychology. *Theory & Psychology, 6*(1), 5–29.

MacMillan, K., & Edwards, D. (1999). Who killed the Princess? Description and blame in the British press. *Discourse Studies, 1*(2), 151–174.

Meredith, J., & Richardson, E. (2019). The use of the political categories of Brexiter and Remainer in online comment threads about the EU referendum. *Journal of Community & Applied Social Psychology, 29*, 43–55.

Moore, M., & Ramsey, G. (2017, May 16). Acrimonious and divisive: The role the media played in Brexit [blog post]. http://blogs.lse.ac.uk/brexit/2017/05/16/ acrimonious-and-divisive-the-role-the-media-played-in-brexit

Potter, J. (1996). *Representing reality: Discourse, rhetoric and social construction.* Sage.

Potter, J. (2012). Discourse analysis and discursive psychology. In H. Cooper (Ed.), *APA handbook of research methods in psychology: Vol. 2. Quantitative, qualitative, neuropsychological and biological* (pp. 111–130). American Psychological Association.

Potter, J., & Edwards, D. (2013). Conversation analysis and psychology. In T. Stivers & J. Sidnell (Eds.), *The handbook of conversation analysis* (pp. 701–725). Routledge.

Potter, J., & Hepburn, A. (2008). Discursive constructionism. In J. A. Holstein & J. F. Gubrium (Eds.), *The handbook of constructionist research* (pp. 275–293). Guildford.

Potter, J., & Wetherell, M. (1987). *Discourse and social psychology: Beyond attitudes and behaviour.* Sage.

Richardson, J. E. (2008). Language and journalism: An expanding research agenda. *Journalism Studies, 9*(2), 152–160.

Sacks, H. (1992). *Lectures on conversation* (Vols. 1 and 2, edited by G. Jefferson). Blackwell.

Sacks, H., & Schegloff, E. A. (1979). Two preferences in the organization of reference to persons in conversation and their interaction. In G. Psathas (Ed.), *Everyday language: Studies in ethnomethodology* (pp. 15–21). Irvington.

Sacks, H., Schegloff, E. A., & Jefferson, G. (1974). A simplest systematics for the organization of turn-taking in conversation. *Language, 50*(4), 696–735.

Simmons, K., & LeCouteur, A. (2008). Modern racism in the media: Constructions of 'the possibility of change' in accounts of two Australian 'riots'. *Discourse & Society, 19*(5), 557–687.

Stokoe, E. (2012). Moving forward with membership categorization analysis: Methods for systematic analysis. *Discourse Studies, 14*(3), 277–303.

Tileagă, C., & Stokoe, E. (Eds.). (2016). *Discursive psychology: Classic and contemporary issues.* Routledge.

Wiggins, S. (2017). *Discursive psychology: Theory, method and applications.* Sage.

11

Visual Communication Through Body Movement

Peter Bull

As we speak, we cannot help but move. Body movement—not just our hand gestures but all parts of the body—is closely synchronized with speech. Even movements of the legs and the feet have been shown to be coordinated with speech (Bull & Connelly, 1981).

Body movement has some highly important features. It is visual; it can be highly visible; it is silent; it is also a form of bodily action. This can make it extremely useful for a variety of communicative functions (Kendon, 1985). We can catch or hold people's attention with flamboyant gestures. We can stress important words or phrases with a movement of the head, a raised eyebrow, or an emphatic gesture. Just as a picture may be worth a thousand words, so miming an action may have much greater impact, or simply be more informative, than a long verbal description. Some things are too delicate to put into words, but you may be able to say it all just with an appropriate gesture or facial expression. Sometimes we do not want to put into words what the assembled company can hear, but because body movement is silent, it is possible to 'catch someone's eye' or 'exchange a meaningful glance' so that they 'get the message'. How we mean others to take our remarks can be conveyed through facial movements. What is intended as a joke may be indicated by a smile: Say it with a smile, and allegedly you can get away with saying almost anything! Conversely, in deadpan humour, these nonverbal indicators are withheld, so deadpan achieves its effect because we are never sure how seriously it should be taken.

From this perspective, nonverbal behaviour can be understood to play an important role in journalism because journalism is heavily reliant on visual forms of communication. In the first section of this chapter, a review is presented of the kinds of information communicated through body movement. In the second section, the role of visuals and nonverbal behaviour is

Peter Bull, *Visual Communication Through Body Movement* In: *The Psychology of Journalism.* Edited by: Sharon Coen and Peter Bull, Oxford University Press. © Oxford University Press 2021. DOI: 10.1093/oso/9780190935856.003.0011 considered in two particular journalistic contexts: print journalism and the television news. Finally, a case study of the television news is reported, based on an analysis of editing techniques utilized for audiovisual material (Bull et al., 2014).

Body Movement as Nonverbal Communication

The term *nonverbal communication* (Bull, 1983) can refer to communication through touch or smell, through various kinds of artefacts such as masks and clothes, or through formalized systems such as semaphore. Sometimes it has been used to include vocal features such as intonation, stress, speech rate, accent, and loudness, although this is more contentious. In addition, it can refer to different forms of body movement—to facial expression, gaze, pupil size, posture, gesture, and interpersonal distance. Because the term nonverbal is a definition only by exclusion, the features it can include are virtually limitless (Bull, 2004). However, the specific focus of this chapter is on communication through body movement.

For communication to occur, nonverbal behaviour does not have to be *intended* as such (Wiener et al., 1972). A person's intentions may not always be clear; furthermore, nonverbal communication may take place even *against* the express intentions of the communicator. A member of a lecture audience might well try hard to appear attentive but still be incapable of suppressing the occasional yawn. To the speaker, the listener may still communicate boredom, despite their best intentions not to do so (Bull, 2004). Communication can also take place without conscious *awareness*, in the sense that neither encoder nor decoder can specify the nonverbal cues through which a message is transmitted. People may be left with the feeling that someone was upset or angry without being able to identify exactly what cues were responsible for that impression (Bull, 1983). Nonverbal communication can also be *idiosyncratic*. Hand gestures, for example, may take their meaning from their visual resemblance to objects or actions that they seek to depict or from the way in which they are used in conjunction with speech (Bull, 2004).

There is now a substantive research literature on nonverbal communication, extending back over several decades (e.g., Argyle, 1988). In this tradition, nonverbal behaviour is typically contrasted with speech, its forte the communication of emotion and interpersonal relationships. But there is

another viewpoint. Given the close interconnectedness of nonverbal behaviour and speech, their separation would appear to be highly artificial. In
particular, hand and facial gestures may be seen as visible acts of meaning
and arguably should be treated as part of natural language (Bavelas & Chovil,
2000). Accordingly, relevant research literature on body movement is reviewed in the following subsections in terms of emotion, interpersonal re
lationships, and body movement and speech. At the same time, nonverbal
behaviour is not always consistent with speech, and it may even give clues to
deception; this is discussed in the subsection on deception detection. Finally,
there is the question of whether nonverbal communication can be taught;
this is discussed in the subsection on communication skills training.

Emotion

Facial Expression

Body movement is of particular importance in communicating emotion.
There are at least six facial expressions of emotion that are universal (Ekman,
1972). That is, the emotions of happiness, sadness, surprise, disgust, anger,
and fear are recognized in much the same way by members of different cultures throughout the world. This is supported by findings from cross-cultural
experiments showing that observers from both literate and preliterate cultures can identify these six different emotions from photographed facial
expressions (Ekman, 1972). A possible seventh universal emotion is contempt (Ekman & Friesen, 1986). In addition, Tracy and Matsumoto (2008)
have provided evidence indicating that pride and shame are also characterized by universal facial expressions. From all this evidence for universality,
it has been hypothesized that the facial expressions of emotion are innate,
a view further supported by studies that have shown that blind individuals
demonstrate the same spontaneous expressions as sighted individuals (e.g.,
Matsumoto & Willingham, 2009). As such, these expressions may well be a
highly informative guide as to how we feel.

At the same time, we can also learn to control our facial expressions.
According to the so-called neurocultural model of emotional expression, although at least six facial expressions of emotion are innate, individuals may
also modify these expressions in accordance with the norms/customs of their
own culture or society through what are called display rules (Ekman, 1972).
According to Ekman, there are four such rules: *amplification* (exaggerating

the intensity of the expression), *attenuation* (weakening the intensity of the expression), *concealment* (hiding an expression by adopting a neutral face), and *substitution* (displaying an expression other than the emotion being experienced). So, for example, traditionally in Japan there has been a taboo regarding the expression of negative emotions (e.g., anger) in public, whereas in the United States, no such taboo exists. This can lead to difficulties in communication between different cultures when some are more expressive than others.

Thus, the neurocultural model is based on a distinction between two principal types of facial expression: those that are spontaneous and those that are under voluntary control. A great deal of evidence based on neuropsychological case studies is consistent with this proposal (Rinn, 1991). Thus, there are reports of patients who lose the capacity to produce voluntary facial movements (e.g., retracting the corners of the mouth on command) but can still smile spontaneously on the paralysed side if something strikes them as amusing. Conversely, there are patients whose capacity to produce spontaneous facial expressions is paralysed, but they still retain the ability to exercise voluntary control over facial movements. This supports the view that at a neuropsychological level, there are two parallel systems for producing facial expressions.

Is there any way we can determine the difference between learned and spontaneous expressions? In a posed smile, people often only raise the corners of the mouth; in a spontaneous smile, smile lines (so-called crow's feet wrinkles) may appear at the corners of the eyes. Again, a posed smile may be produced almost as if turning on and off a light switch, whereas the onset and offset of a spontaneous smile may be more gradual (Ekman & Friesen, 1982). Thus, there are clues that can indicate physical differences between posed and spontaneous expressions, such that facial expressions can provide important guides to the feelings of others.

In the second section of this chapter, the role of facial expressions of emotion in print journalism is considered with reference to photojournalism. As an illustrative example, a photograph from the Vietnam War of the so-called Saigon execution is discussed, where a photographer caught the look of terror on the face of a suspected Viet Cong collaborator just as he was shot by South Vietnam's chief of police. The enormous impact of this photo is considered as part of a wider discussion of the role of emotive photos in print journalism.

Nonfacial Movements

Emotion can be perceived from other body movements besides facial expression. For example, in a study by Atkinson et al. (2004), the researchers created two sets of stimuli (point-light and full-light displays[1]) from video footage of encoders demonstrating emotional whole-body expressions. Static images representing the 'peak' of the emotional displays were also produced. The emotions expressed by the encoders were anger, fear, happiness, disgust, and sadness. It was found that decoders could accurately decode all these emotions from all three displays (full-light, point-light, and static). However, emotional expressions were more readily identifiable from dynamic than from static stimuli. Other researchers have found comparable results, utilizing both point-light displays (e.g., Clarke et al., 2003, 2005; Dittrich et al., 1996) and full-light displays (e.g., Boone & Cunningham, 1998; Van Meel et al., 1993; Wallbott, 1998).

Posture

A series of studies by the author showed that different emotions/attitudes could be identified from posture (Bull, 1987). Participants were asked to rate videos intended to evoke interest/boredom and disagreement/agreement. These ratings were then used to interpret postures displayed by the participants while watching the videos. Interest was associated with leaning forward and drawing back the legs; boredom was associated with leaning back, stretching out the legs, turning the head away from the video monitor, and supporting the head on one hand; and disagreement was associated with folding the arms and tightly crossing the legs so that the knee of the lower leg was visible. Thus, the results showed distinctive postural profiles to be associated with the three emotions/attitudes, which given that they were perceived by another group of participants as conveying these three emotions/attitudes, could legitimately be regarded as a form of nonverbal communication.

In the second section of this chapter, two further illustrative examples are given of the power of bodily images in the context of photojournalism. One, which has to be the most iconic photo from the Vietnam War (the so-called napalm girl), showed a group of children running away, including a naked girl—naked because she had torn off her clothes, which were covered

---

[1] In the point-light display, approximately 12 small lights were attached to various joints and other parts of an actor's body, with the body itself not being visible. In the full-light and static displays, the actor's body (fully covered) was visible, but the face was masked.

in burning napalm. The second is the tragic photo of the dead Syrian refugee Aylan Kurdi, a boy found washed up on a beach in Turkey. Both these photos had a massive public impact, and they are discussed in much greater detail in the section on print journalism.

Interpersonal Relationships

Posture

Posture has also been shown to be of importance in interpersonal relationships. In one study, its role in speed dating was investigated (Vacharkulksemsuk et al., 2016). Participants met prospective partners for just 4 minutes. The investigators were interested in the effects of what they called expansive versus contractive body postures. Expansive postures might be arms open and legs stretched out, whereas contractive postures were 'closed' body postures (arms folded and legs crossed). Confederates (both male and female) posed both expansive and contracted postures, and the expansive postures were found to significantly increase the chance of getting a 'yes' response from a participant (i.e., they would like to meet again on a future occasion). There were significant effects for both male and female confederates, although the effect was more pronounced for males. Interestingly, there were no significant effects for traditional nonverbal measures of affiliation (smiling, laughing, and head nodding).

Another aspect of posture is so-called *postural congruence*, which refers to people adopting similar postures (Scheflen, 1964). It is taken to indicate similarity of views or roles in a group, whereas noncongruence may indicate marked divergence in attitude or status. A further distinction is made between mirror-image congruent postures, where one person's left side is equivalent to the other person's right side, and identical postures, where right matches right and left matches left. Postural congruence has been investigated, for example, in the context of American college seminars. In one study, a significant positive correlation was found between mirror-congruent postures and a questionnaire intended to measure rapport, a significant negative correlation was found between noncongruent postures and rapport, and no significant relationship was found between identical postures and rapport (LaFrance & Broadbent, 1976). In another study (LaFrance, 1979), it was found that mirror-congruent postures as measured on a first occasion predicted rapport as measured on a second occasion (6 weeks later).

Interactional Synchrony

A broader concept than postural congruence is *interactional synchrony*, which refers to a process whereby speaker and listener appear to move in close harmony with one another (Condon & Ogston, 1966). It is believed to be a characteristic feature of everyday interaction (Condon & Ogston, 1971), as well as a fundamental, universal characteristic of human communication evident from the day of birth (Condon, 1975). This effect has been observed between mothers and their children (Bernieri et al., 1988) and between students and teachers (Bernieri, 1988; LaFrance & Broadbent, 1976). It has also been observed in clinical interviews (Geerts et al., 2006) and psychotherapeutic settings (Charny, 1966; Ramseyer & Tschacher, 2006; Scheflen, 1964). According to Holler and Wilkin (2011), co-speech gestures (gestures tightly linked to speech semantically, pragmatically, and temporally) often become synchronized between interlocutors during face-to-face dialogue. They are also believed to provide constant feedback from the listener to the speaker concerning the listener's level of attention and interest, and hence may be a sign of rapport (Condon, 1975). However, the concept of interactional synchrony has been open to dispute. Critics claim that congruent movements between individuals occur at a frequency no greater than expected by chance (e.g., Gatewood & Rosenwein, 1981).

Marriage and Divorce

A series of studies have been conducted on nonverbal communication in the context of marriage: Skill in both encoding and decoding nonverbal cues correlates with the quality of the relationship. Thus, experiments have been conducted to assess the nonverbal communication skills of husbands and wives, based on a task that involves asking them to send standardized verbal messages to one another (Noller, 1984). Given the predetermined verbal content of the message, the success in the task is entirely dependent on the couple's skills in nonverbal communication. Accuracy is measured in terms of whether the other partner can perceive the intent of the message. Results showed not only that unhappy couples misunderstood one another's messages significantly more often, but also that they were significantly worse at decoding messages from their spouses than from strangers (Noller, 1981).

Research has also been conducted on factors that predict divorce (Gottman, 1994). Interactions between marital partners have been videorecorded in a laboratory setting and the videotapes coded by trained observers, including measures of nonverbal communication. Facial displays of contempt and disgust in particular can indicate trouble for the relationship (Gottman, 1994). The husband's facial expressions of contempt are a powerful predictor of physical illness reported by the wife four years later. The wife's facial expressions of disgust were highly correlated with the number of months the couple will be separated in the next four years.

Summary

The previously presented data indicates that nonverbal communication is extremely important in the context of interpersonal relationships. Indeed, in one study, participants were requested to give an account of their own intimate experiences, and they often *defined* intimacy in terms of related nonverbal behaviours. For example, one individual wrote that 'a touch of the hand ... the meeting of our eyes, a kiss, conveyed our intimacy better than a thousand words' (Register & Henley, 1992).

Furthermore, not only are nonverbal cues important within a relationship but also, to an outside observer, they can provide important signals about relatedness (Grahe & Bernieri, 1999). Thus, it has been shown that observers can accurately identify important information about an unseen conversational partner from the nonverbal behaviour of one participant alone. Even very young children can do this; they can determine whether their mother is conversing with a friend or a stranger (Abramovitch, 1977). Adult observers can identify not only the gender of the unseen conversational partner but also whether the person was a friend or a stranger and whether or not the person was of the same age as the other conversationalist (Benjamin & Creider, 1975).

The significance of nonverbal cues as indicators of relatedness is particularly important in the context of photojournalism, as discussed in the second section of this chapter. The illustrative example is given of celebrity photos, where a telling photo can provide immediate and powerful information about celebrity relationships and degrees of relatedness.

Body Movement and Speech

Nonverbal communication has often been regarded as a kind of language of emotion and interpersonal relationships, but microanalytic studies have also shown that a person's body movement is closely synchronized with their speech, a phenomenon often referred to as *self-synchrony* (e.g., Condon &

Ogston, 1967; Dittman, 1972). One principal way in which self-synchrony occurs is through the close relationship between body movement and vocal stress. In spoken English, speech is typically produced in groups of words, with each group averaging approximately five words, where there is one primary vocal stress, conveyed principally through changes in pitch but also in loudness and rhythm. In a study of student conversations, it was found from a detailed microanalysis of the videorecordings that movements of all parts of the body were related to vocal stress (Bull & Connelly, 1981).

Such movements may have a variety of meanings. Head movements, for example, can signal a great deal more than just 'yes' or 'no' (McClave, 2000). Vigorous head shakes may accompany emphatic words such as 'a lot', 'great', or 'really'. A wide sweep of the head may be used to indicate inclusiveness, accompanying such words as 'everyone' or 'everything'. When a person starts to quote directly from someone else's speech, a shift in head orientation may slightly precede or directly accompany the quotation. Such nonverbal behaviour can be integral to the spoken message, figuratively referred to as 'mixed syntax'.

Indeed, body movement is arguably as fundamental as speech for the representation of meaning (Kendon, 1985). Thus, the use of hand gesture has been shown to develop simultaneously with speech in children and to dissolve together with speech in aphasia (McNeill, 1985). Speech and gesture can be seen to interact with one another in creating meaning: Not only does gesture clarify the meaning of speech but also speech can clarify the meaning of the gesture. In short, body movement may be viewed not just as an alternative to speech but also as an additional resource—as part of a multichannel system of communication, which allows the skilled speaker further options through which to convey meaning.

At the same time, it must be acknowledged that nonverbal behaviour is not always consistent with speech. Experiments have been conducted systematically comparing messages delivered in different verbal and nonverbal styles, both independently of one another and in combination. One study focussed on inferior and superior attitudes (Argyle et al., 1970), and another focussed on friendly and hostile attitudes (Argyle et al., 1971). Overall judgements of messages were significantly more affected by the nonverbal than by the verbal style. So, for example, the following friendly verbal message was given to participants:

I enjoy meeting the subjects who take part in these experiments and find I usually get on well with them. I hope you will be able to stay on afterwards to have a chat about the experiment. In fact, the people who have come as subjects in the past always seemed to be very pleasant.

However, when combined with a hostile nonverbal message (harsh voice, frown with teeth showing, and tense posture), the overall message was judged as hostile, and the verbal content was simply ignored.

From this perspective, communication researchers have been very interested in inconsistencies between speech and nonverbal behaviour, as one possible cue to deception. The role of nonverbal cues in deception detection is discussed next.

Deception

He that has eyes to see and ears to hear may convince himself that no mortal can keep a secret. If his lips are silent, he chatters with his finger-tips; betrayal oozes out of him at every pore.
                    —Sigmund Freud (1901/1955, pp. 77–78)

A similar point was made by the famous 16th-century Protestant reformer Martin Luther when he advised 'not to watch a person's mouth but his fists' (as quoted in Ansbacher & Ansbacher, 1958, p. 18).

This abiding belief, that movements of the body can give vital cues to deception, has been picturesquely referred to as *nonverbal leakage* (Ekman & Friesen, 1969). The concept was based on the proposal that different parts of the body vary in their capacity to send messages. Three indices of sending capacity were proposed: average transmission time, number of discriminable patterns, and visibility. According to these criteria, the face is the best sender, and the legs/feet are the worst. Facial muscle changes are rapid, they allow for a wide variety of expressions, and they are usually clearly visible; the feet and legs move much less quickly, they are capable of only a limited number of movements, and they are often screened from view by articles of furniture. Paradoxically, it was hypothesized that because of the greater sending capacity of the face, it may be a poorer source of information about deception, precisely because people are more careful to control their facial movements.

Hence, attempts at deception may often be 'leaked' through movements of the legs and feet (Ekman & Friesen, 1969).

However, research evidence does not seem to support these claims, finding only reduced body movement in deception (e.g., Ekman et al., 1988; Vrij, 2000). In contrast, it is facial expressions that may be an important source of nonverbal leakage. Two principal sources of such leakage have been proposed: so-called *subtle expressions* and *microexpressions*. Subtle expressions are fragments of otherwise suppressed or masked displays of emotion using only part of the normally associated musculature. Microexpressions are full muscular expressions of affect that occur for only a brief instant, typically approximately 1/25th of a second (Ekman & Friesen, 1969; Frank & Ekman, 1997). Due to insufficient suppression of emotional facial expressions, both micro- and subtle expressions have been hypothesized to provide valuable cues to deception, as forms of nonverbal leakage.

So, for example, someone might be extremely surprised by a novel piece of information but not wish others to be aware of this. Although that person on hearing this news might start to raise their eyebrows and start to let their mouth fall open, both movements might be quickly inhibited. Hence, they might show the surprise expression very briefly (microexpression), or they might show a fragment of the expression (subtle expression). However, a skilled observer might notice these expressions and would also be highly sceptical if the other person subsequently denied feeling surprised.

Arguably, subtle and microexpressions may be due to so-called *reliable* groups of facial muscles, notably around the forehead and brow, which are difficult to control voluntarily. As such, these will not be present in fabricated emotional expressions, nor will they be inhibited by suppression or masking, thus providing valuable leakage cues as to genuine emotion (Ekman & Friesen, 1975). However, it is also claimed that some people are capable of voluntarily manipulating these muscles, for whom these movements will not be reliable indicators of deception (Ekman, 2001).

Two studies have shown that for college students and professional lie catchers, the ability to identify microexpressions correlated significantly with deception detection accuracy (Ekman & O'Sullivan, 1991; Frank & Ekman, 1997), and a third study showed that the ability to identify subtle expressions correlated significantly with deception detection accuracy (Warren et al., 2011). A further study (based on individuals making emotional pleas to the public for the return of a missing relative) showed that on the basis of their facial actions, genuine pleaders could be distinguished from those subsequently convicted of murder (Ten Brinke et al., 2012). In the genuine pleaders, the so-called grief muscles (corrugator supercilii and the depressor anguli oris) were more often contracted, producing vertical wrinkles and drawing the corners of the mouth downwards. In contrast, deceptive communicators were more likely to show masking smiles (through contraction of the zygomatic major) and horizontal wrinkles across the forehead (through full contraction of the frontalis).

If nonverbal cues provide useful cues to deception, the question naturally arises as to whether observers (and possibly journalists) can be trained to improve their abilities in recognition. This question can be considered in the broader context of what has become known as communication skills training (CST), which is discussed next.

Communication Skills Training

There is no doubt that nonverbal communication research does have considerable practical significance. Of enormous influence has been the proposal that social behaviour can be regarded as a skill (Argyle & Kendon, 1967). Social behaviour, it was argued, involves processes comparable to those involved in motor skills, such as driving a vehicle or playing a game of tennis. More recently, this model has been significantly refined and updated by Hargie (e.g., Hargie & Marshall, 1986; Hargie, 1997, 2006a, 2006b).

Not only has the social skills model contributed to our understanding of social interaction and interpersonal communication (Bull, 2002) but it also has significant practical applications. If social interaction is a skill, then it should be possible for people to learn to interact with others more effectively, just as it is possible to improve performance on any other skill (Argyle & Kendon, 1967). This proposal was formalized in what was termed social skills training, currently better known as CST. CST has been used extensively in a wide variety of social contexts (e.g., Hargie, 2006c)—for example, employment interviews; therapy with psychiatric patients; intercultural communication; and occupational training with groups such as teachers, doctors, nurses, and police officers (Bull, 2002).

From this perspective, instruction in nonverbal communication can be regarded as a form of CST, characterized in particular by training people in the perception of nonverbal cues. So, for example, in a study of medical students, those already considered to be good communicators showed after training a significant improvement in their recognition of microexpressions (Endres & Laidlaw, 2009). In another study, both students and security officers after training showed significant improvement in microexpression recognition (Hurley et al., 2014). On a video test devised to improve recognition of emotional facial expressions (the Patient Emotion Cue Test), practice with feedback (getting the correct answer after viewing each video clip) was found to be a more effective form of training than just practice alone (Blanch-Hartigan, 2012).

Research and training in nonverbal communication skills is easily applicable to a wide variety of social settings. The analysis of deception detection might be of particular relevance to journalists, especially in the form of interviews. For example, journalists interviewing a potential source may find nonverbal cues to provide valuable indicators as to the genuineness of a response and also possible clues to so-called potential 'hot spots'—issues that may be of emotional concern or might cause potential embarrassment for an interviewee. In the case of television broadcasts, during which so-called *news interviews* take place with politicians, celebrities, or ordinary members of the public, nonverbal cues may also provide useful information as to the genuineness with which an interviewee responds to a question. The role of nonverbal behaviour in the television news is considered in much greater depth in the next section.

The Journalistic Context

The focus of this section is on two particular journalistic contexts: print journalism (with reference to photojournalism) and the television news.

Print Journalism and Photojournalism

'A picture is worth a thousand words' has become something of a cliché, but for all that it expresses a profound truth. Sometimes ascribed to the Chinese and their most famous philosopher Confucius, it was in fact popularized in the 1920s by an American, Fred R. Barnard, who used the phrase to discuss the use of drawn and photographic images to illustrate advertising (he also used the phrase 'a picture is worth ten thousand words', but it is the 'thousand words' version that is most well known) (Grammarist, n.d.).

Photojournalism is the counterpart of print journalism, the use of visual images to tell a story. In the 19th century, the development of photography made it possible for the first time to produce visual images of war, most notably the Crimean War (1853–1856) and the American Civil War (1861–1865). Ever since, war has been a central theme of photojournalism, and its influence is graphically illustrated by its role in the Vietnam War (1961–1975)—the long, bloody, and costly conflict that pitted the communist government of North Vietnam against South Vietnam and its principal ally, the United States.

Two celebrated photos from the Vietnam War were particularly influential. The first showed the shooting of a suspected Viet Cong collaborator by South Vietnam's chief of police (1 February 1968). In this photo, the photographer (Eddie Adams) catches the look of terror on the man's face just before his execution (Stepan, 2013, pp. 114–115). In the first section of this chapter, the importance of facial expressions of emotion was stressed. It was proposed that there are at least six innate expressions of emotion (surprise, disgust, happiness, sadness, anger, and fear), and in this photo, the victim shows a classic look of fear, his mouth stretched wide, his eyebrows drawn together.

The photo had a profound impact. A police chief had fired a bullet, point-blank, into the head of a handcuffed man, in likely violation of the Geneva Conventions. The executioner was not a communist but, rather, a member of South Vietnam's government, the ally of the United States. The Vietnam War has often been described as 'the living room war', 'fought in living rooms around the world' (Stepan, 2013, p. 114). Photos such as that of the Saigon execution were to become key elements in the anti-war campaign and a rallying call for Americans to question the legitimacy of their government's involvement in Vietnam (Stepan, 2013, p. 114). According to Christian G. Appy (professor of history at the University of Massachusetts, Amherst), 'It [the photo] really introduced a set of moral questions that would increasingly shape debate about the Vietnam War: Is our presence in Vietnam legitimate or just, and are we conducting the war in a way that is moral?' (as cited in Astor, 2018).

According to *TIME Magazine* (n.d.),

The act was stunning in its casualness. . . . Adams' photo ushered in a more intimate level of war photojournalism. He won a Pulitzer Prize for this image, and as he commented three decades later about the reach of his work, 'Still photographs are the most powerful weapon in the world'.

A second photo from the Vietnam War (that of the so-called 'napalm girl') is, if anything, even better known than that of the Saigon execution. On 8 June 1972, a South Vietnamese plane attacked the village of Trang Bang outside of Saigon, believed to have been infiltrated by enemy forces. By mistake, napalm[2] bombs were dropped on a cluster of American soldiers and on women and children hiding from the fighting. A photo, first seen on the cover of *TIME Magazine*, showed a group of children running down an empty road, followed by soldiers. The children's mouths are open, screaming in pain, but the central figure is a naked girl—naked because she has torn off her clothes, which were covered in burning napalm.

The use of napalm had a powerful effect on the anti-war movement in the United States. One target was the Dow Chemical Company, which manufactured napalm for the U.S. government from 1965 to 1969. Protests against Dow and boycotts of its products occurred throughout the country. Company recruiters faced virulent protests on college campuses, in some cases finding themselves barricaded in buildings (Silverman, n.d.). The photo of the napalm girl was claimed to 'have shifted public opinion and perhaps even the course of the war' (Berger, 2018).

However, one systematic empirical study of the impact of Vietnam War photos on public opinion presented a rather different picture. In this study, war photos published in *TIME Magazine*, *Life*, and *Newsweek* were compared with shifts in public opinion as measured by Gallup polls (Sherer, 1989). Images were categorized according to three time periods: one in which public support for the war was strong, one when it was shifting, and one when it was weak. When support was high, images mostly depicted American forces but principally in noncombat situations. When support was in transition with a near even split in support for the war, images changed dramatically, mostly depicting combat-related situations involving American forces caught in life-threatening activities. Finally, once public opposition to the war became the majority view, images placed more importance on the allies and less on American forces, with a slightly greater emphasis on life-threatening and combat-related moments. Thus, in effect, Scherer argues that war photos followed public opinion rather than changing it. Nevertheless, these two photos (the execution in Saigon and the so-called napalm girl) are arguably still the most iconic, well-known, and unforgettable images of the Vietnam War, even

---

[2] Napalm is a highly flammable, jelly-like substance that sticks easily to the skin and burns at very high temperatures.

if it is difficult to assess their exact influence on American public opinion at that time.

Another major theme of photojournalism has been the coverage of social issues. In Chapter 7, the treatment of refugees in the media was discussed, with particular reference to the tragic photo of a Syrian boy, Aylan Kurdi, a drowned child who had been found washed up on a beach in Turkey. This photo made the front pages of newspapers throughout the world, regardless of their political leaning (Berry et al., 2016). The *Daily Mail* in the United Kingdom, which had previously been very aggressive in tone toward refugees, published the photo with the headline 'Tiny Victim of a Human Catastrophe' (3 September 2015).

Notably, one effect of the photo's publication was an immediate and dramatic change in the language used to refer to 'migrants' and 'refugees'. Researchers at the University of Sheffield's Social Media Lab analysed approximately 3 million social media posts, comparing the use of these two words (University of Sheffield, 2015). For most of 2015 (prior to the publication of the photo), both words were used with comparable frequency ('migrants' appeared in 5.2 million tweets 'refugees' in 5.3 million tweets). From September 2nd, this radically changed to a clear preference for the word 'refugees' (6.5 million tweets) rather than 'migrants' (2.9 million tweets).

However, a further study indicated that the impact of the photo was not long-lasting. An analysis of refugee policy preferences was conducted in Sweden, based on 32,517 participants from the Swedish Citizen Panel (Sohlberg et al., 2019). Attitudes toward refugees were measured on four occasions in 2015: May (before the publication of the photo), September (immediately after the publication of the photo), and then on two subsequent occasions in October and December. On the second occasion of testing (in September), public opinion attitudes showed a highly significant change toward more generous, liberal refugee policies. However, by October, this had reduced significantly (although still more positive than in the previous testing in May), but by December, attitudes had reverted to the same levels as previously found in May. Thus, although the results indicated that the publication of the photo did have a significant and dramatic effect on attitudes toward refugees, the data indicate that the effect was short-lived.

A third major theme for photojournalism has been the celebrity photo. In the first section of this chapter, it was noted that not only are nonverbal cues important within a relationship but also, to an outside observer, they can provide important signals about relatedness. In this context, given the voracious public appetite for copy about celebrities, photos can provide dramatic and immediate impact about celebrity interrelationships and degrees of relatedness. Top of the list have been photos of the British Royal Family, and top of that list were photos of the late Princess Diana, Princess of Wales.

On 29 July 1981, Diana married Prince Charles (heir to the British throne) in a so-called fairy-tale royal wedding. In a photo that became one of the most published images in the world, the couple appeared on a balcony at Buckingham Palace (Stepan, 2013, p. 151). Even at this time, there was a stark contrast between them—between Diana's seemingly passionate kiss and the marked lack of reciprocity in Charles' response, which seemed little more than just a formal peck. Perhaps this was a sign of things to come.

Eleven years later, the couple's formal separation was announced by Prime Minister John Major to a packed House of Commons (9 December 1992). Earlier in that year, the couple's marital difficulties had been given the widest possible publicity following the publication of the book *Diana: Her True Story* by the journalist Andrew Morton (1992). The book was based on named interviews with Diana's family and closest friends, detailing her bulimia and suicide attempts, as well as the accusations of her husband's infidelity. The book was accompanied by a deluge of press and television coverage, and it created a sensation. Subsequently, in 1995 (20 November), a television interview with Diana was broadcast (see Bull, 1997), in which for the first time she publicly acknowledged her 5-year affair with army officer James Hewitt. After that broadcast, events moved very rapidly. In February 1996, Diana announced that she was agreeable to a divorce, which was announced on July 12 of the same year; the marriage was terminated on 28 August 1996. The following year (31 August 1997), Diana tragically died in a car accident.

The last official tour by Charles and Diana had taken place in November 1992, when they visited South Korea. Nicknamed at this time by the media as 'The Glums' (Darbyshire, 2018), photos of the couple show them stony-faced, unsmiling, and physically distant; not only are they not making eye contact but also their heads are turned away from one another. No one seeing these photos would have been the least surprised by the announcement of their formal separation the following month. Words were not necessary; the photos said it all—the breakdown of their relationship was manifest for all to see.

All the previous examples (the Vietnam War, the Syrian refugee crisis, and the divorce of Princess Diana and Prince Charles) illustrate the highly salient role played by photojournalism in print journalism. The focus of the next subsection is on the television news. In a recent analysis by Ofcom (2019) of news consumption in the United Kingdom, it was reported that television remained the most used platform for news by UK adults, although that had dropped (from 79% in 2018 to 75% in 2019), and the use of social media had increased (from 44% in 2018 to 49% in 2019). Thus, given the continued pre-eminence of television news as the prime source of information in the United Kingdom about public affairs, it is discussed next, with particular reference to the utilization and editing of audiovisual recordings.

Television News

According to a substantive body of research, there has been a marked shift in journalistic practice from a fact-based to a more interpretive style in the presentation of television news (e.g., Ekström, 2001; Eriksson, 2011; Salgado & Strömbäck, 2012). This is characterized by a 'greater emphasis on the "meaning" of news beyond the facts and statements of sources' (Salgado & Strömbäck, 2012, p. 145). According to Eriksson (2011, p. 66), politicians in old-style news journalism were 'set up to talk more directly to the viewer', such that viewers could formulate their own judgements about politicians' utterances. Today, however, 'viewers are given ready-made packages of ideas of what is going on in politics and how it should be understood' (p. 66). Although there is still ongoing debate about what interpretive journalism means in practice (e.g., Salgado & Strömbäck, 2012), the interpretive view of contemporary television news has in recent years come to the fore (Bull et al., 2014). This was clearly demonstrated in a series of studies of news broadcasts in Sweden conducted over a 25-year period by Ekström and Eriksson.

In the context of this Swedish research, it is important to appreciate the impact of recent technological changes on news journalism. In news bulletins broadcast in 1978, answers were fully synchronized with pictures of the politicians so that viewers could observe the answers from start to finish. News journalism functioned primarily as a mediator or interrogator, with the aim of bringing political arguments out in public. In later periods (1993, 2003), the politician's answers may be covered with pictures, or the viewers may hear politicians speaking before they see the image on the screen, or the picture may shift to something else before the politicians have finished talking. Clips from two originally separate parts of one response (or even from two different responses) may be spliced together to form what appears to be one continuous response. Thus, through this technology, news journalism has greater power than ever before over what constitutes an answer to a question. In these later periods, news journalism functions more both as an interpreter (explaining what is going on in politics) and as a critical interrogator (seeking out hidden agendas and underlying motives behind politicians' decisions and proposals).

Notably, Eriksson (2011) has built on this research to develop the concept of news broadcasts as a narrative, defined as the way 'different sequences or elements of talk are organized in news stories' (p. 54). These elements of talk are the narrators (usually the anchor or a journalist) and different characters, such as politicians and other interviewees. These narratives comprise edited clips from different events that are fitted into the broadcast, as well as a narration that provides the overall framework to provide a coherent news story. Notably, clips may be removed from their original context (decontextualized) and set in a new one by the journalist (recontextualized).

The studies by Ekström (2001) and Eriksson (2011) described previously were conducted in the context of news journalism in Sweden. To investigate the extent to which their findings would be replicated in the context of British news journalism, a further analysis was conducted of editing techniques in news coverage of the 2009 British parliamentary 'expenses scandal' (Bull et al., 2014). This is presented as a case study next.

Case Study: The British Parliamentary Expenses Scandal of 2009

The British parliamentary expenses scandal of 2009 was triggered by the leak and subsequent publication in the broadsheet *The Daily Telegraph* of expenses claims made over several years by Members of Parliament (MPs) in the House of Commons and by peers in the House of Lords.

Allegedly, these claims showed blatant misuse of the expenses system for personal gain by many MPs across all parties, including government and shadow cabinet ministers. The scandal dominated the British media for weeks, with headlines on all the major television news programs over a three-week period (11 May–3 June 2009), notably *BBC1*, *Ten O Clock News*, *Sky News at Ten*, and *Channel Four News*.

Claims for tax allowances on second homes were a centrepiece of this scandal, whereby it was alleged that politicians were playing the system for their own financial advantage. In addition, there were some claims that were patently ridiculous. Infamously, the Conservative MP Sir Peter Viggers was reported to have received more than £30,000 for gardening expenses over three years. This included £1,645 for what was identified as a 'floating duck island' (a house for his ducks!). The duck house became an iconic emblem of the expenses scandal.

In our study of the television news coverage (Bull et al., 2014), an innovative methodological approach was introduced. Specific audiovisual clips were identified that had been utilized by more than one news channel. Thereby, analyses could be conducted of how identical audiovisual content (or parts thereof) was interpreted across different news bulletins. In addition, audiovisual recordings of House of Commons debates were compared with Hansard (the written transcript of parliamentary proceedings) to assess whether any video editing had taken place. The overall aim was to investigate the extent to which techniques of decontextualization and recontextualization analysed in Swedish news broadcasts (Eriksson, 2011) could be identified in the use of audiovisual content in British news broadcasts.

The study was based on 53 news bulletins from Sky, BBC, and Channel 4 News (11 May–3 June 2009) that all included news items on the scandal, and these were all transcribed in full. Nine scenarios were identified in which the same clip of film was utilized by more than one news channel; in total, there were 23 such clips. With only one exception, all these clips were decontextualized—that is, neither the source nor the location of each clip was acknowledged. All the clips were then content analysed for editorial comment by the anchor and/or journalist.

On the basis of these analyses, a fourfold typology of editing techniques was devised and applied to each of the nine scenarios as follows:

- Contextualization before and after the utterance: Each of the 23 clips was contextualized by the journalist or news anchor providing an introduction before the utterance, with in most cases a further comment from the narrator afterwards.
- Interpolation: The narrator acts as a storyteller through interpolating at various points within the extract in the form of a voiceover to explain or interpret what is happening on screen. This was the second most frequently used technique, utilized in relation to four of the scenarios.

- Elimination of text from the utterance: Text may be edited out from the original utterance, thereby in effect creating a new utterance.
- Editing the order of utterances: Extracts from different speakers may be presented in one order on one channel and in a different order on another channel. This aspect of framing only occurred once, specifically in the exchanges between the leaders of the three main political parties at that time: Gordon Brown (Labour Prime Minister), David Cameron (Leader of the Conservative Opposition), and Nick Clegg (Leader of the minority Liberal Democrats). This represented the most drastic form of editing, in effect creating an entirely imaginary dialogue, as could be shown from the Hansard record. Not only was it based on edited extracts selected from different points in one session of Prime Minister's Questions but also the actual order of the extracts varied between the two channels (Channel 4 and BBC1). Notably, when the order changed, the argument itself changed, thereby making it seem as if a different politician had the upper hand.

Overall, the results of this study strongly corroborated those found in the studies of Swedish news broadcasts and the view that contemporary news journalism is highly interpretive. The editing of British news broadcasts was not just comparable to that in Sweden; if anything, it was even more pronounced. In all nine scenarios, the politicians' remarks were decontextualized and recontextualized by the journalists' introductory and summary comments, and some clips were recycled and further recontextualized for later broadcasts. Interpolation went beyond this kind of contextualization, with the journalist acting as a narrator, telling the story through the interpretation of events. Finally, there was one scenario in which textual editing effectively created an 'imaginary dialogue' between three political leaders.

In the use of these audiovisual clips, visual nonverbal behaviour played an important role. As an illustrative example, one of the nine scenarios is discussed here in greater detail. This is the case of a former Labour MP, Hazel Blears, who according to a report in *The Daily Telegraph* (8 May 2009) had made a £45,000 profit on the sale of a London flat without paying capital gains tax. Following this report, Blears volunteered to pay the £13,332 capital gains tax she had avoided on the sale of her 'second home'. As a result of these allegations, she appeared on both Sky and BBC News (twice), showcasing her cheque to the Inland Revenue. Despite this attempt to appease her constituents, Blears announced her resignation as Secretary of State for Communities and Local Government on 3 June 2009.

A comparison of the Sky News and the BBC reports illuminates the BBC's use of de- and recontextualization. From the Sky report, it is perfectly clear that Blears is participating in an interview: She can be seen and heard responding to audible questions from a journalist. This is not the case in either of the BBC broadcasts because interviewer questions are edited out. In the first use of the clip, Blears appears to identify with her constituents and sympathize with the public to maintain their support, while at the same time showing her cheque to the camera. In the second use of the clip, Blears' verbal response is no longer broadcast. She is just seen waving her cheque in what appears to be a rather pathetic and failed attempt to win back public support because viewers by this time would already have known of her resignation. In this second viewing, the nonverbal is paramount, and the politician's actual words are no longer to be heard.

Conclusion

Nonverbal behaviour plays an important role in journalism because of its heavy reliance on visual forms of communication. Awareness of the importance of nonverbal communication dates back to classical civilization, whereas its scientific investigation has a relatively short history. In the first section of this chapter, academic research on body movement was discussed in terms of the following topics: the communication of emotion and interpersonal relationships, the synchronization of body movement and speech, deception detection, and CST.

The second section of this chapter focussed on the use of visuals and nonverbal behaviour in two specific journalistic contexts: print journalism and the television news. Photojournalism, the use of visual images to tell a story, is arguably the counterpart of print journalism. Illustrative examples were discussed, based on the impact of photos of the Vietnam War and the dead Syrian boy Aylan Kurdi; celebrity photos of Prince Charles and the late Princess Diana were also considered. This was followed by an analysis of the television news, focussed primarily on recent changes in editing techniques, which arguably utilize highly edited audiovisual content to tell a story rather than leaving viewers to make up their own minds on particular issues. This section concluded with a case study based on television news coverage of the British parliamentary expenses scandal of 2009.

Photojournalism and the editing of the television news are but two illustrative examples of the role that visuals and nonverbal behaviour play in the practice of journalism. The interface between them has barely been explored, but it represents a fertile and fascinating field for future investigation. It is proposed that academic research on nonverbal behaviour and nonverbal communication has manifest applications and implications for enhancing our understanding not only of journalism and journalistic practice but also of the impact of visual images and nonverbal behaviour on the wider society as a whole.

References

Abramovitch, R. (1977). Children's recognition of situational aspects of facial expression. *Child Development, 48*, 459–463.

Ansbacher, H. L., & Ansbacher, K. R. (1958). *The individual psychology of Alfred Adler.* Allen & Unwin.

Argyle, M. (1988). *Bodily communication* (2nd ed.). Methuen.

Argyle, M., & Kendon, A. (1967). The experimental analysis of social performance. *Advances in Experimental Social Psychology, 3*, 55–97.

Argyle, M., Alkema, F., & Gilmour, R. (1971). The communication of friendly and hostile attitudes by verbal and non-verbal signals. *European Journal of Social Psychology, 1*(3), 385–402.

Argyle, M., Salter, V., Nicholson, H., Williams, M., & Burgess, P. (1970). The communication of inferior and superior attitudes by verbal and non-verbal signals. *British journal of social and clinical psychology, 9*(3), 222–231.

Astor, M. (2018, February 1). *A photo that changed the course of the Vietnam War.* Retrieved 29 April 2020 from https://www.nytimes.com/2018/02/01/world/asia/vietnam-execution-photo.html

Atkinson, A. P., Winand D., Gemmell, A., & Young, A. (2004). Emotion perception from dynamic and static body expressions in point-light and full-light displays. *Perception, 33*, 717–746.

Bavelas, J. B., & Chovil, N. (2000). Visible acts of meaning: An integrated message model of language in face-to-face dialogue. *Journal of Language and Social Psychology, 19*, 163–194.

Benjamin, G. R., & Creider, C. A. (1975). Social distinctions in nonverbal behaviour. *Semiotica, 14*, 52–60.

Berger, S. (2018, February 14). War images: 'Napalm girl'. *Confluence.* Retrieved 29 April 020 from https://confluence.gallatin.nyu.edu/sections/research/war-images-napalm-girl

Bernieri, F. (1988). Coordinated movement and rapport in teacher–student interactions. *Journal of Nonverbal Behavior, 12*, 120–138.

Bernieri, F., Reznick, S., & Rosenthal, R. (1988). Synchrony, pseudosynchrony, and dissynchrony: Measuring the entrainment process in mother–infant interactions. *Journal of Personality and Social Psychology, 54*, 243–253.

Berry, M., Garcia-Blanco, I., & Moore, K. (2016). *Press coverage of the refugee and migrant crisis in the EU: A content analysis of five European countries.* United Nations High Commissioner for Refugees. http://www.unhcr.org/56bb369c9.html

Blanch-Hartigan, D. (2012). An effective training to increase accurate recognition of patient emotion cues. *Patient Education and Counseling, 89*(2), 274–280.

Boone, R. T., & Cunningham, J. (1998). Children's decoding of emotion in expressive body movement: The development of cue attunement. *Developmental Psychology, 34*, 1007–1016.

Bull, P. (1983). *Body movement and interpersonal communication.* Wiley.

Bull, P. (1987). *Pergamon international series in experimental social psychology: Vol. 16. Posture and gesture.* Pergamon.

Bull, P. (1997). Queen of Hearts or Queen of the Arts of Implication? Implicit criticisms and their implications for equivocation theory in the interview between Martin Bashir and Diana, Princess of Wales. *Social Psychological Review, 1*, 27–36.

Bull, P. (2002). *Communication under the microscope; The theory and practice of microanalysis.* Psychology Press.

Bull, P. (2004). Nonverbal communication. In A. Kuper & J. Kuper (Eds.), *The social science encyclopedia* (3rd ed., Vol. 2, pp. 692–695). Routledge.

Bull, P., & Connelly, G. (1985). Body movement and emphasis in speech. *Journal of Nonverbal Behaviour, 9*, 169–187.

Bull, P., Negrine, R., & Hawn, K. (2014). Telling it like it is or just telling a good story? Editing techniques in news coverage of the British parliamentary expenses scandal. *Language & Dialogue, 4*(2), 213–233.

Charny, J. E. (1966). Psychosomatic manifestations of rapport in psychotherapy. *Psychosomatic Medicine, 28*, 305–315.

Clarke, T., Bradshaw, M., Field, D., Hampson, S., & Rose, D. (2005). The perception of emotion from body-movement in point-light displays of interpersonal dialogue. *Perception, 34*, C1171–C1180.

Clarke, T., Rose, R., Bradshaw, M., Hampson, S., & Field, D. (2003). Perceiving emotion from point-light displays of interpersonal communication behaviours. *Perception, 32*(Suppl. S), 143–154.

Condon, W. S. (1975). Multiple response to sound in dysfunctional children. *Journal of Autism and Childhood Schizophrenia, 5*, 37–56.

Condon, W. S., & Ogston, W. D. (1966). Sound film analysis of normal and pathological behaviour patterns. *Journal of Nervous and Mental Disease, 143*, 338–347.

Condon, W. S., & Ogston, W. D. (1971). Speech and body motion synchrony of the speaker-hearer. In D. L. Horton & J. J. Jenkins (Eds.), *Perceptions of language* (pp. 150–173). Merrill.

Darbyshire, R. (2018, September 29). *Inside Diana and Charles' final tour before their separation—where they looked 'miserable' together.* Retrieved 29 April 2020 from https://www.mirror.co.uk/news/uk-news/inside-diana-charles-final-tour-13329058

Dittman, A. (1972). The body movement-speech rhythm relationship as a cue to speech encoding. In A. Seigman & B. Pope (Eds.), *Studies in dyadic communication* (pp. 135–152). Pergamon.

Dittrich, W., Troscianko, T., Lea, S., & Morgan, D. (1996). Perception of emotion from dynamic point-light displays represented in dance. *Perception, 25*, 727–738.

Ekman, P. (1972). Universal and cultural differences in facial expressions of emotion. In J. R. Cole (Ed.), *Nebraska Symposium on Motivation 1971* (pp. 207–283). University of Nebraska Press.

Ekman, P. (2001). *Telling lies: Clues to deceit in the marketplace, politics, and marriage.* Norton.

Ekman, P., & Friesen, W. V. (1969). Nonverbal leakage and clues to deception. *Psychiatry, 32*, 88–106.

Ekman, P., & Friesen, W. V. (1975). *Unmasking the face: A guide to recognising emotions from facial clues.* Prentice Hall.

Ekman, P., & Friesen, W. V. (1982). Felt, false and miserable smiles. *Journal of Nonverbal Behaviour, 6*, 238–252.

Ekman, P., & Friesen, W. V. (1986). A new pan-cultural facial expression of emotion. *Motivation and Emotion, 10*, 159–168.

Ekman, P., Friesen, W. V., & O'Sullivan, M. (1988). Smiles when lying. *Journal of Personality and Social Psychology, 54*, 414–420.

Ekman, P., & O'Sullivan, M. (1991). Who can catch a liar? *American Psychologist, 46*, 913–920.

Ekström, M. (2001). Politicians interviewed on television news. *Discourse and Society, 12*(5), 563–584.

Endres, J., & Laidlaw, A. (2009). Micro-expression recognition training in medical students: A pilot study. *BMC Medical Education, 9*, 47.

Eriksson, G. (2011). Adversarial moments: A study of short-form interviews in the news. *Journalism, 12*(1), 51–69.

Frank, M. G., & Ekman, P. (1997). The ability to detect deceit generalises across different types of high-stake lies. *Journal of Personality and Social Psychology, 72*, 1429–1439.

Freud, S. (1955). Fragment of an analysis of a case of hysteria. In *Collected papers* (Vol. 7, pp. 77–78). Hogarth. (Original work published 1901)

Gatewood, J., & Rosenwein, R. (1981). Interactional synchrony: Genuine or spurious? A critique of recent research. *Journal of Nonverbal Behavior, 6*, 12–29.

Geerts, E., van Os, T., Ormel, J., & Bouhuys, N. (2006). Nonverbal behavioral similarity between patients with depression in remission and interviewers in relation to satisfaction and recurrence of depression. *Depression and Anxiety, 23*, 200–209.

Gottman, J. M. (1994). *What predicts divorce? The relationship between marital processes and marital outcomes.* Erlbaum.

Grahe, J. E., & Bernieri, F. J. (1999). The importance of nonverbal cues in judging rapport. *Journal of Nonverbal Behaviour, 23*, 253–269.

Grammarist. (n.d.). *A picture is worth a thousand words.* Retrieved 17 April 2020 from https://grammarist.com/proverb/a-picture-is-worth-a-thousand-words

Hargie, O. D. W. (1997). Training in communication skills: Research, theory and practice. In O. D. W. Hargie (Ed.), *The handbook of communication skills* (2nd ed., pp. 473–482). Routledge.

Hargie, O. D. W. (2006a). Skill in practice: An operational model of communicative performance. In O. D. W. Hargie (Ed.), *The handbook of communication skills* (3rd ed., pp. 37–70). Routledge.

Hargie, O. D. W. (2006b). Training in communication skills: Research, theory and practice. In O. D. W. Hargie (Ed.), *The handbook of communication skills* (3rd ed., pp. 553–565). Routledge.

Hargie, O. D. W. (Ed.). (2006c). *The handbook of communication skills* (3rd ed.). Routledge.

Hargie, O. D. W., & Marshall, P. (1986). Interpersonal communication: A theoretical framework. In O. D. W. Hargie (Ed.), *The handbook of communication skills* (pp. 22–56). Croom Helm.

Hurley, C. M., Anker, A. E., Frank, M. D., Matsumoto, D., & Hwang, H. C. (2014). Background factors predicting accuracy and improvement in micro expression recognition. *Motivation and Emotion, 38,* 700–714.

Kendon, A. (1985). Some uses of gesture. In O. Tannen & M. Saville-Troike (Eds.), *Perspectives on silence* (pp. 215–234). Ablex.

LaFrance, M. (1979). Nonverbal synchrony and rapport: Analysis by the cross-lag panel technique. *Social Psychology Quarterly, 42,* 66–70.

LaFrance, M., & Broadbent, M. (1976). Group rapport: Posture sharing as a nonverbal indicator. *Group and Organisation Studies, 1,* 328–333.

Matsumoto, D., & Willingham, B. (2009). Spontaneous facial expressions of emotion of blind individuals. *Journal of Personality and Social Psychology, 96,* 1–10.

McClave, E. Z. (2000). Linguistic functions of head movements in the context of speech. *Pragmatics, 32*(7), 855–878.

McNeill, D. (1985). So you think gestures are nonverbal? *Psychological Review, 92,* 350–371.

Morton, A. (1992), *Diana: Her true story.* O'Mara.

Noller, P. (1981). Gender and marital adjustment level differences in decoding messages from spouses and strangers. *Journal of Personality and Social Psychology, 41,* 272–278.

Noller, P. (1984). *Nonverbal communication and marital interaction.* Pergamon.

Ofcom. (2019). *News consumption in the UK.* Retrieved 29 April 2020 from https://www.ofcom.org.uk/research-and-data/tv-radio-and-on-demand/news-media/news-consumption

Ramseyer, F., & Tschacher, W. (2006). Synchrony: A core concept for a constructivist approach to psychotherapy. *Constructivism in the Human Sciences, 11,* 150–171.

Register, L. M., & Henley, T. B. (1992). The phenomenology of intimacy. *Journal of Social and Personal Relationships, 9,* 467–481.

Rinn, W. E. (1991). Neuropsychology of facial expression. In R. S. Feldman & B. Rimé (Eds.), *Fundamentals of nonverbal behaviour* (pp. 3–30). Cambridge University Press.

Salgado, S., & Strömbäck, J. (2012). Interpretive journalism: A review of concepts, operationalizations and key findings. *Journalism, 13*(2), 144–161.

Scheflen, A. E. (1964). The significance of posture in communication systems. *Psychiatry, 27,* 316–331.

Sherer, M. D. (1989). Vietnam War photos and public opinion. *Journalism Quarterly, 66*(2), 391–396.

Silverman, J. (n.d.). *How napalm works.* Retrieved 29 April 2020 from https://science.howstuffworks.com/napalm.htm

Sohlberg, J., Esaiasson, P., & Martinsson, J. (2019). The changing political impact of compassion-evoking pictures: The case of the drowned toddler Alan Kurdi. *Journal of Ethnic and Migration Studies, 45*(13), 2275–2288. https://www.tandfonline.com/doi/full/10.1080/1369183X.2018.1538773

Stepan, P. (Ed.). (2013). *Photos that changed the world* (2nd ed.). Prestel.

Ten Brinke, L., Porter, S., & Baker, A. (2012). Darwin the detective: Observable facial muscle contractions reveal emotional high-stakes lies. *Evolution & Human Behaviour, 33*(4), 411–416.

TIME Magazine. (n.d.). Saigon execution: Eddie Adams, 1968. Retrieved 29 April 2020 from http://100photos.time.com/photos/eddie-adams-saigon-execution

Tracy, J., & Matsumoto, D. (2008). The spontaneous expression of pride and shame: Evidence for biologically innate nonverbal displays. *Proceedings of the National Academy of Sciences of the USA, 105,* 11655–11660

University of Sheffield. (2015, December 14). *Aylan Kurdi: How a single image transformed the debate on immigration.* Retrieved 29 April 2020 from https://www.sheffield.ac.uk/news/nr/aylan-kurdi-social-media-report-1.533951

Vacharkulksemsuk, T., Reit, E., Khambatta, P., Eastwick, P. W., Finkel, E. J., & Carney, D. R. (2016). Dominant, open nonverbal displays are attractive at zero acquaintance. *Proceedings of the National Academy of Sciences of the USA, 113*(15), 4009–4014. https://doi.org/10.1073/pnas.1508932113

Van Meel, J., Verburgh, H., & DeMeijer, M. (1993). Children's interpretation of dance expressions. *Empirical Studies of the Arts, 11,* 117–133.

Vrij, A. (2000). *Detecting lies and deceit.* Wiley.

Wallbott, H. (1998). Bodily expression of emotion. *European Journal of Social Psychology, 28,* 879–896.

Warren, G., Schertler, E., & Bull, P. (2011). Detecting deception from emotional and unemotional cues. *Journal of Nonverbal Behaviour, 33*(1), 59–69.

Wiener, M., Devoe, S., Robinson, S., & Geller, J. (1972). Nonverbal behaviour and nonverbal communication. *Psychological Review, 79,* 185–214.

12

Conclusion

Sharon Coen and Peter Bull

Psychology as Subjectivity

Psychology is about subjectivity (Tuma, R. personal communication, 2014). It is about understanding how our brains work, how we perceive and attend the world around us, how it makes us feel, and how we interact with it. It is about understanding how we construct our world and how we think and feel about it—and about ourselves in interaction with it.

Media psychology—understood as the study of individuals' thoughts, feelings, and actions in interaction with media and communication technology—can also offer important insights on what still needs to be understood about the way in which individuals work. For example, the way in which groups form and communicate online, online hate crimes, and anonymity give—in our opinion—interesting insight on 'crowds' and on the role perceived social norms play in human interaction, as well as how ideas about ourselves and new social identities emerge from the interaction with others online.

With regard to professional practice, as in the case of journalism, insights from psychological research and evidence can complement and expand existing paradigms in the media and communication field. They can help us understand the way in which aspects of production and consumption of media in the current—shifting—climate can affect the way in which journalists select information to report as well as present the information to their audiences. A psychological lens can help us understand how the audience is likely to relate to and make sense of such information. Furthermore, it can help us understand how news production and the making of meaning play out within different sociocultural and organizational contexts.

One of the key messages we hope this book can give is to challenge our understanding of who a journalist or a news 'user' is and how their experience forms and informs the way in which they relate to the world around them.

Sharon Coen and Peter Bull, *Conclusion* In: *The Psychology of Journalism*. Edited by: Sharon Coen and Peter Bull, Oxford University Press. © Oxford University Press 2021. DOI: 10.1093/oso/9780190935856.003.0012

Identity

Understanding who we are—and who others are—is a core aspect of psychological research and theory. Throughout this book, we have seen how our identity and our beliefs concerning others' identity shapes the way in which we interact with media and with each other. Hardy showed in Chapter 2 how the structural and contextual changes in news media production have posed important questions concerning who journalists are, what journalists believe their industry is about, and what the public expects from journalists. In Chapter 6, Oni showed how these beliefs shape the ways in which we enact our roles in society. Thus, research has shown how journalists and news producers justify the type and quality of information they provide in the news, based on their beliefs about what people are most interested in, as indicated by metrics such as the 'most read' articles. Indeed, online metrics have been used as a way to justify editorial and journalistic practices (Lee & Tandoc, 2017). However, research has shown that people are still very aware of 'what news should be about', in terms of informing citizenship and providing 'solid' information (Schrøder, 2019). Indeed, Grabe et al. (2003) have shown how the public is discerning with regard to 'tabloidized' content, and they judge it as less trustworthy, although they tend to pay more attention to it and remember it better.

In Chapter 3, it was demonstrated how there is a competition for the attention of online users, who are often facing competing demands on their limited processing capacity when interacting with media. We have also seen how motivation plays an important role in directing people's attention. Research by Vignoles and colleagues (for a summary, see Vignoles, 2011) has shown how motivation plays an important role in driving not only our choice of groups with which we identify but also the way in which we use media (and social media in particular; e.g., see Manzi et al., 2018). We have seen in Chapter 7 by Lido, Swyer, and De Amicis how the choices we make about the groups with which we will identify and the beliefs we attach to our—and other—groups will shape the way we think, feel, and act in our social world and the way that is likely to inform our sense making of current affairs and events. In Chapter 9, Hichy and Di Marco showed us how these decisions about who we are and who others are have (often unintended) consequences for the way in which we talk about events involving the groups to which we do and do not belong. Meredith in Chapter 10 showed the complex processes of identity construction that often are articulated in media discourses. And we have seen in Chapter 8 how ideologies and cultural contexts often drive our interpretations of who we are and who others are, as well as what is and is not desirable from a member of our community.

Thus, as stated previously, examining subjectivity in journalism entails looking at how we construct our idea of who we (and others) are in interaction with media and how we use media to express our beliefs about ourselves and others. For example, an old tension between media and psychology is that many media professionals are often concerned with what they believe their work is about: beauty and craft. These will be the standards they will use to judge other people's performance in that particular role. On the other hand, social scientists and psychologists are more interested in the way in which media impacts on society. Thus, with regard to media violence, for example, a media professional and a psychologist would look at different aspects. The media professional might be more interested in whether, and how, the violent scene fits in the narrative and how well executed it is, in terms of being able to achieve the desired suspense, fear, or anger reaction in the audience (for a summary of research in the area, see Neroni, 2012). It is perfectly acceptable for media experts to evaluate the product in terms of its artistry and/or its ability to capture 'reality'. A psychologist, on the other hand, might be more interested in understanding why and how the producer, director, and actors chose to portray violence the way they did; how the audience makes sense of it; and what are the consequences (effects) of these choices on the audience (e.g., Ferguson & Kilburn, 2009).

Again, one important take-home message from what we have learned so far is that who we are, the groups with whom we identify, what we hold as crucial for our role in society, and what we believe about others inform the way in which we think, feel, and act in interaction with the world.

Motivation

A second, very important construct in psychology is that of motivation. Motivation can be conceptualized as the drive people have in pursuing goals they set for themselves (Conroy et al., 2009). Psychologists have been trying to identify the key motivations driving human behaviour; where these come from; and the consequences of such motivations in relation to people's thoughts, feelings, and behaviours about themselves and others (e.g., Ryan, 2012). Chapter 7 discussed how humans seem to have a series of universal motives driving the way in which they define themselves and the groups to which they belong. Importantly, Vignoles (2011) notes that although the motives are universal, the way in which they are expressed and satisfied varies significantly across cultures (see Chapter 8). We have seen how motivation shapes the way in which we explore and react to the world around us. Indeed, literature on motivated cognition shows how our attention and the way we process information is guided by our motivation (see Chapter 3). Our motivation will also inform what and how we learn: the example of news grazers discussed in Chapter 4 is an excellent illustration of this process. But motivation will also inform our emotional reactions to events; for example, the same event can be associated by a positive emotional response if we perceive it as being in line with our goals, or it can be associated with negative emotions if we perceive it as an obstacle (see Chapter 5).

With regard to media consumption, the uses and gratifications perspective (see Chapter 1) builds on work on motivation by showing how the 'effects' media will have on us are dependent on the reasons why we are consuming media. Regarding news, Schrøder (2019) highlights that although it is indeed the case that people are often attracted by news that is not traditionally deemed as important for democratic purposes (e.g., celebrity, entertainment, and 'weird' news), they are still very well aware—and demanding—of 'quality' journalism.

This book has demonstrated how group membership norms and role conceptions (Chapter 6), identity and group membership (Chapter 7), and ideology and culture (Chapter 8) function as important motivators that will influence the way in which we interact with media, whether to produce messages or to interpret them.

Emotions

Chapter 2 provided an overview of the fundamental structural changes faced by news media, with the increased use of the internet as a form of delivery and distribution of news and its impact on other forms of broadcasting. We have seen how this entails changes in journalistic practices, as well as the type and amount of demands posed on journalists. In particular, Chapter 3 taught us how the changing climate discussed previously may have implications for the way in which journalists try to capture people's attention in an increasingly competitive environment and regarding the extent to which these 'tricks' to capture attention may be effective. For example, we have seen how psychological research suggesting that negative information tends to be more attended to than positive information applies also to news (Soroka, 2014) and how the use of a more complex delivery, which includes news crawls, seems to be effective in capturing attention but also hinders the processing of the message (Bergen et al., 2005). We have also seen how the arousal deriving from the adoption of more sensationalistic news coverage (typical of tabloidization) is successful in attracting more attention but hinders processing and recall of the content (Grabe et al., 2003). Psychology can therefore help in understanding the mechanisms by which both journalists and audience members select (in the sense of allocating attention to) information and also how the features of the medium can plausibly impact on this process—for example, by overloading the user with information and hindering processing.

But does it mean that the content needs to be delivered in a dull and boring way in order to be informative? In Chapter 5, Bachleda and Soroka suggested this is not the case. It was shown in Chapter 3 how emotions are important drivers of attention and guide our understanding and interpretation of issues and also how this happens at both an individual level and a collective level (Chapters 4, 7, 9–11). Bachleda and Soroka clearly showed how emotions are featured in journalistic content and in people's reaction to the content. And it is true that—as the authors recognize—trying to trigger strong emotion is a typical feature of tabloidization and sensationalistic coverage. However, as the authors further noted, this does not have to be the case, and it is possible to create emotionally moving stories while at the same time maintaining a high-quality[1] level of coverage.

Psychological research and evidence can therefore support the understanding of the role of emotions in the way in which people interact with media and can also indicate the challenges and opportunities offered by emotional appeals in journalism.

---

[1] By quality coverage, we intend coverage providing accurate information and an account of the events contextualized in the more general context (e.g., the circumstances surrounding the event, its meaning, likely causes, and/or implications for citizens).

Interpersonal Processes

Strong Versus Weak Ties and News

In Chapter 4, Grabe and Bas discussed how the new formats of news delivery (particularly with regard to social media) seem to have significant impact on the type and amount of news that citizens come across, with a significant increase in 'incidental exposure' to—more or less accurate—information. Interestingly, from a psychological standpoint, the impact of accidental exposure varies, depending on where people come across the news. In particular, accidental exposure to information increases through exposure to posts made by people connected through weak ties (i.e., acquaintances rather than close friends). This supports extant literature on interpersonal relationships in social psychology, which suggests that we tend to form stronger ties with like-minded people (for a review, see Montoya et al., 2008). A clear implication is that using social media as a tool to expand the range of one's connections (as opposed to simply consolidating existing connections) has the potential to help individuals expand the range of information they come across and increase their knowledge (Tewksbury et al., 2001). But it also has implications for journalists as professionals: the wider their network, the more likely they will come across information they would not otherwise see.

Attribution

Another important area of research in psychology that has clear applications to journalism—and that has emerged in the course of this book (although seldom mentioned directly)—is attribution. Attribution is the explanation we give to the motivations leading an individual to behave in a certain way. The literature on attribution in psychology is vast, especially with regard to the biases (i.e., systematic mistakes) we have when explaining others' behaviour. For example; according to the so-called fundamental attribution error (Ross, 1977), people have a tendency to overemphasize dispositional or personality-based explanations of behaviour while underemphasizing the role of situational factors. A classic example is the so-called blame the victim (McLeod, 2018) whereby observers tend to view actors as personally responsible for their own misfortunes, pain, or suffering and pay insufficient account to the circumstances in which victims (or indeed offenders) may find themselves (e.g., Maruna & Mann, 2006). In this book, Hichy and Di Stefano in Chapter 9 explain key dynamics of attribution when illustrating the linguistic intergroup biases: we tend to explain others' behaviours in terms of internal predispositions and our own as responses to specific circumstances. Hichy and Di Marco might have tapped into the cognitive basis of these biases when illustrating the induction–deduction asymmetry and how we tend to erroneously ascribe behaviours to traits more often than we assign traits to behaviours.

In summary, although literature suggests that we tend to prefer interacting with similar others, the ability to establish and maintain links with people who are different from us and view the world differently can help us gain access to information we would not otherwise come across. Interacting with different others might also help reduce our systematic biases in attribution. However, there are limits to the ability of news producers to foster this kind of engagement when focussing on the commercial viability of news as opposed to the social function of news.

Subjectivity in Journalism

Based on what we have read so far—and on what we can learn from psychology in general—an important lesson from the study of media is that the idea of journalism as an 'objective' window to the world is more a myth than reality. The choice of which events are covered and how, the selection of sources to quote, and the images, sound bites, videos, and formats of delivery are the results of coordinated subjectivities. In other words, the way in which news is selected and presented to the audience is the result of the interaction between the subjective experiences of those operating within a particular medium and their cultural system. This means that—from a psychological viewpoint—there is no such a thing as 'objectivity' in journalism.

Does this mean that journalists should stop trying to be objective and just give in to their subjectivity? Of course not. Apart from columns and features, where there is an expectation that the opinions of the authors or interviewees will be presented, news-making is about reporting events that are deemed interesting and important to the audience (see Chapter 6 on norms). When journalism incorporates a psychological understanding of media— that is, when it recognizes the role of subjectivity—it is not less 'factual' but is less 'judgemental'. It does not hide from acknowledging the role our internal world plays in the way in which we talk about the world. It is our tenet that only by recognizing the enormous role subjectivity plays in the way we make sense of reality are we in a better position to provide a richer range of information and views and to try to step out of our shoes in order to see the world from another's point of view.

Journalism—like any kind of communication—can be otherwise perceived as an attempt at persuasion. It is not surprising, from this viewpoint, that with increased access to information and with an overcrowded marketplace of ideas, such as the internet, news media are increasingly facing challenges and criticism regarding their choice of coverage. It is our tenet that failing to recognize the role of subjectivity in the way in which news is produced while at the same time claiming objectivity and freedom from bias can be seen as a form of imposed etic (see Chapter 8), in which the journalist's viewpoint is presented as the one objective standard to which readers should abide.

Sources in Journalism

The previous discussion offers an interesting interpretation of how and why the inclusion of a broader number of sources in the news seems to be associated with an increased level of political self-efficacy in the audience. Curran et al. (2014) found a correspondence between the variety of sources quoted in the news and people's knowledge (in terms of performance on a recognition task of key figures, events, and issues) of current affairs across countries. In Chapter 4, Grabe and Bas presented research showing how the incorporation of testimonies from ordinary citizens was associated with improved recall and willingness to participate in political action. The media psychological construct of parasocial relationships (Giles, 2002) can help in understanding this: presenting news in a way that fosters identification with the actors can also foster the establishment of parasocial relationships with them, and we can more easily learn from their experiences (e.g., see Howard Gola et al., 2013), as we do from our own experiences or those of our acquaintances.

Literature on imagined contact (for a meta-analysis, see Miles & Crisp, 2014) and indirect contact (for a meta-analysis, see Lemmer & Wagner, 2015) also helps by showing how, when we come into contact with out-groups (even just imagining it or via someone we know and trust), we are less inclined to rely on stereotyping and prejudice. In other words, the wider the variety of voices we hear, and with which we establish positive relationships, the more understanding and knowledgeable we become. It is therefore not surprising that—for example—with regard to coverage of immigration news, 'quality' journalism is characterized by the provision of a wider range of actors and the presentation of different viewpoints (Masini et al., 2018).

Listening to the stories of a wider range of people can help journalists develop a deeper understanding of the events on which they report. Obviously, there are serious impediments to this idealistic form of coverage, such as the incredible time pressure journalists are under and the difficulties of getting access to sources. Another impediment is the now standard practice of interviewing people to get a specific viewpoint. During the editors' careers, journalists have often approached us with a pre-existing angle (e.g., social media is bad for you, news is good for you) searching for someone to corroborate their view. At other times, they were searching for representatives of different viewpoints (they already had someone holding one view, and they were searching for someone with a different view). In our opinion, the former is dangerous in that it merely supports the journalist's view and does not present the scientific consensus on a particular issue, whereas the latter is a very interesting way to foster debate, provided the focus is on different interpretations rather than on conflict per se.

Subjectivity in Context

Data from research on journalistic norms from both journalists and audiences show that journalism is still viewed as having an important function in the service of public interest (intended as informing citizens and holding powers to account; see Chapter 6).

A caveat emerging clearly from Chapter 4 is that in order to serve the public interest and contribute to the creation of an informed citizenry, journalists must uphold the standards of newsworthiness, fairness, and truth that they apply in their more traditional work. Obviously, this is in direct contrast with the search for 'clicks' as a mandate for much of the current media business model, as eloquently illustrated by Hardy in Chapter 2. Indeed, Cable and Mottershead (2018) review how major football outlets tend to use 'clickbait' in order to attract audience interaction online via Twitter. They claim that this occurs at the expenses of quality football journalism.

So there are glaring tensions in the profession of journalism, driven by competing demands. But there are also more subtle forces at play, such as the way in which our language (see Chapters 9 and 10), nonverbal communication (see Chapter 11), and culture (see Chapter 8) shape and express our beliefs and interpretations of the events occurring around us, often in the way in which we define ourselves and others, the goals we are trying to achieve, the emotions we are experiencing, and the perspectives with which we are familiar.

The future of journalism, and its role in our societies, depends on how these tensions are managed and resolved. We believe (in line with Beattie, 2019) that insights from psychology in general, and media psychology in particular, can help in this enterprise.

References

Beattie, P. (2019). *Social evolution, political psychology, and the media in democracy*. Palgrave Macmillan.

Bergen, L., Grimes, T., & Potter, D. (2005). How attention partitions itself during simultaneous message presentations. *Human Communication Research, 31*(3), 311–336.

Cable, J., & Mottershead, G. (2018). 'Can I click it? Yes you can': Football journalism, Twitter, and clickbait. *Ethical Space, 15*(1–2), 69–80.

Conroy, D. E., Elliot, A. J., & Thrash, T. M. (2009). Achievement motivation. In M. R. Leary & R. H. Hoyle (Eds.), *Handbook of individual differences in social behavior* (pp. 382–399). Guilford.

Curran, J., Coen, S., Soroka, S., Aalberg, T., Hayashi, K., Hichy, Z., Iyengar, S., Jones, P., Mazzoleni, G., Papathanassopoulos, S., Rhee, J. W., Rojas, H., Rowe, D., & Tiffen, R. (2014). Reconsidering 'virtuous circle' and 'media malaise' theories of the media: An 11-nation study. *Journalism, 15*(7), 815–833.

Ferguson, C. J., & Kilburn, J. (2009). The public health risks of media violence: A meta-analytic review. *Journal of Pediatrics, 154*(5), 759–763.

Giles, D. C. (2002). Parasocial interaction: A review of the literature and a model for future research. *Media psychology, 4*(3), 279–305.

Grabe, M. E., Lang, A., & Zhao, X. (2003). News content and form: Implications for memory and audience evaluations. *Communication Research, 30*(4), 387–413.

Howard Gola, A. A., Richards, M. N., Lauricella, A. R., & Calvert, S. L. (2013). Building meaningful parasocial relationships between toddlers and media characters to teach early mathematical skills. *Media Psychology, 16*(4), 390–411.

Lee, E.-J., & Tandoc, E. C. (2017). When news meets the audience: How audience feedback online affects news production and consumption. *Human Communication Research, 43*, 436–449.

Lemmer, G., & Wagner, U. (2015). Can we really reduce ethnic prejudice outside the lab? A meta-analysis of direct and indirect contact interventions. *European Journal of Social Psychology, 45*(2), 152–168.

Manzi, C., Coen, S., Regalia, C., Yévenes, A. M., Giuliani, C., & Vignoles, V. L. (2018). Being in the social: A cross-cultural and cross-generational study on identity processes related to Facebook use. *Computers in Human Behavior, 80*, 81–87.

Maruna, S., & Mann, R. E. (2006). A fundamental attribution error? Rethinking cognitive distortions. *Legal and Criminological Psychology, 11*, 155–177.

Masini, A., Van Aelst, P., Zerback, T., Reinemann, C., Mancini, P., Mazzoni, M., Damiani, M., & Coen, S. (2018). Measuring and explaining the diversity of voices and viewpoints in the news: A comparative study on the determinants of content diversity of immigration news. *Journalism Studies, 19*(15), 2324–2343.

McLeod, S. A. (2018, October 31). Fundamental attribution error. Simply Psychology. https://www.simplypsychology.org/fundamental-attribution.html

Miles, E., & Crisp, R. J. (2014). A meta-analytic test of the imagined contact hypothesis. *Group Processes & Intergroup Relations, 17*(1), 3–26. https://doi.org/10.1177/1368430213510573

Montoya, R. M., Horton, R. S., & Kirchner, J. (2008). Is actual similarity necessary for attraction? A meta-analysis of actual and perceived similarity. *Journal of Social and Personal Relationships, 25*(6), 889–922.

Neroni, H. (2012). *Violence and cinema.* In K. Gabbard (Ed.), *Oxford bibliographies in cinema and media studies.* Oxford University Press. doi:10.1093/obo/9780199791286-0148

Ross, L. (1977). The intuitive psychologist and his shortcomings: Distortions in the attribution process. *Advances in Experimental Social Psychology, 10*, 173–220.

Ryan, R. M. (Ed.). (2012). *The Oxford handbook of human motivation.* Oxford University Press..

Schrøder, K. C. (2019). *What do news readers really want to read about? How relevance works for news audiences.* http://www.digitalnewsreport.org/publications/2019/news-readers-really-want-read-relevance-works-news-audiences/#1-recent-research-on-news-preferences

Soroka, S. N. (2014). *Negativity in democratic politics: Causes and consequences.* Cambridge University Press.

Vignoles, V. L. (2011). Identity motives. In S. J. Schwartz, K. Luyckx, & V. L. Vignoles (Eds.), *Handbook of identity theory and research* (pp. 403–432). Springer.

Tewksbury, D., Weaver, A. J., & Maddex, B. D. (2001). Accidentally informed: Incidental news exposure on the World Wide Web. *Journalism & Mass Communication Quarterly, 78*(3), 533–554.

Index

For the benefit of digital users, indexed terms that span two pages (e.g., 52–53) may, on occasion, appear on only one of those pages.

Page numbers followed by n indicate footnotes. Tables and figures are indicated by t and f following the page number